AMERICA REDISCOVERED

GARLAND REFERENCE LIBRARY
OF THE HUMANITIES
(VOL. 986)

AMERICA REDISCOVERED
Critical Essays on Literature and Film of the Vietnam War

edited by
Owen W. Gilman, Jr.
Lorrie Smith

GARLAND PUBLISHING, INC. • NEW YORK & LONDON
1990

Library of Congress Cataloging-in-Publication Data

America rediscovered : critical essays on literature and film of the
Vietnam War / [edited by] Owen W. Gilman, Jr., Lorrie Smith.
    p. cm. — (Garland reference library of the humanities ; vol.
986)
    Includes bibliographical references.
    ISBN 0-8240-1942-3
    1. American literature—20th century—History and criticism.
2. Vietnamese Conflict, 1961–1975—Literature and the conflict.
3. Vietnamese Conflict, 1961-1975—Motion pictures and the conflict.
4. War stories, American—History and criticism. 5. War poetry,
American—History and criticism. 6. War films—History and
criticism. I. Gilman, Owen W. II. Smith, Lorrie, 1953-   .
III. Series.
PS228.V5A44   1990
810'.9'358—dc20
                                                    89–38457
                                                    CIP

Printed on acid-free, 250-year-life paper
Manufactured in the United States of America

CONTENTS

PREFACE

As surely as we are moving along toward a new millennium, the American interest in studying Vietnam grows with each passing year. In the decade of the 1980s, now at an end, Vietnam studies came of age. Philip Beidler's *American Literature and the Experience of Vietnam* (University of Georgia Press,1982), a provocative and ferociously written study, gave immediate purpose to consideration of the literary dimension of recent public experience, and subsequent developments in serious scholarship on the enduring impact of the Vietnam war have been both abundant and consequential. John Hellmann's *American Myth and the Legacy of Vietnam* (Columbia University Press, 1986) and Thomas Myers's *Walking Point* (Oxford University Press, 1988) attest handily to the fact that the legacy of the war is still very much with us.

The Vietnam section of the Popular Culture Association, begun with encouragement from Peter Rollins, guided recently by William Searle, and now in the hands of Jacqueline Lawson, reflects the broad sweep of interest in the subject. Every year now the PCA National Meeting offers dozens and dozens of papers on diverse aspects of the Vietnam war. Some of these papers are naturally stronger than others, but the whole spread of offerings suggests healthy vitality in this new field. Sometimes in explaining our work with Vietnam texts to more conservatively oriented colleagues, we note--only partially in jest--that we are engaged in building a new American canon.

Several times in the past few years, this canon has managed to place some rounds in the annual gatherings of the Modern Language Association and the American Studies Association. In the best of this work, we can see and hear refreshing styles of scholarly writing. The subject seems to demand a response in kind. What Thomas Carlyle felt obliged to do in his effort to comprehend the French Revolution is evident in much of the primary literature of Vietnam, and more heartening yet, the same spirit of feisty contentiousness is palpable in many scholarly explorations. We have been honored with an opportunity to gather a set of studies which carry such a spirit. Based on this experience with so many distinguished colleagues, we are confident that the future of Vietnam studies is indeed bright--a fine light at the end of that once dark tunnel.

ACKNOWLEDGMENTS

Grateful acknowledgment is made to the following authors, publishers, and journals for permission to reprint previously published material:

D.C. Berry, "[the way popcorn pops is]," from *saigon cemetery* by D.C. Berry (Athens: University of Georgia Press, 1972). Copyright 1972 by D.C. Berry. Reprinted by permission of the author.

Michael Casey, "The LZ Gator Body Collector," from *Obscenities* by Michael Casey (New Haven: Yale University Press, 1972). Copyright 1972 by Yale University Press. Reprinted by permission of Yale University Press.

W.D. Ehrhart, "Soldier-Poets of the Vietnam War," Copyright 1987 by *Virginia Quarterly Review*. Reprinted by permission of the author and *Virginia Quarterly Review*.

W.D. Ehrhart, "To Those Who Have Gone Home Tired," from *To Those Who Have Gone Home Tired* by W.D. Ehrhart (New York: Thunder's Mouth Press, 1984). Copyright by W.D. Ehrhart. Reprinted by permission of the author.

Robert Graves, "Broken Images." Copyright 1955 by Robert Graves. Reprinted by permission of Curtis Brown, Ltd.

Yusef Komunyakaa, "2527th Birthday of the Buddha," "Camouflaging the Chimera," "You and I are Disappearing," "Nude Pictures," "Tunnels," "Starlight Scope Myopia," "Fragging," "Re-Creating the Scene," "Hanoi Hannah," "Combat Pay for Jody," "Facing It," from *Dien Cai Dau* by Yusef Komunyakaa (Middletown, CT: Wesleyan University Press, 1988). Copyright 1988 by Yusef Komunyakaa. Reprinted by permission of the author.

Tim O'Brien, "Going After Cacciato," from *Ploughshares* 3.1 (1976). Copyright by Tim O'Brien. Reprinted by permission of the author. "The Way It Mostly Was," copyright 1976 by Washington and Lee University, reprinted from *Shenandoah:* The Washington and Lee University Review with the permission of the Editor. "Speaking of

We want to thank our home institutions for providing direct support toward this project; Saint Joseph's University assisted the early editing stage with a 1988 summer grant for research; Saint Michael's College contributed a research grant and released time to complete the project. We also owe a huge debt to Amy Beattie, who took on the enormous task of formatting and printing the manuscript.

And finally--beyond the immediate, timely, and specific assistance noted above--there stands another kind of support which truly made this endeavor possible. We have been fortunate beyond belief in having the help of generous loved ones, Mary and Wayne, who have made time available, tended children, and offered wise counsel whenever problems surfaced in the making of this book. For all that help, we are especially grateful.

Owen W. Gilman, Jr.   Lorrie Smith
Saint Joseph's University   Saint Michael's College

INTRODUCTION: WHY READ VIETNAM WAR TEXTS?

Owen W. Gilman, Jr.

In the beginning--or maybe it was rather well toward the end--there was a war, a little war between a giant power and a midget power, a little war that seemed everlasting, a little war that veered finally toward the soul of sorrow. Things happened in the war that demanded more than one look. History had provided a fiendishly ample prefiguration of the war's necessary outcome; the Vietnam war, after all, mirrored the diverse tactics of the colonists and the British soldiers during the American Revolutionary War. However, history in this case proved no comfort at all for the American side. As a consequence, initial scrutiny of the Vietnam war by Americans had not much to do with history. But everything to do with being an American.

The shaping principle of this collection of essays is to bring together a set of insights about the condition of being an American--past, present, and future. Illumination on this matter comes by means of careful consideration of various texts that have emerged from the experience of war in Vietnam. Times of duress often afford opportunities for reassessment of both principles and practices. In the process, which involves careful tracing of old issues and motifs, a certain recovery of fundamentals in the nature, character, and function of the American becomes conceivable, even as new slants emerge. Thus a new land is found in an old one--indeed, a place with a past--and America itself might be recovered from the dark, nightmarishly turbulent storms of the little war that happened not so long ago, far away on the edge of a darkly alien continent.

The Vietnam war has been a protean subject, and texts about the experience have proliferated in the past two decades. In many of these texts, surface details alone speak for the whole experience. That the surface should predominate is not surprising. When you first look at something, you see the surface. As Hemingway understood well, getting the surface right is not easy, and a kind of truth resides in mastering the surface of a moment in time. Thus wars trail streams of realistic detail, all assembled to give immediate access to what is being represented. The spirit of realism becomes momentarily privileged by war, a point addressed directly by John M. Del Vecchio in the "acknowledgements" for his novel *The 13th Valley:*

Grateful acknowledgement is made to: A soldier
on Firebase Rendezvous at the edge of the A Shau
Valley during Lam Son 719, Spring 1971.
He said to me, "You can do it, Man. You write
about this place. You been here a long time.
People gotta know what it was really like." And thus
this book began.[1]

Anyone who has read around a bit in the fiction of Vietnam knows the
extent of efforts made to recreate "what it was really like" in a full
deluge of details. In more than one case, details prove to be
everything, noisy and annoying. Sometimes, however, the package
comes with latent meaning--hints and clues of a people suspended
perilously in time. It all depends upon the form assumed by the
material in a given text.

The essays of this collection serve the original texts of Vietnam
with honor. Whether guided by well established principles of analysis
or by relatively new theories of interpretation, they work to make sense
of the discoveries lurking in creative encounters with the Vietnam war.
In doing this, they explore far beyond the limits of realism implicit in
comments made by John Del Vecchio to the Asia Society in its
conference of 7-9 May 1985. Del Vecchio acknowledged there the
complexity and diversity of human experience in the war. The war was
not one. To make this point, he developed a three dimensional scheme
for representing diversity in all its possibilities. One axis was drawn
from John Clark Pratt's time continuum model, with seven stages
(prologue, Five Acts, and an epilogue) of development, all dependent
upon absolute confidence in chronology--year by year, a war evolving
in real historical time. Another axis was drawn from cartography itself,
with assured reference to the seven military regions of the war as it was
fought in country--the real of maps. The final axis came from a set of
individual variables (age, rank, race, education, military job)--the real
of people doing things.[2] Del Vecchio concluded that these many
variables were responsible for the apparent fragmentation in the
literature of Vietnam, fragmentation which could be dismaying to some
but comforting to others.

However, Del Vecchio's scheme sadly neglects the profound weight
that the *form* of a creative text carries, and there is no suggestion in his
comments that American culture--seldom more substantial than a
dream-- has been just as elusive, as hard to pin down, as meaning in
the war. Finding the ephemeral requires a multitude of voices and a
surfeit of styles. Slowly, incrementally, the Vietnam war in literature
and film has come to be known in a play of language that knows no

boundaries, and the war has become shockingly paradigmatic of life in the modern world. To know the American in our time, therefore, we must read the texts of Vietnam.

In the first section of this collection, a series of essays survey in rather broad ways the placement of Vietnam in American culture. With reference to Tim O'Brien's *Going After Cacciato* and Stephen Wright's *Meditations in Green*, both dazzlingly fanciful in form and substance, Philip Beidler's essay makes a brief case for the idea that the texts of Vietnam may well have embedded in them the seeds for altered visions and priorities in American life as we find our way into the future. Beidler's "new dimensions of imaginative possibility" are clearly forward oriented, even as he responds to "experiential and cultural memory" as found in two provocative novels from the war. Michael Bellamy reflects a similar interest in determining the conditions for forward movement, but he sweeps across a wide array of texts in order to locate the primary conditions that would bring a new America out of Vietnam; he finds a culture uneasy with ludic delight--a culture which has suffered considerably as a result of this uneasiness. From Hawthorne's "The Maypole of Merry Mount" story to *Apocalypse Now* and a host of other Vietnam texts, Bellamy examines the structural dichotomies of American culture to find clues for successful resolution of past problems.

Milton Bates offers another study of dichotomies, this time with men and women representing the diverse options. Bates reviews the evolution of ideas about the roles of men and women through the turbulence of the sixties and then assesses the impact of the Vietnam war on the battle of the sexes, with extensive reference to *Coming Home* and Donald Pfarrer's *Neverlight*, a novel which takes up the task of exploring "in the individual psyche those areas where social constructions of gender overlap or fail to account for feelings and behavior." Perhaps a certain confusion reigns in such exploration, but for Donald Rignalda, confusion--or chaos--is the essential point. With Michael Foucault's *The Archaeology of Knowledge* and James Gleick's *Chaos* (chaos being the newest field of physics) in the background, Ringnalda posits Michael Herr's *Dispatches* as a signpost to truth in a world where Newtonian logic no longer is safe or helpful.

In Philip Jason's view, an essential distinction in considering Vietnam texts must be made along formal lines, and his analysis of six novels develops along two diverging tracks--one with narratives bound to conventions/traditions of the past, one with narratives given to visionary explorations (texts that merge elements of "lyricism, psychological realism, and naturalism") that carry the culture into new realms. Lorrie Smith draws a similar distinction in order to uncover the political ramifications of narrative form and style. She contends that conventionally realistic war stories "are often implicated in unexamined assumptions, fantasies, and myths rooted deep in the American psyche," whereas the war's more "aggressively non-rational" narratives destabilize the social codes and myths which support the acceptability of war.

Marilyn Durham shifts the emphasis away from cultural/political gestalt to the compact between writer and reader as managed by narrative form. Durham looks at three post-combat adjustment stories --Larry Heinemann's *Paco's Story*, Philip Caputo's *Indian Country*, and Bobbie Ann Mason's *In Country*. She considers the storytelling voice present in each text and concludes that the insider's perspective (achieved by Heinemann and Mason) offers the most satisfying means of bringing readers through the impact of the war to deepened understanding of it. Using similar formalist critical methods, David DeRose probes the limits of realism and authenticity. With reference to *Platoon*, David Rabe's Vietnam trilogy, and Amlin Gray's *How I Got That Story*, DeRose explores the use of first-person voice-overs in film and drama to create a dual presence, an epic voice which interprets events for us and illuminates "the emotional truth of the experience." An America of "emotional truth" is not a very settled place; Americans of the post-Vietnam era are obliged to keep on raising questions, and hence our world is one of mandated discovery. The old is constantly turned inside out.

In "'Vietnam and Sexual Violence': The Movie," Cynthia Fuchs introduces some "postmodernist and feminist theories which identify the crisis of cultural authority as a crisis of representation." *Full Metal Jacket* is the central text in Fuch's discussion, but she surveys a range of movies and her discussion has sweeping implications. Kubrick's film reflects the collapse of cultural meaning in the moral void of Vietnam, and thus, ironically, is a step beyond many Vietnam films that conflate death and the female as unrepresentable, invisible others.

J. T. Hansen considers Vietnam as a function of language. Hansen assumes the inherent value of "authenticity" and posits narrative coherence as something desireable and achieveable. With close textual analysis of diction and with concern for various speech communities, he examines the efforts of veteran writers (fiction and nonfiction) to juxtapose different "vocabularies" (standard American English, military, conversational) that together constitute the war in a reader's experience.   H. Palmer Hall, in contrast, is concerned with understanding how two symbols that are found in many war texts carry a cautionary message about technology.   Thoreau advised his readers to pursue simplicity, and simplicity is what made the punji stick so powerful an answer to the technology of the American role in Vietnam, represented by the ubiquitous helicopter in countless narratives. Whether we might ever be set free from the hovering chopper is a question left hanging implicitly at the close of Hall's essay.

Through the second section of this collection, the focus is rather more specific, often located on a given work or corpus of work by individual writers. Robert Bourdette scrutinizes the reactions to *The Deer Hunter* and then presents a revisionist examination of the film, cued throughout to Arisotelian notions of epic. By tracking the central tension between community and isolation, he shows how Cimino "breaks radically with the tradition he invigorates." More modern theories--particularly those of Bakhtin and others in sociolinguistics-- shape Matthew Stewart's discussion of Michael Herr's *Dispatches*. Stewart finds that Herr's radical style of new journalism "recovers" the war; Herr jostles languages in a "multivocal" text which allows him to speak on behalf of less articulate grunts, undermine official journalistic "facts," and use metafictional, novelistic techniques.

Two studies here are devoted to Tim O'Brien's *Going After Cacciato*, one text certain to survive as a major document of the imagination in the late twentieth century. Robert Slabey carefully weighs O'Brien's combination of "realistic war scenes, absurdist events, along with fantasy" as a means of "celebrating the imagination's way of resisting the destructive powers of immediate experience" and, simultaneously, of questioning the imagination. Catherine Calloway probes *Cacciato* by measuring its text against other versions of the narrative that appeared in short story form. She finds that O'Brien's inconsistency is instructive--an argument "against viewing reality in terms of fixed perceptions." O'Brien "demonstrates the need of American culture to reject any over-simplifications of the Vietnam war's inconsistencies and discrepancies."

David Whillock applies the structuralist methodology of Levi-Strauss to work through the complexities of *Apocalypse Now*; culture and nature are found to be locked in opposition, and Willard's journey up the Nung River to Kurtz's compound becomes a mediating device that ultimately serves the purpose of allowing "our culture to articulate interpretations of a historical event through narrative forms to new members of our society." In similar fashion, Kate Meyers finds "the basic dichotomies of American culture"--the myth of the "hunter/warrior" and the "shaman"--embedded in Emily Mann's play *Still Life*. Richard Slotkin's views on myth are coupled with close textual analysis by Meyers to illuminate the play's characters who are emblems of large segments of our culture still not able to talk together about the war.

William Palmer's exploration of *Platoon* finds the "ultimate deconstruction of the Vietnam War" to be provocatively located in the film's final battle scene. After categorizing earlier cinematic treatments of the war (the "epic" and "comic book" phases), Palmer focuses on the films of 1987-88, with *Platoon* being the key to the "symbolic nihilism" phase of representing the war, a phase which opens up the conclusion that meaning itself "seems to be utterly non-existent." Nancy Anisfield also takes up a particular text, *Paco's Story*, with an eye to establishing it as a break with prior patterns in narrative structure. In the main, Vietnam fictions have been built to arrive at an apocalyptic moment; *Paco's Story* rebukes that sequence, moving ever away from an action climax, leaving the reader at the end with a sense of Paco "as the subject of a text within a text, further removed from the rest of the world." The new narrative structure "rejects apocalyptic closure and encourages careful examination of not only the Vietnam War, but also the aftermath of that war and the texts that will hold that war in America's collective memory." There is diminution. . . but no end.

The last "looking glass text," Yusef Komunyakaa's *Dien Cai Dau*, is taken by Vicente Gotera as an "aesthetic advance not only of poetry about the Vietnam War but also of war literature in general." Komunyakaa's particular lyric and surrealistic talents create a poetry of consolation, self-renewal, and transformation that moves beyond the documentary and polemical urge of most veterans' poetic texts.

The final section of this collection, "Genre Overviews," is meant to serve the needs of anyone inclined to carry the spirit of rediscovery forward. Reasonably comprehensive bibliographic guides to the fiction of Vietnam have been available for some time, but other genres are not served so well. Four essays here are aimed at correcting that problem. David Whillock begins by reviewing the problem of defining exactly what a "Vietnam" film is; he then adopts a classification model based on narrative structure, which results in a filmography exploring five types of Vietnam war film: Pre-*The Green Berets*, the Vietnam Veteran/Coming Home, the Effects Film, Incountry Films, and the Revenge Film. W. D. Ehrhart brings an insider's perspective to his delineation of the canon of Vietnam war poetry; Ehrhart argues that the war has produced an impressive and distinctive body of poetry, and he traces the development from the first carthartic poems to more recent, more complex poems. Anyone mentioned by Ehrhart deserves further study.

Of all the genres, drama of the Vietnam war has been the hardest to assess. Many works exist in hard-to-find manuscript form, and many have fallen into obscurity. Many have appeared only in minimalist productions. But as Weldon Durham so capably reveals, many texts exist for eventual scrutiny, and several good books may yet come from those willing to pursue the contribution of drama to rediscovering America in Vietnam. The nonfiction literature of Vietnam is better known than the drama, but as Jacqueline Lawson shows, the material is rich in possibilities for provocative scrutiny. Lawson's overview is admirably comprehensive, putting the "avalanche of dairies, journals, memoirs, chronicles, anthologies, oral histories" and a few other forms into quick perspective. Lawson finds that "the Vietnam narrative is an intensely personal statement written out of each veteran's desperate need to give shape, definition, meaning, and purpose to an experience that was, for most of the war's participants, inscrutable, surreal, fragmented, terrifying, devoid of meaning and filled with anguish." Still, as Lawson concludes, "in the personal narratives of Vietnam's veterans reside the 'truths' that may prevent another generation of Americans from fighting the next war." In the end, then, another America may be discovered, one with peace prevalent--chaos confronted and transcended by dint of the fury inherent in imagination. Perhaps the story of Vietnam, never to be finished, has redemptive value. As this story goes, so goes the American.

Notes

1. John M. Del Vecchio, *The 13th Valley* (New York: Bantam Books, 1983), p. ix.

2. Del Vecchio's observations are recounted by Timothy Lomperis in *"Reading the Wind": The Literature of the Vietnam War* (Durham, N.C.: Duke University Press, 1987), p. 45, and they anchor one side of a debate which engaged quite a few of the conference participants; on the other side were several writers who argued for the primary importance of fancy, not fact, in constructing deeply meaningful texts about the Vietnam war.

PART I

TEXT, VIETNAM CONTEXT, AND AMERICAN CULTURE

RE-WRITING AMERICA: LITERATURE AS CULTURAL REVISION IN THE NEW VIETNAM FICTION

Philip D. Beidler

"We can truly be transformed, and even possibly redeemed, by electing to write at times of what happened--but also of what might have happened, what could have happened, what should have happened, and also what can be kept from happening or what can be made to happen . . . . Words are all we have" (Lomperis 87). These words happen to be mine, although they have their origin in the words of the fine novelist, Tim O'Brien, who in turn had earlier made them the words, in his *Going After Cacciato*, of the fictional protagonist, Paul Berlin. In them we find a call and a challenge to a new art that would be a kind of ultimate cultural revision, an art that, even as it acknowledges the painful memory of the experience of Vietnam, would make possible the imaginative projection of that memory into new dimensions of consciousness, individual and collective, often providing equally new insights into knowledge, meaning, and value. It is a call, in the fullest terms of artistic possibility, to do nothing less than re-write ourselves, and apace, to re-write America.

The project of cultural revision so defined supplies the artistic agenda for Vietnam fiction even in a number of extremely early and highly experimental works such as Norman Mailer's *Why Are We in Vietnam?*, James Crumley's *One to Count Cadence*, and William Eastlake's *The Bamboo Bed*. It certainly continues to dictate the evolution of variously experimental styles in subsequent novels such as Charles Durden's *No Bugles, No Drums*, John Clark Pratt's *The Laotian Fragments*, and David Winn's *Gangland*, not to mention, on the other side of what might be called the meta-fictive coin, Michael Herr's *Dispatches*. It is in Tim O'Brien's award-winning *Going After Cacciato*, however, and in Stephen Wright's more recent and comparably acclaimed *Meditations in Green*, that we find the issue most fully elaborated. In them, we are confronted with the prospect of a new imaginative fiction of the American experience of Vietnam that indeed might ultimately reify itself into redemptory cultural fact.

The better known of the two works, *Going After Cacciato*, makes its creative task clear from the outset:

> Paul Berlin, whose only goal was to live long enough
> to establish goals worth living for still longer, stood

> high in the tower by the sea, the night soft all around
> him, and wondered, not for the first time, about the
> immense powers of his own imagination. A truly
> awesome notion. Not a dream, an idea. An idea to
> develop, to tinker with and build and sustain, to draw
> out as an artist draws out his visions. (27-28)

Thus begins a novel that, as one quickly sees, is actually two, or possibly three, novels, each of which, moreover, can be read only in terms of its other or others. In a guard tower by the South China Sea, Specialist Fourth Class Paul Berlin stands lonely vigil and thinks out at once a fact-book and a fantasy-book, a book of memory and a book of imagination. Connected by frequent interchapters in what perhaps might be considered a third book--entitled, appropriately, "The Observation Post,"-- the other two flow in and out of each other at will until all boundaries of consciousness seem dissolved. What results is a whole far greater than the sum of its parts, one in which Berlin re-writes himself and his America into new realms of individual and collective insight.

The domain of fact or memory is a nightmare-continuum of particular horrors. Frenchie Tucker gets shot through the nose. Bernie Lynn dies of a tunnel wound, shot from his chest straight down into his vitals. Billy Boy Watkins dies of fright on the field of battle, screaming his dreadful scream, trying to lace back on the boot that holds what used to be his foot. Buff winds up ass-high in the air, "like a praying Arab in Mecca" (283), his upturned helmet holding all that remains of his disposable humanity in the muck of his shot-away face.

Then, as if all along, enter *and* exit Cacciato. "Dumb as a bullet," says one G.I. "Dumb as a month-old oyster fart," says another (2). Dumb, perhaps, but apparently not crazy. Or maybe just dumb and crazy enough to think he can pull it off. "Split, departed," says Doc Peret, and somehow, incredibly, miraculously, "Gone to Paris" (2-3). So, in *Going After Cacciato*, the real quickly begins to meld into the imaginative, the factually just plausible into the fictively just possible. Cacciato goes. Berlin and the others follow. Apace, Berlin ponders: "what part was fact and what part was the extension of fact? And how were facts separated from possibilities? What had really happened and what merely might have happened? How did it end?" (28).

The fictive road to Paris does somehow magically end there, and in the negotiations that ultimately terminate American participation in the war. At the same time, the novel remains firmly anchored in the experience of the battlefield and centered on the movement of Berlin's particular experiential consciousness toward the recognition of new possibilities of acceptance and understanding. Within this twofold movement, the complex play of style re-engenders that whole vast collocation of memory, myth, metaphor, slogan, political shibboleth, and popular cliché that was in fact America in Vietnam.

It will be remembered, for example, that "The Road to Paris" was the literal expression used by bureaucratic and journalistic phrase-makers to describe the tortuous, and often nearly absurd labors--including some prolonged squabbling over the shape and dimensions of a conference table--of getting the peace talks set in motion. It will also be remembered that "The Road to" any number of places once supplied the title to any number of innocently ridiculous American movies that made comedy, in some of the the bleakest times of war, out of danger and dire predicament. Here Berlin finds his Dorothy Lamour--it is hard in fact to think of the new model as being clothed in anything but a sarong--in Sarkin Aung Wan, his Vietnamese companion and spiritual guide. He persistently finds himself playing pensive Crosby to wisecracking Hope in the nimble Doc Peret. Peril mixes with pratfall all the way. They and the rest of Cacciato's pursuers barely escape death at the hands of the Shah's dreaded Savak. They miraculously avoid detection as they slip ashore in Greece. They traverse the breadth of Europe looking over their shoulders for pursuers.

In Asia itself, they have already fallen, Alice-in-Wonderland-like, through "A Hole in the Road to Paris" (82) and have wound up seeing "the Light" at the end of General Westmoreland's "Tunnel" (111). The "Light" turns out to be a periscope manned by an aged Vietnamese who is himself a deserter condemned there now for ten years. Berlin, looking through the eyepiece and seeing in imagination, he realizes, Bernie Lynn and Frenchie Tucker in precisely the same moment of his experiential memory of their descent and death, understands for a split second that here the Americans have the chance to see the war from the other side. It is too late. Berlin's platoon commander, a sick, aging relic of American wars, destroys the periscope with six rounds from his M-16 (84). Shortly, they all fall back out of the Hole on the Road to Paris, and, the lesson of perspective lost, continue on their weary, imperiled way.

Such fantasy wordplay is also grounded in mythic memories of other times and other wars and empires as well. One of the roads on the Road to Paris turns out to be the Road to Mandalay (111). What they ultimately seek, the most recent in a long line of historical belligerents, is the "Peace of Paris" (290). Shortly after they arrive, Berlin finds a *New York Herald-Tribune* carrying news of the death of Eisenhower. On the front page are two pictures, one of Eisenhower as a cadet at West Point, the other of "him riding into Paris, the famous grin, the jeep swamped by happy Frenchmen" (304).

Berlin reads on. So at the end, even as at the beginning, he sees, it remains all of a piece, the world, himself, his America: "The world went on. Old facts warmed over. Nixon was President. In Chicago, a federal grand jury had handed down indictments against eight demonstrators at the Democratic convention the previous summer. He'd missed that--the whole thing had happened while he was in basic training. Tear gas and cops, something like that. No matter: Dagwood still battled Mr. Dithers. What changed? The war went on. 'In an effort to bring the Peace Talks to a higher level of dialogue, the Secretary of Defense has ordered the number of B-52 missions over the North to be dropped from 1,800 to 1,600 a month;' meanwhile, in the South, it was a quiet week, with sporadic and light action confined to the Central Highlands and Delta. Only 204 more dead men. And Ike. Ike was dead and an era had ended" (304).

So it goes in "The Observation Post." Still, if nothing has really changed, a very great deal may have been learned and gained. The mythic cycle may persist, but one may also still elect not to succumb to its grim dominion. Like Yossarian, Berlin elects to persevere. "Insight, vision. What you remember is what you see, and what you see depends on what you remember. A cycle, Doc Peret had said. A cycle that has to be broken. And this requires a fierce concentration on the process itself: focus on the order of things, sort out the flow of events so as to understand how one thing led to another, search for that point at which what happened had been extended into a vision of what might have happened" (207). Persevere. Seek the possibility in the face of all of it still to be able to say the two words with which the novel ends: "Maybe so" (338).

Apropos of the mode of fiction that over the last two decades or so we have come to call "magical realism," an alternate title for *Going After Cacciato* might be "Henry Fleming meets Jorge Luis Borges and/or Gabriel Garcia Marqez and/or Italo Calvino." A comparable gloss on Stephen Wright's *Meditations in Green* might be something like "Johnny Appleseed meets the Fabulous Furry Freak Brothers." It is a drug-addled American pastorale, a whole lurid apocalypse of collective myth. At the same time, this general nightmare, through the shaping and transforming process of imaginative art, ultimately does come, magically, miraculously, by the novel's end, to bear also the generative promise of new creation.

As with *Going After Cacciato*, *Meditations in Green* quickly turns out to be a novel that is several novels, again each of which can only be read in terms of the others. It begins with one of a series of interchapters entitled "Meditations in Green." It then moves to two other narratives, one emanating from a first-person narrator and another from a third-person narrator. The former announces himself early on: "I, your genial narrator, wreathed in a beard of smoke, look into the light and recite strange tales from the war back in the long ago time" (8). It is, as we soon find out, perhaps one of the most familiar of Vietnam litanies: "Dear Mom, Stoned Again." His book is a book of imagination. At the same time, he is also the other narrator as well. There, his book is a book of memory. The two merge and interflow in and out of each other to form, as the interchapters remind us, a series of meditations in green, and one ultimately in which the institutional war-green, the olive drab of death and old destruction becomes the fruitional green of promise, the peace-green of life and new creation.

In the book of memory--Vietnam--we are given the whole stoned, lurid spectacle. The setting is in a military intelligence unit that specializes in photo-interpretation and physical torture. The narrator-protagonist, Griffin, and his fellow draftees who work there spend their lives in a near-permanent state of drugged hallucination. The unit commander dies on take-off in a plane most likely sabotaged by a homicidal G.I. Grunts from the Spook House drive around in their jeep with decomposing Viet Cong corpses sitting in the back seat. The corpses are wearing party hats. Weird Wendell, enlisting fellow G.I.'s and base-camp Vietnamese, makes a make-believe war-movie with a cast of thousands. During the last scene the idiotic make-believe comes hideously real. His creative endeavors interrupted by an actual Viet Cong attack on the base camp, Wendell keeps filming. A plane takes a direct hit from a mortar round. He films the pilot being incinerated in his cockpit. He films a U.S. Captain and "a genuine VC in black shorts locked in a lover's clench on the gravel outside the O club and stabbing one another at intervals with long knives" (332). In an ensuing explosion, Wendell himself falls, mangled, mortally wounded. He dies giving camera directions and quoting from a cherished copy of *Atlas Shrugged* (334). Over in in the chapel, a real film has been playing all the while, spectatorless. Griffin wonders how it came out. He does not know that it has self-destructed, as has Wendell's, on the last frame. In fact, as in fantasy,--or, if you will, in fantasy as in fact,--it is Vietnam, the movie: "The screen was blank, a rectangle of burning light" (338).

Back in the world, both initially and for a good part of the novel to come, we are forced to comprehend what seems an equally nightmarish mixup of fact *and* phantasmagoria. Literally and literarily, they blend across a whole stoned, echolalic spectrum. Trips, Griffin's war buddy, endlessly stalks after and plots lovingly various forms of demise for a

figure he takes to be his old NCO nemesis, Sergeant Antrim. Griffin
finds a friend and possible soulmate named Huette Mirandella. Her
nickname: Huey. More neo-Shakespearean horseplay shows up in a
botanic psychologist named Arden. As in Vietnam, so back in the
world, it can only get crazier and crazier. Trips continues his mad
quest. Huey pronounces "all this plant jive" thus far but "words, words,
words." It is time, she challenges Griffin, to "test how green your
thumb really is" (264).

As the novel would have it, the exhortation is, both figuratively and
quite literally, the crucial seed planted in the fertile ground of ever-
creating consciousness. Out of a nightmare memory of old death
comes a generative thrusting forth of imagination into imagings and
envisionings of new life.

As in *Going After Cacciato*, the book of fact and the book of
imagination in *Meditations in Green* merge at the novel's end, and with
comparable result. Outside, nothing much probably does change a very
great deal. Given the way the world goes, the operative question may
well always be the one recorded at the bottom line of the last of the
novel's meditations in green: "Who has a question for Mr. Memory?"
(340). In life, this may indeed always be the basic issue. At the same
time, however, through the generative power of art, there has now
emerged also the possibility that such a going back might become the
stuff of a going ahead as well. And that going ahead for Stephen
Wright, as with Dylan Thomas, will lie in "the green fuse that drives the
flower," the vision of an art that would come to touch on nothing less
than the eternal springs of creation. Here may yet reside, one may be
bold enough to believe, the answer to what Griffin announces near the
end as "Problem of the Age." Question: "how to occupy the
diminishing interval between fire and wind and flags" (340). Answer:
Imagine. Create. Make it happen. "I think my thumb has always been
green" (340), he exclaims. The dream of a new imaginative possibility
has come to germination:

> In the spring I'll wander national highways, leather
> breeches around my legs, pot on my head, sowing
> seeds from the burlap bag across my shoulder, resting
> in the afternoon in the shade of a laurel tree. At night
> I carve peace pipes from old cypress branches.
> Everywhere the green fuses are burning and look now,
> snipping rapidly ahead of your leaping eye, the forged
> blades cutting through the page, the transformation of
> this printed sheet twisted about a metal stem for your
> lapel your hat your antenna, a paper emblem of the

widow's hope, the doctor's apothecary, the veteran's
friend: a modest flower. (340-341)

In the play of the text, the extending of experiential and cultural
memory into new dimensions of imaginative possibility, the veteran's
flower newly engenders itself out of the the memorial of death into the
promise of new life. Flower Power indeed. The veteran's friend, his
dream, his creation, his gift to you: peace.

Works Cited

Lomperis, Timothy J. *"Reading the Wind:"* The Literature of the Vietnam
War. Durham: Duke UP, 1987.

O'Brien, Tim. *Going After Cacciato*. New York: Delacorte
Press/Seymour Lawrence, 1978.

Wright, Stephen. *Meditations in Green*. New York: Scribner's, 1983.

CARNIVAL AND CARNAGE:
FALLING LIKE ROCK STARS AND SECOND LIEUTENANTS

Michael Bellamy

> "Vietnam by implication was 'un-world,' another place.
> Two common names for Vietnam were 'Brown
> Disneyland' and 'Six Flags Over Nothing;' the country
> was a playground or amusement park where social
> rules had been suspended, but the fun was gone."
> (Gibson 199)

Americana, a little-known film starring David Carradine, begins as a Vietnam veteran wanders into a Kansas town where he finds a broken-down merry-go-round sitting in an otherwise abandoned field. The rest of the movie depicts the various struggles of the hero with the very community for whom, it turns out, he is trying to refurbish, reconstruct, and regenerate that broken carrousel. Much of the resistance to his scheme results from his refusal to attend the cockfights regularly held in the abandoned church across the street from his merry-go-round. The climax of that conflict occurs when the hero kills a dog in a wrestling match in the arena where the cockfights ordinarily take place; he has to kill the dog to get the crucial gear assembly to complete the resuscitation of the carrousel. Carradine leaves town without commenting on the mission he has accomplished. Indeed, he is even less communicative in this film than he was in *Kung Fu*.

I'd like to begin by speaking for Carradine--since he will not speak for himself--by considering the implications of his enterprise in the context of typical American attitudes toward carnival and war. The gift of the carrousel suggests a joyful alternative to the cockfights that go on across the street: bringing the carnival back to life signals the end of the war. It is 1973, the year the last American troops returned from Vietnam. The same antithesis between carnival play and the violence of war is suggested by the visual similarity of the top of the merry-go-round and the helicopter rotor Carradine hears at stressful moments throughout the film. The dialectic of the film alternates between the jaunty melody of the carrousel and jittery fantods of the Huey, the straightforward enjoyment of carnival and the perverted savagery of the cockfights across the street, the carefree diversion of play and the deadly game of war. In a larger context, my essay will concern the implications of Carradine's restoration of the carrousel as a reversal of the process by which the carnival energy of the Sixties was so tragically and perversely enacted in the war.

My subject is the vitality of the Sixties, an abundance of energy first articulated in Kennedy's vigorous rhetoric of the challenges of the new frontier. In retrospect, it seems obvious that our frenetic energy would culminate in fire power that displayed all the markings of a Fourth of July celebration gone berserk: even our national anthem's spectacular description of aerial bombardment reveals a characteristic conflation of carnival and war. Our venture in Vietnam, originally conceived as an agonistic demonstration of superior energy, character, and technology brought this characteristic confusion to the fore. Our attitude, so evidently displayed by the mystique of counter-insurgency, implied a ludic, playful version of war. In this light, war, evolving from a sense of energetic excess rather than from a desperate need for survival, corresponds with what John Huizinga calls "*homo ludens*," man the player--at law, at ritual, at carnival, even at war. Much of the commentary about America in Vietnam clearly reveals a characteristic tendency to confuse the two ludic activities of carnival and war that predominated in those years. Although the conventional wisdom identifies carnival with irresponsible infantile shenanigans at home, and war with our tragic duty abroad, the two games are often conflated, a conflation I attribute largely to our cultural devaluation of other forms of carnival. In a sense, our Puritan heritage declares war the only carnival game in town, or at least the only one sanctioned as both adult and righteous. I will focus in this essay on the significance of this reductive tendency, a tendency often alluded to on the periphery of commentary about Vietnam, but never extensively discussed. What were the implications of the common assumption that Vietnam was a kind of Disneyland? The answers reveal a great deal about the intensity of the townspeople's intolerance for Carradine's carnival, a carnival they presume is a mockery of their cockfights across the street. More generally, America's tendency to reduce carnival to carnage tells us a great deal about the Sixties. More significantly yet, it speaks volumes about an abiding aspect of American culture that has haunted us from the beginning.

Before examining the conflation of carnival and war in specific works about Vietnam, I want to adumbrate briefly what I mean by "carnival." Mikhail Bakhtin's work on Rabelais is most helpful in this respect. Generally speaking, carnival's irreverence playfully inverts the everyday official hierarchies of customary usage. Ultimately democratic, it refuses to observe the most fundamental boundaries between upper and lower social classes, sacred and profane rituals, even between people and animals, or creatures and things. For example, what Bakhtin awkwardly refers to as the functions of the "lower bodily stratum," usually suppressed in ordinary times, are celebrated for their crucial role in the on-going generation of man. Carnival celebrates life by acknowledging the significance of sex, excrement, and death as natural aspects of the on-going evolvement of man, readily acknowledging, in fact reveling in the incompleteness of life. Usually tolerated, but certainly never encouraged by the official Roman Catholic Church, carnival lost much of its life-enhancing quality after its suppression by the Puritans. Since then, according to Bakhtin, carnival's life-affirming belly laugh has been replaced by the sardonic sneer of satire directed either at the established order or at the "unsavory" physicality of life itself. Thus, although the class origins and the psychological impulse for carnival have remained largely the same (the grunts in Vietnam the modern-day equivalent of Bakhtin's folk) the tendency to reduce carnival to the violence of war prophetically fulfills Bakhtin's supposition about post-Puritan degradation.

Perhaps the most illuminating account of the Puritan's war on carnival is Nathaniel Hawthorne's historical romance, "The Maypole of Merry Mount." Hawthorne describes the unhappy fate of a pagan cult of Europeans, Indians, and animals living outside the Puritan settlements in the primordial wilderness. The tale emphatically demonstrates the official American attitude toward carnival. The Puritans at the Bay Colony simply could not tolerate any alternative, especially a merry one, to their New Jerusalem. Hawthorne describes this intolerance as the result of the Puritan's belief in the revelers' mockery: "The Puritans affirmed that, when a psalm was pealing from their place of worship, the echo which the forest sent them back seemed often like the chorus of a jolly catch, closing with a roar of laughter" (205). Governor Endicott leads his "men of iron"--iron in both their austerity and in their military attire--out into the "howling wilderness," as the Puritans called it, to obliterate this jolly alternative to their gloomy settlement. They cut down the maypole and erect, in its stead, a whipping post, cropping the wilderness, some long hair and a few ears for good measure. Hawthorne's historical romance demonstrates a crucial American assumption: both of these cultures cannot exist in the same world. One must be *either* gloomy or jolly, a grizzled saint or a gay sinner, always attired in heavy armor or sensuous silk.

Hawthorne's ultimate concurrence with the outcome at Merry Mount comes through in both the tone of the tale and the thematic evocation of the fortunate fall. As Adam and Eve had to leave Eden, so too we have to grow up and assume adult responsibilities. This, in any event, sums up the lesson learned by the couple who were going to be crowned lord and lady of the May until they are properly chastised and joined in wedlock by the Puritans. Initially reluctant to accept the gloomy responsibilities of their new lot, the couple "never wasted one regretful thought on the vanities of Merry Mount" (210). Clearly, festival time ends with the end of childhood: adults don't go out masking on halloween.

The victory of the Puritans was cultural and historical. The psyche does not, however, respond so readily to purification by fiat. In Hawthorne's tale, it is the Puritans who are described as shadows, though Jung's term for the split off and denied part of the psyche might more properly have been identified with the revelers. In any event, disowned parts of the self tend to follow us around like our shadows. We might well say that the psyche allowed the Puritans to believe they had destroyed communities in Vietnam in order to save them. Meanwhile, the carnival impulse keeps coming back. (Perhaps the Puritans might better have deracinated the maypole, rather than just cropping it.) As the failure of prohibition so convincingly demonstrated during the Twenties--the other carnival decade in this century-- legislating against merriment merely drives it underground. Carnival re-surfaced, willy-nilly, within the very settlements of the establishment, albeit in the form of bootlegged whiskey that left some terrible hangovers in its wake; so too did the excesses of the Sixties. When the party does get going in America, it's hard to stop. Hence, the high attrition rate for rock stars. The more dramatically self-destructive carnival of war is, of course, complicated by the necessity for disguising the fun. Still, the gloomy mask of the dutiful warrior often slipped in Vietnam, momentarily revealing the ecstasy of those whose maypole has become a whipping post.

The abrupt termination of the carnival in the forest by the cropping of hair and the appropriation of the couple amounts, for the young man, to a draft notice. As Hawthorne says, the Puritans were either *fighting*, working or praying (209). As the stasis of permanent commitment in the settlement replaces the flux of life in the forest, so too lambent, silken clothing gives way to the uniform of iron. Since then, our culture maintains that the best way--many would say the only way--for males to join the community of responsible adults is to go into the armed services. The norms that prevail during the rite of passage to adulthood--most dramatically evident during basic training, but typically continuing throughout the tour of duty--are virtually synonymous with the carnival norms of festive time. As Gennep, Turner and Eliade have shown, the liminal or threshold time betwixt- and-between childhood and adulthood during initiatory passage suspends the customary norms of behavior and perception. Only by going through this sort of void can the novice actually separate from childhood. So too carnival time suspends established procedures to encourage the free play of imagination. Thus, even before the shooting starts, the similarity between the liminal time of initiatory passage and carnival flux encourages our cultural conflation of carnival and war. After all, the three--initiation, carnival, and war--all temporarily rescind the rules of ordinary time. Vietnam was so bizarre for many of our combat troops that they never emerged from the liminal flux of that initiatory experience; even now, post-combat stress disorders continue to haunt the veteran. Less obvious, but no less real, is the more pervasive flash-back, the more general lingering nation-wide inability to emerge from the liminal haze of the Sixties. The works I will consider tend to acknowledge, to one degree or another, our continuing confusion in this liminal miasma. Related to this acknowledgment is the assumption that transitional, liminal states can best be enacted by re-creation of the carnival climate that characterized our national psyche during that era.

Even Ron Kovic's autobiographical novel, for all its prosaic prose, reflects the author's liminal rite of passage from naive patriot to embittered war veteran by refusing to be either an autobiography or a novel. As soon as it looks like one, it becomes another; "I" becomes "he" becomes "I"...and so on. But my main concern here with *Born on the Fourth of July* is with its unequivocally announced theme. Whether rooting for the Yankees, watching July 4th fireworks, or joining the marines, the young Kovic incessantly demonstrates the American tendency to identify the carnival energy of youth with chauvinistic display. His conversion later in the book lies in the recognition of this reductive confusion. In retrospect we can see that the seemingly limitless, and certainly optimistic, Kennedy vigor of Camelot and the carnival energy of the counter-culture he joined later that same decade were both energized by the same dionysian source. Kovic's odyssey from gung-ho marine to crippled war protestor chronicles the change in his allegiance from one kind of carnival to another. The turning point in his gradual transformation occurs when he realizes that he and another wounded veteran are being exploited as exhibits in a Memorial Day parade (96-110). His later joining what he initially calls the "weird carnival" (137) of a protest demonstration signals, in effect, his "un-enlistment" from the marines, and his simultaneous joining with a collective life-force of another kind. As Kovic puts it, there was, at the protest rally, a "togetherness here just as there had been in Vietnam, but it was a togetherness of a different kind of people and for a much different reason" (140). Perhaps the most telling enactment of this sort of conversion experience was suggested by the frequent invitation to make love, not war--the protestors placing flowers in the gun barrels of the National Guard troops who witnessed so many of these carnivals. Unfortunately, this kind of gesture came too late for Ron Kovic, paralyzed as he was from the waist down, to reverse the consequences of his earlier belief in that basic training jingle

> This is my rifle
> This is my gun;
> This is for shooting
> And this is for fun.

It is too late for a number of reasons. Coupled with America's abiding infatuation with violence is the characteristic confusion of carnival's celebration of life's abundance with insistence that life is inexhaustible, whether "life" means a wilderness itself, or the people who happen to live there. If life is inexhaustible, so the "thinking" goes, then life is cheap. Why not waste it? This implicit syllogism was especially enticing in jungles of Southeast Asia. The most dramatic demonstration of this ideology of waste--and I do have the grunt's slang for killing in mind here--was no doubt Michael Cimino's metaphor of Russian roulette, the ultimate carnival game played throughout his film *The Deerhunter*. Foiling this conspicuous waste of life are the wedding feast at the beginning and the funeral breakfast at the end of the film, this last ceremony a muted, heart-rending, paradoxical reminder that life, both abundant and precious, should not be confused with an exploding firecracker in a bizarre carnival game.

Even when Americans are invited to join traditional carnival in full folk swing, the upshot is sometimes violent. Take *Southern Comfort*, a film ostensibly about an ill-fated National Guard contingent on week-end maneuvers in Southern Louisiana. From the very start, the film parabolizes American experience in Vietnam. Before long, the war game maneuvers become real, deadly war with the locals. The only two guardsmen to emerge alive from a running battle with the swamp folk find themselves at a Cajun festival, complete with slaughtered pigs (we hope as sublimated offerings to substitute for the perhaps still-in-jeopardy surviving guardsmen) dancing, and Cajun music. But as the tempo of the festival mounts, some more swamp folk join the party by joining in battle with the two guardsmen. On this level, the film, also set in the pivotal year 1973, ironically recalls Hawthorne's historical romance. The guardsmen, modern-day Puritans, whose motto as the standing militia is "civilians in peace, soldiers in war," are out of their element in the wilderness of the swamp, just as our troops were out of their depth in the jungles of Vietnam. The guardsmen arrogantly disregard the local customs--they cut fish nets, "borrow" boats without asking the owners' permission, destroy a local's house after beating him up and taking him prisoner without any evidence that he has been shooting at them. All this only-too-familiar kind of arrogance is remarkably ironic: it effectively ensures that the guardsmen will not be able to enjoy the festival, a golden opportunity in Southern Louisiana, the only area in America that has maintained traditional carnival. Though invited to join the festival by some of the locals, the guardsmen depart in haste--little Southern Comfort for them--not as their Puritan ancestors were refusers of pleasure, but as the only way to survive.

Though largely limiting the national guardsmen to blanks during their maneuvers in *Southern Comfort* symbolizes brilliantly our ineffectiveness in Vietnam, we were hardly without sufficient ammunition in the "real" situation. Indeed, we were only-too-well-equipped for celebrating our fire power with hubristically tragic effect. While the hippies at home enjoyed light shows, the grunts, like Prometheus, found ways to steal fire from the establishment, reveling in aerial bombardment. Perhaps the most direct, and certainly one of the most typical, specific manifestations of this kind of carnival occurs when several grunts, perched on top of their bunker, enjoy the spectacle of an especially breath-taking battle in *Meditations in Green*: "The distant fire fight proceeded in eerie silence. It was like watching the electronic display of a fancy pinball machine on which all the bells and buzzers had been disconnected" (175-76). All Griffin, the main character, can do is utter, "God, it's beautiful" (176) or "God, it's so beautiful" (178). To which his friend replies, "it's better than acid" (178):

> Off in the distance beyond the clustered lights of the base the smooth rock surface of night was split by--he [Griffin] paused to count--five magnesium flares, hung like lamps at various altitudes, each dangling on a parachute between a twisting coil of gray smoke and a cascade of sparks, artificial suns drifting down into extinction, their replacements bursting brightly into illumination further up above, the whole show like a student's model of genesis and apocalypse, planets spawning and dying in unbroken succession, a parody of eternity. From below a long red line of tracer fire arched back and forth like a sluggish windshield wiper. A second red line appeared, the two swung slowly toward each other, intersected with no perceptible effect, swung slowly away. (175)

America lights up the sky, tracing its reduction of carnival's double celebration of the on-going death of the old and birth of the new to the carnage of war. Energetically begun, the show ends entropically, "like a sluggish windshield wiper," the tracer rounds swinging slowly toward each other, intersecting, but not meeting or revealing any perceptible effect. Life no more issues from this spectacle of death than from the carnival of the grunt who observes the same display from the privacy of the bunker, "stretched out on his bunk, masturbating" (176).

One of the most impressive analyses of the spectacle of fire power as carnival display occurs in William Broyles's disturbing essay "Why Men Love War." He describes these pyrotechnics like an opera buff sharing the fine points of a particularly spectacular performance of a favorite work:

> War *is* beautiful. There is something about a firefight at night...the red tracers go out into the blackness as if you were drawing with a light pen. The little dots of light start winking back, and green tracers from AK-47s begin to weave in with the red brilliant patterns...Daytime offers nothing so spectacular, but it also has its charms. Many men loved napalm... but I always thought napalm was greatly overrated unless you enjoy watching tires burn. I preferred white phosphorous, which exploded with a fulsome elegance, wreathing its target in intense and billowing smoke, throwing out glowing red comets trailing brilliant white plumes. (62)

Michael Herr, in *Dispatches*, captures the same shocking sentiment in his quotation of the remarks of Tim Page, a British war correspondent, who expresses disgust at the suggestion that he supply photographs for a book that would "take the glamour out of war....'You can't take the glamour out of that. It's like trying to take the glamour out of sex, trying to take the glamour out of the Rolling Stones.'" Not only disgusted, Page finds such naivete incredible: "'I mean, you *know* that, it just *can't be done*! The very *idea*. Ohhh, what a laugh! Take the bloody *glamour* out of bloody *war*!'" (265-66).

The most glamorous version of the war in Vietnam in this sense of "glamour" is undoubtedly *Apocalypse Now*. Even the title of the film reveals America's tendency to confuse carnival display--this time its napalm, though it could, of course, be nuclear holocaust--with apocalyptic destruction. As the patrol boat goes up the river toward Kurtz's temple of death at the heart of darkness, the action becomes more explicitly carnivalesque. Perhaps most memorable is the U.S.O. show in the jungle that culminates in a riot. The chaos begins when the go-go-playboy bunny dancers, suggestively reminiscent of Dallas Cowboy cheerleaders, mime sexual intercourse with their toy M-16s. At the climax, the troops storm the stage, the members of the show hastily departing in a helicopter swirl of chaos highly reminiscent of America's undignified withdrawal from Vietnam. We are, no doubt, inclined to agree with Captain Willard's (Martin Sheen's) comment on this episode that we are trying to win a war run, "by a bunch of four-star clowns who were going to wind up giving the circus away."

That the war in Vietnam was, at least from the American point of view, a carnival is the final revelation of *Apocalypse Now*. Lieutenant Colonel Billy "Duke" (as in John Wayne) Kilgore of the Air Calvary, the napalm buff, explicitly demonstrates this reality by bringing his Wagnerian, flying circus to town, a village that imprudently locates itself adjacent to a good surfing area. (Colonel Kilgore wants to go surfing.) The children who leave school early as Kilgore's circus descends actually run away from, not towards, Kilgore's kind of fun. Farther up the river, what begins as a carnival also ends in carnage, demonstrating, as Captain Willard puts it, that the boys on the patrol boat are, indeed, "rock and rollers with one foot in their graves." The attack actually begins in the haze of two smoke grenades the surfer Lance B. Johnson (or L.B.J.) has ignited to demonstrate Vietnam's spectacular superiority to Disneyland. The first fight that interrupts this display is brief, but fatal. As the boat continues quietly up the river, the enemy never seen, a young boy, who moments before danced in ecstasy to the Rolling Stones, lies dead. A tape-letter from his mother drones reassuringly as his cassette player plays on. The fireworks have turned to a fire fight with the super-sensible speed of a bullet. It's difficult to distinguish the carnival from the carnage until the smoke clears, and even then, the violence occurs far too fast for us to be entirely clear about exactly what did happen.

The condition of the men on the boat at that confusing moment is not altogether unfamiliar when we think about our experience in Vietnam even now. Much of the obfuscation results, no doubt, from the category conflation that has characterized our perspective from the start. Having observed innumerable war movies before going to Vietnam, the tendency was to re-enact those movies and those movie roles all the while the "real" war was going on. Official hallucinatory sightings of lights at the end of tunnels further contributed to the liminal haze. For all of our fire power, we *were*, in a sense, using blanks in the real war, rarely able even to see, never mind reconstruct what actually occurred: shooting blanks and going blank. But of course the enemy was not. They knew only too well they were not living in Disney cartoons where characters pop back up no matter how many times they are flattened. As Captain Willard sardonically says, after referring to the clowns running the American circus, the Viet Cong had no U.S.O. shows: no way out but death or victory. The screeching cognitive dissonance that resulted from the American experience still reverberates today. Take, for example, the central issue of *"Reading the Wind": The Literature of the Vietnam War*, an interpretative commentary on the 1985 Asia Society conference: How can we best "get at" the war, in fact or in fancy?

This struggle between the Puritan quest for the plain facts literally interpreted and the aesthetes' conviction that reality is, must be, imaginatively reconstructed has always been the central issue of American's attempt to come to terms with Vietnam. Even Robin Moore changed his mind about whether *The Green Berets* was to be a factual or fictional account. Philip Caputo, David Halberstam, and Tim O'Brien all struggled with this issue. Michael Herr's compromise, literary journalism, perhaps best allows for both the startling facts and the sort of imaginative formal transformation needed to deconstruct cultural assumptions about the nature of war. The imagination is, in this sense, homeopathic, in that only an added dose of carnival can demonstrate that we have all the while been carnivalizing. American writers have been, in this respect, in much the same situation as those who write about the Holocaust, a reality that far exceeded what they could imagine even while it was happening. So too, Philip Roth complained that the evening news in the American Sixties was far more bizarre than anything the writer of fiction could possibly imagine (120): how could one better describe the fate of the artist living in a culture unconsciously indulging in carnival, the very indulgence it has most emphatically condemned?

Although the usual tendency was to identify the uncanny quality of American experience in Vietnam with the (un)reality of that place, much of this sense was doubtless a projection of the dissonance we brought to the scene. Reading about that experience even today can cause the same sensation. Consider the habit of collecting body parts as trophies of personal victory. Ears were customary--a traditional Puritan favorite--though other appendages were sometimes preferred. A lieutenant in *Dispatches*, typically located at the nexus of official versions of what war is supposed to be and the bizarre thing the grunts know it to be, reveals this discrepancy when he scolds one of his men who wants to skin a dead enemy soldier in the presence of a journalist: "'We had this gook and we was gonna skin him' (a grunt told me), 'I mean he was already dead and everything, and the lieutenant comes over and says, "Hey asshole, there's a reporter in the TOC, use your fucking heads, there's a time and a place for everything..."' (69-70). The lieutenant says, in effect, that carnival is only appropriate in carnival time. Even more sensational is the rumor of the attempt to construct a sort of composite "gook" somewhere out in the wilderness of the highlands (35). But perhaps most troubling of all is Broyles's account of what his men did to a North Vietnamese soldier they had brought back after a successful ambush:

> I later found the dead man propped up against some
> C-ration boxes. He had on sunglasses, and a *Playboy*
> magazine open in his lap; a cigarette dangled jauntily
> from his mouth, and on his head was perched a large
> and perfectly formed piece of shit. (61)

It seems this kind of imaginative play was commonplace. The gruesome games of the grunts display an uncanny similarity to what Bakhtin sees as carnival's preoccupation with grotesque, with lower bodily strata, with all aspects and manifestations of life that the established order ordinarily wants to repress. But as Bakhtin would have predicted, though the grunts' freak shows unconsciously enact carnival's celebration of life's amorphous multiplicity, they also reverse its ultimate meaning. Whereas traditional carnival celebrated the simultaneous death of the old and birth of the new in the ongoing evolution of life forms, the grunts' carnivals reflect the post-Puritan tendency to see only death and degradation in the same process. We might say that the grunts' insistence on brute enactment of the freak show betrays a defective (Puritan) imagination, the sort of crippled sensibility that e.e. cummings and Ferlinghetti never tire of trying to entice us out of. In any event, the point of the freak show in Vietnam, as Broyles tells us, was not to remind us of our participation in life's mind-boggling multiplicity, but rather to distance us from our (dead) brothers. We are not involved in mankind, because we are not (yet) dead. Here is his confessional commentary on the desecrated enemy soldier:

> I pretended to be outraged, since desecration of bodies
> was frowned upon and un-American and unproductive.
> But it wasn't outrage I felt. I kept my officer's face on,
> but inside I was...laughing. I laughed--I believe now
> --in part because of some subconscious appreciation of
> this obscene linkage of sex and excrement and death;
> and in part in exultant realization that he--whoever he

had been--was dead and I--special unique me--was
alive. He was my brother and I knew him not. (61-
62)

What, then, are we to make of all this? In the most general sense,
war, as Broyles rightly says in his essay, is "like lifting up the corner of
the universe and looking at what's underneath" (61). In this respect it
resembles C. L. Barber's formulation of the essence of carnival in his
essay on Shakespeare's festive comedy. He writes that the characters
in festive time go "through release to clarification" (6). In other words,
temporarily suspending the ordinary constraints of behavior and the
customary modes of perception can be a learning experience. To step
out of our ordinary roles is to see what is usually disguised or even
invisible. So too war, especially a lost war, uncovers much that might
otherwise remain hidden. For all of its horror, the anonymous account
of a young man's literal indulgence in "carnival" by delving into the flesh
of his dead comrades *is* a kind of carnal knowledge, not only about
human anatomy, but also about man's boundless curiosity:

> Watching guys die is a drag, but there's a weird
> educational side to war, too. Like the first time I seen
> a guy's guts laying on top of him, as disgusting as it
> was, I said to myself, "Oh, wow. So that's what they
> look like.' If you want, you can go in there and help
> yourself to a handful, you can wash them off and keep
> them. You can perform major surgery right there.....
>
> I used to love to go over to guys who would catch
> rounds in the chest or the guts and pretend I was a
> doctor. You had a license to do whatever you
> wanted....I would sort of experiment. You know, I
> couldn't do nothing to hurt these guys, they were dead.
> But there was something about sticking my hands in
> warm blood that I used to love especially during the
> monsoon seasons. (Baker 75)

In the broadest sense, we not only lost the war in Vietnam; we lost our
innocence as well. Thus Colonel Kurtz, purest of Puritans dedicated to
the eradication of evil, ends the carnival impresario of his death camp
in Cambodia. Marlon Brando, playing Ambassador MacWhite in the
film version of *The Ugly American*, comes full circle as the demented
Colonel Kurtz, the demon merely the shadow of the pure knight in

shining armor that was repressed at the beginning of this powerful enactment of the American Romance.

To acknowledge carnival, in this context, is to acknowledge the arbitrary and often self-serving nature of our established modes of ordering our experience. Carnival's celebration of flux undermines the tendency to rest complacently in inherited shibboleths: that, for example, the Puritans were good, the wilderness bad (why else would the devil lurk there? what else could all that howling be about?), or to cite a more recent formulation of the Romance, that America is Godly, Russia the Empire of Evil. Carnival helps maintain a sense of humor to combat this sort of naive equation. (In this respect, *Good Morning Vietnam* demonstrates sound instincts.)

So too, *Americana* demonstrates a healthy awareness that we are humorous in another sense: human beings, and cultures too, are mixtures of the same stuff; all are capable of carnival and carnage. To appreciate this is to achieve a sense of balance that involves integration, not purification. Traditional carnival reminds us that, "the highest truth is not the negation of evil, but the most inclusive good" (Stewart 161). The carrousel functions as an especially effective metaphor for the shift from war to peace. A carrousel was originally a tournament in which horses went through ritualized paces, a sublimation, in effect, of their normal use in war. The carnival carrousel, even more remote from war, innocently celebrates life's cosmic cyclical rhythm in exuberant play. Carradine's gesture signals the shift from his war-time experience in air calvary to the reinstatement of carnival joy in the heart of the heart of the country. Individuals, and countries as well, can, as the film implies over and over again, go either way: to carnage or to carnival. The informing energy is the same.

The title of the book upon which *Americana* was based, *The Perfect Round,* says much about the thematic significance of carnival. In a general way, the round configuration signifies the restoration of the dance round the maypole with all the fecund implications of that celebration of life's bounty. Roundness also implies the full dimension of human complexity, a complexity demanding a cycle that incorporates times for both work and play. Much of the carnage of the Sixties resulted from the characteristic tendency to repress half that cycle. Both wars and carnivals involve "lifting off the corner of the universe and looking at what's underneath." We might rather say, given the American tendency to repress traditional carnival, that the pressure built up until the lid blew off. Still, both Broyles' metaphor and Barber's formula imply the possibility of learning from the temporary revocation of peace-time restraints. In fact, we not only covered the war in the media, but also discovered something of importance about our unconscious mythical fantasies and beliefs. We will have grown up as a result of the disillusionment occasioned by this knowledge to the extent that we have learned to distinguish between the carnival escapism typical of World War II propaganda and the grim realities of carnage that are inevitably thrust upon us when we lift up the corner of the universe by going to war. This means we will have to stop insisting that the war didn't mean anything--it meant only too much--or that there is no way to connect what happened over there with "the World" back here.

It was because of its concern with establishing this connection that I began with *Americana*. The hero repudiates the nightmare of Vietnam, but he does not attempt to escape its implications by going back to sleep. He performs a gesture that suggests, however cryptically, an alternative version of carnival. This version represents a confidence in life's possibilities clearly distinguished from the typical frenzied forms of carnival madness that raged during the Sixties. Herr sums up this destructiveness with characteristic eloquence:

> The Sixties had made so many casualties, its war and
> its music had run power off the same circuit for so
> long they didn't even have to fuse. The war primed
> you for the lame years while rock and roll turned more
> dangerous than bullfighting, rock stars started falling
> like second lieutenants. (276)

This carnage might have been mitigated if the need for carnival release had been acknowledged before repression accumulated to produce the explosive pressures we witnessed in Vietnam. Both gods, Apollo and Dionysus, insist on recognition. To deny one is to wallow in regression, to stifle in repression, or, worse yet, to spawn monstrous combinations of both: Kilgore carnage, Kurtz's cult, Manson's crew. Once the party did begin in those dionysian times, nobody wanted to stop. Absolute power, absolute freedom, absolute everything was demanded, *now*. What we got instead was an endless, tedious dance around the maypole, or seemingly endless, and certainly pointless, marches around the swamp, bad drug trips that wouldn't end and a nightmarish war that never had officially even begun. Robert A. Johnson, in his study *Ecstasy*, eloquently describes the futility and the danger of attempting to reinstate Dionysus without rendering Apollo his due:

> Remember the hippie movement, which degenerated
> from the innocence of Woodstock to the violence of
> Altamont in the space of a year....It is not enough to

> throw the whole society over and go dance naked on
> the beach.   Such   experiments,   however   well
> intentioned, are doomed to failure. We cannot simply
> move from the realm of rationality to the irrational
> realm of Dionysus and think that everything will be
> solved. This is either/or thinking. Jung has said that
> for us the choice is no longer either/or, but either-
> *and*-or. We must touch Dionysus, we must bring him
> back into our lives in a humanized form, or in denying
> him we will destroy ourselves. (27)

We can return to Hawthorne's romance to see how the problem
inheres in its very formulation. The prevailing assumption was we must
be either full-time grim Puritans *or* full-time irresponsible merrymakers.
No integration is possible, because the stakes are absolute: "Jollity and
gloom were contending for an empire" (198). Without a dialectical
point of reference to limit and contextualize carnival, the Sixties
exploded. If we had a carnival tradition besides war, a sort of cyclical
release valve, Broyles's metaphor and Barber's formula might have
been apt. But as I said, we did not so much lift up a corner of the
universe in those years as witness an eruption when the lid blew off.
And, of course, when the fragments came down, people got hurt. If we
did plan to lift up the corner periodically, who knows but we might see
something brewing that is not the next war.
    Perhaps the most useful hint as to how to lift up the corner
periodically occurs in *Americana* where Carradine has to re-balance the
carrousel by wedging up one end to get it back on track. When he
finally does get the merry-go-round going at the end of the film, the
very people who have so stupidly and cruelly interfered with his project
go for a ride, joining the carnival at the end of the war. Balance here
integrates standard American dichotomies: ecstasy and control;
wilderness and settlement; the garden and the machine. *Americana*
suggests a revision of both history and Hawthorne's grim tale as the
Puritans of Kansas abandon their abandoned church/cockfighting
arena, cross the street, and join, however temporarily, the perfect dance
round Carradine's rejuvenated maypole.

Works Cited

Bakhtin, Mikhail. *Rabelais and His World*. Trans. Helene Iswolsky.
    Bloomington: Indiana University Press, 1984.

Barber, C. L. *Shakespeare's Festive Comedy*. Princeton: Princeton University Press, 1972.

Baker, Mark. *Nam*. New York: Berkley Books, 1981.

Broyles, William Jr. "Why Men Love War." *Esquire*, Nov. 1984. 55-65.

Caputo, Philip. *A Rumor of War*. New York: Ballantine Books, 1977.

Caputo, Philip. *Indian Country*. New York: Bantam, 1987.

Eliade, Mircea. *Rites and Symbols of Initiation*. Trans. Willard R. Trask. New York: Harper and Row, 1958.

Gibson, James William. *The Perfect War: The War We Couldn't Lose and How We Did*. New York: Random House, 1988.

Gennep, Arnold van. *The Rites of Passage*. Trans. Monika B. Vizedom and Gabrielle L. Caffee. Chicago: The University of Chicago Press, 1960.

Halberstam, David. *One Very Hot Day*. Boston: Houghton Mifflin, 1968.

---. *The Best and the Brightest*. New York: Random House, 1972.

Hawthorne, Nathaniel. "The Maypole of Merry Mount." *Hawthorne: Selected Tales and Sketches*. Ed. Hyatt H. Waggoner. New York: Holt, Rinehart and Winston, 1970. 198-210.

Herr, Michael. *Dispatches*. New York: Avon, 1980.

Huizinga, Johan. *Homo Ludens: A Study of the Play-Element in Culture*. Boston: Beacon Press, 1955.

Johnson, Robert A. *Ecstasy: Understanding the Psychology of Joy*. San Francisco: Harper and Row, 1987.

Kovic, Ron. *Born on the Fourth of July*. New York: Pocket Books, 1976.

Lomperis, Timothy J. *"Reading the Wind"*: *The Literature of the Vietnam War*. Durham: Duke University Press, 1987.

Moore, Robin. *The Green Berets*. New York: Avon, 1965.

O'Brien, Tim. *Going After Cacciato*. New York: Delacorte Press, 1978.

---. *If I Die in a Combat Zone*. New York: Delacorte Press, 1973.

Robinson, Henry Morton. *The Perfect Round*. New York: Harcourt, Brace and Company, 1945.

Roth, Philip. *Reading Myself and Others*. New York: Farrar, Strauss and Giroux, 1975.

Stewart, Marilyn. "Carnival and *Don Quixote*: The Folk Tradition of Comedy." *The Terrain of Comedy*. Ed. Louise Cowan. Dallas: The Dallas Institute of Humanities and Culture, 1984, 42-62.

Turner, Victor. *The Ritual Process: Structure and Anti-Structure*. Ithaca: Cornell University Press, 1969.

Wright, Stephen. *Meditations in Green*. New York: Bantam, 1984.

MEN, WOMEN, AND VIETNAM

Milton J. Bates

> A man and a woman
> Are one.
> A man and a woman and a blackbird
> Are one.
> --Wallace Stevens, "Thirteen Ways of
> Looking at a Blackbird"

I

The blackbird in Wallace Stevens' familiar poem is both a unifying device, involved in all the speaker knows and perceives, and an intrusive, rather sinister presence. Though men and women are said to be still "one" after the blackbird joins them, the second configuration seems less stable than the first. Two is company, three a social contract. During the nineteen sixties, the Vietnam War played a role analogous to Stevens' blackbird in relationships between men and women. Superficially, it was a time of unprecedented androgyny in dress, hair styles, and activities. But beneath the surface lay differences of outlook and purpose that emerged toward the end of the decade as the women's liberation movement. While the War did not cause these differences, it served in some cases to disclose them, as an x-ray reveals an unsuspected stress fracture, in other cases to exacerbate them.

The blackbird casts its shadow over much of the film and literature dealing with men and women of the Vietnam generation, sometimes long after the last American troops returned home. Among the many clichés in *The Big Chill* (1983), directed by Lawrence Kasdan, is the sexually wounded veteran played by William Hurt.[1] Nick, whose very name links him to Hemingway and thereby to another Hemingway protagonist, the impotent Jake Barnes, had been something of a ladies' man in college. When he joins his classmates for the funeral of one of their friends, a suicide who symbolizes the played-out idealism of the sixties, he is approached by an old girlfriend with an embarrassing proposition. Meg (Mary Kay Place), now a lawyer, sees in Nick an opportunity to add motherhood to her resumé; but she is forced to look elsewhere when he tells her what happened to him in Vietnam. Nick eventually takes up with Chloe (Meg Tilly), the girlfriend of the suicide, who accepts him even though he can't, as he puts it, "do anything." He decides to forego his current line of work as a drug dealer in order to build a new life with Chloe in a backwoods cabin.

Why Chloe rather than Meg? The answer has as much to do with the generation gap as it does with the nature of Nick's wound. Meg is just about Nick's age and bent on success in a career once dominated by men. She dresses in a "power suit" and, not anticipating that the funeral will turn into a weekend-long post-mortem on the sixties, arrives with an attaché case stuffed with legal briefs rather than such domestic comforts as a toothbrush or change of clothing. Chloe, by contrast, is a belated flower child of the younger generation, devoted to physical rather than mental culture and blissfully ignorant of the past. She is a throwback to the stereotypical American helpmate of the forties and fifties, perhaps even to the Asian bride favored by some veterans of World War II and Korea. Nick will not have to re-fight the sex wars of the sixties with Chloe.

Much the same story is told, though with greater finesse, in Bobbie Ann Mason's critically acclaimed novel *In Country* (1985). The events of the novel are seen through the eyes of Samantha Hughes, a seventeen-year-old girl living with her uncle Emmett in Kentucky. Like Chloe, Sam is both bemused by the antics of the sixties generation and strongly attracted to them as shapers of her identity. While her peers cruise the "mating range" between the Burger Boy and McDonald's restaurants, she becomes infatuated with an older man, a Vietnam veteran who has the advantage of resembling Bruce Springsteen. At the crucial moment, however, Tom Hudson proves to be impotent, though he tells her that the problem is psychological rather than physiological. This episode seems to epitomize--perhaps in some cases to explain--a pattern Sam had observed in men and women of the older generation: their relationships seem always to be troubled, often by effects of the Vietnam War.

This is most literally true of her own parents, inasmuch as her father had been killed in Vietnam before she was born; but it is also true of her uncle and his veteran friends. When Sam visits Emmett's girlfriend Anita in her apartment, she is struck by Anita's expectant posture: "It was as though she were sitting in a perfectly arranged setting, waiting for something to happen, like a stage set just before the curtain goes up" (62). Anita will have to wait indefinitely, it appears, since her leading man is not ready to commit himself to a life with her or anyone else. Emmett, Sam learns later, had lost most of his comrades on a patrol in Vietnam and now fears intimacy with another human being--one of the classic symptoms of post-traumatic stress disorder. Though some of Emmett's fellow veterans have married, none has found domestic tranquility. One of them would rather be in Vietnam and is perpetually feuding with his wife over matters related to the War. Another, the president of the local Vietnam veterans' organization, is devastated when his wife leaves him for a career in computer programing. Speculating about the source of these tensions, Sam wonders whether men might not differ fundamentally from women in the value they place on human life. During an overnight campout in a swamp preserve, which she undertakes in order to experience some of the things soldiers had experienced in Vietnam, she concedes that women, too, occasionally wage war and even kill their own babies (208, 215). But she decides that such behavior is the exception; as a rule, men kill and women don't (209-10).

In the novel's concluding episode, both Sam and Emmett find a measure of healing when they make a pilgrimage to the Vietnam Veterans' Memorial in Washington. Will this experience enable Emmett to connect with Anita and Sam with Tom Hudson? We never know, and to that extent *In Country* declines the easy solution offered by *The Big Chill*, the pat epithalamial closure of comedy and sentimental romance. The novel implies, however, that neither Sam nor Anita will be quite complete until she gets her man. Sam's mother has achieved the consummation they devoutly desire. Irene Hughes, having survived her phases as war widow and antiwar activist, is now blissfully advanced in her "yuppie" phase. Her accoutrements include an IBM executive husband, a ranch home in suburban Lexington, a red Trans Am, and a new baby named Heather. Sam initially regards her mother's transformation as a rejection not merely of the sixties, to which Sam belongs in spirit, but also of herself. By the end, however, mother and daughter are reconciled and Sam plans to move in with Irene while attending college.

Like *The Big Chill*, then, *In Country* disposes of the sixties tension between the sexes by reaffirming, albeit with a dose of conscious irony, a version of the feminine mystique. Though both allude to sexual conflict and imply a connection with the Vietnam War, they are framed in such a way as to preclude serious engagement with the conflict. *The Big Chill* is a comedy of manners, calculated to mine the vein of nostalgia uncovered by a similar and better film, John Sayles' *The Return of the Secaucus Seven* (1980). Mason, having elected to tell her story from a teenage girl's point of view, cannot realistically venture a more mature critique of the War or sexual roles. Why inflict such a handicap on one's narrative? Very likely, Mason was simply respecting the limits of her experience. Her own war story, she remarked in an interview (7), is the same one Anita tells in the novel: sharing a bus with soldiers on their way to Vietnam (115-16). *In Country*'s chief strength, its convincing representation of a particular character's point of view, remains its chief weakness.

I propose in this essay to fill in some of the blanks in these two popular works. After tracing the history of the sexual revolution of the sixties and early seventies in broad outline, I will turn to some of the literature and film in which this revolution and its attendant conflicts are represented. If I am correct, the more thoughtful literary and cinematic treatments of the War suggest how men and women of the Vietnam generation can still be "one" in the company of that insidious blackbird.

II

Precisely what is meant by "sexual revolution," and when did it take place? If the phrase is used to describe a significant increase in nonmarital (that is, pre- or extra-marital) sex, then few historians or sociologists would date the revolution before the late sixties.[2] The Kinsey Institute, for example, found little more sexual experience among college students in 1968 than in 1948, despite the relaxation of policies restricting dormitory visitation (O'Neill 300n). At the end of the decade, however, surveys and opinion polls began to register the shift toward sexual permissiveness that became manifest in the seventies. One mid-seventies poll of students in eight colleges indicates that three-fourths of both men and women had experienced intercourse by their junior year, and that the women were more active sexually than the men (Chafe 437, Jones 176-77).

Another kind of sexual revolution can be dated somewhat earlier, and it tended to curtail or at least draw attention away from genital sexual activity. This was of course the revolution in culturally defined gender roles. During the years following World War II, Betty Friedan pointed out in *The Feminine Mystique* (1963), American women were becoming wives and mothers at a progressively younger average age, contrary to the trend in other industrialized nations and many underdeveloped countries (16, 150, 162-63, 385, 386). The traditional dichotomy between virgin and whore had been supplanted by the dichotomy between "the feminine woman, whose goodness includes the desires of the flesh, and the career woman, whose evil includes every desire of the separate self" (46).[3] Friedan found that "feminine" women often became obsessed with sex, demanding from their husbands and lovers a kind of fulfillment they could not possibly provide (258-81). She urged women to cure their malaise by venturing into the workplace. Why should they not have what men had always had, both career and family? They would in fact be better wives and mothers once they had satisfied those desires of the "separate self."

As the conservative logic of that last statement suggests, *The Feminine Mystique* was a product of its time--and therefore of the feminine mystique--as well as a catalyst for change. Later, when Friedan looked back on the sixties from the vantage point of the eighties, she had to concede that a career is not always the solution to "the problem that has no name."[4] Many women lack the skills or freedom to pursue the more challenging careers she envisioned, and those who have the opportunity often discover that yesterday's glamorous career is today's routine job. *The Feminine Mystique* nevertheless opened new worlds to a particular group of young women-- generally white, middle-class, well-educated--and set the stage for direct political action affecting many more women. Its publication was timely, coming just before the Civil Rights Act of 1964 banned discrimination in employment on the basis of sex as well as race. When the government failed to act on cases of sex discrimination, Friedan and several other women formed the National Organization for Women as a pressure group. Due partly to their efforts, Congress passed the Equal Rights Amendment in 1972 and sent it to the states for ratification.

That the ERA is not yet the law of the land (an extension of the usual seven-year period for ratification expired in 1982) is due both to external opposition, particularly from pro-family and pro-life groups, and to dissent within the ranks of NOW and the women's movement generally. Even before the founding of NOW, a group of younger women were learning a very different lesson from the civil rights movement, one that led them to reject the careerism of the NOW group. Casey Hayden, Mary King, and other white women who worked with the Student Non-Violent Coordinating Committee during "freedom summer" of 1964 identified not with the successful journalists, lawyers, and politicians who formed the inner coterie of NOW but with the victims of the American Dream, poor blacks in the rural South. In the urban centers of the North other young women, mostly college students, were simultaneously working with blacks and the poor under the auspices of the Economic Research and Action Projects organized by Students for a Democratic Society.

SNCC and SDS nurtured in their women an ideology they would later sum up in the slogan, "The personal is political." Politics was not merely a matter of passing laws and winning votes; politics suffused relationships with family, friends, and fellow activists in the "participatory democracy" of the movement. But it was precisely here that the women in SNCC and SDS noted a contradiction between ideology and practice. The new left, as one historian of the women's movement has observed, "embodied the heritage of the feminine mystique far more strongly than the older left had" (Evans 116). Men occupied the positions of leadership and expected their women to do the "chickwork"--running the mimeograph machine, stamping envelopes, dispensing peanut butter sandwiches and even sex on demand. When Hayden and King protested this treatment in a position paper presented at a SNCC staff retreat in 1964, Stokely Carmichael's reply was crude but to the point: "The only position for women in SNCC is prone."

Carmichael's remark, which provoked both outrage and laughter at the time, is the most salient of many bits of mid-sixties folklore all expressing the same truth--that young men and women who shared the same goals, worked side by side, and even dressed alike were still separated by an abyss of sexism. At first, the women appealed to shared ideals as a way of bridging the gap, comparing themselves to the oppressed classes and races that groups like SNCC and SDS were committed to helping.[5] If this comparison appeared ludicrous to poor blacks in the rural South and northern cities, coming as it did from college-educated whites, it nevertheless reflected the level of desperation among these women shortly before they struck off on their own to start the women's liberation movement. That movement first attracted national media attention in 1968, when a group of radical feminists protested the Miss America pageant. Over the course of the following year, women's liberation became a staple news item in the popular press.

These were also the peak months of protest against the Vietnam War, framed on one side by the Tet Offensive of January 1968 and on the other by the draft lottery of December 1969. Surely the War was an issue that could bring the sexes back together? News footage and photographs of antiwar demonstrations, featuring women as conspicuously as men, suggest that it did. But the appearance is again deceptive. Examining the role played by women at the March on the Pentagon in the fall of 1967, Norman Mailer implies in *The Armies of the Night* (1968) that they were merely pawns in the real contest between soldiers and male demonstrators. The real issue, according to Mailer, was the virility of men on either side of the line. The antiwar males were in effect saying to the soldiers, "I will steal your élan, and your brawn, and the very animal of your charm because I am right and you are wrong and the balance of existence is such that the meat of your life is now attached to my spirit, I am stealing your balls" (288). In reply, the soldiers appeared to single out female demonstrators with their rifle butts, humiliating the male demonstrators who sat helplessly by, unable to defend their women (308).

Even allowing for the avowedly "novelistic" latitude of these passages from *Armies*, one has to grant their kernel of truth. Young men who joined the civil rights movement or the new left had to forego or at least postpone a conventional mode of demonstrating manhood through success in a career. By way of compensation, some adopted the exaggerated machismo of Third-World revolutionaries or (in the case of whites) of the racial minorities among whom they worked (O'Neill 195-97, Evans 150). This accounts for some of the sexism of men in SNCC and SDS; it also helps to account for their growing impatience with nonviolence as a political strategy. Opposing the Vietnam War precipitated a further crisis of masculinity, since it precluded another traditional male rite of passage, one their fathers had undergone in World War II. Some feigned homosexuality so as to be declared unfit for service, only to wonder later how much was pretense and how much truth. There was finally no way to feel morally justified without also feeling sexually compromised.

The SNCC-SDS pattern of conflict between the sexes was repeated in the antiwar movement. Women were not allowed to forget that they had less at stake in opposing the War, since they were exempt from the draft. They were to be, in effect, camp followers of the antiwarriors. As in the civil rights movement, their support was implicitly sexual as well as moral. The slogan emblazoned across a British propaganda poster of World War I, "Women of Britain Say--Go!," was revised to read, "Girls Say Yes to Guys Who Say No." Eventually it occurred to "girls" of the new left that when they said yes they reaffirmed the pattern of exploitation they were protesting in Southeast Asia. The War taught them that they were not merely a disadvantaged race or class but a politically and economically oppressed segment of the world's population. "As we analyze the position of women in capitalist society and especially in the United States," reads a paper drafted in a women's liberation workshop in 1967 and published in *New Left Notes*, "we find that women are in a colonial relationship to men and we recognize ourselves as part of the Third World. . . . Women, because of their colonial relationship to men, have to fight for their own independence" (quoted in Evans 240-41).

Does the word fight seem misplaced in a document drafted by women opposed to the War? If so, it reflects the contradictory history of feminist responses to war and the military. In 1971 a NOW national conference held in Los Angeles passed a resolution calling for an immediate end to the Vietnam War and all other wars, which the delegates regarded as an expression of the "masculine mystique" (Van Breems 12). But when registration for the draft was reinstated nine years later, during a time of peace, NOW protested male-only registration as a form of discrimination against women. This prompted one Veterans Administration official to wonder whether NOW was acting in good faith when it overlooked such discrimination during the

Vietnam era (MacPherson 560). Whatever its attitude toward war as a masculine enterprise, however, the equal rights faction is generally committed to the "right to fight." Betty Friedan, who spent three days observing the progress of women cadets at West Point in 1980, is troubled by the attitude of women who seek equal rights without also accepting equal responsibilities (*Second Stage* 23, 164). At the opposite end of the feminist spectrum are the radical pacifists who maintain that war is a pathological behavior peculiar to men and that any "militarization" of women's lives is a form of male oppression.[6] Between such antithetical views, what common ground? According to Jean Bethke Elshtain, all varieties of feminism share a taboo against "sleeping with soldiers," which she defines as "the age-old union of Eros with Mars that makes of men in uniform attractive targets for libidinal fixation" (232).

I will return to this taboo below, when I consider two major imaginative responses to the Vietnam War. First, however, I want to turn from the liberated woman's view of the soldier to the soldier's view of women.

An American male becomes a soldier not only by submitting to military discipline and acquiring combat skills but also, as many have remarked, by systematically rejecting traits our culture considers to be feminine. (This is true even if the soldier happens to be a woman. For the purposes of this discussion, however, I speak as though all soldiers are men.[7]) Prominent among the motives that prompt a young man to enlist in the military are the need to prove his manhood and desire for adventure, coupled with distaste for the safe, well-regulated, rather tedious routine of civilian life--a life traditionally regarded as feminine. Before he can embark on his adventures, however, the martial Huck Finn must first undergo a period of training more highly regimented than anything he has known in civilian life. Until he completes that training he will be called a "girl," a "lady," a "pussy."[8] Marching from the confidence course to the rifle range, from the rifle range to the mess hall, from the mess hall to instruction in hand-to-hand combat, he memorizes a repertoire of marching songs that fulfill the feminists' worst suspicions about their affinity with the Third World. "There is no thing named love in the world," writes Tim O'Brien in *If I Die in a Combat Zone* (1973), summing up the trainee's catechism. "Women are dinks. Women are villains. They are creatures akin to Communists and yellow-skinned people and hippies" (52). Philip Caputo recalls in *A Rumor of War* (1977) how he shunned marginal recruits and "unsats" who might carry the "virus" of weakness. He could not imagine a fate worse than having to drop out of Marine basic and return home to the "emasculating" affection of his family (10).

The soldier is taught to identify with his rifle in its hardness, precision, and capacity for inflicting death without remorse. This obviously phallic identification is underscored in a little ditty the neophyte must recite, with appropriate gestures, if he fails to distinguish between the militarily correct word for his weapon and the slang word for penis:

> This is my rifle,
> This is my gun;
> This is for fighting,
> This is for fun.

The rifle does double duty as a female surrogate. "I don't want no teenage queen," goes one marching song. "All I want is my M-14." In Gustav Hasford's *The Short-Timers* (1979), translated to the movie screen in Stanley Kubrick's *Full Metal Jacket* (1987), Sergeant Gerheim orders his Marine recruits to give their rifles feminine names, saying, "This is the only pussy you people are going to get. ... You're married to this piece, this weapon of iron and wood, and you will be faithful" (13). By the end of basic training, the men not only sleep with their rifles but also fantasize intimate conversations with them. Leonard Pratt, who rises from platoon goat to outstanding recruit during basic, shoots Gerheim through the heart when the sergeant attempts to take "Charlene" away from him. A moment later he blows his own brains out with "Charlene."

To the extent that military training succeeds in shaping the imagination of teenage males, then, it inculcates a pornographic view of women: women are the passive objects of a lust often mixed with violent aggression. Woman is Jane Fonda in Roger Vadim's *Barbarella* (1968), not the same actress in Hanoi four years later. Tim O'Brien, who recalls that *Barbarella* ran for three weeks straight at the Fort Lewis movie theater while he went through advanced infantry training (69), sought to defend the integrity of his imagination against this assault by conjuring up muse-like figures. He memorized letters from his girlfriend and imagined that she had written the Auden poem she sent him (41-42). When he decided to desert to Sweden, he went first to a sorority house at the University of Washington for moral support, then abandoned his carefully researched plans when he failed to get a date. In effect, he used one stereotype of the feminine to counter another, pitting his muse against the prostitute of the military imagination.

When O'Brien recounts his experiences in Vietnam, however, his female figures turn sinister. Though he cannot recall his girlfriend-muse's face while in country, he does remember in vivid detail a teenage dream of a beautiful snake-charmer who betrayed him into captivity (95, 92-93). The factual counterpart to his dream-lamia is a Korean stripper who entertains Alpha Company on the eve of a combat assault into Pinkville, a VC-infested section of Quang Ngai Province:

> She did it to Paul Simon and Arthur Garfunkel's music. *Homeward bound, I wish I was, homeward bound.* She had big breasts, big for a gook everyone said, damn sure. Pinkville. Christ, of all the places in the world, it would be Pinkville. The mines. Sullen, twisted dinks.
>
> The Korean stripped suddenly, poked a tan and prime-lean thigh through a slit in the black gown. She was the prettiest woman in the Orient. Her beastly, unnaturally large breasts quivered like Jello. (110)

The Korean stripper is Pinkville, Indochina, the Third World in all their ambiguity.   She is at once seductive and repulsive.   She personifies home, yet is also dangerously exotic. Tonight she can be dominated visually by the leering soldiers; tomorrow she will unman them with the shrapnel from Bouncing Betty mines, popping up from the soil of Vietnam and exploding at waist level.

When Vietnam was still part of French Indochina, Graham Greene implies in *The Quiet American* (1955), American counter-insurgency experts regarded the colony in much the way Alden Pyle sees Phuong: compliant, childlike, and eminently available. She had only to be wooed away from the Old World colonials represented in Greene's novel by Thomas Fowler. American soldiers of the sixties saw a less delicate, less mandarin Vietnam, though her gender remained the same. She was the VC prostitute in the local Dogpatch who waited for GIs with razor blades concealed in her vagina. Whatever the factual basis of this obsessively recounted bit of folklore (most soldiers knew someone who had heard from someone else whose buddy had bled to death in just this way), it has obvious symbolic import.[9] It tells what is for many the essential Vietnam War story, a story of emasculation.

The story begins with the Marines who landed near Danang to replace ARVN troops on the defensive perimeter, thus freeing the ARVN to pursue the enemy. It was disappointing and unmanly duty for soldiers schooled in the "offensive spirit," not unlike the trench warfare of World War I in its psychological effects.[10] Their cafard lifted briefly when they were allowed to go on patrols beyond the concertina wire and later engage in large-scale combat assaults (Caputo 65-66). These aggressive modes of engagement occasionally confirmed their masculinity, and their reminiscences are suffused with appropriately sexual imagery. Philip Caputo, for example, recalls the "ache as profound as the ache of orgasm" he experienced when leading his platoon in a surprise attack on the Viet Cong (254). In *Dispatches* Michael Herr, a journalist, compares a firefight more voyeuristically to undressing a girl for the first time (144).

More often, however, their masculinity was challenged rather than confirmed in encounters with the Viet Cong and NVA. Classic maneuvers like the hammer and anvil rarely succeeded against an enemy who disappeared into tunnels and friendly villages when attacked, then harassed them invisibly with sniper fire, rocket and mortar attacks, booby traps, ambushes, and nighttime sapper probes. It was generally the VC and NVA rather than American military strategists who determined where and when skirmishes were to be fought. One psychologist puts it succinctly: American soldiers used aggressive means to produce passive results while the enemy used passive means to achieve aggressive results (Levy 20).

The Bouncing Betty (not Billy or Bobby, though either would have preserved the alliteration) and the VC prostitute were thus apt symbols. Each invited an aggressive act on the part of the American soldier, one he paid for with his manhood and sometimes his life. He was becoming the very thing he had learned to despise during basic training, and every woman he saw was a reminder of his impotence. In retrospect, it seems inevitable that he should have vented his frustration on targets that mirrored his enforced passivity and weakness. This accounts for some of the American animus against ARVN soldiers, who were thought to be effeminate or homosexual because they held hands as a sign of friendship. It also helps to account for violence against Vietnamese women, whether or not they were suspected of being enemy soldiers or nurses. The massacre at My Lai (located in Tim O'Brien's Pinkville) was among other things a catharsis of masculine frustration. After weeks of taking casualties in the local mine fields, the soldiers were briefed for their mission in such a way that they expected finally to take revenge on the enemy (Lifton 48). Subliminally speaking, the women and children of My Lai were the enemy. They were to Charlie Company what Moby Dick is to Captain Ahab--a dreaded and denied facet of the self "visibly personified and made practically assailable" (Melville 160).[11]

Had basic and advanced infantry training succeeded in obliterating the last vestiges of human feeling and respect for women, American soldiers returning from Vietnam would have felt little guilt over episodes like the one at My Lai, whether they had participated in such episodes or only heard about them. But seventeen or eighteen years of family life, even in a culture some feminists deem oppressively patriarchal, cannot be canceled in a few months. The literature (including *If I Die In a Combat Zone*) recounts numerous factual and imaginary instances of the soldiers' kindness to women and remorse on discovering that an enemy casualty is a woman. Returning veterans were often disillusioned not merely with the military and political conduct of the War but also with the American conception of manhood that had betrayed them into enlisting or had shaped their behavior once drafted. They fixed on John Wayne, the hero of films like *The Sands of Iwo Jima* (1949) and *The Green Berets* (1968), as the embodiment of the specious masculinity they had come to detest.[12] In March 1972, while many of their fellow soldiers were still in Indochina, Vietnam Veterans Against the War held a workshop on the theme, *"How Much of John Wayne Is Still In Us?"* Robert J. Lifton has described how the veterans in his rap group strove against what they called "the John Wayne thing," even though they frequently reverted to John Wayne postures in their antiwar activities (94, 238-39, 251-56).

The youth counterculture of the sixties, Lifton observes, provided some veterans with alternative models of masculinity (239). Unfortunately, they often had to reconstruct their sexual identity at a time when their relationships with women were most troubled.[13] Some wives and girlfriends had gone off with the legendary Jody of basic training marching songs. Others had taken a different political or spiritual path. Others reflected the maddening indifference of the American majority. The stewardess in the concluding chapter of O'Brien's *If I Die in a Combat Zone*, for example, is as deadly in her own way as the Korean stripper described earlier:

> The airplane smells and feels artificial. The stewardess, her carefree smile and boredom flickering like bad lightning, doesn't understand. It's enraging, because you sense she doesn't want to understand. . . .

> The stewardess comes through the cabin, spraying a mist of invisible sterility into the pressurized, scrubbed, filtered, temperature-controlled air, killing mosquitoes and unknown diseases, protecting herself and America from Asian evils, cleansing us all forever.

> The stewardess is a stranger. No Hermes, no guide to anything. She is not even a peeping tom. She is as carefree and beautiful and sublime as a junior-high girl friend. (202-203)

The women who still waited for their husbands and lovers were unprepared for the purgatory that lay ahead--the inexplicable rages, self-destructive behavior, and emotional remoteness associated with post-traumatic stress disorder. The Disabled American Veterans organization estimates that 38% of married veterans were divorced within six months after their return, and less formal relationships dissolved without leaving a statistical trace (MacPherson 306).

Since the veteran typically belonged to the socio-economic class most thoroughly imbued with traditional sexual stereotypes, he was ill-prepared to understand the causes and implications of the women's liberation movement that monopolized media attention in the late sixties and early seventies. Conversely, the educated middle-class feminist regarded the veteran with a revulsion usually uncomplicated by first-hand acquaintance. In him she saw the chauvinism of his class compounded with crimes against women and children in a racist, colonialist war. During the early seventies, when veterans were having difficulty finding and holding jobs, NOW and other women's organizations opposed laws that awarded extra points to veterans applying for civil service positions. Dean Philips, who served as special assistant to the director of the Veterans Administration in 1977- 1981, believes that veterans' groups helped to defeat the ERA in several crucial states in direct response to NOW's opposition (MacPherson 560).

Nor have women's groups been particularly generous to veterans of their own sex. When Bobby Muller, the founder and first president of Vietnam Veterans of America, encouraged Lynda Van Devanter to form a Women Veterans Project, the former army nurse sought financial backing from an organization she identifies only as "one of the foremost women's groups in the country." She was turned down, on the grounds that "women veterans were not enough of a cutting edge feminist issue" (*Home Before Morning* 345). With an irony that Gloria Steinem could appreciate fully, she received her first contribution from the Playboy Foundation (351). Among the early members of the Women Veterans Project was Mary R. Stout, who went on to become the second president of the VVA in 1987 and the first woman to head a major American veterans' organization.[14]

Residual tension between feminists (and women who share feminist objectives) and veterans of both sexes is a disturbing legacy of the Vietnam War--the more so because the two groups share experiences and a relationship to mainstream American culture that could provide a basis for communication and possibly concerted action toward common political and economic goals. The young women who joined the civil rights movement or labored among the urban poor in the mid-sixties were motivated by a vision of self-transcending sacrifice. They sought not just to improve the lives of those among whom they worked but also to identify with them insofar as that was possible. "Personal politics" meant putting one's entire life on the line. This led, as some historians of the movement have noted, to a romantic cult of the victim, and it was of course easier to be a victim if one knew that this was more a role than an identity.[15] When these women noticed that their male co-workers were treating them much as white middle-class America was treating its poor and its racial minorities, they regrouped to fight for their own liberation. When the Vietnam War succeeded poverty and racial discrimination as a national issue, it was natural for them to transfer the cult of the victim to the North Vietnamese and associate the American soldier with the forces of patriarchy, racism, and capitalistic exploitation. This simplistic juxtaposition of "noble Viet Cong" and American brute mars otherwise intelligent accounts of the War by Mary McCarthy, Susan Sontag, and Frances FitzGerald.[16]

Ironically, many Vietnam veterans have followed a path parallel to that of many feminists. Especially in the early sixties, it was possible to join the military and go to Vietnam for idealistic reasons. When President Kennedy exhorted the youth of America to ask not what their country could do for them but what they could do for their country, many responded by joining the army rather than the Peace Corps, VISTA, or religious volunteer organizations. Like the young women in SNCC and SDS, soldiers in Vietnam eventually learned that they were being used by the very institutions to which they had dedicated their energy and idealism. Unlike the women, however, they came late to a sense of group solidarity, in part because they returned from Vietnam as they had been sent over--one by one. Though a small minority joined groups like Vietnam Veterans Against the War, where they could work through their guilt and disillusionment in therapeutic rap sessions while engaging in purposeful political activity, most tried to blend into the indifferent crowd.

Popular films like *Coming Home* (1978), *The Deer Hunter* (1978), and *Apocalypse Now* (1979) marked the beginning of general public interest in the War and helped individual veterans to confront their experiences in Vietnam. But if there was a single public episode that galvanized large numbers of veterans, it was the release of the Iranian hostages in January 1981. Veterans were stunned and outraged by the contrast between the hostages' welcome home and their own. It was also a moment of self-recognition. Hadn't they too been hostages of American policy in Vietnam? Hadn't they been victims of one institution or another ever since their return? One veteran, former army nurse Saralee McGoran, recalls breaking into tears on hearing of the hostages' release; it was the beginning of her own release, a process she compares to the gradual relaxation of muscles that had remained painfully contracted for over a decade (Marshall 256). Among veterans, the period since 1981 has been one of consciousness-raising and organization-building similar to that which took place in the women's movement after 1968.

Vietnam and the sex wars of the sixties produced yet another category of victims, though their plight is harder to take seriously: men who evaded or were simply passed over by the draft. "I have often wondered," journalist Susan Jacoby remarked in the course of a 1980 symposium on the War, "whether the millions of men my age who avoided the draft may feel 'unmanned' in a way that no woman can truly understand" (199). Soon after, as though in response to her conjecture, one of those young men in his mid-thirties published an essay in the *New York Times*, recalling how he had revived a childhood case of bronchial asthma in 1969 by inhaling canvas dust from the sewing tables of a tent factory. Michael Blumenthal, poet and assistant to the chairman of the National Endowment for the Humanities, suspected that he had failed more than his pre-induction physical. Setting aside the question of the War's morality (a question that was seldom answered unselfishly, he claims), he confessed to feeling inadequate in the company of veterans:

> To put it bluntly, they have something that we haven't got. It is, to be sure, somewhat vague, but nonetheless real, and can be embraced under several headings: realism, discipline, masculinity (kind of a dirty word these days), resilience, tenacity, resourcefulness. We may have turned out to be better dancers, choreographers, and painters (though not necessarily), but I'm not at all sure that they didn't turn out to be better men, in the best sense of the word. (23)

Blumenthal did not invent the genre that has come to be known as "Viet Guilt Chic." James Fallows' *"What Did You Do In the Class War, Daddy?,"* for example, had appeared almost six years earlier. But his essay represents a significant variation on the form: whereas Fallows was concerned with the social injustice of a system that allowed the educated white middle class to send "proles" of all colors to die in Vietnam in their place, Blumenthal focuses chiefly on the personal consequences suffered by a beneficiary of such discrimination. He and others who have written in this vein now feel cheated of their manhood, not so much by their own choices as by the inequities of the draft law and the political climate of the sixties. Now embarked on the years of mid-life crisis, they have begun to romanticize the Vietnam veteran in much the way they romanticized the Viet Cong in their youth. "I don't think I'll ever have what they have," Christopher Buckley writes of his veteran friends, "the aura of I have been weighed on the scales and have not been found wanting, and my sense at this point is that I will always feel the lack of it and will try to compensate for it, sometimes in good, other times in ludicrous, ways" (72).

Writing confessional essays is one kind of compensation. Another is seeking physical risks that normally lie outside one's chosen career. When one graduate of Wesleyan got a high number in the draft lottery, he went out West and became a logger to experience the "element of macho and danger" in the work (MacPherson 176). It may well be Robert Bly, however, who takes the prize for the most ludicrous form of compensation. At a time when many Vietnam veterans are searching for less deadly modes of masculinity, Bly, who made his reputation as an antiwar poet during the sixties, is urging men to counter the rise of feminism by returning to the "primitive roots" of their maleness. He delivers this message at rallies that feature conga drummers and men capering about in fearsome masks (Carroll and Chapple). What men like Bly seek, according to psychotherapist Edward Tick, is a definitive rite of male passage equivalent to war. In a *New York Times Magazine* essay melodramatically entitled "Apocalypse Continued," Tick concedes that Vietnam veterans have little to feel good about, even today. But nonveterans, he argues from professional and personal experience, are no better off:

> Those like me who, for one reason or another, did not
> serve, suffer because we chose not to perform a primary
> and expected rite of passage. We were never inducted,
> not merely into the Army, but into manhood. . . . I have
> had some of the usual rites--marriage, educational and
> professional recognition. But no matter how many
> passages or accomplishments I garner, I never quite feel
> complete (60).

Men like Blumenthal, Buckley, Bly, and Tick are in some respects the saddest if also the most comic casualties of the sixties sex war. They are also a reminder, if one is needed, that little was accomplished in that war- -partly because, like Vietnam, it lacked front lines and clear objectives. Masculinity and femininity (as distinct from male and female physiology) are now generally thought to be defined by human communities. The community embodies these definitions in myths whose social function is rather to preserve than to challenge the status quo. Not infrequently, a myth of gender reinforces traditional attitudes and behavior even when it appears to undermine them. Jean Bethke Elshtain has shown, for example, how the discourse of radical feminist pacifism shores up the traditional Western myth of woman as "Beautiful Soul." Never mind that history repeatedly supplies fresh examples of women who take part in combat, urge their husbands and sons to fight, or appropriate the language of war to describe womanly functions like childbirth. The myth of the Beautiful Soul requires that women invest men with the human capacity for violence and destruction, reserving to themselves the function of peacemakers and nourishers of life (140-49, 163-93).[17]

Elshtain, though she spoke out against the war in Vietnam, was put off by antiwar activists who called for a North Vietnamese victory. These protestors merely affirmed what she calls "the paradigmatic narrative of war discourse" by dividing the world into heroes and villains, good guys and bad guys, wicked imperialists and noble peasants (37). She remarks that feminist discourse--and one could say the same of the "masculinist" discourse of Robert Bly--is beset with the polarities of warrior and peacemaker, life-taker and life-giver, active aggressor and passive victim, and so forth. Such discourse must be deconstructed as a prelude to rational discussion and conduct. This has long been the task not only of philosophers and political scientists like Elshtain but also of storytellers.

Given the conservative function of myth, it is not surprising that most retellings of the Vietnam War story embody traditional myths of gender. William Eastlake seems to endorse one such myth in *The Bamboo Bed* (1969), where he has Appelfinger assert that "every soldier hears death ticking off inside him." "Not only every soldier," he corrects himself, "but every male human being. Not every female human being. They don't hear death ticking off inside them because they feel life ticking inside them. . . . A female would rather fuck than fight" (225). Tim O'Brien says much the same thing, though less crudely, in a novel published two years after *If I Die in a Combat Zone*. Paul Perry, the central protagonist of *Northern Lights*, is a nonveteran torn between the masculine values of his veteran brother, Harvey, and the feminine values of his wife Grace. Though Paul becomes a man during a winter ordeal in the woods of northern Minnesota with Harvey (whose death wish almost kills them both), he discovers that he is unsatisfied with this new identity. The novel climaxes with a second rite of passage, this time into the "feminine" values of love and nurturing represented by Grace.[18]

Eastlake and O'Brien are both male writers, both former soldiers. Neither would be likely to describe himself as a political radical. Their antithesis would seem to be Susan Sontag, whose *Styles of Radical Will* reprints two essays dealing with gender and the Vietnam War. The first, "What's Happening in America?" (1966) is in part a response to an essay by Leslie Fiedler criticizing the androgyny of the youth counterculture of the sixties. Sontag takes the side of the young people, arguing that the ills of Western white civilization, including the war in Vietnam, can ultimately be traced to its excessively "masculine" character structure. In particular, she defends the counterculture's attraction to Oriental modes of thought, which Fiedler considered "feminine" and "passive" (199-202). Ironically, when Sontag traveled to Hanoi two years later, she was troubled by the apparent sexlessness of the North Vietnamese (227). In the conclusion of her memoir "Trip to Hanoi" she nevertheless reiterates her call for "radical change" in the West, change that will result in a new and presumably less "masculine" version of human nature (272).

Different as their writings seem at first, Eastlake, O'Brien, and Sontag are all working within a conventional discourse and mythology of gender. They either imply or state outright that the survival of the human race depends on a feminization of the dominant male character type. Short of direct surgical or genetic interference, this will have to be accomplished through the continued revision of gender as it is culturally constructed. Unfortunately, all three writers confirm the very myths they consider deadly. A more radical critique of the mythology of gender may require the violation of a taboo mentioned above-- namely, the feminist taboo against "sleeping with soldiers." Here I wish to consider two Vietnam stories that address this taboo: Hal Ashby's film *Coming Home* (1978) and Donald Pfarrer's novel *Neverlight* (1982).

III

Perhaps because Jane Fonda was cast in the lead role, *Coming Home* was widely regarded as the story of a woman who sheds her conservative upbringing and becomes an antiwar feminist. In fact, one reviewer praised the film yet thought it "too ambitious for its own good" in attempting to chronicle not only Sally Hyde's love affair with Luke Martin (Jon Voight) but also her "political radicalization" and "feminist-styled friendship with another woman" (Rich 68). Regarding Sally's initial conservatism there can be no doubt. Though the film is set in 1968 and conscientiously plotted against the significant events of that year (the Tet Offensive and the assassinations of Martin Luther King and Robert Kennedy), her clothing and hairstyle belong to the Kennedy years, when patriotism was still fashionable and the feminine mystique still in force. She is upset when a friend treats the American flag and the national anthem too casually. According to her high school yearbook, the one thing she would want to have on a desert island is a husband. Years later, she has her wish: the desert island is a Marine base in California and the husband is Bob Hyde (Bruce Dern), a captain who expects to be promoted to major after his tour in Vietnam.

It is appropriate that we should first see Bob as he is jogging on the base, since he regards the War as an athletic event. Back in the officers' club he confides to his wife and another couple that he feels "competitive nervousness" as he prepares to go "off to the Olympic Games, representing the United States." The combination of patriotism, physical health, and Marine uniform is apparently irresistible, to judge from the words another officer's wife whispers to Sally: "Bob is very sexy." Unfortunately, his sexiness doesn't manifest itself in bed, where Sally stares vacantly at the ceiling while he satisfies himself. This departure from the ideal enshrined in the feminine mystique seems not to trouble her, however. She presents Bob with a new wedding ring just before he ships out for Vietnam and tells him that she's proud of him.

Sally might eventually have repudiated her role as "cheery Sally, the captain's wife" regardless what happened to Bob. But the Marine Corps inadvertently sets this process in motion when it orders him to Vietnam and banishes her from the desert island. Initially disgruntled at the policy requiring that she move out of government quarters, she comes to savor her liberation. She moves into an oceanside apartment with Vi Munson (Penelope Milford), who works in the kitchen of the base hospital to stay close to her emotionally disabled brother. She trades her conservative sedan for a black Porsche, her leisure for volunteer work in the hospital, her teased and straightened hair for "natural" curls, her dresses and pants suits for less bourgeois attire. Knowing that Bob might regard any or all of these as mutiny, she reverts to type before meeting him for R & R in Hong Kong. Though she has begun to fall in love with Luke Martin, a wounded veteran she had known when he was the captain of their high school football team, she urges Bob's friend Dink Mobley (Robert Ginty) to formalize his relationship with Vi: "Like women and dogs, you have to have a license to show you're the owner."

Sally's "owner," however, has become moody and remote as a result of his war experience, and he further disapproves of her work with the "basket cases" in the hospital. Shortly after her return from Hong Kong she initiates an affair with Luke. Though apparently emasculated by the War--he is paralyzed from the waist down--he provides her with her

first satisfying sexual experience.   As the date of Bob's return
approaches, she begins to face the possibility that their marriage may
belong, like the old Sally, to the past.   In a poignant scene occasioned
by a letter from Bob, she tells Luke that she doesn't know what will
happen to them, only that she has changed.   The film signals this
change visually and aurally: there she stands on a beach by the Pacific,
dressed in a white cotton tunic and blue bell-bottom pants, holding a
frisbee and a bottle of beer; her natural curls toss in the wind as the
sound track delivers the Beatles' "Strawberry Fields Forever."

At this point if not earlier, the viewer may well be troubled. How,
precisely, has Sally changed?   What does her migration from Bob to
Luke say in terms of "personal politics"?   Specifically, are the counter-
culture props meant to reflect counter-culture attitudes toward the
Vietnam War and relations between the sexes?   For the purpose of
discussion, we might separate the War from sexual politics, though the
the two are finally of a piece.

Bob Hyde is old enough to have known the Marine Corps before
the Vietnam War had begun to tarnish its reputation as an elite fighting
unit. He also associates his manliness and sex appeal with the Marine
uniform. "Would you have married me if I wasn't a Marine?" he asks
Sally on R & R. "In a second," she replies. But Bob has heard only
what he expected to hear. Turning to Dink he crows, "What'd I tell ya,
huh? Didn't I tell ya the uniform always used to mean something?"
He and Dink then lament the recent deterioration of the Corps. Bob
had regarded Vietnam as an opportunity not only for promotion but
also for heroism. Once in country, he learns that it is the heart of
darkness rather than glory, a place where his men want to cut off the
heads of enemy corpses and place them on stakes to spook the VC. A
freak accident further mocks his quest for heroism. On the way to the
shower he stumbles and shoots himself in the calf with his M-16. He
is sent home to recuperate and also recommended for a medal (it
appears to be the all-purpose Bronze Star rather than a Purple Heart)
he knows he doesn't deserve.

Bob's self-inflicted leg wound may stand for the entire American
venture in Vietnam. That it is also a sexual maiming is made explicit
when he confronts his wife and her lover back in California. In a final,
enraged assertion of masculinity, he threatens them with a rifle and
bayonet, calling them the names sanctioned by basic training marching
songs: "Jody motherfucker" and "slope cunt." When his anger subsides,
he slumps against the wall as Luke deliberately and noisily folds the
bayonet and ejects the cartridges from the rifle. "I want to go out a
hero," Bob tells Sally. "That way I would have done something that was
mine, that I'd done." He may still be seeking a measure of heroism

when we last see him. After removing his uniform and wedding ring, symbols of the two institutions that have betrayed him, he jogs with no hint of an injury into the Pacific and swims to his death.

In drifting away from Bob, Sally would seem to be liberating herself from American militarism and male subordination of women. If so, one wonders what she sees in Luke Martin. Luke is more deeply embittered by the War than Bob, due to his paralysis and daily association with other handicapped veterans. When Vi's brother commits suicide, Luke is moved to protest the War publicly, by chaining himself and his wheelchair to the entry gate of a recruit depot. He uses media attention to this episode to protest the mass suicide of Americans in Vietnam. A local high school then invites him to speak at an assembly, following a pitch by a Marine recruiter. "When I was your age," he tells the students, ". . . I was really in good shape then, man, I was the captain of the football team and I wanted to be a war hero, man; I wanted to go out and kill for my country." Conspicuous on the front of Luke's jacket are the words "War Hero," a decoration he wears with the some of the same sense of irony Bob feels in wearing his Bronze Star. Like all irony, however, it affirms even as it undercuts. For Luke understands that his authority as an antiwar spokesman depends precisely on the mystique of the athlete and the soldier wounded in action.[19] His jacket is the more eloquent because Luke is unable to mount a real argument against the war beyond saying that war is hell and there is "not enough reason" for anyone to go to Vietnam. Pauline Kael accurately labels this pure pacifism and observes that the politics of the film, as expounded by Luke, are "extremely naïve, and possibly disingenuous" (119).

Perhaps it is unrealistic to expect Luke to think politically at a time when he is still coping with personal loss. One wonders, however, whether he is capable of thinking in larger terms. According to his high school yearbook, his classmates believed that the one thing he would want on his desert island is a mirror. Narcissism colors not only his view of the War but also his relationship with Sally. In the early weeks of their friendship he calls her Bender, which is both her maiden name and the key term in a crude sexual joke. When she doesn't immediately succumb to his amorous advances, he becomes peevish and sullen. Though more sensitive to her sexual needs than Bob, he is just as intent on possessing her body and soul. He can afford to be generous to Bob on his return because he suspects that he has won the prize in their contest.

Sally, then, never ceases to be what she had been in high school and what she becomes again during a Fourth-of-July football game for handicapped vets: a cheerleader for the status quo. Apart from her sexual awakening, which is no challenge to the feminine mystique, she changes in superficial ways. The "greening" of America in the sixties is reflected in her new foliage, but never goes to the root. Since we can imagine only the most conventional future for her and Luke, the film does well to stop where it does. Indeed, it should probably conclude with Bob's suicidal swim and spare us the cuteness of its final scene, which shows Sally and Vi shopping for steaks to celebrate Bob's medal. The door of the supermarket opens and they exit offscreen, leaving two words (one of them the name of the supermarket chain) emblazoned on the screen: "Lucky Out." Lucky out for whom? For Bob, who has escaped his shame and emotional pain? For Sally, who is spared having to choose between two men? Or for Hal Ashby and his screenwriters, who have brought their characters to this impasse?

Donald Pfarrer's *Neverlight* is a novel, not a film, and that in itself would explain why it commanded far less popular attention than *Coming Home*, which won Academy Awards for best actor, best actress, and best screenplay. Even in the book world, however, *Neverlight* caused scarcely a ripple when it appeared in 1982. It shared space with another Vietnam novel in a review in the back pages of the *New York Times Book Review* (Cheuse 31), but otherwise went virtually unnoticed outside of publishing trade journals. This may have been due partly to its politics--or, as the author would have it, to its attempt to steer clear of politics. When Pfarrer was trying to find a publisher for the book, he recalls, "Many of the editors were looking for a political view--and it was obvious which view they were looking for. To be apolitical about Vietnam was to them abhorrent. They wanted a denunciation of our war policy" (Interview 1). *Neverlight* is by no means a denunciation of American war policy in Vietnam. Yet the reader who trusts the tale rather than the teller will find it to be a highly political book, especially if read in the light of the feminist axiom that the personal is political.

The musical sound track of *Coming Home* opens and closes with the Rolling Stones' "Out of Time," a song about a woman who has stepped out of a familiar social milieu and is unable to return; it applies with some modifications to Sally and every other character in that time-obsessed film. *Neverlight* is set in another temporal dimension altogether. From the novel's rare allusions to calendar time, one learns that it covers a period of about twenty months spanning the years 1965-1967. Though this was a period of growing antiwar sentiment, the main characters appear determined not to allow public controversy over the merits of the War to influence their thinking. Katherine Vail, for example, reads "whole forests" of books and articles about the War, yet hesitates before entering a laundromat when she notices that the television carries footage of a clergyman exhorting antiwar marchers.

Not wanting to be swayed by the passion in his voice, she waits till the next day to read the text of his speech in the *New York Times* (140). Much of the novel is set in rural New England, where the political upheaval of the big cities seems remote and time is measured by the stately progress of the seasons (267).

The seasonal cycle determines, somehow, the kinds of questions Katherine and her husband Richard ask about their roles in the war. There is little discussion of issues specific to Vietnam; they move instead to a loftier philosophical plane to consider freedom, the sanctity of human life, and the nature of one's civic duties. These are not merely academic questions for the Vails. Richard is a naval gunnery officer assigned to a Marine infantry unit on shore. Wounded in an ambush, he is sent home to recuperate for several idyllic weeks with his wife and young daughter Terry on a farm in New Hampshire. During that time he decides to request reassignment to Vietnam, though Navy policy doesn't require this of him. The decision opens a breach of misunderstanding between Richard and his wife which their letters cannot fully bridge before he is killed in another ambush. The final chapters of the novel record Katherine's effort to absorb this shock, envision a future for herself and Terry, and comprehend her husband's fatal decision.

Neverlight is more thoughtful and less cliché-ridden than *Coming Home*, and this is particularly evident in the way Pfarrer relates war to gender and the relationships between men and women. At the center of the novel are Richard and Katherine Vail, whose complex love affair is framed by the more polarized relationship between Katherine's brother, John Ashley, and his wife Ella. John is the stereotypical male, a college athlete who goes on to become a Marine platoon leader in Vietnam. For him, there are only two kinds of men: "the unfinished and the complete, those who have not fought and those who have" (8). John goes to Vietnam in obedience to orders, and feels no compunction about killing. Ella, a competitive diver of stunning grace and beauty, seems at first to be the perfect feminine counterpart to John. Katherine, assuming that anyone as physically gifted as Ella must be deficient in mind and spirit, initially tries to save her brother from this "suppleton." Only later does she learn that it is Ella who must be saved from John. In a conversation with his wife and sister just before he leaves for Vietnam, John cruelly suggests that Ella is looking forward to a furlough from marital fidelity. In the aftermath of that gibe, Ella confides to Katherine that she feels unloved, unnecessary, and virtually invisible in her marriage (133-34, 191). Katherine suspects that John will use Ella as long as she helps to advance his career, then discard her.

By contrast, the relationship between the Vails is intensely romantic. Their bodies are perfectly congruent in bed, a physical sympathy which has its psychic equivalent (251). Though they are separated by thousands of miles when he is in Vietnam, their experiences are at times uncannily similar. In Chapter Five, for example, Richard is mesmerized by a corpse lying against a paddy dike; in the following chapter, Katherine becomes equally fascinated with a freshly killed deer (107-8, 111-12, 123). Each of the lovers confirms the other's identity and sexual role. Katherine senses that Richard derives his peculiar power from her love for him, while he in turn is the force that fuses her body and soul (56, 64). Were the Vails of one mind regarding the merits of war in general and the Vietnam War in particular, their story might resemble that of Frederick Henry and Catherine Barkley in Hemingway's *A Farewell to Arms*, with New Hampshire taking the place of Montreux as the lovers' refuge. In their case, however, war serves initially to divide rather than unite them. Katherine regards Vietnam as merely another move in the "monstrous game" played by politicians who care nothing for human life. The United States has no business interfering in a civil war, particularly not on behalf of the "little military gangsters" in South Vietnam (80-81). Even supposing there were some good to be accomplished in Vietnam, how could it possibly offset the loss to Richard's family if he were killed? Katherine still feels keenly the loss of her own father in the Korean War, and does not want to see their daughter deprived in the same way.

When Katherine realizes that Richard has made up his mind to return, she wants to know why. His "You know why" throws her into a rage; she leaves their cabin, slamming the door hard enough to break the glass, and goes stomping through the woods. What grotesque variety of machismo, she wonders, lay behind his response? Previously, she had joked about the "Platonic Idea of Balls" that allied Richard with their male cat, whose "cruising" had also disrupted their domestic arrangements (42). Now, glimpsing the sinister side of the male animal, she bitterly reconstructs the dialogue implicit in his reply:

> "You see, my poor little cunt, it's not my fault. It's the mystique of combat. How can I explain it to you?
> "Well, try, try. Maybe I could grasp one little part of it.
> "I doubt it, since you're nothing but a girl. A female. In the brief intervals between being depressed because of your period, you stupid little shit, and

> being nervous because you're ovulating, there's hardly
> any time for you to learn anything about the world,
> is there?   (74-75)

Sexual identity, normally a cooperative venture in the Vails' relationship, here becomes a source of antagonism. Katherine mentally answers Richard's "mystique of combat" with the mystique of motherhood: what did he know about carrying a baby for five months and then losing it, as she had when she miscarried during her second pregnancy? Her anger cools to sarcasm by the time she returns to the cabin, and she tries once again to probe for Richard's motive. Is he going so as to prove he isn't a coward? For glory or patriotism? To live life to the full? To kill a commie for Christ? Richard doggedly resists entering into an argument, in part because he cannot fully comprehend his own motive. He feels that he should return, that this is what a "good and strong" man would do. During their lovemaking, however, his doubts return, and it is Katherine who must bolster his resolution (86-87).

The Vails' relationship is nearly as polarized as John and Ella's when Richard departs for Vietnam. But unlike the Ashleys--or, for that matter, the Hydes in *Coming Home*--they gradually come closer together during their physical separation, both in their views of the War and in their sensitivity to the full range of "masculine" and "feminine" feelings. This rapprochement is achieved not so much through their letters, though these are frequent, lengthy, and thoughtful, as through their day-to-day experiences in rural New Hampshire and Vietnam. Rather than return to their apartment in Washington, Katherine decides to remain on the farm, which adjoins land her father had worked during the interlude between World War II and Korea. As a child, she had been a daddy's girl and something of a tomboy, given to reading and unfeminine pursuits like hunting. At fourteen she underwent the quintessential male rite of passage in that part of the country, killing and gutting a deer (124-25).

Waiting for Richard to return, Katherine resumes the rural clothing and some of the pastimes of her teens, notably the voracious reading. It is also a period of apprenticeship in the rhythm of the New England seasons. Yielding to this rhythm, she learns more about her own capacity for both asceticism and sensuality. On one occasion in midwinter she bathes in the snow, prolonging and even luxuriating in the denial of her body's craving for warmth and sexual contact (169-73). On another occasion in early spring she bathes in the sun, shocked to discover that her naked body "came forth to meet the sun with every manifestation of its meeting with a man" (187). Under the sun's

influence she even fantasizes a homoerotic encounter with Ella, who
had suggested the sun bath (183-84). Thus Katherine's isolation teaches
her to what extent she is an autonomous, self-reliant being and to what
extent she requires human contact. She is both confirmed in her
female sexual identity and awakened for the first time to more diffuse
and ambiguous erotic feelings.

Katherine's thinking about war, like her sexual awareness, grows in
subtlety during Richard's absence. Reading ancient history, she ponders
the status of the individual human being in civilizations generally
thought to be enlightened. She is disturbed to realize that Greek
temples, roads, and walls were built of stone quarried by slaves--people
who were like herself except that they never knew liberty, peace, or
rest; who could not choose their asceticism as she had chosen hers
(177-78). Life itself was hardly more sacred than liberty. The
Mycenaeans cast their female infants and defective male infants into
Chaos Ravine to die. The Athenians killed all the men of Melos and
enslaved their wives and children. The Romans killed all of a man's
slaves when any one of them dared to kill the master. More recently,
Americans were dropping napalm on the Vietnamese and speaking of
"acceptable losses" of their own soldiers. Katherine recites this dreary
chronicle in a letter to her husband, concluding with the question,
"Dick, I only ask, is life sacred? I write this to you because you are my
friend and husband and also out of fear, in a way, because, forgive me,
you seem willing to kill. If you can take life, how can it be sacred?"
(241).

Before receiving an answer to this question, Katherine is notified
of Richard's death. Pfarrer is at his best in rendering the phases of her
mourning, beginning with disbelief and numbness, proceeding through
acceptance and emotional catharsis to resentment at being abandoned.
If Richard had really loved his family, Katherine wonders, how could he
have left them for an abstraction like "Western Civilization"? (266).
Finally, ten months after his death, she musters the courage to open the
package of his belongings forwarded to her as next-of-kin. In it she
finds his writing tablet, whose first page contains the beginning of a
letter he had started the day before the ambush: "Dear Kit--Yes--"
(284). She cannot imagine what he had meant to affirm until she finds,
in a small bag labeled CONTENTS OF POCKETS, the letter in which
she had demanded, "is life sacred?" Richard's reply from beyond the
grave forces her to confront the contradiction in her own thinking.
She realizes that she too would be willing to kill in a just war,
notwithstanding her belief in the sacredness of life. For Katherine as
for her husband, pacifism is an "abdication of moral responsibility"
(287). True, they disagreed on whether Vietnam was a just war.

Where she was willing to fight when life was threatened, he was willing to fight when freedom was threatened, as he apparently assumed it was in Southeast Asia.

Since Richard had avoided political discussion, Katherine must reconstruct his position--or what she takes to be his position-- tentatively. In this respect the reader has the advantage, being privy to Richard's experiences and inmost thoughts in Vietnam. Having returned to Vietnam to combat communism, he begins to wonder whether communism is the great enemy of the human spirit he had once thought it to be. On consecutive days he contemplates first the corpse of a VC who had attempted to infiltrate the company's night laager armed only with a pistol, then an ancient fortification wall constructed by gangs of human beings and water buffaloes. Though the regimentation implied by the wall oppresses him, the infiltrator's individual courage leads him to conclude, in an imaginary dialogue with Katherine, that "men do not live by freedom alone" (157).

He is also alarmed at the War's effect on his own spirit. With the efficiency and detached precision of an engineer he continues to call in naval gunfire strikes against enemy positions, but cannot escape the guilt which comes with taking human life. Looking into his own heart, he glimpses a Chaos Ravine like the one Katherine had described in her letter, filling up with corpses. Though the men in his unit appreciate the virtue in his performance of his duty, he is more conscious of its contamination-- a contamination he is sure no Christian absolution can remove (243-44). A man either assimilates his guilt, he believes, or is destroyed by it. Though Richard is not destroyed by guilt, he twice imagines placing the muzzle of his pistol in his mouth (226, 245).

On the afternoon following his second suicidal fantasy, he experiences a kind of epiphany while taking a shower. As Paul Fussell has observed, the "soldiers bathing" scene is a set piece in war literature, and is often charged with homoerotic feeling (299-309). Though this feeling remains unacknowledged in Richard's case, he comes up with the answer to Katherine's question while contemplating the naked, vulnerable bodies of his fellow soldiers. Yes, life is sacred, he decides (245-46). But he lacks the time and perhaps the will to recreate for her benefit the tiny point of light he has glimpsed in the darkness of Vietnam. When Richard dies the following morning, Pfarrer ironically echoes the fatuous political and military rhetoric of the day: "There may be victory 'at the end of the tunnel' for some; perhaps only survival; there is never light" (247).

Not surprisingly, *Neverlight* reflects the political views of its author, who also served as a naval gunnery officer in Vietnam. "The conduct

of our national policy in Vietnam," Pfarrer wrote in 1985, was
vacillating, cowardly, spineless and perfidious. I am speaking of the
country into which I was born and which was born into me, which I feel
to be part of myself and my destiny, of the country I cannot but love,
whose evils and blunders stir my deepest emotions and whose triumph
and glory as the inventor of human liberty, and as the homeland of
liberty today, are among the reasons I can affirm life on this Earth

> . . . . I cannot criticize the people who said in 1964 and
> '65 that we should stay out of Vietnam. I agreed with
> them. I was guilty of saying that the whole of Vietnam
> wasn't worth the life of a single American soldier. I may
> have been right strategically but I was wrong morally.
> ("Why" 6)

Vietnam, as Pfarrer sees it and the Vails come to see it, was a bad war
for a good cause. The John Ashleys of the world appreciate neither the
badness of the war nor the goodness of the cause. The characters in
Coming Home, with one exception, understand the badness of the war
but assume there is nothing to be said for the goodness of the cause.
The exception is a disabled veteran who appears in the opening scene.
He claims that he doesn't regret having gone to Vietnam because he
felt a "moral obligation" to defend that nation against the loss of its
freedoms. He is roundly hooted by the other veterans in the room, and
his motive psychologized out of existence: of course he must tell
himself this lie so he can live with his guilt and physical impairment.

Neverlight, inasmuch as it recognizes and credibly recreates a wider
range of responses to the War, is politically richer than *Coming Home*,
notwithstanding Pfarrer's belief that he had written an apolitical novel.
Its major triumph, however, is in the realm of personal and sexual
politics. Sally Hyde neither violates nor affirms the feminist taboo
against sleeping with soldiers, though she goes to bed with a Marine
captain and a former Marine sergeant. Katherine Vail does violate the
taboo. She is not, to be sure, "libidinally fixated" on Richard qua
soldier; and she is repelled by the soldierly business of killing human
beings. Yet she does endorse the soldier's motive. Even before she
comprehends Richard's decision to return to Vietnam, she confirms it
in an act of sexual love. After his death, she comes to understand that
they had both been wedded to the same values and therefore wedded
more deeply to one another.

Sally Hyde is ideologically programed to change as she does. As
Pauline Kael observes in the first sentence of her review, "Jane Fonda
isn't playing a character in '*Coming Home*,' she's playing an abstraction

--a woman being radicalized" (119). Katherine Vail is no abstraction, and she grows toward her final act of reconciliation through a lifetime of experiences, some of which trespass on the masculine side of the culturally inscribed gender line. On the threshold of womanhood she had killed another living creature and so acknowledged one of the less palatable facts of daily existence--that life must sometimes be sustained by the taking of life. This is not the sort of fact that can be learned once and for all. It is obscured not only by the bloodless cuts of meat in the Lucky supermarket but also, as Richard Vail discovers, by the human carnage on the battlefield. The sexist myth of the Beautiful Soul is deconstructed most effectively when Katherine recognizes the practical implications of her belief in the sacredness of life, and again when Richard discovers that this same principle informs his deeds and choices.

IV

Casting a backward glance over the writings and films discussed in this essay, one notices that they sort themselves into three categories, according to the way they treat the relationship between war (particularly the Vietnam War) and gender. *Coming Home, The Big Chill*, and to some extent *In Country* are what we might call complacent works. Regardless of their political stance, they do not use war to challenge conventional notions of manhood and womanhood. Neither do they question the assumption that women are by nature the nurturers of life and men the takers of life. The second category of works presupposes the same mythology of gender as the first, but urges us--usually the males among us--to do something about it. Men should become more feminine for the sake of world peace (Sontag, O'Brien) or more masculine for the sake of personal fulfillment and maturity (Blumenthal, Buckley, Tick, Bly). The former hope, though not unattractive, is probably sentimental and utopian. To feminists who blame war on male physiology, Jean Bethke Elshtain replies, "No scheme that calls for the remaking of human nature has ever panned out" (247).

Neverlight is one of the more fully realized examples of a third category of responses to the Vietnam War: works that explore in the individual psyche those areas where social constructions of gender overlap or fail to account for feelings and behavior. One detects intimations of the same effort to demythologize gender in Lynda Van Devanter's *Home Before Morning* (1983), in some oral histories of nurses and Red Cross workers, and even in those episodes of the television series *China Beach* (first aired in the spring of 1988) based on women's narratives of Vietnam rather than the formulas of soap opera. The ultimate effect of third-category stories is the one suggested by Wallace Stevens. To read or view these works is to feel that a man and a woman can indeed be one, even if the man happens to be a Vietnam veteran and the woman an antiwar feminist. That being so, Stevens' corollary likewise applies. War, though it has often divided the sexes, may serve in the recounting to bring them together in a recognition of their shared, intricate humanity: "A man and a woman and a blackbird / Are one."

Notes

1. The literature of World War I established the convention of the emasculated veteran, as Sandra M. Gilbert notes (198).

2. See Smith 321-35. Like most researchers, Smith detects little change in nonmarital sexual activity between the nineteen twenties and nineteen sixties.

3. Susan Gubar has shown that the image of woman was already thoroughly eroticized in World War II propaganda generated by both the Axis and the Allies (227-59).

4. In *The Second Stage* Friedan recommends that the women's movement address issues of home and family in response to the emptiness many women feel while pursuing careers exclusively.

5. See, for example, the SNCC position paper and "Sex and Caste: A Kind of Memo," both drafted by Hayden and King and reprinted in Evans 233-38.

6. This view informs, for example, Cynthia Enloe's *Does Khaki Become You?: The Militarization of Women's Lives*.

7. During the nineteen eighties, according to the Department of Defense, women have constituted more than 9% of American military services (*Statistical Abstracts* 327, *Report of the Secretary of Defense* 157). During the Vietnam War, between 7,500 (Department of Defense estimate) and 11,000 (Veterans Administration estimate) military women served in Vietnam (Marshall 4). For a discussion of military women and their relation to the masculine mythology of war, see Mithers 79-90.

8. I understand that much of the sexism has been eliminated from military vocabulary and training in the past decade. What I say here applies to the Vietnam era and before.

9. In the version I heard, the razor blades were mounted in a cardboard or plastic tube, with the cutting edges facing inward; the tube could then be inserted in the vagina without injury to the woman.

10. Leed's discussion of the "proletarianization" of the soldier in *No Man's Land* (73-114) applies especially to this phase of the Vietnam war.

11. In Oliver Stone's film *Platoon* (1986), Sargeant Barnes (Tom Berenger) is compared to Ahab as he leads his men into a Vietnamese village to avenge recent losses. Stone elaborates the comparison in his Forward to *Platoon* and *Salvador* (7).

12. Allusions to John Wayne abound in the War fiction and nonfiction. Ron Kovic, for example, mentions Wayne in the epigraph of *Born on the Fourth of July* (1976) and a half-dozen times thereafter (11, 54-55, 74, 86, 112, 171).

13. Joe Klein's *Payback* (1984) tells the story of five Marines whose postwar lives are littered with broken marriages and unhappy relationships with women. One of them read and re-read Vincent Bugliosi's *Helter Skelter*, fascinated by Charles Manson's control over his women (91, 109).

14. At the time of the election, the VVA membership of 35,000 included only 300 women. Yet Stout won 77% of delegation votes, while two other women were elected to the ten at-large positions on the board of directors ("Vote" 9).

15. See Evans 41-42, 127-28; and Gottlieb 64-65. For Betty Friedan, the tendency to identify with the victims rather than the "spirited heroines" portrayed in women's magazines was a disturbing symptom of the feminine mystique (*Mystique* 52-53).

16. See McCarthy's *Vietnam* and *Hanoi*; Sontag's "Trip to Hanoi," reprinted in *Styles of Radical Will*; and FitzGerald's *Fire in the Lake*. What Leo Marx says about Sontag's "revolutionary pastoralism" applies to all three writers. Jane Fonda, whose opposition to the War was also

well-publicized, has acknowledged in an interview that she too "romanticized the Vietnamese" during the War (1).

17. Betty Friedan likewise doubts the value of a separate women's peace movement, since she believes that women are not necessarily less aggressive than men. She speculates that some feminists, unwilling to face their own aggression, instead project it onto men and become obsessed with pornography and rape to the exclusion of other women's issues (*Second Stage* 366, 141).

18. I discuss this novel and its relation to O'Brien's other work in more detail in "Tim O'Brien's Myth of Courage" (263-79).

19. For this reason I am not persuaded by Susan Jeffords' argument that *Coming Home* is addressed primarily to Vietnam veterans, whom it warns, in effect, that they must become "feminized" if they are to be reincorporated into society (19). I suspect that the film is an exercise in self-congratulation, aimed primarily at those who share its politics. As Jeffords observes, however, the film exploits the Vietnam veteran for its own purposes.

Works Cited

Apocalypse Now. Dir. Francis Ford Coppola. United Artists, 1979.

Barbarella. Dir. Roger Vadim. Paramount, 1968.

Bates, Milton J. "Tim O'Brien's Myth of Courage." *Modern Fiction Studies* 33 (1987): 263-79.

The Big Chill. Dir. Lawrence Kasdan. Columbia, 1983.

Blumenthal, Michael. "Of Arms and Men." *New York Times* 11 Jan. 1981, sec. 4: 23.

Buckley, Christopher. "Viet Guilt." *Esquire* Sept. 1983: 68-72.

Caputo, Philip. *A Rumor of War*. 1977. New York: Ballantine, 1978.

Carroll, Jerry. "Father Figure to the New, New Man." *San Francisco Chronicle* 19 Mar. 1986: 36+.

Chafe, William H. *The Unfinished Journey: America Since World War II*. New York: Oxford UP, 1986.

Chapple, Steve. "In Search of the Beast Within." *San Francisco Examiner* 11 Jan. 1987, Image magazine: 12+.

Cheuse, Alan. "Vietnam Revisited." Rev. of *Neverlight*, by Donald Pfarrer; and *The Green Line*, by Tom Molloy. *New York Times Book Review* 19 Sept. 1982: 31.

Coming Home. Dir. Hal Ashby. United Artists, 1978.

The Deer Hunter. Dir. Michael Cimino. EMI/Columbia/Warner, 1978.

Eastlake, William. *The Bamboo Bed*. New York: Simon, 1969.

Elshtain, Jean Bethke. *Women and War*. New York: Basic, 1987.

Enloe, Cynthia. *Does Khaki Become You?: The Militarization of Women's Lives*. Boston: South End, 1983.

Evans, Sara. *Personal Politics: The Roots of Women's Liberation in the Civil Rights Movement and the New Left*. New York: Knopf, 1979.

Fallows, James. "What Did You Do in the Class War, Daddy?" *Washington Monthly* Oct. 1975: 5-19.

FitzGerald, Frances. *Fire in the Lake: The Vietnamese and the Americans in Vietnam*. 1972. New York: Vintage, 1973.

Fonda, Jane. Interview. *Milwaukee Journal* 21 Dec. 1986, sec. E: 1+.

Friedan, Betty. *The Feminine Mystique*. New York: Norton, 1963.

---. *The Second Stage*. Rev. ed. New York: Summit, 1986.

Full Metal Jacket. Dir. Stanley Kubrick. Warner, 1987.

Fussell, Paul. *The Great War and Modern Memory*. New York: Oxford UP, 1975.

Gilbert, Sandra M. "Soldier's Heart: Literary Men, Literary Women, and the Great War." *Higonnet* 197-226.

Gottlieb, Annie. *Do You Believe in Magic?: The Second Coming of the Sixties Generation*. New York: Times, 1987.

The Green Berets. Dir. John Wayne. Batjac/Warner, 1968.

Greene, Graham. *The Quiet American*. 1955. New York: Penguin, 1980.

Gubar, Susan. "'This Is My Rifle, This Is My Gun': World War II and the Blitz on Women." *Higonnet* 227-59.

Hasford, Gustav. *The Short-Timers*. 1979. New York: Bantam, 1980.

Herr, Michael. *Dispatches*. 1977. New York: Discus-Avon, 1980.

Higonnet, Margaret Randolph, et al., eds. *Behind the Lines: Gender and the Two World Wars*. New Haven: Yale UP, 1987.

Jacoby, Susan. "Women and the War." *The Wounded Generation: America After Vietnam*. Ed. A. D. Horne. Englewood Cliffs: Prentice, 1981. 193- 204.

Jeffords, Susan. "Friendly Civilians: Images of Woman and the Feminization of the Audience in Vietnam Films." *Wide Angle 7* (1985): 13-22.

Jones, Landon Y. *Great Expectations: America and the Baby Boom Generation*. New York: Coward, 1980.

Kael, Pauline. "Mythologizing the Sixties." Rev. of *Coming Home*, dir. Hal Ashby. *New Yorker* 20 Feb. 1978: 119-21.

Klein, Joe. *Payback*. 1984. New York: Ballantine, 1985.

Kovic, Ron. *Born on the Fourth of July*. 1976. New York: Pocket, 1977.

Leed, Eric J. *No Man's Land: Combat and Identity in World War I*. New York: Cambridge UP, 1979.

Levy, Charles J. "ARVN as Faggots: Inverted Warfare in Vietnam." *transaction* 8.12 (1971): 18-27.

Lifton, Robert Jay. *Home From the War: Vietnam Veterans: Neither Victims Nor Executioners*. New York: Simon, 1973.

MacPherson, Myra. *Long Time Passing: Vietnam and the Haunted Generation*. 1984. New York: Signet-NAL, 1985.

Mailer, Norman. *The Armies of the Night*. New York: Signet-NAL, 1968.

Marshall, Kathryn. *In the Combat Zone: An Oral History of Women in Vietnam, 1966-1975*. Boston: Little, 1987.

Marx, Leo. "Susan Sontag's 'New Left Pastoral': Notes on Revolutionary Pastoralism." *Literature in Revolution* Ed. George Abbott White and Charles Newman. New York: Holt, 1972. Rpt. in *The Pilot and the Passenger: Essays on Literature, Technology, and Culture in the United States*. New York: Oxford UP, 1988. 291-314.

Mason, Bobbie Ann. *In Country*. 1985. New York: Harper, 1986.

---. Interview. *New York Times Book Review* 15 Sept. 1985: 7.

McCarthy, Mary. *Hanoi*. New York: Harcourt, 1968.

---. *Vietnam*. New York: Harcourt, 1967.

Melville, Herman. *Moby-Dick*. Ed. Harrison Hayford and Hershel Parker. New York: Norton, 1967.

Mithers, Carol Lynn. "Missing in Action: Women Warriors in Vietnam." *Cultural Critique 3* (1986): 79-90.

O'Brien, Tim. *If I Die in a Combat Zone*. 1973. New York: Laurel-Dell, 1979.

---. *Northern Lights*. New York: Delacorte-Seymour Lawrence, 1975.

O'Neill, William L. *Coming Apart: An Informal History of America in the 1960's*. New York: Quadrangle/Times, 1971.

Pfarrer, Donald. Interview. *Milwaukee Journal* 6 June 1982, entertainment sec., 1+.

---. *Neverlight*. 1982. New York: Laurel-Dell, 1984.

---. "Why Did We Lie to Ourselves?" *Milwaukee Journal* 28 Apr. 1985, sec. 2: 6.

Platoon. Dir. Oliver Stone. Orion, 1986.

Report of the Secretary of Defense Frank C. Carlucci to the Congress on the Amended FY 1988/FY 1989 Biennial Budget. Washington: Superintendent of Documents, 1988.

The Return of the Secaucus Seven. Dir. John Sayles. Salsipuedes/Libra, 1980.

Rich, Frank. "The Dark at the End of the Tunnel." Rev. of *Coming Home*, dir. Hal Ashby. Time 20 Feb. 1978: 68.

The Sands of Iwo Jima. Dir. Allan Dwan. Republic, 1949.

Smith, Daniel Scott. "The Dating of the American Sexual Revolution: Evidence and Interpretation." *The American Family in Social-Historical Perspective*. Ed. Michael Gordon. New York: St. Martin's, 1973. 321-35.

Sontag, Susan. *Styles of Radical Will*. 1969. New York: Farrar, 1987.

Statistical Abstract of the United States: 1987. 107th ed. Washington: U. S. Bureau of the Census, 1986.

Stone, Oliver. *Platoon and Salvador: The Original Screenplays*. New York: Vintage, 1987.

Tick, Edward. "Apocalypse Continued." *New York Times Magazine* 13 Jan. 1985: 60.

Van Breems, Arlene. "Feminists Zero In on Volunteerism." *Los Angeles Times* 7 Sept. 1971, sec. 4: 1+.

Van Devanter, Lynda, with Christopher Morgan. *Home Before Morning: The Story of an Army Nurse in Vietnam*. 1983. New York: Warner, 1984.

"The Vote Is In." *Veteran* [pub. by Vietnam Veterans of America] Aug. 1987: 9-11.

UNLEARNING TO REMEMBER VIETNAM

Donald Ringnalda

At the 1978 Vietnam Writers Conference at Macalester College, in St. Paul, Minnesota, celebrated novelist and combat veteran Tim O'Brien voiced two fears--that American would forget the Vietnam War too quickly or remember it too simplistically. More recently he has said that America has tucked Vietnam safely away: "I fear that we are back where we started. I wish we were more troubled" (207).

Indeed, by now it is a cliché to say that the war disappeared down Orwell's memory hole. Indeed, each of our last three presidents has played his part in airbrushing the obscenities and absurdities of the war out of American consciousness. But would O'Brien speak so ominously today after seeing how highly acclaimed movies like *Full Metal Jacket*, *Hamburger Hill*, and especially *Platoon* have galvanized American interest in the war? Yes, I think he would, perhaps even more adamantly. Granted, there has been a bit less airbrushing and a lot less amnesia going around lately, but what is becoming more worrisome is the quality of the remembering. Rarely do we find a book or movie that remembers Vietnam *and* remembers it well--with a radical (as in "root") assessment of American behavior, leading up to, during, and after the war. As we will see, Michael Herr's book *Dispatches* is one of the few exceptions to do both. But most Vietnam War novels and films are seriously flawed by the narrowness of their vision.

Oliver Stone's *Platoon* is a case in point. One might ask, "That same *Platoon* that drew rave reviews and pronouncements all over the country that, at last, we finally have a film that gets the Vietnam War right?" But does it? Does it impart a vision of this monstrous war that enables the audience--non-veterans and veterans alike--to see its own complicity in the violence of Vietnam's "heart of darkness?" Does it have the wisdom to understand the final words of *Dispatches*--"Vietnam Vietnam Vietnam, we've all been there"? Or does it put the war safely behind us as a freakish, isolated aberration, about which we are now properly debriefed and exculpated?

In order to deal with such questions, it is helpful, first of all, to take note of a phenomenon that took place when *Platoon* was first released. All across the country, television and radio stations, magazines, and newspapers solicited the opinions of combat veterans as to whether or not this is a good movie, waiting almost reverentially for their OK. The unexamined assumption here is that just having been in Vietnam bestows the rank of critic on the grunt. Furthermore, in the minds of such "critics" another unexamined assumption manifests itself: what truly matters when making a film or novel about war is accuracy, factualness, faithful attention to details--*not* vision. As Herr points out, in Vietnam there were too *many* facts, and the problem with conventional reporting was that it glutted itself on this excess: "The press got all the facts (more or less), it got too many of them" (229).

Accuracy is a consuming passion for many of the veterans I've gotten to know. And for that very reason, most of them make poor critics. Mired in their own facts, these veterans quite understandably don't want to read great books or see great cinema. Instead, they want to see themselves, their outfits, their Area of Operations, *their* Vietnam. Their reasons for wanting this visualization have little to do with being vindicated or being shown as heroes (this is the language of Hollywood and Washington); they simply want this black hole in American consciousness illuminated. It certainly *needs* illumination. But when these same people write novels and make movies about Vietnam, their beam of light often is so privately narrow that very little illumination takes place. This is because, obsessed by the facts of their Vietnam experiences, they are also victimized by them. At the 1985 Asia Society Conference, Tim O'Brien stated that this victimization results in melodrama and a closure of the imagination (46). Unfortunately, most tellers of war stories do not heed the words of O'Brien, or for that matter, those of the World War I writer, Robert Graves: "The memoirs of a man who went through some of the worst experiences of trench warfare are not truthful if they do not contain a high proportion of falsities" (32).

So what do critics mean when they say that *Platoon* is possibly *the* Vietnam War movie? Quite frankly, I don't know. I even have problems with Stone's "facts"! I've talked to vets who never experienced anything like what we see in *Platoon*--a pitched battle, World War II style?! Depending on where they were when, many vets will tell you they never saw an NVA soldier, much less a battalion of them. Stone's narrow facts may not invalidate the raw power of his movie, but they do point to that problem that flaws most artistic responses to the war: retelling an individual's truth results in a myopic, narrow vision.

Stone's personal facts distort the war in two other ways. First, despite the movie's emphasis on the moral depravity induced by the war, Stone leaves the audience a comfortable way out, thereby perhaps helping set the stage for the next chapter in the history of carnage: war isn't hell after all, because Stone's narrator-hero is allowed successfully to choose good (Sgt. Elias) over evil (Sgt. Barnes). By falling back on the old lie that war offers a time-honored initiation experience to "children ardent for some desperate glory," Stone sanitizes the war and changes its rating from X to PG13. Maybe *Stone's* war was PG13, but any revelation of the war that minimizes the overall moral vacuum created by U.S. involvement and policy is less revelation than cover up.

Secondly, like almost all Vietnam War literature and cinema, Stone's movie--with the dubious exception of the village scene--casts the Vietnamese people as mere extras, stick-figure props that register as little more than malevolent abstractions. Even in the powerful village scene, Stone does not appear to be particularly interested in revealing the moral complexities or the political ambivalences of the South Vietnamese peasants, who were caught in the middle of a war they neither understood nor desired. Instead, Stone uses this scene as a rather awkward contrivance to stage the drama he *is* particularly interested in: the black-and-white moral tug of war between good and evil. Thus, Stone's "facts" do not just restrict and distort the Vietnam War; they are, in effect, racist. Lost in the pathos with which he imbues *American* tragedy is the fact that our losses were miniscule compared to those of Southeast Asians and their soil. To paraphrase the World War I poet Wilfred Owen, *their* losses probably made the devil himself say "enough!" In some ways, therefore, *Platoon* is a tenderized, self-indulgent portrait of the great *American* trauma: America's black eye, America's pulled hamstring, America's impacted wisdom tooth.

The failure to imagine beyond and below the immediate "facts" is what bothers me most about Vietnam War literature and film. It relies almost totally on undifferentiated foregrounding of the individual writer's facts. It is mostly very disturbing close-ups and unshaped raw material without disturbing subtextual *questions* such as, why America behaves the way it does, how war feeds on unexamined fears in order to perpetuate itself, and why, despite repeated advice from many quarters over a long period of time, America naively went to Vietnam anyway.

No response to the Vietnam War raises such questions as relentlessly as Michael Herr's book *Dispatches.* Herr is one of few writers to realize that getting Vietnam right is not a matter of amassing facts; it is a matter of *interpreting* facts, of using both short and long-range lenses, of seeing the facts in the context of America's history, and, finally, it is a matter of looking at his own accustomed way of remembering, with suspicion. So even though Herr certainly does not allow us to forget the facts of Vietnam, his primary genius lies in the way he prevents us from remembering them simplistically. He achieves this by self-example. Several years after leaving Vietnam he came to understand that if he were ever going to really experience and remember the war in its horrible totality, he first had to deconstruct his own consciousness, a consciousness that had been pre-formed by the language of American cultural myths richly fed by the media (Herr talks

about Americans who got wiped out by years and years of war movies
before going to Vietnam to get wiped out for good), a nation's hubris
over its victory in World War II, and its black and white paranoia over
Communist expansionism since then. Moreover, the question implicitly
asked throughout Herr's book is how can we trust facts if those same
facts have been forced to fit this pre-formed consciousness, despite the
glaring gap between language and actuality? Therefore, the knowledge
that *Dispatches* brings home from Vietnam is not the knowledge of the
historian, the memoirist, the journalist, or even the grunt. Rather, it is,
to use Michel Foucault's metaphor, the knowledge of the *archaeologist*
(*The Archaeology of Knowledge*). Herr's book is an excavation down
to the heart of war and the heart of those who wage it and observe it.

Like many other writers, Herr talks about how the civilian and
military leadership abused language with euphemism, "language fix,"
Orwellian "doublespeak," and outright lies. This is as far as most writers
ever go. But Herr digs to a deeper archaeological stratum and discovers
a more fundamental language fix in America's unconscious script. To
his amazement, Herr noticed that this unconsciously-inherited mythic
conditioning was not just distorting his experiences, it was blocking them
out altogether. The facts added up to zero. As Herr says, "Time and
information, rock and roll, life itself--the information isn't frozen, you
are" (20). Thus, while watching a soldier die, Herr feels like he's
viewing a take from a movie scene.

So when Herr says "A lot of things had to be unlearned before you
can learn anything at all" (224), what he is saying is that before he can
write *his* book--become self-authored, as it were--he needs to unwrite
the inherited book of story-telling realism. In Michel Foucault's
terminology, he needs to engage in the insurrection of subjugated
knowledges (82) against the officially sanctioned reality principle.
Throughout his book *The Perfect War*, James William Gibson argues
that in Vietnam this reigning reality principle was determined by an
Aristotelian, Newtonian mindset that filtered and ordered a messy war,
much as this mindset's literary heir--realism--still does. Faced with
chaos in Vietnam, American war managers erected a trillion-dollar
Newtonian model of the universe, a model with a sure, stable
epistemology based on a Westerner's sense of order, predictability,
balance, logic, and the *power* that accrues from such a "sure" knowledge
of reality. The model was very effective: it effectively made it
impossible for our leaders to see around it. They were effectively
trained *not* to see.[1] Wallace Stevens' jar gained total dominion, from
the Oval Office to I Corps Headquarters.

There is a strikingly real (as opposed to metaphorical) parallel
between this blindness of war managers and the blindness of tradition-

bound scientists that James Gleick talks about in his insurrectionist book, *Chaos*. Each is blinded by the same model. Each has traditionally identified chaos with non-meaning. Thus, rather than discerning the patterns within chaos, they deny or disregard the chaos with their superimposed model.

Gibson's observation (and, quite unintentionally, Gleick's) is one of the most trenchant pieces of Vietnam War commentary I have ever encountered. He clearly shows that ill-conceived tactics and strategy were merely symptomatic of a whole mechanistic world view exported to Southeast Asis inviolately. And Gibson is not in the least being eccentric in rooting this in an epistemology spawned by Newtonian physics. Henry Kissinger himself--that great explicator of reality who for years has displayed his pearls for the porcine--writes in *American Foreign Policy* that "The West is deeply committed to the notion that the real world is external to the observer, that knowledge consists of recording and classifying data--the more accurately the better. Cultures which have escaped the early impact of Newtonian thinking have retained the essentially pre-Newtonian view...[which has been] a liability for centuries" (48-49).

Michael Herr, too, became blinded--to the *model*. The "liability" becomes his book's greatest strength (this holds true for a handful of Vietnam War novels, particularly the early *Bamboo Bed*, by William Eastlake, and the more recent *Meditations in Green*, by Stephen Wright). On a microcosmic level, Herr counters the model by writing about an obscene, chaotic collage created by Davies, a flipped-out, insurrectionist door gunner who lived in Vietnam "as far from the papers and the regulations as he could get." The collage acts as an analogue for *Dispatches* in that it sees around the model and thereby also sees the patterns within the officially unrecognized chaos. It sees the whole symbiotic panoply of "winners and losers" in America's farce. Scrapping Newtonian linear order, Davies' collage is a spatial, non-linear equation that lumps together such "coefficients" as burning monks and Cardinal Spellman, Ronald Reagan and cannabis, Mick Jagger and Rap Brown, The American flag and dollar signs, playgirls and hogs, bombs and genitalia. The most important aspect of the collage, however, is its ridicule of America's love of maps and how it tried to superimpose its maps of reality (its old geometry) onto Vietnam: one of the prominent features of Davies' work is a map of the western United States with the shape of Vietnam reversed and fitted over California (187).

Herr's creation in *Dispatches* is a brother of the *new* geometry that James Gleick talks about in *Chaos*. Gleick says "The shapes of classical geometry are lines and planes, circles and spheres, triangles and cones. They represent a powerful abstraction of reality, and they inspired a powerful philosophy of Platonic harmony. Euclid made of them a geometry that lasted two millennia, the only geometry still that most people ever learn [and the dominant "geometry" in Vietnam]...The new geometry mirrors a universe that is rough, not rounded, scabrous, not smooth. It is a geometry of the pitted, pocked, and broken up, the twisted, tangled, and intertwined. The understanding of nature's [or the phenomenology of America's involvement in Vietnam] complexity awaited a suspicion that the complexity was not just random, not just accident...The pits and tangles are more than blemishes distorting the classic shapes of Euclidian geometry. They are often the keys to the essence of a thing" (94).

They certainly are the keys to understanding Davies' collage, and, thereby, Herr's book. Similarly, they are the keys to understanding the 1069th Intelligence Group's collage in Stephen Wright's *Meditations in Green*. This collage,[2] called "subversive junk" by the colonel, assembles the scabrous shards and the broken-up fragments of the war in order to give shadowy form to the underground subjugated knowledges. In doing so, both Herr's and Wright's collages articulate the chaos of the war and of their books. The collages and the books they appear in are counter-epistemologies.

Robert Graves, one of the premier poets of World War I (that earlier "Vietnam War"), precisely delineates this opposition between dominant and subjugated epistemologies in his aptly named poem "Broken Images":

> He is quick, thinking in clear images;
> I am slow, thinking in broken images.
>
> He becomes dull, trusting to his clear images;
> I become sharp, mistrusting my broken images.
>
> Trusting his images, he assumes their relevance;
> Mistrusting my images, I question their relevance.
>
> Assuming their relevance, he assumes the fact;
> Questioning their relevance, I question the fact.
>
> When the fact fails him, he questions his senses;
> When the fact fails me, I approve my senses.
>
> He continues quick and dull in his clear images;
> I continue slow and sharp in my broken images.

He in a new confusion of his understanding;
I in a new understanding of my confusion.

The best Vietnam writers, such as Herr, Wright, O'Brien, Rabe, and Eastlake, fully understand and expressively delineate their confusion. They *use* Gleick's keys, which to the United States civilian and military war managers, the traditional scientist, and the traditional war writer so clearly seem to be barricades to and blemishes upon the understanding. Unusable. Thus, the normative tactic: disregard. Scientists refer to these blemishes as "noise;" strange, unaccounted-for, even monstrous, departures from a mechanistic, periodic Newtonian world. But the artist and the critic perform their jobs *only* when they tune into the noise, *only* when in their unofficial, subjugated status, they insurrect and make noise themselves. Herr is an insurrectionist. He deconstructs the habits of his mind, scraps the reigning normative epistemology, and works his way out of a hermeneutical rut. To borrow a metaphor from Frost's "The Death of the Hired Man," Herr knew that he could not pitch the hay he was standing on. To borrow another metaphor, from Gregory Bitz's novel *War Hangover*, you can't get the bugs off the windshield from inside the car (174).

Thus, in order to create his book of new geometry Herr had to eschew the light of civilization in the official press clubs of the major cities and step aside, *way* outside, into the unmappable, twisted, tangled, and intertwined heart of darkness of Vietnam and the human mind. Herr was afraid of the dark, but he knew that if he was to "report" this war, that is where he had to spend his time. He knew that "Hiding under the fact-figure crossfire there was a secret history, and not a lot of people felt like running in there to bring it out" (51). Herr may not have felt like it either, but he did it. And he did it by refusing to use what Gibson both figuratively and literally calls "the old trails" (11), conventional paths that lead only to the destruction of serious intellectual and artistic inquiry, just as the literal trails ominously assured the likelihood of ambushes, claymore mines, and Bouncing Betties.

Like the Long Range Reconnaissance Patrols (LURPS), that spent days at a time observing the enemy in the darkness of the far reaches of nowhere, so Herr's LURP book pushes itself and the reader off the old trails and away from the artificially-cleared LZ's of convention. *Dispatches* avoids what Eastlake calls the classic American blunder--of giving the Indians the cover (22). The book is a deep "recon" probe (without fire support) into murky questions such as who we are and how we know what we think we know. Herr could ask such questions because he pushed himself far beyond the lighted civilized comforts of official facts, information, "war stories," and the "5:00 o'clock follies." Far beyond the comfort of Stone's good vs. evil geometry. Far beyond any sense of epistemological or ontological security. Far beyond any compromise with the official "book." Knowing that the medium is the message, Herr replaces the filtered, laundered narrative of sense-making, old-trail realism with a camera dropped (224) in the bush that catches the weird, secret subtext of the war. To paraphrase Herr, his book is a fabulous warp that takes the journey first, then departs. His book takes the meat and potatoes of war stories and turns them into word salad. It is a book in which the phrase "How are you tomorrow" makes sense. It is a book in which the conventional geometries of space and time melt like Dali's clocks.

Someone once said that in Vietnam a grunt learned to live in the bush; a LURP learned to *be* a bush, so thoroughly did he cut himself off and meld with his surroundings. Herr's book is a bush. It is not so much *about* Vietnam as it, in frightening ways, *is* Vietnam. In both form and content, *Dispatches* is serpentine, unpredictable, explosive, chaotic, hot, and as different from conventional war stories as Jimi Hendrix is different from the Beach Boys.

Both Herr and the LURPs realized that rather than "throw the book" at the enemy, they needed to throw the book away, look below and within, and write a new script. They needed to be archaeologists. They knew that conventional writing and conventional warfare were square pegs in amorphous holes. As a writer of the new geometry, Herr seems to have come to the realization that it makes no sense to set up ambushes, as it were, to go out on sweeps and search and destroy missions when the enemy has in fact already tunneled through the strata beneath your base camp. It makes even less sense than closing the barn doors after the horses have run away. Bad timing is one thing, stubborn blindness, quite another.

Freed from the snare of conventionalized facts, Herr's deconstruction and excavation make his book the most frighteningly valid revelation of the war. He discovered for himself that anything short of such radical thinking would leave him as impervious to the hallucinatory reality of the war as is Colonel Kilgore in the only great Vietnam War film, Coppola's blend of satire and Lurpism, *Apocalypse Now*. *I* call it great, but many veterans hate it. In fact, John Del Vecchio cites this grossly unfactual affront to the Newtonian world as the primary inspiration for writing his novel *The 13th Valley*. The film's Kilgore scene strikes many veterans as a ridiculous lie, almost as bad as the unfactual Russian roulette scenes in *The Deer Hunter*. With Kilgore it is not so much that he brought the American book with him as he never left America. (How many Americans really did "leave"

America?) With mortars, flares, and machine gun fire zinging all around him, he acts as if he were on his own ordered, private Malibu Beach, surfing, barbecuing, playing the guitar and shooting the latest John Wayne cavalry movie (now with Huey helicopters instead of horses), killing America's latest Indians (now named "gooks," "dinks," "slants," and "slopes"). Kilgore's first-edition book is like his clothes (the suffocating heat and humidity notwithstanding): in mint condition, impeccable, clean.

So what happened to America's book of facts, its old geometry? If O'Brien is right, we would have to conclude that it was remaindered and temporarily forced out of print during and after the war. But it has been reissued, particularly in the political realm. Macho-mythic, messianic, "immaculate deceptions" seem to be on the rise, while the fundamentally disturbing meditations of people like Herr and Stephen Wright are on the decline. Once again, opponents of America's "book" are condescendingly dismissed as naive liberals who desperately need a "reality sandwich" to wake them up to the facts. Are we once again becoming impervious to the suffering brought about when nations-- imprisoned by the "facts" of their scripts--slavishly and unknowingly play out their mythic fantasies?

Finally, has an authentic, non-simplistically-remembered, unlearned book been written? Herr's likely comes as close as one can get. However, one could argue that it too is flawed by its failure to incorporate the whole *Vietnamese* side of the war. But C. D. B. Bryan, author of *Friendly Fire*, says that even if the authentic Vietnam War Book *were* written, we wouldn't be able to read it, nor would be want to, because

> It would not be available at bookstores. Instead it would be helicopter-assaulted onto readers' front lawns; it would come videotaped, computerized, and Dolby-stereoed, with acetate overlays and a warning that eight or so years after being exposed to it, the reader stood a good chance of getting cancer (72).

Perhaps the Vietnam War was simply too monstrous for import. Perhaps like Picasso's immense 12' by 26' *Guernica*, Vietnam won't fit into America's living rooms. Perhaps it simply is *too* chaotic. Perhaps even if the Vietnam War were shown in our living rooms, it would appear to us as does David Nelson's home movie in David Rabe's play *Sticks and Bones*--flickering shadows and shades of green, not underexposed, as Ozzie Nelson says, but overexposed. Perhaps if we ever do hear the Vietnam War story, it will be as inscrutable as the

LURP story that Herr relates: "Patrol went up the mountain. Only one man came back. He died before he could tell us what happened." Perhaps Amlin Gray is right, for the story in his fine play *How I Got That Story* is that there *is* no story fit for Newton's prime-time world. To extrapolate from Tim O'Brien, perhaps the lesson we need to learn from Vietnam is that as a literary subject, war must not be adjusted to fit within the narrow artificial confines of war stories. Finally, as John Irvin and Jim Carabatsos seem to have realized in their *Hamburger Hill*, perhaps you can't make a war story if your only epistemological certainty is that "It don't mean nothin'. It don't mean nothin'. It don't mean nothin'."

But once we unlearn to simplistically remember Vietnam according to the old untroubling geometry, it means altogether too much.

Notes

1. For a full exposé of this ingrained myopia, see Neil Sheehan's *A Bright Shining Lie: John Paul Vann and America in Vietnam*, first serialized as "Annals of War (An American Soldier in Vietnam")" in the June 20, 27, July 4, and 11 1988 issues of *The New Yorker*.

2. For fuller discussions of the collage as a structuring analogue in Vietnam War literature, see my "Chlorophyll Overdose: Stephen Wright's *Meditations in Green*," *Western Humanities Review*, Summer, 1986, 130f.; and "Fighting and Writing: America's Vietnam War Literature," *Journal of American Studies*, April, 1988, 39f.; see also John Clark Pratt and Timothy J. Lomperis in *"Reading the Wind": The Literature of the Vietnam War*, 1987, 90f.

Works Cited

Bitz, Gregory W. *War Hangover*. Minneapolis: Angel Wing Press, 1987.

Bryan, C.D.B. "Barely Suppressed Screams." *Harpers*, June, 1984.

Eastlake, William. *The Bamboo Bed*. New York: Avon, 1969.

Foucault, Michel. *The Archaeology of Knowledge*. New York: Pantheon Books, 1972.

---. *Power/Knowledge: Selected Interviews and Other Writings*. Ed. Colin Gordon. New York: Pantheon Books, 1980.

Gibson, James William. *The Perfect War: The War We Couldn't Lose and How We Did*. New York: Random House, 1988.

Gleick, James. *Chaos*. New York: Viking, 1987.

Graves, Robert. *But It Still Goes On*. New York: 1931.

Gray, Amlin. *How I Got That Story*. New York: Dramatists Play Service, 1981.

Herr, Michael. *Dispatches*. New York: Avon, 1980.

O'Brien, Tim. "We've Adjusted Too Well." In *The Wounded Generation: America After Vietnam*. Ed. A.D. Horne. Englewood Cliffs: Prentice-Hall, 1981.

Lomperis, Timothy J. *Reading the Wind: The Literature of the Vietnam War*. Durham: Duke University Press, 1987.

Rabe, David. *Sticks and Bones*. New York: Penguin, 1978.

Sheehan, Neil. *A Bright Shining Lie: John Paul Vann and America in Vietnam*. New York: Random House, 1988.

Wright, Stephen. *Meditations in Green*. New York: Bantam, 1984.

VISION AND TRADITION IN VIETNAM WAR FICTION

Philip K. Jason

If one goal of literature is to render convincingly a vision of life, to depict it so compellingly that readers are led to share the author's notion of experience, then literary form--as it uses and departs from tradition--is a key means to that end. While the fictions that have come out of the Vietnam War tend to share an absurd vision of the war itself, not very many find the innovations in form or technique with which to communicate that vision. The perceived absurdities of the war are manifold: They include confusion over the nature and identity of the enemy, the abandonment of objectives--territory or positions--soon after obtaining them at great cost, conflicting or unreliable information about the goals and status of the war, and constant mismatches of ends and means. If there was, finally, something "unreal" about the fighting man's experience in Vietnam, how best communicate that unreality? The conventions of realism are intertwined with recent, non-romantic traditions of war literature, but they somehow fail to capture the ways in which this war was felt to be different from its predecessors. I intend to review this issue of vision and method by reference to six novels distributed into two categories.

The features of the first group include third person narration with shifting focal characters; a representation that emphasizes the experience of the group, the fighting unit, more than the experience of the individual; the backgrounding of a large cast of characters; and fairly convention handling of time, place, action, and causality. These are fictions in the realist tradition, filled with the boredom, blood, and pain of men at war. Though each novelist is clearly conscious of absurd conditions, of a unique set of circumstances, the techniques employed are similar to those employed by Norman Mailer in *The Naked and the Dead*. And Mailer, I'm sure, found much of what he needed in the novels of John Dos Passos. The works I include here are John Del Vecchio's *The Thirteenth Valley* (1982), James Webb's *Fields of Fire* (1978), and William Turner Huggett's *Body Count* (1973).

The novels in the second group share the following characteristics: a severely limited perspective (two are first person narrations, the other channeled through a single character though cast in the third person); passages of lyrical, surreal description that create distortions of time, place, and action (or illusions of such distortion); and little or no backgrounding of characters. They shred cause and effect assumptions, leaving us wondering what, if anything, governs human life on this planet. These novels include Gustaf Hasford's *The Short-Timers* (1979), Larry Heinemann's *Close Quarters* (1977), and Tim O'Brien's *Going After Cacciato* (1978).

In the first group, there is an enslavement to some conventional demands: where the characters come from, what pre-war circumstances shaped them, what they might have to return to. The degree to which these pasts, presented through set stretches of exposition or labored flashbacks, inform the present is rarely questioned. They seem offered as a "given" necessity of characterization. The fighting units are rendered along socio-economic lines as we are reminded about who fought this war for us. Though these novels show us the discontinuities that the war brings to individual lives, they nonetheless work to suggest connections between the characters' experience of war and their larger (or broader) range of experiences. Indeed, the structures of these novels reflect the assuring notion of coherence.

The novels of the second group seem more claustrophobic, more internal, the characters more detached from any sense of the past's relevance to who they are now. By defying certain expectations, they may be said to force something closer to the absurd experience upon the reader. These novels blend various components of lyricism, psychological realism, and naturalism.

I

Del Vecchio's work, the most recent of the first group, is also the most ambitious. *The Thirteenth Valley* slowly but engagingly relates the tale of a major operation, the taking of a North Vietnamese stronghold in the Khe Ta Laou valley in 1970. The cast of characters includes, most notably, Lt. Brooks, a black intellectual who is torn between his duty to his wife, his duty to his men and his country, and his deep concern for the human condition, and Sgt. Egan, the perfect fighter and point man, a hero to others but a man with nightmares. This calloused cynic becomes a mentor to his "Cherry," a radio man without battle experience who slowly turns into a fighting monster. "Cherry" seems to be the author's surrogate.

The characterizations of Brooks and Egan are fairly rich, and the flashback triggers that usher in "the world" are usually plausible and they are certainly well-spaced, keeping us in touch with the larger life story of which the current military engagement is only a part.

The novel plays close attention to the details of strategy and tactics, leadership, the effects of battlefield conditions on a wide range of personalities, and the political and moral issues of this and other wars. Del Vecchio provides clear presentations of the various levels of command and their interaction. In fact, Del Vecchio is probably too ambitious, trying to cover too much intellectual ground while maintaining the "feel" of the various engagements and situations. The political discussions among the men become awkward substitutes for authorial comment, and at many points their debates are simply unbelievable.

All in all, this is an impressive achievement, but the broad range of concerns leaves effects diffused, even though there are extraordinary accounts of discomfort, pain, and fortitude. Like many similar constructions, this novel uses the past--the backgrounding of a wide range of characters--to suggest the kind of melting pot or cross-section of American society that makes up a fighting unit. Additionally, the more or less conventional past of each character (a fairly predictable sequence of events, purposes, and outcomes) serves to set off the discontinuities of all sorts that characterize the war experience. The inference we may draw is that the characters bring irrelevant pasts to an unparalleled, unpredictable set of experiences.

One of the longest fictional narratives of the war, this book, in fact, is focused on a relatively short period of time. And it is the orderly marking out of events and behavior within a rigid and conventional temporal sequence that overwhelms Del Vecchio's presentation of the flow of experience, a presentation that in certain long passages is handled quite effectively.

Nowhere is this irony of how the realistic tradition fails the novelist's essential vision clearer than in *The Thirteenth Valley*, which pays such meticulous attention to time, place, strategy, and tactics.   The juxtaposition of maps and "official" reports of the campaign's progress with invented passages representing the "real" flow and feel of events shows Del Vecchio's constant awareness of this irony. Still, his conventional handling of plot, time, and point of view does not serve to create the "new thing"--the absurd experience--within the reader.   His method is a sieve that cannot hold the essential truths of the experience.

Often represented as a vehicle for the celebration of combat, James Webb's *Fields of Fire* is not so easy to pin down. Certainly Webb suggests that for many of his characters the sharing of life-and-death experience gives them a sense of purpose and relationship that nothing outside of combat can provide. However, combat is not a prescription for what ails the world or even the individual psyches of these men.

The special complications of the Vietnam War as they affected the fighting men are seen cleanly, especially the nature of the enemy. Other topics include the corruption of those sitting behind desks and the horrors of battle itself.   Many sections of this narrative are gruesome.

The inset biographies of the characters, once again, owe much to Mailer's *The Naked and the Dead*. The two main characters, Lt. Hodges and Snake, share our attention and provide our points of reference through the first hundred pages of the novel. Clearly Hodges is the dominant perspective for the novel as a whole, and thus his absence from some of the key actions creates a perspective void. In fact, the unsteadiness of point of view is one of the novel's weaknesses.

The backgrounds of the other characters--Goodrich, Phony, Dan (the Vietnamese scout), Gilliland, Bagger, Cat Man, and Cannonball --are layered in at reasonable intervals. And with the introduction of each comes a brief attempt at following the war from this character's point of view. However, each such attempt quickly finds the narrator stepping back into a neutral territory or swinging once again toward Hodges. When we follow Hodges on his Okinawa time out--the second stage of his romance with Mitsuko--we see, perhaps, Webb's failure to separate the autobiographical "what happened" from the novelist's "what does this story need."

But what are the consequences of the various pasts Webb draws for us? Few of the characters are driven by patriotism or any other ideal. We see them doing what must be done, curiously leveled in spite of all their differences. Is this the message? The war has found them and remade them, and each is equally capable of dying.

Webb is concerned with creating contexts that blur moral issues, often making conventional moral stances irrelevant. Yet his work is at times patently and narrowly argumentative. His "patsy" is Goodrich, who, though treated with some sympathy, is nonetheless the target of Webb's disdain for intellectuals. Goodrich's attempts at rational perspectives are found wanting, and this part of his character is somehow coupled with his physical cowardice. This treatment of Goodrich--a character so obviously drawn to argue a point-- compromises Webb's hold on the reader's imagination. Though this case stands out, it does not represent a general tendency of the novel.

Although Webb sometimes seems concerned with characterization as it is found in the best serious literature, more often the characters are there for the sake of the action--the major way in which the popular genres of adventure and war fiction distort esthetic priorities. If the war seems to have discovered and remade these people, then the effort put into giving them pasts becomes an ironically mechanical effort, one which--perhaps unintentionally--underscores the failure of Webb's approach to contain or release his vision. Or is it a failure of vision? These tensions, complicated by the strangely decentralized point of view and the clock-time march of events, underscore the special problems of form and content found in the body of Vietnam War fiction, problems handled even less effectively in *The Thirteenth Valley* and met more sure-handedly in *Body Count*.

One of the most conventionally plotted novels of the war, William Turner Huggett's *Body Count* traces the career of Lt. Hawkins from the time he arrives as a green officer intimidated by his veteran sergeant and eyed skeptically by his men through the various ordeals that prove him worthy of their loyalty and respect. The story of Hawkins' development as a leader helps to give the book a solid shape. Rooted in the realistic tradition, this novel follows a number of vivid supporting characters through major combat operations as well as the lulls in between. The action scenes portray significant stages in the conduct of the war, so that the plot as military history and the plot as officer coming-of-age run side by side.

Much of the standard lunacy of the war is portrayed, particularly the quick abandonment of positions achieved at tremendous cost and the consequent attitude of men who fought hard, sustained injuries, and saw their buddies die for that most temporary objective. Huggett also nails down the tension between the experience of the combat soldier (Marine) and the soft life of those assigned to administrative or supply units. Though Huggett's treatment of the obligatory sex scenes with Oriental women seems to break faith with the texture and unity of the novel, *Body Count* has plenty of saving graces.

Characterization is one of this novel's strengths, but how much of it resides in the "backgrounding" materials? For me, this relatively unheralded work makes the most effective use of a realistic mode of characterization in handling the absurd elements. This success is achieved because the range of characters' reactions to the absurdities is detailed and compelling. Huggett allows his narrator to stand behind a half dozen or more key characters, telling parts of the story from the perspective of each (though not in the words of each). By alternating focal characters, Huggett is able to extend the depth of characterization while at the same time fragmenting the "truth" of the Vietnam experience.

Del Vecchio lets Lt. Brooks and St. Egan carry almost all of the introspective material (with Cherry representing another pole), and Webb's narrator pushes through the serial presentation of Snake, Hodges, and then the others in a systematic yet self-conscious way. Huggett, on the other hand, cycles and recycles through his main characters, alternating several segments seen through the eyes of Lt. Hawkins, Wilson, and LeBlanc with segments in which various lesser characters are allowed to shape the reader's understanding. There are even segments headed "The Platoon" in which the narrator stands behind the shared outlook of the group. Because Huggett has his plot under control, he is able to find the best character to reveal the nuances of particular events. This technique reminds us of the fact that there were innumerable Vietnam Wars, not one.

Hawkins, Huggett's main character, just barely manages to dominate over the others. Huggett's technique emphasizes the separate identities of the men, even while it is related to the technique of Webb and Del Vecchio that, to various degrees, demonstrates how individual identities are submerged in the group identity of the fighting unit or ground down by the depravations and exhaustion of the combat situation.

The representations of time, place, and action are realistic, but it is the rich interiority of this novel that makes it so much more than just another fictionalized battle report.

The achievements of Huggett, Webb, and Del Vecchio are genuine, and each novel in its own way is at least a partial success. The scope of *The Thirteenth Valley*, the power and pace of *Fields of Fire*, the rounded characters and perspectives of *Body Count* show us the war according to the conventions of popular and literary realism. In many ways, these novels are more "finished"--more complete as fictional structures--than those to be discussed next. Yet the abandonment of clocktime structures for more experiential renditions of "what happened" brings us fictional constructions that seem more capable of recreating the absurd and grotesque awarenesses that each of the six novelists needs to share.

II

After a powerful treatment of Marine boot camp, Hasford's *The Short-Timers* loses any kind of standard plot development. The Vietnam material in the sections called "Body Count" and "Grunts" is often beautifully written, sometimes poetic, but rarely directed or shaped beyond what one might expect from autobiographical writing. Events follow one another, but they don't seem to lead anywhere. There is little sense of causality--a feature of the novels more squarely centered in the realist tradition--and, thus, little sense of rationality. Whether these features of the book are intentional or merely the limitations of Hasford's art, they evoke the madness of the war more compellingly than the more programmatically plotted fictions discussed earlier.

The key characters are well displayed, and the brutal and brutalizing aspects of warfare are handled in a convincing and powerful fashion in a style more lyrical than realistic. There is no heroism in this novel--only survival and the ironically dehumanized "being" whose existence is the price of survival. The recognition of this empty, hollowed-out, ghoulish existence is conveyed by the recurring images of werewolves and vampires as well as by the cynical, worldy, inarticulate refrain that says it all: "There it is." An eerie mixture of the apocalyptic and the realistic, this novel is the basis for the film *Full Metal Jacket* directed by Stanley Kubrick.

One of a handful of first-person fictions, Hasford's vision is presented as that of Corporal Joker. Joker, however, is not as vivid as many of those he describes: Rafter Man, Cowboy, and Animal Mother. The self-effacing narrator often provides a feeling of merged experience, a sort of a first-person plural ("we") perspective that bears some resemblance to "the platoon" sections of *Body Count*.

The Short-Timers hovers between the Maileresque fictions that envision characters formed by carefully etched histories and works like *Cacciato* and *Close Quarters* that seem to detach their characters from the past. The first section, in boot camp, is conventionally but effectively told, and the variety of characters--of American types--is systematically introduced. While many of these characters are moved into the battle scenes that follow, somehow the two halves of the book are sharply severed. Corporal Joker, the narrator, undergoes changes that turn him into a more powerfully lyrical stylist, and the back-grounding done in the first part loses its relevance as the characters are redefined by the experience of war, an experience that has little association with that of boot camp.

Even the boot camp section is unusual as it presents the characters only in the here and now, as formed identities detached from the freight of history. Hasford's use of the present tense heightens his lyrical thrusting forward. Parris Island is a first rebirth, complete with its own absurdity and brutality. The war itself is a second, its terrors strangely beautiful and other-worldly.

As the novel progresses, Joker's sense of humor becomes more and more grotesque, a dark chuckle at despair. Charged with obtaining atrocity photographs as evidence of the enemies' inhuman cruelty, Joker and Rafter Man approach a mass grave:

> We see corpses of Vietnamese civilians who have been buried alive, faces frozen in mid-scream, hands like claws, the fingernails bloody and caked with damp earth. All of the dead people are grinning that hideous, joyless grin of those who have heard the joke, of those who have seen the terrible secrets of the earth. There's even the

> corpse of a dog which Victor Charlie could not
> separate from its master.
>
> There are no corpses with their hands tied
> behind their backs. However, the green ghouls
> assure us that they have seen such corpses
> everywhere. So I borrow some demolition wire
> from the Arvin snuffies and, crushing the stiff
> bodies with my knee until dry bones crack, I bind
> up a family, assembled at random from the
> multitude -- a man, his wife, a little boy, a little
> girl, and, of course, their dog. As a final touch
> I wire the dog's feet together. (126-127)

In sections like this, and in the searing, nightmarish account of the
skirmish with a sniper who turns out to be a fifteen year old girl,
Hasford finds the style and the highly charged detail to project his
vision. His images are not the images of mere realism, but rather the
dream symbols of a funhouse for ghouls and madmen.

Though *The Short-Timers* is a novel made out of fragments, at best
those fragments become prose poems of unrivaled power. And it is
when Hasford is making us experience what is most unreal that he tells
us so much: "I try to dream something beautiful. . . . My grandmother
sits in a rocking chair on her front porch shooting Viet Cong who have
stepped on her roses" (144). There is more in this fleeting dream than
in many pages and chapters of "authentic" documentary realism.

Larry Heinemann's *Close Quarters* is a highly stylized first person
narrative that reports Philip Dosier's year of combat. We meet Dosier
as he joins a team of soldiers who drive or man armored personnel
carriers--"tracks"--and follow him through a series of ambushes,
bodycounts, and major skirmishes.   We witness the spiritual
disintegration of Dosier that accompanies his experiences in this war.
Dosier's drinking, dope-taking, capacity for mindless violence and
cruelty are seen as the inevitable consequences of what he must learn
in order to survive. In this way, Heinemann's work is closest to the
conventions of naturalism, with its insistence on seeing man as a
creature controlled by instinct and environment and circumstance.
Dosier is not to be judged, for without free will there can be no moral
judgment.

This is not an original theme, but Heinemann's strategy of keeping
a narrow focus through his protagonist's narration gives this treatment
heightened power. Many passages attain a poetic elegance unmatched
by any other fiction of the war. Heinemann's presentation of fatigue,

hallucination, the chaos of combat, and the upwelling of powerful emotions is remarkable. Lyricism, ironically, handles the inner states that tell us so much about what counts in this war.

Also of special interest is his handling of Dosier's tenuous re-entry into "the world," a prefiguring of Heinemann's recent critical success, *Paco's Story* (1986).

Like many of the other novels, this one gives us an understanding of the powerful bonds formed among the soldiers, and also the motivations behind their individual and collective hostilities. Unlike the novels in the first group, *Close Quarters* does not depend very much on flashbacks or backgrounding. It's only when we come close to Dosier's future that we get a sense of his past, or in the brief flashback to his relationship with his girlfriend, Jenny, that occurs half-way through the novel--and only then through the trigger mechanism of Dosier's escapade with "Susie," a bar girl he meets while on R & R. What makes him is the strenuous, demanding present. Memory serves that present, joins it, and then dissolves in the rush of events. Only rarely will it become a relevant instrument of identity.

This sense of Dosier as a man recreated in the war, a man who in a special sense has no relevant past, is a significant part of Heinemann's vision. He simply "appears," ready to play his part, already molded of the strange stuff that will allow for some kind of appropriate functioning in an absurd predicament.

Repetition of action--the seemingly meaningless cycle of behaviors in which the characters are defined--is caught in the novel's patterns but hardly given editorial comment. The repetition of incident, the endless nerve-numbing or nerve-shattering routines from which there is little relief and for which there is no justifying outcome, this is the full measure of Dosier's experience. Though arbitrarily confined to what the world would call a year, the time of the novel has nothing at all to do with the passage of months but rather with spiraling rounds of madness.

Like many of the novels of this war, *Close Quarters* has a good deal of raw language and raw sex, but it is all convincing and well-integrated into Heinemann's determinist vision, a vision in which those best prepared to survive can't make it through while the bunglers somehow hold on.

It is not so much the borrowed authenticity of first-person narration that makes a work like *Close Quarters* so compelling, but the narrowed scale of concerns. While a novel that puts a sharp focus on the individual may not satisfy our demand for explanations of larger political or military issues, it allows us to feel who we might be--or become--as the record of internal events balances or overrides the external record.

Internal event, projected outward as a picaresque romp, is the main concern of Tim O'Brien's *Going After Cacciato*, perhaps the most inventive (along with Stephen Wright's 1983 *Meditations in Green*) of the Vietnam novels. This surreal fantasy follows a squad's alleged pursuit of a deserter who leads them to Paris on his own naive separate peace. The men at first believe--or almost believe--in the legitimacy of their mission, but soon come to understand it as a rationalization for their own wishes.

The central intelligence is Paul Berlin, an effective, fully-drawn character surrounded by interesting cut-outs. Through flashbacks that occur during Paul's duty at the Observation Post, we come to understand what the men have been through that makes their zany chase after Cacciato plausible. The insanity of the war is transformed into their Cacciato obsession, at the same time making that obsessional flight acceptable to the reader. Or are these passages really a hallucination, the presentation of Paul's fantasies during Observation Post periods or between them? After all, if only one could get up and walk away. If only. Daring to think such thoughts, we allow ourselves to participate in a joyful victory over the war itself.

A consistent explication of *Cacciato* is difficult in part because the temporal relationships between segments of the novel are hard to pin down. The chapters that record the pursuit after Cacciato form a consistent sequence, always moving forward in a picaresque manner. The Observation Post segments interrupt the chase story, but in themselves don't seem necessarily consecutive (though time markers are given for the passage of a single night). Even if they were, they contain Paul Berlin's memories of battle as well as his contemplations of Cacciato--memories that blur any sure chronology.

More than any other fiction of this war, *Going After Cacciato* develops a complex allegory of the human condition out of its materials. While the specific nature of this war is always in focus, O'Brien's art reaches out to embrace much more. His novel finally leaves the war behind, just as Cacciato does. One thread of this allegory spins off the image of the tunnel.

It is into the Vietcong tunnels that Lt. Sidney Martin urges his men to climb. First blow them with grenades; then search for the enemy or any intelligence about the enemy. Standard Operating Procedure. After two men die following Martin's orders, the others start to organize a rebellion whose goal is to frag Martin in order to save their own lives. Paul Berlin is sent to find Cacciato and bring him into solidarity with the group by having him grasp the grenade. Cacciato, found fishing in a rain-filled crater, refuses to participate--more concerned with whether or not there is a nibble at the end of his fishing line. Berlin says, "They say you better touch it. It's hopeless--it'll be done no matter what. And it's for your own good" (286). These are words that ironically argue the call to war itself. Though Berlin presses the grenade into Cacciato's hand, Cacciato never holds it or even feels it. In his excitement over catching a fish, the simple-minded Cacciato escapes complicity in the fragging incident. And in his flight to Paris --or is it Paul Berlin's flight to capture Cacciato's innocence?--he escapes once again, but this time the group follows him. Cacciato, the "dumb kid," becomes their ironic leader.

The journey the men take in pursuit of Cacciato includes episodes called "A Hole in the Road to Paris," "Fire in the Hole," "Falling Through a Hole in the Road to Paris," "Tunneling Toward Paris," and "Light at the End of the Tunnel to Paris." The sequence becomes an allegory of spiritual trial and renewal, of death and rebirth, ironically mirroring the story of blowing up and searching through the mysterious network of enemy tunnels in Vietnam. The men's resistance to Lt. Martin's SOP orders, orders that had already killed their comrades, is linked to their tunnelled passage through the sewers to Paris--the Paris of romance and Peace Conferences--towards which Cacciato lures them.

The ending is difficult to sort out. It suggests a number of rethinkings of the story's pattern and meaning. What is unquestionable is the power of O'Brien's work with its mixture of fable and realistic detail that flashes back and forth between literal and imaginative flight. The real and the unreal lose distinction over and over again, becoming part of one another, and this slipperiness is part of the novel's truth about the war.

This lyrical, surreal treatment--with its suspension of time and its provocative Pan myth underpinning--releases understandings of this war's absurd nature far more effectively than traditional or modified realist methods.

* * *

The novels by Del Vecchio, Webb, and Huggett, even while they would argue to the contrary, most often create links with previous war literature. Furthermore, by striving after scale and scope, they forsake the intensity that can only come through a narrowing of focus. O'Brien's work and, to a lesser extent, the work of Heinemann and Hasford convey the differences by less conventional methods of presentation. These approaches--mixtures of the naturalistic, the lyrical, and the psychological--are handled with sufficient skill to allow for a transformation of reality, or of realism, into something visionary and profound.

Works Cited

Del Vecchio, John M. *The Thirteenth Valley*. New York: Bantam Books, 1982.

Hasford, Gustav. *The Short-Timers*. New York: Harper and Row, 1979.

Heinemann, Larry. *Close Quarters*. New York: Farrar, Straus, Giroux, 1977.

Heinemann, Larry. *Paco's Story*. New York: Farrar, Straus, Giroux, 1986.

Huggett, William Turner. *Body Count*. New York: Putnam, 1973.

O'Brien, Tim. *Going After Cacciato*. New York: Delacorte Press, 1978.

Webb, James. *Fields of Fire*. New York: Prentice-Hall, 1978.

Wright, Stephen. *Meditations in Green*. New York: Scribner's, 1983.

DISARMING THE WAR STORY

Lorrie Smith

In 1969, Thomas Merton published "War and the Crisis of Language," an essay which extends the more genteel observations of George Orwell's "Politics and the English Language" to America's catastrophe in Indochina. Writing, he claims, more as a poet than a philosopher, Merton describes the moral vacuum and political bad faith created by "the gap between words and actions that is characteristic of modern war" (100). Unravelling the "narcissistic tautology of war," which constructs its own hermetic system of meaning, Merton shows how this gap helped perpetuate a war "fought to vindicate the assumptions upon which it [was] being fought"--assumptions based on America's solipsistic delusions about its mission in the world. The real tragedy of the war, Merton points out, is that America "decided to rule the world without paying serious attention to anybody else's view of what the world is all about" (116). Such power can be maintained only through a dictatorial monologue characterized by "double-talk, tautology, ambiguous cliché, self-righteous and doctrinaire pomposity, and pseudoscientific jargon that mask a total callousness and moral insensitivity, indeed a basic contempt for man" (117).

Of course, this language did not spring into being *sui generis*. Before the military ever destroyed a Vietnamese village to save it, the gaps between words and actions had been inscribed in the language of official American history and politics: the genocide of a native population and the theft of their land are still conceived as an "errand into the wilderness" or, more secularly, as "expansion" and "manifest destiny"; revolution and self-determination in the New World colonies are noble and enlightened, in the Third World evil and benighted; dropping atomic bombs on Hiroshima and Nagasaki makes the world "safe for democracy"; the invasion of Cambodia is an "incursion"; the suppression of self-determination in Nicaragua is a "freedom fight" using the techniques of "post-Vietnam low-intensity conflict." As historian Samuel P. Huntington points out, the gap between the rhetoric of democratic ideals and the realities of history "condemns Americans to co-exist with a peculiarly American form of cognitive dissonance" (4).

For a while during the Vietnam War, it seemed that our tolerance for this disjunction had finally run out. After Tet, public disapproval rose as the credibility of official language eroded in the face of a war which obviously did not match the version created by the power elite. (The Nixon/Kissinger slogan, "Peace with honor," was a last-ditch effort to recover popular support for the war.) Conceived within a system of ethnocentric, Cold War cowboy fantasies and perpetrated through political and semantic deception, the Vietnam War finally gave the lie to America's most misguided national myths[1]. Though the war spawned a generation wary, if not outright contemptuous of, the debased public language of the government which exploits these myths and the media which feeds on them, the force of this disillusionment has been absorbed by the mainstream and converted into impotent apathy or cynicism. We have recouped, in the eighties, the comfortable rhetoric of patriotic and patriarchal myths, which are shaping the values of a generation born after the war. As David M. Berman points out, the cycle of myth-making which led us into the quagmire in the first place remains unbroken: "The narratives of the Vietnam War which appear in [high school] textbooks are the results of a process of remaking history in the image of the myths upon which a culture depends. . . National mythology justifies the war in Vietnam as a war for a noble cause; but this mythology is unable to encompass the savage and painful conflict in which American sons died inglorious deaths for obscure reasons." We studiously avoid studying "the political and cultural realities of Vietnam" and "the fundamental premises upon which the war was fought" (63). That is, we are still trapped by the tautologies Merton speaks of. There is once again tacit support for militaristic intervention, and war remains as alluring to young men as ever.

If language and reality rarely crossed paths during the war, then the search for retrospective meaning inevitably leads us into a linguistic minefield. We have now reached a crucial stage in our collective enterprise of constructing the history of the Vietnam War and understanding its significance in American cultural and political life. Since the erection of the Vietnam Veterans Memorial and the "celebration" of the tenth anniversary of the "fall" of Saigon, it's no longer taboo to mention Vietnam in polite company; in fact, it's a hot topic, which is both a boon and a curse. The venting of ideas and feelings has been healthy, but as with anything that reaches the surface of American consciousness through the contaminated channels of the mass media, the war itself--its messy lived experience and memory-- gets boxed in a tidy package, labeled, and shipped to every living room. We have produced "Vietnam" the movie, the TV series, the HBO special, the video documentary, the comic book, the board game; "Vietnam" the best seller, the spectator sport, the commodity, the academic field, the band-wagon. The tag, "Vietnam" (a country's name), comes to stand for a whole complicated web of *American* feelings, actions, and memories.

While it is tempting to dismiss the current visibility of Vietnam as mere commodity fetish, we cannot ignore the real power of mass media productions like movies and Marvel comics. Nor can we ignore the complicated interplay between popular culture and "serious" literature. Even the most polished and well-meaning literary treatments of the war are often implicated in unexamined assumptions, fantasies, and myths rooted deep in the American psyche: the war was solely an American tragedy; our mission was worthy but our means were misguided; the war was "good" before Tet; meaning resides in the individual soldier's angst rather than collective complicity; we learned our lesson in Vietnam; trial by fire in battle makes boys men. Such beliefs and values--particularly the last one--often form the stock themes of conventional war stories, whose tragic, ironic, or serio-comic formulas displace the real emotional and political complexity of the war.

If we are ever to free ourselves from the hermetic illogic of war-making and the myths which promote battle as the ultimate test of manhood, then we must bring to consciousness our "peculiarly American form of cognitive dissonance." In narrative writing, this demands more than the techniques of realism, which inevitably produce war stories shaped by the values and ideologies of the dominant culture. Real changes--both political and psychic--require active resistance of those values and ideologies, and active disruption of the modes of representation which maintain them. For many Vietnam veteran writers--betrayed by the patriarchal system which sent them to fight-- the gaps between the war as they lived and remember it and cultural constructions of "Vietnam" are precisely the places where a truly subversive imaginative literature flourishes. The most successful veteran writers interrogate the assumptions of realism and resist the mystique of war perpetuated in conventional war stories.

Traditionally, literary realism has flourished during periods of social flux and confusion, and it is not surprising that realistic novels, films, and memoirs about Vietnam have wide popular appeal while the large body of poetry and drama about the war remains obscure. Realistic narrative relies on organic form and verisimilitude to create the illusion that literary representation and what Henry James called the "myriad forms" of reality are seamlessly intermeshed. In actuality, mimetic writing mirrors a representative reality defined by consensus and delimited by social norms, thus assuring the stability of moral and political codes. Mimetic stories have spatial symmetry and temporal order; they impose upon random experience beginnings, middles, and ends, causes and effects, heroes and antagonists, dramatic tension and resolution. However shocking and defamiliarizing the details of the stories may be, the very orderliness and safe enclosure of traditional plot structures maintain established social codes and hierarchies. If enough individual stories repeat the same motifs, they may come to form larger patterns which the culture comes to perceive as "natural" or "archetypal" or "universal." The "story" of World War II, for instance, has meaning for our culture as a heroic quest, and it forms a coherent narrative in which the soldier's sacrifices are redemptive.

When we apply the traditional war story pattern to the Vietnam War, we feel acutely the disjunction between ideals and realities. Yet few realistic Vietnam novels or films challenge the tacit elevation of war as an honorable rite of passage for young men. In most treatments of this stock theme, American presence in Vietnam is a given and larger moral and political questions about intervention or cultural constructions of masculinity are rarely raised. Books like James Webb's *Fields of Fire* and John Del Vecchio's *The Thirteenth Valley* encode war as a noble mission for the nation and for men. Though they can portray the war itself in all its absurdity and horror, mimetic narratives rarely challenge the status quo, for they tend to fit their absurd and horrifying material into structures of conventional symbolic meaning. Many films and novels of the war have been praised for their accuracy, as if verisimilitude alone yields truth. But realistic techniques have no inherent value unless the work also investigates the cultural assumptions which animate and give meaning to its images. The images themselves too easily seduce us with glamor and titillate us with terror, too easily detach themselves from the more indeterminate historical and political contexts of the war.

For example, many viewers of Oliver Stone's *Platoon* conflate the authentic depiction of the war's texture (all but the smell, some veterans say) with the highly stylized plot, which imposes Christian humanist meanings on the random, disjointed experiences of the foot soldier. Even as slice-of-life naturalism, the film parades a predictable sequence of Manichean conflicts in front of us: sensitive college kid vs. working class tough guys, black vs. white, officer vs. enlisted man, volunteer vs. draftee, new guy vs. short timer, and, of course, pragmatic Barnes vs. humanistic Elias. The details of the war are selected, composed, and framed in a political vacuum and yield coherent and comforting resolutions on a symbolic level where a hero named Chris T. comes of age by passing all the tests of courage, discovering and then overcoming his brutal instincts, killing off the evil father, and gaining the moral amplitude to synthesize good and evil. The patriarchal world of war is preserved, glorified, and reproduced, as Chris admits at the end that he was miraculously born again of "two fathers." Finally, he *tells* us about it all in a most lugubrious voice-over meant, apparently, to deepen our identification with the hero and give continuity to his developing manhood [2]. Such war stories, because of their wide appeal, both sustain and widen the gaps between myth and reality. A generation too young to remember the war is now forming its image of it from movies such as *Platoon*, just as many who enlisted to fight in Vietnam imagined the war as a high-tech re-make of *The Sands of Iwo Jima*. Both rest on and promote the assumption that war is an ugly but necessary and inevitable fact of life.

In some realistic narratives, the gaps between language and reality take the form of more complicated subtextual conflicts, as if their writers were subliminally aware that the conventions of realism were exhausted and inappropriate but didn't know how else to tell their stories. In *A Rumor of War*, Philip Caputo bitterly denounces the "splendid little war" in the dramatic unfolding of his *Bildungsroman* but glorifies battle in his highly earnest tone, elevated diction, and self-consciously literary epigraphs from the Bible, Shakespeare, Owen, and Sassoon. (The corollary to this elevation in film is the camera's fixed gaze on the spectacle of battle, which the established tradition of war movies has privileged.) On one page, Caputo describes battle as "that primary sacrament of war, baptism by fire" (120) and on the next page as a physical horror which "burst the religious myths of my Catholic childhood" (121). One might think this shift was intentionally ironic except that Caputo recovers religious metaphors (and hence reconstructs the myths which had supposedly "burst") later in his narrative: "hooded and bowed, the marines resembled a column of hunchbacked, penitent monks" (221); "The platoon rose as one, like a congregation at a Mass" (239). He decries throughout his story how men were betrayed by John Wayne fantasies of heroism but admits that a well-executed fire-fight gives him "an ache as profound as the ache of orgasm" (254). Caputo is even confused about his feelings for the men he commands, admitting "some of them were not so decent or good" (128). He feels a fraternal bond with "the men with whom I had shared the heat and dust, the tense, watchful nights, the risks of patrolling some desolate jungle trail" (129). But he also "decided there were good reasons for barriers between officers and enlisted men" (134).

Such confusions are, indeed, built into the nature of combat and the received language of warfare, which Caputo appropriates without the least resistance. His intent, like Oliver Stone's, is to dramatize how the military turns ordinary men into brutal killing animals, but also to acknowledge frankly the erotic allure of battle. To the extent that he tries to capture this ambiguity--shades of gray rumors rather than black and white truths--his narrative is more effective than Stone's. But one senses the conflicts in Caputo's narrative are not fully realized or articulated. The confusion comes with his impulse to reconcile the inherent paradoxes of the war by forcing them into traditional structures of meaning. The real anguish and anger beneath the surface of Caputo's story are tamed and subsumed within compensatory myths. Primarily, he resurrects nostalgic images of heroic sacrifice, as in his eulogistic apostrophe to Walter Neville Levy: "Yours was the greater love. You died for the man you tried to save, and you died *pro patria*. It was not altogether sweet and fitting, your death, but I'm sure you died *pro patria*. You were faithful. Your country is not" (213). But what exactly does such sacrifice and betrayal mean in this war? Caputo can not quite bring himself to say it means nothing but waste. Indeed, finding a way to pay tribute to individual acts of courage without buying into larger myths which glorify war is one of the major dilemmas facing the veteran writer.

"Honor the warrior, not the war" is a well-meaning phrase often invoked by and on behalf of Vietnam veterans since the heated disputes over the memorial. But can the two really be separated? This stance, as it is played out in many realistic narratives like *Platoon* and *A Rumor of War*, begs crucial ethical questions and belies fundamental confusions about the extent to which men raised in patriarchal culture perpetuate its values: in story after story, men are simultaneously appalled by the atrocities and absurdities of war and enthralled by what our culture has enshrined as the ultimate, most intense test of manhood. Readers of the stories are vicariously allowed to have the same cake and eat it too. Rather than *use* this paradox to point up the violence and oppression of patriarchal culture or to formulate political judgments about America's behavior in the world, neither Caputo nor Stone can resist the temptation to contain these confusions in comforting mythic patterns and narrative boundaries. Their protagonists, while fallen and betrayed, are nonetheless allowed to gain knowledge and attain heroic stature. As veteran writer Daniel M. Swain has written: "No matter how much you show the inequity of war, no matter how terrible you make the events, no matter how completely you show the Vietnam soldier as the victim of politicians, you still glorify him by making him the tragic figure in your dramas" (107).

How, then, can the veteran writer *use* his witnessing experience without directly or inadvertently reproducing the glamour and glory of war? Tim O'Brien, who has grappled with this dilemma more deeply and self-consciously than any other war writer, asserts the value of the war story in his memoir, *If I Die in a Combat Zone*. But he also guards against drawing facile "lessons" from his experience and imposing false order and "themes" upon it:

> I would wish this book could take the form of a plea
> for everlasting peace, a plea from one who knows, from
> one who's been there and come back, an old soldier
> looking back at a dying war.
>   That would be good. It would be fine to integrate it
> all to persuade my younger brothers and perhaps some
> others to say no to wrong wars.
>   Or it would be fine to confirm the old beliefs about
> war: It's horrible, but it's a crucible of men and events
> and, in the end, it makes more of a man out of you.
>   But, still, none of this seems right.
>   Now, war ended, all I am left with are simple,
> unprofound scraps of truth....Can the foot soldier teach
> anything important about war, merely for having been
> there? I think not. He can tell war stories. (31-32)

In the stories which follow, O'Brien assiduously resists the
temptation to revert to old patterns and meanings and instead lets his
"scraps of truth" speak for themselves--a creative risk more traditional
story-tellers don't take. What O'Brien realizes, even in his non-fiction,
is that the *manner* of telling creates meaning. His stories are expressed
lyrically and constructed as much of "dreams" and "nightmares" as of
facts. For O'Brien, imagination is "a real thing" which yields "a kind of
truth or clarity" (Lomperis 54). The "truths" he ends up with in his
memoir are contradictory and complicated; a passage near the end
suggests they may never "add up":

> You add things up. You lost a friend to the war, and
> you gained a friend. You compromised one principle
> and fulfilled another. You learned, as old men tell it
> in front of the courthouse, that war is not all bad; it
> may not make a man of you, but it teaches you that
> manhood is not something to scoff; some stories of
> valor are true; dead bodies are heavy, and it's better
> not to touch them; fear is paralysis, but it is better to
> be afraid than to move out to die, all limbs functioning
> and heart thumping and charging and having your
> chest torn open for all the work; you have to pick the
> times not to be afraid, but when you are afraid you
> must hide it to save respect and reputation. You
> learned that the old men had lives of their own and
> that they valued them enough to try not to lose them;
> anyone can die in a war if he tries. (204)

O'Brien has gone on, of course, to explore and "stretch the fictive possibilities" (Lomperis 46) inherent in these experiences, though he limits his scope to the phenomenological "truths" of war rather than exploiting the war's larger political implications.

The most provocative and subversive narratives of the war succeed precisely because they capitalize on war's contradictions and do not labor to resolve them through narrative coherence or by turning "scraps of truth" into grandiose heroic myths. Instead of glossing over the spaces between myths and realities, experimental narratives like O'Brien's *Going After Cacciato*, Michael Herr's *Dispatches*, Stephen Wright's *Meditations in Green*, Larry Heinemann's *Paco's Story*, Gustav Hasford's *The Short-Timers* and its film version, Kubrick's *Full Metal Jacket*, bring those gaps to the foreground. These non-linear books are often hailed as the most profoundly *realistic* treatments of the war's craziness, chaos, and illogic. Though they may be truly mimetic, their deeper value lies, I believe, in their destabilization of the social order as it is perceived and understood by popular consensus. It is important to realize that none of these narratives breaks completely free of the male fascination with battle. But each acknowledges its grip and at least implicitly interrogates that fascination and critiques the values which support traditional war stories. Most importantly, perhaps, they relinquish the traditional authority of the "invisible," omniscient narrator and pull the reader into a collaborative construction/deconstruction of meaning. By dislocating conventional meanings, these books force us to decode our own preconceptions about war. Their formal and linguistic experiments consciously overturn the comforting illusions of realism--chronological plot, meaningful character development, a distinct moral center, climax and resolution, closure. By subverting mythic patterns which valorize the mystique of war, these anti-war stories strip the experience of the Vietnam war down to its most chaotic core. Heinemann, Herr, and O'Brien, in particular, concentrate on the self-reflexivity of story-telling, engaging in the simultaneous narrative processes of constructing and unravelling traditional war stories.

It is no accident, for example, that *Paco's Story* opens with a wildly playful, darkly disturbing meditation (published separately as "The First Clean Fact") which simultaneously discards the traditional war story and preserves its detritus in the marginal world of carny geeks--thus staking out Paco's place in the social order:

> Let's begin with the first clean fact, James. This ain't
> no war story. War stories are out--one, two, three,

and a heave-ho, into the lake you go with all the
other alewife scuz and foamy harbor scum. But isn't
it a pity. All those crinkly, soggy sorts of laid-by
tellings crowded together as thick and pitiful as street
cobbles, floating mushy bellies up, like so much
moldy shag rug (dead as rusty-ass doornails and
smelling so peculiar and un-Christian). Just isn't it
a pity, because here and there and yonder among the
corpses are some prize-winning, leg-pulling daisies
--some real pop-in-the-oven muffins, so to speak,
some real softly lobbed, easy-out line drives. (3)

Though the war story is a dead genre, it cannot be completely buried
but continues to insinuate itself into the writer's consciousness in
perverse and ghoulish permutations; likewise, the book's narrator, a
corpse, finds a voice outside the bounds of decorous and traditional
discourse. Metaphors of pollution, cobbles, dead fish, shag rugs, frozen
food, and baseball are "crowded together" in an impossible collocation,
an outrageous yoking together of incongruities which defies any
coherent logic or meaning but does, in fact, express truths about *this*
illogical war. The introduction then goes on to play with the reader's
expectations, claiming "folks do not want to hear" about Paco's story but
giving "folks" what he knows they really want anyway in gruesome
detail.   Instead of merely satisfying the reader's voyeuristic and
lascivious desire for war stories, the narrator turns that voyeurism back
upon the reader and thematizes it within the narrative. Paradoxically,
this war story "ain't no war story." Though the poetry is still in the
"pity," neither the pity nor the terror of Paco's story leads to
regenerative catharsis.

Stephen Wright, like Heinemann, brings the war's past into the
reader's present through the mediation of a narrator whose language
contains impossible incongruities. Like *Paco's Story*, *Meditations in
Green* continually challenges the reader's complacency and emphasizes
our complicity: "What are we to do when the darkness comes on and
we wait for something to happen, as Huey, who never even knew she
shared her name with a ten-thousand-pound assault helicopter, sprawls
on the floor with her sketchbook, making pastel pictures of floating
cities, sleek spaceships, planets of ice, and I, your genial storyteller,
wreathed in a beard of smoke, look into the light and recite strange
tales from the war back in the long ago time" (5-6). Such cynical self-
consciousness about tale-telling keeps us off-balance and calls into
question all the premises of conventional war stories.

With similar self-reflexivity, Michael Herr places his enigmatic Lurp's "story" at the beginning of *Dispatches*, a book whose main impulse is to undermine and overturn all the implicit social and political values supporting conventional war stories and reportage. What we are meant to "read" is all that is not told: "'Patrol went up the mountain. One man came back. He died before he could tell us what happened'" (7). "So what happened?" we're dying to ask. The Lurp won't tell Herr, and Herr won't tell us. This skeletal narrative, stripped of all the elaboration and closure we desire in stories, frustrates our expectations and thus forces us to admit that the grit and gore and heroics and heightened intensity we associate with war stories in fact provide a good deal of visceral reading pleasure. And that admission pushes us towards a deeper understanding of our own complicated feelings about war, whether we have fought in one or not. While the Lurp's story is partly about the unspoken language of fellow initiates (since Herr admits that only later does he understand the story), it is also about the impossibility of capturing experience in words--especially experience which confounds socially-sanctioned categories of meaning and sense.

Several pages later Herr explains the lesson of his anecdote: "In war more than in other life you don't really know what you're doing most of the time, you're just behaving, and afterward you can make up any kind of bullshit you want to about it, say you felt good or bad, loved it or hated it, did this or that, the right thing or the wrong thing; still, what happened happened" (21). We had better be careful, Herr cautions, how we interpret and draw meaning from "what happened." Or, as Tim O'Brien writes in "How to Tell a True War Story," "happeningness is irrelevant. A thing may happen and be a total lie; another thing may not happen and be truer than the truth" (214). The war itself will always elude our war stories. Neither Herr's "dark revelations" nor O'Brien's "scraps of truth" will ever add up to a coherent, logical plot; one meaning will always qualify or reverse another. Such an ontological condition requires fluid language and indeterminate forms.

While Heinemann, Wright, and Herr each use their own outrageous patois composed of counter-culture drug slang, obscenity, and soldier's argot to turn the artificial logic of war inside out, Tim O'Brien relies on elegant metafictional structures to resist fixed meanings. In both his short stories and *Going After Cacciato*, O'Brien simultaneously satisfies the impulse to tell traditional war stories-- relating tales of fraggings and atrocities, thousand-yard stares and lost innocence, AWOL fantasies, and comaraderie--and undercuts that satisfaction by blurring the boundaries between fact, memory, and fantasy. Any easy morals or conclusions we may draw from his stories are intercepted by a constantly shifting and decentered narrative which leaves us in a slippery realm of ambiguity; the recurring phrase, "anything was possible," refers as much to the generative process of story-telling as it does to Paul Berlin's escapist imaginings. One point of O'Brien's short metafiction, "How to Tell a True War Story," is that we are prisoners of the conventions of the war story, which in its truest form is also "a love story" and a "ghost story" (214). Though these writers may not resolve war's experiential conflicts any more than Caputo does, they bring them squarely into the open, forcing the reader to take an active role in tracing out the meanings within paradoxical material and calling attention to how insistently our perceptions and values are determined by cultural norms, literary conventions, and received language. Pulling simultaneously in several directions and refusing to reconcile their paradoxes, these narratives subvert the old schemes where warfare is noble and soldiers are heroic.

The linguistic dislocations and formal indeterminacy destabilize the very modes of thinking which permitted American intervention in Indochina in the first place and which distort that experience for us now. Their fractured surfaces both reflect a fragmented experience and release new perceptions. Multi-valent and multi-vocal, they actively resist the monologue of war-making described by Merton. Their irreverent narrators--the inscrutable Private Joker in *The Short-Timers/Full Metal Jacket*, the hallucinatory James Griffin in *Meditations in Green*, the jive-rapping ghost in *Paco's Story*--speak from a dual position as inside initiates of the war's "dark revelations" and outside agitators bent on dismantling official war stories. They shock, cajole, taunt, and challenge us with their defiance of proper language, conventional wisdom, and logical plot. Revelling in word play, shifting voices, multiple perspectives, illogical transitions, metaphoric elaboration, temporal disjunctions, and other experimental techniques, these narratives resist hierarchy, linear history, and binary oppositions. They ask us to participate in their decreations and invite us to imagine new social orders, new modes of thinking, new roles, new ways of remembering the war. In short, they overturn all the expectations and satisfactions of conventional war stories. They do not fix the war in a gaze of horror or wonder, but thrust us into the real flux and chaos of history.

The aggressively non-rational styles of writers like Herr, O'Brien, Wright, and Heinemann support subversive political imperatives, though none places his work in an explicitly political context. Only when the old stories have been stripped of power and meaning can new forms of life emerge. The ending of *Meditations in Green* opens up such possibility through its free-floating, lyrical language. Without denying war's horror, the plenitude of poetry offers the hope of metamorphosis and regeneration by making a new thing out of old materials, as the Vietnamese have turned old artillery shells into sculptures and water troughs. Wright's self-consuming text itself becomes the red paper poppy of the D.A.V., uprooted from Flanders, replanted by the wounded Vietnam veteran, and offered up to the reader: "Everywhere the green fuses are burning and look now, snipping rapidly ahead of your leaping eye, the forged blades cutting through the page, the transformation of this printed sheet twisted about a metal stem for your lapel your hat your antenna, a paper emblem of the widow's hope, the doctor's apothecary, the veteran's friend: a modest flower" (322). Though few of these narratives work their way past chaos and dissolution, their immersions help us realize, with Paul Berlin, that "anything is possible"--perhaps even peace.

Notes

1. For a full analysis of how "the triangulation of myth, politics, and bureaucracy might locate" American involvement in Vietnam, see Loren Baritz, *Backfire: A History of How American Culture Led Us into Vietnam and Made Us Fight the Way We Did.* He focuses particularly on the myth of the "city upon a hill" and America's sense of missionary zeal in saving the rest of the world. His premise is that "We cannot understand war without understanding culture" (9). I would agree, and add that the reverse, unfortunately, is also true. For a literary analysis of American myth and war, see John Hellman, *American Myth and the Legacy of Vietnam.*

2. For an excellent analysis of how *Platoon's* techniques of realism mask "the elevation of the warrior hero and the glamorization of combat" see Thomas Prasch, "*Platoon* and the Mythology of Realism" in William J. Searle, ed. *Search and Clear: Critical Responses to Selected Literature and Films of the Vietnam War.*

Works Cited

Baritz, Loren. *Backfire: A History of How American Culture Led Us into Vietnam and Made Us Fight the Way We Did.* New York: William Morrow, 1985.

Berman, David M. "In Cold Blood: The Vietnam War in Textbooks." *Vietnam Generation* 1.1 (Winter 1989): 61-80.

Caputo, Philip. *A Rumor of War*. NY: Ballantine Books, 1977.

Hasford, Gustav. *The Short Timers*. NY: Bantam, 1979.

Heinemann, Larry. *Paco's Story*. NY: Penguin, 1987.

Hellman, John. *American Myth and the Legacy of Vietnam*. NY: Columbia U. Press, 1986.

Herr, Michael. *Dispatches*. NY: Avon Books, 1978.

Huntington, Samuel P. *American Politics: The Promise of Disharmony*. Cambridge: Harvard University Press, 1981.

Lomperis, Timothy. *"Reading the Wind": The Literature of the Vietnam War*. Durham: Duke University Press, 1987.

Merton, Thomas. "War and the Crisis of Language." In Robert Ginsberg, ed. *The Critique of War*. Chicago: Henry Regnery Co., 1969.

O'Brien, Tim. *Going After Cacciato*. NY: Dell, 1978.

------------. "How to Tell a True War Story." *Esquire* 108.4 (October, 1987): 208-215.

------------. *If I Die in a Combat Zone (Box Me Up and Ship Me Home)*. NY: Dell, 1973.

Swain, Daniel M. "Brothers in Arms." In Reese Williams, ed., *Unwinding the Vietnam War: From War into Peace*. Seattle: The Real Comet Press, 1987: 107-110.

Wright, Stephen. *Meditations in Green*. NY: Bantam Books, 1983.

NARRATIVE STRATEGIES IN RECENT VIETNAM WAR FICTION

Marilyn Durham

Literature of the Vietnam War, since it concerns experiences most readers have not personally lived through, must face an initial obstacle in engaging not only our interest, but more crucially our participation, in constructing its singular reality.   As in all literary encounters, communication between writer and audience is a result of their active partnership, but Vietnam may be an especially difficult environment to share in that it is not only excessively foreign to most of us, but it may also be intensely painful. The war is a world which the majority of readers will not have physically entered, and if we are to make sense of it we must do more than read about it; we must become complicit in mentally rebuilding it and imaginatively living in it. One wedge into an unknown universe is narrative point of view.

This strategy is handled variously, and with different results, in three novels which explore the impact of the war on veterans and their families. *Paco's Story* by Larry Heinemann, *Indian Country* by Philip Caputo, and *In Country* by Bobbie Ann Mason all focus on the efforts of a returning soldier to reinsert himself into normal life. We learn much about the war experiences of each veteran, but we learn more about the emotional and physical fallout of Vietnam for themselves and the people they come home to.   In each book, narrative strategy calibrates the intensity of our engagement in each story and its truth. Heinemann and Mason isolate one voice to draw us into their narrative structures, and this focus invites our sympathy, identification, and ultimate insight into the speaker's experience. We feel privileged to know the storyteller's world from the inside, to see it from behind his own eyes. Caputo's detached and omniscient narrator, on the other hand, and the author's movement from one character's consciousness to another, separate a reader from that one insistent vision necessary to our complete understanding. This resulting distance between story and reader precludes our full participation in *Indian Country*.

The voice which narrates *Paco's Story* does so with a special authority: he was there with Paco, at Fire Base Harriette, when the company was attacked, leaving Paco the only survivor. The soldier who speaks to us was killed we learn, and Paco's story is told to us by a ghost, surrounded by the other ghosts of Paco's company. We don't know the ghost's name and we don't know who James is (the speaker constantly addresses this friend), but we do know these are men who fought with Paco, who humped the jungle with him, who set the ambushes, and who raped the VC prisoner. The unstinting realism and concreteness of the narrative conjures an image of a ghostly storyteller, surrounded by a circle of intimates, concerned with revealing the truth. This authority and experiential immediacy draws us in; the expression is so vital and heartfelt because so intensely *lived* that we experience its pain and its beauty through a special lens. It is the lens of a friend, of a loving commentator, a wistful voice which sounds its loss while following the survivor. It is in no way what omniscient narration often becomes: a detached Olympian voice, surveying and reporting. This speaker was on that hill when it was attacked, he lost his life while Paco held on to his, and every fact he reports about Paco resonates with the narrator's awareness of his own dissolution.

While this intimacy is encouraged between reader and narrator, however, his haunting revelations assume a cosmic significance, increasing his stature and diminishing our own. While on the one hand we might imagine we were listening in on a terrifying yet eloquent conversation among intimates, at the same time we are reminded that this is a conversation in heaven or hell--somewhere in the after life--in another world where soldiers gather to stand vigil over survivors of firefights. This tells us that the events at Fire Base Harriette were no mere local affair, but form part of a global even universal perspective. This is a broadening of our consciousness. But we simultaneously hear, smell, taste, and feel the moment concretely--which is a way of focusing our consciousness. The narrative strategy in *Paco's Story* makes us feel as if we'd been there--in detail--while at the same time forcing us to locate "there" in a larger meaning. Narrative voice and language work to narrow and expand the center of consciousness, and this rhythm akin to the inhale-exhale of the human body, breathes life into *Paco's Story*.

The narrator begins his account with "the first clean fact" and follows it with a riotous series of facts about life in Vietnam. But the central fact of the massacre, that night when Alpha Company was evaporated, leaving behind only Paco alive, that fact is withheld until the end of the first chapter. After following the man's patter, happily drawn into his rollicking account and even laughing with him, we begin to squirm for we now learn *he* was one of the "disappeared": "When the mother fuckers hit we didn't go *poof* of a piece; rather, we disappeared like sand dunes in a stiff and steady offshore ocean breeze--one goddamned grain at a time" (Heinemann 16). The individual crystals of the imagery point to each soldier's separate consciousness and the speaker makes us feel each shell's impact and each life extinguished. But lest we conclude this was an isolated event with only local import, he ends the chapter implying that, on the contrary, it resounds throughout the universe. The cosmic range of

Alpha Company's dissolution is suggested when the ghost says: "Oh, we dissolved all right, everybody but Paco, but our screams burst through the ozone . . . the aurora borealis . . . frequency-perfect out into God's Everlasting Cosmos." And, he adds, "we're pushing up daisies for half a handful of millenia" while that "blood-curdling scream is rattling all over God's ever-loving Creation like a BB in a boxcar, only louder" (17). We know now that this voice ranges over "God's ever-loving Creation" and is uttering a terrible truth. We have reveled in his chattiness throughout the first chapter, then we are brought up short when we realize he speaks from the dead. You'd better believe that we begin to listen more closely to the rest.

It is striking, given this awful solemnity and power our narrator suddenly seems to assume, that over the course of the story he creates an intimacy among reader, Paco, and storyteller which directly engages our senses and emotions. After Paco's return to the United States, he rides a bus as far as his money will take him and alights at a small town named Boone. And, here, incredibly, beauty enters this story as the narrator lovingly describes the arrival of spring and the birth of new life Paco perceives around him. The small ugly town where Paco bitterly encounters prejudice and rejection is yet suffused with a luminosity and energy which nature cannot withhold even where a blighted humanity has set up shop. Spots of beauty enter the narrative as Paco enters Boone and stands at the edge of a "broad panorama of farmland and woods, greening up, with the warmth of the lowering sun full in his face, the shadows elongated. The bright spring sky is beginning to cloud over, and a clean moist rain smell fills the air" (40).

The ghostly voice pauses often to look about, and these introspective interruptions invite us to share his wonder at nature's loveliness, as, for example, when Paco stops to watch the rainbows in the mist playing below the bridge. As the story progresses, James is not mentioned as often, the attention lavished on the tactile effect of words increases, and this caress of the landscape enables us to live in Paco's pores. We are again in the midst of an ordinary life. Before we meet Paco on the bus and enter the green world with him, the disembodied voice of the narrator dissolving into the cosmos has clothed the story in apocalyptic colors. However, when we travel behind Paco's eyes, we luxuriate in the ripeness of the warm plums a fellow-traveller hugs to herself in sleep.

The sensual awareness intensifies when Paco enters The Texas Lunch and brings the spring sunshine in the door with him:

> And just now that strong, clean, spring-
> showery yellowy light streaks straight in the

> back door, a sudden sharp presence that
> makes everyone blind, startled, lighting up
> everything. (97)

The narrator invites us to take "this whole image" into our hearts and
feel its life-force: "Right this moment, James we could stand in the
middle of the street at the edge of the shadow of that bright, late-
afternoon light . . ." (98). Although this voice has constantly intruded
on the story and reminded us of his ghostly role, we are brought up
short at this heightening of the experiential immediacy of the narrative.
"We could stand"--he says, it's like we're right there, James, so *feel* it.
He urgently brings home Paco's sensations to us, but his intrusion
evokes the gathering of the dead Alpha Company. Part of what he
wants us to notice is the beauty of young, rain-drenched Betsy
Sherburne, her shining locks catching the light as Paco gazes at her.
And yes, we savor her loveliness at the same time that we feel the loss
of this earthly beauty by the narrator and his cronies. Thus, the
concrete sensual enjoyment we gain from the minute observation of
this day and our awareness of the narrator's distance from this earthly
pleasure reinforces the tragedy of Paco's story. It is a moment in time
which transports us beyond time and keeps our eyes firmly fixed on the
ghosts of those who no longer live in our time.

This lifelike narrative strategy controls the force of the impact, and
while Heinemann achieves a visceral thrust with his ghostly narrator,
Philip Caputo creates a highly gripping but somehow artificial structure
which manages to maintain its distance from a reader. The omniscient
voice of *Indian Country* relates Chris Starkman's tale with the sweep of
a camera's eye rather than the passion of a participant. The point of
view changes and throughout the book this move through a series of
voices is logical but repels our efforts to identify with any one voice.
We listen to an external and all-knowing consciousness, to Chris'
thoughts, to the mind of his wife June, and to the ruminations of the
old Ojibwa Indian Louis, grandfather to Bonny George St. Germaine
who was Chris's best friend. This consistent shift in narrative focus
allows the story to be told from many different angles but at the same
time has an alienating effect. The change in focus reminds us that a
narrative construct is being built and diminishes our ability to absorb
the persona of the teller and thus make the story our own. There is no
central witness to whom we can attach our emotions. While reading
Indian Country we are always aware that revelations are orchestrated;
we are being shown rather than immersed in experience.

Chris, naturally, is the character whose thoughts we explore most
frequently. We often find ourselves understanding the man as he

explains himself, but the insightful--yet sanitized--voice of the omniscient narrator repeatedly intrudes on Chris's speculations to clarify a point or strengthen a moral lesson. For example, Chris wrestles with the injustice of a society in which his Indian friend Bonny George must go to Vietnam while he, a middle-class white kid of the same age, can stay home and go to college. We witness this struggle in Chris's mind and become a part of it when our sympathies are pulled toward Bonny; then the narrator breaks in to comment sonorously on the social and political realities of modern America. We are again reminded that these people are characters in a novel and we are being manipulated to feel something for them. We lose sight of Chris because his protective storyteller who knows all has dwarfed the young man's role.

In a special moment of beauty and communion between Chris and Bonny, with the aurora borealis splashed across the night sky, the narrator breaks the spell by observing:

> they stood as silent and transfixed as the first human
> beings ever to behold the wonder of creation . . . for
> what was he and what was Bonny George? (30)

Chris doesn't think to himself "what am *I*," instead we watch Chris staring at the stars and notice conspicuously philosophic and didactic statement being put into his head. The intrusion closes the moment off--we have not felt it from inside Chris.

Another distancing technique is the series of long retrospective sections which explain how these characters became the people they are. So, for example, we follow Chris into the woods and spend the day with him "cruising timber" for a lumber company, and when he breaks for lunch he suddenly "remembers" in great detail the events between the last time we saw him in the woods with Bonny George and the present walk through the forest.

Our immediate reactions are similarly blunted by the way sentences from the Bible will suddenly enter the narrative when Chris thinks of his father. Lucius Starkman, a pacifist minister who bitterly disapproved of Chris's enlistment, casts his son out of his heart when Chris returns from Vietnam, and much of *Indian Country* concerns Chris's efforts to reconcile himself to the differences between his father and himself. Biblical quotations, always in italicized print, intrude on Chris' stream of consciousness, and although they often fit the context of Chris's thoughts, they don't seem fully integrated, breaking our absorption in the way Chris' mind is presently working. Chris may be hearing his father's voice, but the words have no flesh for us because we don't know the man who spoke them well enough. The device is finally artificial and ineffective, rendering the distance between reader and story palpable.

The most destructively intrusive narrative element is Caputo's handling of the ghosts. As Chris's mental state deteriorates, he retreats into the safe camaraderie he felt in Vietnam among his fellow soldiers, D.J., Hutch and Ramos. He begins by simply talking to them, but as his withdrawal from reality intensifies, he hallucinates the three figures. Their appearance is not revealed "from the inside" however, as they grow before Chris's disturbed mind, but we experience them from a clinical perspective (as if a psychiatrist were observing a patient). The emphasis on insanity reminds us, again, that we are watching Chris twist in the wind rather than understanding the source of the movement. Chris lashes himself with this fear of insanity when he first sees the ghosts, then blacks out. When he awakens, the narrator reports, he had relaxed

> and his mind, working with supernatural speed, grasped the truth in the apparent contradiction that the three men were real and illusory at the same time. He had entered a realm in which distinctions between the imaginary and its opposite did not exist. The instantaneousness with which he came to this understanding astonished him. (248)

The narrator explains that Chris had grasped this truth rather than showing Chris's mind moving toward it. The "instantaneousness" is indeed astonishing because the reader has not been made to see how it happened, and this explanatory mode generated by the intrusive narrator lessens the impact of the ghosts' appearance and conventionalizes their role in the narrative.

Bobbie Ann Mason makes us feel the impact of the war by firmly centering her narrative perspective in the awakening consciousness of Samantha Hughes, aged 17. *In Country* differs from *Paco's Story* and *Indian Country* in that the focal character is not a returning soldier, but the daughter of a soldier killed in Vietnam before she was born. The story reveals Sam's discovery, through his letters and journals and her own "growing up," of the father she never knew and the war which killed him. Living in Sam's mind allows us to participate in her learning process and forces us to recognize our own difficulties in sorting out Vietnam. She is no soldier and neither are most of us; thus, her move toward insight replicates our own epistemological journey, and her personal connection with the war deepens our emotional response. Mason guides Sam, and us, through the paces logically by filtering all input through Sam's eyes and finally through her heart. When the book ends with Sam's visit to the Vietnam War memorial in Washington, we feel that each step on the road to this climactic encounter has been earned by both Sam and reader.

In the beginning of the story we find Sam living with her uncle Emmett, another Vietnam veteran, whose behavior frightens her because she can't understand the source of his conflicts--the war. One effect she becomes fairly sure of, however, is his poor health: the skin rash, headaches and digestive problems she attributes to his exposure to Agent Orange. We follow her efforts to draw Emmett out on his war experiences and her increasing involvement with his vet friends, all of whom exhibit permanent scars from the war. As she grows closer to Emmett and his friends, her reflections on the world are colored by her knowledge of what happened to these men in Vietnam and what continues to happen to them and their families "back in the world."

Mason collects Sam's conclusions in one short scene when she shows us how Sam's stream of consciousness is continually invaded by the war. The veterans organize a dance to benefit the son of Buddy Mangrum, a child recently hospitalized due to complications arising from his father's contamination by Agent Orange. Sam's thoughts are these as she sits in the darkened gymnasium:

> The entwined red and white and blue streamers flowed
> in the breeze from the air conditioner. Buddy
> Mangrum's kid's intestines were twisted like that. (120)

Sam's world has been darkened by realizing the impact of the war on soldiers and their families, and because we are close companions of her mind, we share her insights. We have no need for instruction because we have collected the same data due to Mason's narrative strategy.

Sitting and watching the vets at the dance, Sam thinks of a party she decided not to attend and to the present she never bought.

> You could work hard wrapping a package and buy
> some pretty paper and a nice ribbon and a name tag,
> but the person would just rip it all up to see what was
> inside. Packaging was supposed to deceive, Sam
> thought, but it never did. (120)

One kind of packaging reminds her of another sort and she muses, "Her father came back from the war in a plastic bag. Attractive and efficient. A good disguise" (120). The shadows in the gymnasium are unsettling because "in the corners it was dark, like a foxhole where an infantryman would lie crouched for the night, under his poncho, spread above" (120). Sam vividly imagines the nocturnal scramblings of jungle creatures, frequently illuminated by "the tracers beaming across the sky, identifying the crisscross path of a distant firefight. The strobe light was like that. The pain in Emmett's head" (120). She moves from the gym to Vietnam, then back again as she collides with the fallout from that jungle experience: her uncle's psychological scars.

Sam's thoughts are impinged upon by her new knowledge about her father, and the transitions between ideas seem logical, almost organic. The lessons we draw maintain the narrative integrity and avoid the artificial imposition we felt occasionally in *Indian Country*. Mason's method is a gentler entangling of reader in the narrative web than Heinemann's shocking entrapment of the reader with his ghostly scream. Both books, though, involve us in an intimate exploration of the truth.

We share Sam's awareness of at least one painful truth: the sheer waste of human lives, among those killed in Vietnam and among those who returned. She feels the hurt most deeply due to her desire for Tom, a veteran whose memories prevent him from making love to Sam. His impotence brings home the war to Sam:

> The sadness of his affliction hit her then like a truck. She thought of all the lives wasted by the war. She wanted to cry, but then she wanted to yell and scream and kick. She could imagine fighting, but only against the war. All the boys getting killed, on both sides. And boys getting mutilated. And then not being allowed to grow up. That was it--they didn't get to grow up and become regular people. (140)

Sam has aged considerably throughout *In Country*, and it is our participation in her growing up which renders the cut-off of young lives even more poignant, and at the same time, more tangible. College students identify with Sam and the meaning of Vietnam is brought home to them, with a special urgency, it seems, because Mason's narrative strategy invites them into Sam's consciousness.

In *Walking Point: American Narratives of Vietnam*, Thomas Myers comments on the importance of this collusion between writer and reader:

> . . . there is in even the most powerful writing something that language cannot reach or explicate, an

experience that words point toward but that only the reader's own creative energies can begin to trace. (32)

The aesthetic rendering of experience which *Paco's Story* and *In Country* employ makes the most of these "creative energies." Our partnerships with these authors result in concrete connections with the narrative universe of Heinemann and Mason, while Caputo's *Indian Country* remains, at least for this reader, largely unknown territory.

Works Cited

Caputo, Philip. *Indian Country*. New York: Bantam Books, 1987.

Heinemann, Larry. *Paco's Story*. New York: Farrar Straus Giroux, 1986.

Mason, Bobbie Ann. *In Country*. New York: Harper and Row, 1984.

Myers, Thomas. *Walking Point: American Narratives of Vietnam*. New York: Oxford University Press, 1988.

A DUAL PERSPECTIVE:
FIRST-PERSON NARRATIVE IN VIETNAM FILM AND DRAMA

David J. DeRose

In one of the earliest, and what is still considered one of the finest Vietnam war dramas, David Rabe's *Sticks and Bones*, a blind veteran shows his Vietnam "home movies" to his parents. But his camera has malfunctioned; the supposedly horrifying footage is nothing more than a green flickering screen. Although the screen remains blank, what horrifies is the soldier's own narration of the images he assumes his family is watching. This veteran's subjective impressions of the Vietnam war, Rabe is telling us, are far more powerful than any film image, however graphic.

While Rabe's stance has often been criticized as extreme,[1] this scene from his play might well stand as a reminder to dramatists and film makers of the most meaningful method of expressing the experience of American soldiers in Vietnam. Both stage and screen have struggled for twenty years to bring the essence of this experience to life. During that time, one thing has been made clear: that the real story of the Vietnam war lies with those who fought there, and that their personal stories, their impressions, must serve as guide in any artistic exploration of Vietnam.

The film industry is currently pursuing the creation of the definitive Vietnam film. Despite the great variety within the recent crop of Vietnam war films, one common thread holds them together: the desire to tell "the real story" of America's men in Vietnam. "The impossible longing for a satisfactory conclusion tempts each Viet film to sell itself as definitive," comments J. Hoberman in a *Village Voice* review of *Hamburger Hill* (57). In a similar vein, Bill Couturie, director of the recent Vietnam war documentary *Dear America: Letters Home From Vietnam*, confesses his desire to "make the definitive film on Vietnam from an emotional level" (qtd. in Freedman, 34). Certainly, *Dear America* is an overwhelming emotional experience, capturing the most intimate expressions of soldiers in Vietnam. One need not look very hard to identify the categories which other new films have claimed for themselves, or into which they have been placed by the public and the press. *Platoon* has quickly become the "benchmark Vietnam War movie" (McGillan 12). *The Hanoi Hilton* is the POW film; *Good Morning, Vietnam* is the Vietnam comedy; *Hamburger Hill* is the revisionist, "John Wayne" film; and *Full Metal Jacket* will probably be unjustly reduced in the near future to the film containing the Marine training camp sequence.

These grand aspirations on the part of film-makers, and this pigeon-holing on the part of film-goers, reduce the war to a codified series of "accurate" or "true" images. The fact that no such universal codified standards existed either during the Vietnam war or since has not kept us from measuring all war narratives against them. In particular, the accurate reproduction of the physical conditions of Vietnam, or "showing it like it really was," has become the suppositional yardstick by which Vietnam combat films like *Platoon*, *Full Metal Jacket*, or even *Hamburger Hill*, are measured.[2] In these films, veracity is measured in terms of physical verisimilitude or "authenticity"--the graphic representation of the conditions of war. In Vietnam, those conditions included a physical arena of dense tropical jungles, oppressive temperatures and humidity, voracious insects, and a thoroughly acclimated and seemingly invisible enemy. *Platoon*, says Vietnam journalist David Halberstam, "understands something that the architects of the war never did: how the foliage, the thickness of the jungle, negated U.S. technological superiority. You can see how the forest sucks in American soldiers; they just disappear" (qtd. in Corliss 57). Still, veracity must also be defined in terms of the life-stories of those who fought in Vietnam. *Platoon* has been singled out not only for its physical accuracy, but also because it presents many of the human elements which made fighting in Vietnam unique: the drug abuse, the inexperienced junior officers, the racial imbalances, the in-fighting, and, most importantly, the loss of America's belief in its own "essential morality" (Cawly 18).

In the words of one Vietnam scholar, James Reston Jr., the important issue of any Vietnam narrative is to get "to the interior of the thing." Reston, in his introduction to the Vietnam drama anthology, *Coming to Terms*, proposes that all Vietnam narratives should be responsible for relating "the most accurate, most profound memory of Vietnam," namely, the "emotional truth of the experience" (ix). Reston's choice of plays in that anthology--only two of seven actually take place in Vietnam--demonstrates that emotional truth is not always to be found in the representation of authentic combat images. Emotional truth means that people and events must be viewed, not only through the impartial eye of the camera, but from the personal perspective of those who fought in Vietnam.

As a model for Vietnam narratives (albeit a non-fiction one), *Dear America* touches that emotional truth by combining "mail sent by 37 of the 3 million Americans who served in Vietnam...and a visual montage of still photographs, home movies, Department of Defense footage and

TV newscasts from the period" (Freedman 33). These historical documents are combined with the most intimate thoughts and feelings expressed in the letters of the continuous voice-over. This combination of physical reality with emotional consciousness creates a dual-presence in the film, manifesting one of the most underrated techniques of Vietnam narratives: the first person narrator or voice-over.

First person narrators or similarly subjective or familiar narrative voices come as no surprise in Vietnam prose. [3] The evocative power of language being the primary tool of prose, the first person voice is a widely accepted and utilized means of personalizing prose accounts. In film, however, the voice-over is considered an impurity which draws attention to the limitations of the cinematic medium as a pure narrative form. [4] Nevertheless, the majority of acclaimed Vietnam war films use a first person voice-over narrator. The presence of this "impurity" arises from the need to balance or to comment upon the physical violence in such films. In this age of cinematic wizardry, films such as *Platoon*, *Full Metal Jacket*, and even the decade-old *Apocalypse Now* depend on language to compensate for the cinematic appeal of the high-tech, hyper-real portrayal of violence. The cinematic representation of combat violence cannot help but glamorize war. As one war film critic has noted: "however bloody and violent filmmakers have portrayed combat on screen, the action and excitement have become escapist entertainment rather than creating a revulsion against the war" (Suid 24).

In war films, it is easy to confuse cinematic authenticity with objectivity. The old assumption that film is an impartial medium, that "the camera does not lie," does not take into consideration film's obsession with its own craft and technology. There is nothing impartial (or, perhaps one should say "artless") about *Full Metal Jacket*'s slow-motion shootouts, splattering gunshot wounds, and grimacing faces; they are far too alluring as artistic screen spectacles to convey the repulsive violence of war. Through the use of the first person voice-over, Vietnam war films are able to comment upon what is seen; they bring to the events of the war and the individual film a new, thoughtful perspective. The narrator evokes a sobering personal perspective upon what is, cinematically, high-tech adventure. [5]

The ability of the first person narrator to offer a contemplative perspective is due to an epic quality frequently present in the narration. The epic voice, in the Brechtian sense of the term, allows for the presence of the action and of a simultaneous narrative voice which speaks from the future. Thus, the events and experiences conveyed in the narrative are viewed from a future (sometimes omniscient) perspective which incorporates insights gathered during the time between the event itself and the eventual story-telling. In film, the combination of immediate visual event and future contemplative voice-over greatly enhances the audience's perception and understanding of complex emotional events.

First person narration may also take the form of a self-objectification in which the narrator perceives himself both as participant in and observer of his own actions. In Vietnam veteran Charles Durden's outstanding novel, *No Bugles No Drums*, such moments of insight and contemplation occasionally take on the characteristics of film-viewing. In one instance, the narrator, "Hawk" Hawkins notes that "my mind separated from my body and I could see us as we were, like lookin' at a freeze-frame on a movie screen" (237). Elsewhere, Hawk sees himself "through a camera lens, a long, slightly out-of-focus shot that slowly zoomed in, sharper 'n' sharper" (235). While it is ironic in the context of this essay that Hawk sees himself on a movie screen, it is significant that he is cognizant of himself as active participant in and removed observer of his own experience.

Playwright and veteran David Rabe, whose three Vietnam war dramas, *Streamers* (1976), *The Basic Training of Pavlo Hummel* (1969), and *Sticks and Bones* (1969), respectively portray Vietnam soldiers before, during, and after their war experiences, articulates the need for a dual presence when discussing his Vietnam experience. In Rabe's case, unlike "Hawk" Hawkins', the contemplation comes after a "sinking-in" period.

> While in Vietnam, I felt I should keep some sort of journal...But all my efforts brought me nothing, or very little...writing requires a kind of double focus that I could not then quite handle. If you encounter an auto accident and then go home to write of it seriously, you must bring your full sensibility to bear on all elements of that accident. To do this in Vietnam (though there are men who have done it) was a task I didn't try...I was living then in a high, brittle part of my mind. I skimmed over things and hoped they would skim over me...All I knew in Vietnam were facts, nothing more: all simple facts of such complexity that the job of communicating any part of them accurately seemed impossible beyond my reach. (Rabe, *Basic Training* xvii)

Rabe makes two points: first, that the experiences of the war were something over which one attempted to skim--that is, one avoided close scrutiny in order to maintain one's sanity. Secondly, when one did begin to think and write about those experiences, a "double focus"--a simultaneous involvement in and contemplative distance from the events--was necessary.

This double-focus, or self-objectification, further justifies the presence of the first person narrator in Vietnam combat films. The powerful and often exhilarating portrayal of combat situations is commented upon by the discriminating presence of the voice-over narrator. The voice-over in Vietnam veteran Oliver Stone's *Platoon*, for instance, creates a highly contemplative and personalized narrative perspective, establishing a moral framework through which one views the atrocities of the film. This framework is especially apparent in the film's final scene:

> I think now, looking back, we did not fight the enemy, we fought ourselves--and the enemy was in us...The war is over for me now, but it will always be there-- the rest of my days. As I am sure Elias will be-- fighting with Barnes for what Rhah called possession of my soul...There are times since I have felt like the child born of those two fathers...(129)

Here, the narrator both analyzes and gives coherence to the film's events from a personal perspective that transcends the moment--i.e., leaving Vietnam in a helicopter. He speaks with the voice of a veteran looking back over several years and struggling to make sense of his experience.

The first person narrator, common to the Vietnam war film, is a virtual stranger to the theater, where the convention of direct address exploits the powerful live presence of the actor. The theatrical equivalent of film's on-location authenticity is the physical presence of the actor. When actor and character simultaneously inhabit the stage, they create a dual presence far more ambiguous than the near-total subjugation of the film actor to his role. This presence allows for a type of self-objectification in which the actor has the ability to split from his role and comment upon it without ever leaving the stage.

Such self-objectification can take place in an unobtrusive manner within a naturalistic stage situation, as when one of the characters in David Rabe's *Streamers* finds himself face to face with his own potential violence and articulates his new sensation to the other characters in the play:

> I'm a twenty-four-year-old goddamn college
> graduate...and I got a razor in my hand. I'm thinkin'
> about comin' up behind one black human being and
> I'm thinkin' nigger this and nigger that--I wanna cut
> his throat. (53)

Characters can just as easily break the theater's "fourth wall" and talk directly to the audience. They have the ability to include the audience in the fictional universe of the play, as in veteran Amlin Gray's *How I Got That Story*, or they may acknowledge the active presence of the audience and step out of the fictional action of the play, as in the Vietnam Veterans Ensemble Theatre production of *Tracers*.

In Gray's two-actor/twenty-one-character Vietnam fantasy, a wire service reporter serves as narrator, treating the audience as if they were his readers or radio audience:

> Hello there. This is Am-bo Land. My new job with
> the Trans-PanGlobal Wire Service brought me here.
> It's not the safest place right now, but this is how I
> figure it...It's what the world is like. If I just keep my
> eyes wide open I can understand the whole world.
> That's how I figure it. (82)

The quality of this narrative is not epic, but journalistic. The reporter speaks from the moment, not from any point in the future. His comments are in no way contemplative since, as he repeatedly tells the audience, he is in Vietnam to impartially record and report events. Here, it is the narrator's sheer lack of a contemplative consciousness which gives the audience a greater insight into the stage events. The strain of remaining impartial in the face of the atrocities portrayed in the play eventually drives the narrator to distraction. He is consumed by the war he came to observe and the audience, his readers, are left to make sense of his story.

In *Tracers*, the actor/characters are anything but impartial. The play was created out of group improvisations and is based on the Vietnam experiences of its original all-veteran cast. Actors regularly step out of the fictional framework of the play and directly address the audience. One character, a black platoon leader called Habu, freely expresses his opinion to the audience:

> They call 'em patrols. I call them hunting parties.
> That's what we do, you know...hunt 'em, kill 'em, and
> count 'em. If we lose any, we count them, too. Then

we call in the count and we get points. Where does
it all go? I think it goes to a big computerized
scoreboard, and every day the big brass go in and they
look at it. They nod their big heads and they say, "Ah,
very good hunting, boys." How do I feel? It's my
team against his. And a kill is just a touchdown. (55-
56)

Tracers is one of the few Vietnam war plays to actually take its
audience out on patrol. Like the film *Platoon*, *Tracers* explores daily
life within an infantry unit, except that in *Tracers*, the highly theatrical
stylization of all performance elements must replace cinematic realism.
With no jungle setting or enemy soliders to aid in the presentation of
the experience, the burden in *Tracers* falls upon the live actors and their
mastery of language, sound, and movement. In one scene, an FNG
(Fucking New Guy) nicknamed Dinky Dau (Vietnamese for "Crazy"),
relives his first patrol and his first contact with the enemy. The scene
in many ways resembles the narrator's first patrol in *Platoon*. But, in
Tracers, direct address replaces the close-up and the point-of-view shot;
Dinky Dau speaks to the audience while the members of the seven-
man cast assume patrol formation, fanning-out in slow motion across
the bare stage. When the point man freezes and points into the
audience, Dinky Dau describes the dozen Vietcong who have appeared
on the trail in front of them:

> I watched the point man as he raised his weapon. It
> was like a movie in slow motion. The point man
> opened up on the first two or three VC...I watched the
> first two or three VC go down, and then I opened up
> on full automatic. I creamed one of 'em with an
> entire clip. I watched my bullets as they ripped across
> his torso. Everybody was up. Everybody was hyper.
> Everybody was hittin'... (37-38)

This slow motion sequence is seen entirely through Dinky Dau's eyes.
He is the perceptual force shaping the images and sounds on stage. As
in *No Bugles No Drums*, a character uses film as a metaphor for self-
objectification. But on stage, Dinky Dau is both mentally hovering
above the scene, watching it in slow motion and physically involved in
it.
    Only after Dinky Dau starts shooting does the stage image snap
from an expressionistic slow-motion back to normal speed. Likewise,

the scene resumes an impartial point of view. Later, Dinky Dau
comments upon the events the audience has witnessed:

> I really lost it there for a minute. I was shooting at
> dead bodies. I was shooting at men I knew were
> already dead. It's a terrible sight to see a man's body
> get ripped apart like that. It was a frenzy that I got
> caught up in. (44)

Throughout the play members of the veteran cast turn to the audience
in moments like this one, commenting from a point of view which
encompasses both their experiences in Vietnam and their subsequent
insights into those experiences. "I know he would have killed me if he
had the chance," justifies one character. "I lost my sense of judgement
yesterday," laments another. "I feel like I'm reading a book about this
dude in Vietnam, but it isn't a book--it's real, it's me, and I'm here."
There is a self-reflection and an attempt to analyze and express the
emotional truth of the situation in this type of confessional drama which
combines the contemplative voice-overs of *Platoon* with the slow-motion
shoot-outs of *Full Metal Jacket*. Characters can telescope an event for
the audience in a manner which allows them to act out a scene while
they speak thoughts and express emotions which they may not have
understood or recognized at the time.

The epic narrative voice, juxtaposed to moments of high emotional
intensity in a play like *Tracers* or a film like *Platoon*, enables the
veteran artist to communicate his war experiences via his eventual grasp
of their significance and consequences. Such veteran artists are, in
essence, doing our thinking for us, interpreting events for us. As one
critic said of David Rabe's work: "[Rabe] prefers the role of the artist-
narrator-playwright who interprets from his own sense of moral
outrage, to that of the journalist, who presents without representing and
offers his audience no moral guide to what they see" (Cooper 615).
This subjective manipulation of our perception on the part of veteran
artists comes from a belief that audiences will only appreciate the
experience of soldiers in Vietnam by understanding the impact that
experience has had on them. French poet Stephan Mallarmé once
wrote "Do not paint the thing, but rather the effect it produces." The
goal of the various forms of epic and contemplative narrative in the
Vietnam war films and plays here discussed is to supplement, to
expound upon, or perhaps even to justify the live presentation of
combat experience, thus accurately communicating the "emotional truth"
of the Vietnam experience.

"All I knew in Vietnam were facts," comments David Rabe. "all simple facts of such complexity that the job of communicating any part of them accurately seemed impossibly beyond my reach."

Notes

1. Rabe has both been criticized (see Asahina 35, 36 and Brustein 24) and satirized (see Durang).

2. *Platoon* was proclaimed on the cover of *Time* (26 Sept. 1987) as "Viet Nam As It Really Was."

3. Since far more attention has been paid to Vietnam prose than either film or drama, I do not feel the need to elaborate on the contribution of prose to the topic of this essay.

Among the well-known Vietnam novels and prose accounts to use a first-person or familiar narrator are *A Rumor of War*, Philip Caputo; *No Bugles No Drums*, Charles Durden; *Dear America*, Bernard Edelman, ed.; *The Short-Timers*, Gustav Hasford; *Dispatches*, Michael Herr; *Everything We Had*, Al Santoli, ed.

4. McGilligan, for one, laments that both *Apocalypse Now* and *Platoon* are "burdened with disconnected voice-over narration" (12).

5. One need only look at a film like *Hamburger Hill* to see how easily a combat film can become an adventure film when no guiding consciousness balances the dramatic action. On the few occasions that characters in the film do attempt to add some personal insight to the action, their dialogue is contrived; their attempts at profundity have no place in the battle zone.

Works Cited

Asahina, Robert. "The Basic Training of American Playwrights: Theater and the Vietnam War." *Theater* 9.2 (1978): 30-37.

Brustein, Robert. "The Crack in the Chimney: Reflections on Contemporary American Playwrighting." *Theater* 9.2 (1987): 21-29.

Cawley, Leo. "Refighting The War: Why the Movies Are in Vietnam." *Village Voice* 8 Sept. 1978: 18, 20-23.

Cooper, Pamela. "David Rabe's *Sticks and Bones*: The Adventures of Ozzie and Harriet." *Modern Drama* 29.4 (1986): 611-625.

Corlis, Richard. "Platoon: Vietnam, the way it really was, on   film." *Time* 26 Jan. 1987: 55-61.

DiFusco, John, Vincent Caristi, Richard Chaves, Eric E. Emerson, Rick Gallavan, Merlin Marston, Harry Stephens, with Sheldon Lettich. *Tracers*. New York: Hill and Wang, 1986.

Durang, Christopher. *The Vietnamization of New Jersey*. New York: Dramatists Play Service, 1978.

Durden, Charles. *No Bugles No Drums*. New York: Avon, 1984.

Freedman, Samuel G. "Vietnam Echoes: 'We Are All Afraid to Die'." *New York Times* 3 April, 1988: H33-34.

Gray, Amlin. *How I Got That Story*. *Coming to Terms: American Plays & the Vietnam War*. Ed. James Reston, Jr. New York: TCG, 1985, 77-117.

Hoberman, J. "Hollywood on the Mekong." *Village Voice* 8 Sept. 1987: 19, 57.

McGilligan, Pat. "Point Man." *Film Comment* 23.1 (1987): 11-20, 60.

Rabe, David. *The Basic Training of Pavlo Hummel* and *Sticks and Bones*. New York: Viking, 1973.

----. *Streamers*. *Coming to Terms: American Plays & the Vietnam War*. Ed. James Reston, Jr. New York: TCG, 1985, 1-66.

Reston, James, Jr., ed. *Coming to Terms: American Plays & the Vietnam War*. New York: TCG, 1985.

Stone, Oliver, Richard Boyle. *Oliver Stone's Platoon; and Salvador*
    "The Original Screenplays". New York: Vintage, 1987.

Suid, Lawrence. "Hollywood and Vietnam." *Film Comment* 15.5
    (1979): 20-25.

"VIETNAM AND SEXUAL VIOLENCE": THE MOVIE

Cynthia J. Fuchs

"The first casualty of war is innocence," say the advertisements for Oliver Stone's *Platoon* (1986). And on a very basic level, films about the Vietnam War have repeatedly focused on the death of an American ideological and moral faith. The representation of this implacable, intangible death has been a complicated business, though not for lack of "realism": contemporary special effects and make-up make dying look "real" enough in the movies.[1] Rather, the problem has been the representation and interpretation of the profound intimacy of this personal and cultural death--the simultaneous closeness and distance that relentlessly brought Vietnam home.

The dilemma of representation hinges on showing something which is absent; to present the terrible void of death is in one sense the quintessential act of representation. While the cinematic figure of (symbolic or literal) death in Vietnam has taken various forms--military machinery, pyrotechnic effects, the (often faceless) enemy--all of these representations are grounded in a basic dichotomy: death is the other to the (living) self. As the collective American nightmare of Vietnam becomes more thinkable, more speakable and more visible in movie theaters and on television, the challenge to this definitional opposition is frequently delineated in moral terms.

Again and again, writers and filmmakers have described the American experience in Vietnam as a collapse of the longstanding national self-image which defined itself as good, right, and opposed to an other. The concept of the other is of course not an American military invention. Western ideologies (for example, those analyses formulated by Descartes, Hegel, Saussure, and Freud) have long been organized around binary oppositions of self and other. The correspondence between configurations of non-self and non-male in a patriarchy is likewise well-rehearsed,[2] and leads back to the question of representation. "Men say," writes Hélène Cixous, "that there are two unrepresentable things: death and the feminine sex" ("Medusa" 225). The connection between death and sex is an old one, to be sure, but Cixous' observation bears particular weight with regard to representations of Vietnam on screen.

Where in World War II movies John Wayne and Audie Murphy could represent gallant American heroism in opposition to evil "Japs" and "Krauts," in Vietnam movies the moral distinction between "us" and "them" becomes confusing. While "gooks" remain decidedly other in almost all their screen incarnations, the image of an honorable and self-perpetuating American manhood can no longer be securely located in an unquestioned icon like Wayne. Instead, as the *Platoon* poster reminds us, in Vietnam men lost their ethical virginity. If the initial Hollywood versions of the Vietnam War (*First Blood, Missing in Action*) tried to restore the glorious vision of righteous American virility in action, more recent movies have challenged the insular cultural mythology which created this self-image. Many of these films have explored, however obliquely (and however unintentionally), the cultural construction of war as a means to virtuous manhood and morality.

My analysis of sexual violence in Vietnam movies, and particularly in Stanley Kubrick's *Full Metal Jacket*, begins by examining the representation of manhood opposed to non-manhood, and has its roots in the conflation of those postmodernist and feminist theories which identify the crisis of cultural authority as a crisis of representation. This intersection of theoretical discourses emerges with the space of "unrepresentability," where, in the words of Craig Owens, it becomes possible to "conceive difference without opposition" (62). In using the concept of visibility to describe and analyze postmodernism, theorists posit the invisible, what Jacqueline Rose calls the "vanishing-point of [any system's] attempt to construct itself as a system." This point regularly occurs, according to Rose and other feminist theorists, with reference to the female figure in a phallocentric discourse.[3]

In American Vietnam movies, the unknown, unknowable alien that threatens the "system" of the American military commonly appears as the multiple and anonymous guerilla gook, feminine in stature and dress, appallingly amoral and unmanly in fighting technique and ferocity. The insistent, unseeable vacuum behind this visible (feminine) otherness is death--again, *the* threat to virile manhood. Where most American films about the War have yet to address the triple collapse of Otherness onto Enemy onto Woman, *Full Metal Jacket* directly engages the cultural configuration of the unrepresentable as female.

No matter what their ideological stance, Vietnam movies have generally followed the sexual political course set by Joseph L. Mankiewicz's *The Quiet American* (1958), with Audie Murphy in the title role, and John Wayne's own *The Green Berets* (1968). In the first, the inscrutable child-woman Phuong embodies the impossibility of understanding or recuperating the alien culture. With the incipient American involvement in the War as backdrop, Phuong resists all attempts to render her redeemable. By the time of Wayne's film, the overt War is figured as a kind of World War II test of manhood. Men become men by going to war and waking up to a few things:

Communists are bad, Americans are good, and women are prostitutes, willing to sell their bodies and their "honor," a price no real man would pay. That this film is widely regarded as right-wing propaganda has had little bearing on its depiction of women's place in the cultural and moral hierarchy, which is recounted again and again in films which follow it.

The lesser known and more cynical *Go Tell the Spartans* (1978), directed by Ted Post, casts Burt Lancaster as Barker, a career major undone by "booze and pudenda," busted because of his affair with a general's wife. Major Barker's crude equation of women with moral corruption becomes the film's central image, reinforced and extended when a fifteen-year-old North Vietnamese girl (whom the American men have ridiculed for "making eyes" at Corporal Corsey [Craig Wasson]) pinpoints the American-ARVN outpost for obliteration by the NVA. In the prescriptive view of the military, her betrayal has more to do with her gender than with her political beliefs, which are no doubt fickle--she's a gook and a girl and so, by definition, unstable and unreliable.

More interesting because more troubled, the confused sexual relations in Michael Cimino's *The Deer Hunter* (1978) correspond to the moral and political confusion of Vietnam. Ostensibly the film celebrates the camaraderie of young manhood while charting the disillusionment brought on by the War. But at the same time, it describes that camaraderie as disturbed from the start. The wedding which opens the film inscribes a breakdown in the all-male hunting party, and the relationship between Nick (Christopher Walken) and Linda (Meryl Streep) upsets Mike (Robert De Niro) and Nick's friendship. Nick's eventual inability to face her aligns Linda with the World to which he cannot return--he has become too "other" due to his experiences in Vietnam.

That they each sleep with Linda both affirms and severs the men's bond--she is the figure for the unrepresentability of their relationship. If, as Robin Wood suggests, the film's central concern is a "male love story" that can't admit its sexuality, Nick's suicide suggests his compulsion to destroy what he perceives as his own (female) otherness (292). As Wood points out, Nick responds to Mike's cue of "one shot" by shooting himself, signalling the men's incapacity to reconcile or admit their connection except in the intimate unrepresentable space of death.

Francis Ford Coppola's *Apocalypse Now* (1979) invokes a mythology of men disillusioned and de-humanized by the savagery of war, embodied by the "slopes" who ostensibly bring out the beast in Marlon Brando's Kurtz. But during the early part of his mission to terminate the "insane" Kurtz, Willard (Martin Sheen) observes the last vestiges of civilization--a USO show featuring Playboy Dancers. After being brought in by helicopter, three "playmates" (barely dressed as an Indian, a cowboy, and a cavalry soldier) perform for a massive crowd of lusting GIs: the women pump their pelvises at rifles and dance in isolated areas of a stage which is shadowed by phallic missiles. When the frenzied men swarm onto the stage and engulf the dancers, Willard considers their weakness compared to Charlie, who "has no USO." He implies that the lurid display of women's bodies preys on the homesickness and vulnerability of emotionally and ideologically starved soldiers.

For Willard, survival depends on abandoning home and denying the women who represent it (his one word to his wife is "yes to a divorce"). The gunner on Willard's boat, "Mr. Clean," is indeed shot down while listening to his mother's tape-recorded voice; and at Kurtz's compound, his Cambodian mistress watches while he oversees Willard's debilitation (emasculation), and then as Willard ritually slaughters him. Remembered as the impossible return to the World, dismembered as performing body parts, or silenced as the unrepresentable horror at heart of darkness, women in Coppola's film are portrayed as the dangerous, seductive, and insidiously passive other.

By the time we get to Stone's *Platoon* (1986), the specific relation between Vietnam as female other to the American male self becomes overtly violent. Rape surfaces as a metaphor for American action in the war, but just below the frame line: after Sargeant Barnes' (Tom Berenger's) My Lai-like murder of a village civilian, the overcharged platoon gang-rapes a woman, much to the disgust of our college-educated narrator and moral center, Chris (Charlie Sheen). Here the woman, living in a village that is hiding North Vietnamese artillery, is regarded by the troops as fair game, part of the spoils of war ("She's only a gook, man!"), object of a "natural" masculine need. That this incident rouses Chris to action (he rescues her from the men, signalling his ethical superiority) underlines the rape's centrality to the film's moral(istic) vision.

Barry Levinson's *Good Morning, Vietnam!* (1987) and *Off Limits* (1988, written and directed by Christopher Crowe) both schematize women as figures for the American experience in Vietnam. In the first, Adrian Cronauer (Robin Williams) adores an ethereally pristine, white-dressed Vietnamese girl-woman who represents the untouchable alien culture (much like Phuong in *The Quiet American*). Her doppleganger/brother, initially Cronauer's friend, turns out to be a VC terrorist. Set in Saigon, 1964, the movie parallels Cronauer's initial naivete and subsequent education to the political realities of Vietnam with the beginnings of American involvement in the War. The object of Cronauer's interest, the woman is finally left behind in her rice paddied village while the betrayed American rides away in a military jeep. U.S. technology (Cronauer as a voice on the radio) is unable to comprehend the very culture it proposes to rescue.

The romantic vision of the Asian woman as inaccessible undermines *Good Morning, Vietnam!*'s unusually positive representation of Vietnamese people. Less forgivable is the more manifestly racist *Off Limits*, which offers a generalized treatment of women as victimized non-humans. Here, the "good" woman is a French nun, the only white woman amid "a sea of slant-eyed pussy." She helps the CID police (McGriff/Willem Dafoe and Perkins/Gregory Hines) find a high-ranking American military official who is murdering Vietnamese prostitutes who have Amerasian children.[4] One witness they seek out is an "exotic dancer" at a strip joint: on stage she strokes and squats on a red U.S. mortar shell/giant dildo (recalling *Apocalypse Now*'s gun-swinging dancers). *Off Limits'* near-indictment of rampant American military abuse and destruction of (a feminine) Vietnam is lost in the moral righteousness attributed to Dafoe (who was, after all, the Christ figure in *Platoon*). As usual, the Vietnamese whores are undeveloped stereotypes who have VD, speak pidgin English, and offer the investigators blow jobs to avoid prosecution; the morally driven cops regard them with loathing, even as they purport to "save" them.

In contrast to these cinematic evasions of the cultural processes which (in)form sexual violence at home and at war, *Full Metal Jacket* is fiercely complex and polemic. The film engages the problematic relation of women to a patriarchal ideology which consistently represses them and renders them unrepresentable through its rhetoric, imagery, and erection of meaning. While some critics have complained about the film's deliberate distance from its audience, I suggest that the film articulates this "alienation" in order to represent the experience of the war, for the (foreign) American soldiers as well as for the (South and North) Vietnamese condemned as enemies in their own land. The film's construction of an unstable narrator, Private Joker (Matthew Modine), is also a deconstruction of audience expectations. Joker undermines our identification with a sympathetic "protagonist" and disrupts narrative coherence and closure. Most significantly, the film forces us to confront difference in its cinematic representation--the enemy in *Full Metal Jacket* is specifically female.

The difference inscribed by this film is disturbingly indescribable in conventional visual and verbal terms. A series of narrative upheavals and an accumulation of impossible contradictions indicate a dangerous collapse of cultural meaning. The credits roll over a scene in South

Carolina's Parris Island Marine Corps Training Camp, where the recruits ritually exchange "normal" sexuality for violent sexuality: while they lose their long, effeminate civilian hair to the Marine barbers, Johnny Wright sings on the soundtrack, bidding farewell to social amenities and girlfriends, "hello" to Vietnam--the site of chaos and savagery, where only men survive. The newcomers are stripped of domesticity (or more precisely, femininity) and individuality, and are made anonymous and alike in uniforms and buzz cuts.

The first scene takes place in the oppressive and eerily lit barracks, where the booming voice of Gunnery Sergeant Hartman (Lee Ermey) assaults the recruits with verbal obscenities. An early casualty of war, everyday language cannot contain or describe the experience of real manhood. Instead, the recruits learn to speak in extreme terms of "us" and "them": "If you ladies leave my island," roars Hartman, "if you survive recruit training, you will be a weapon, you will be a minister of death, praying for war. But until that day you are pukes... You are not even fucking human beings!"[6]

Violence, patriarchal religion, and the universally desired gender --male--elide in this introduction to the Corps, the body of men. To be a man (a human being) means to overcome being a "lady." In this Norman Mailer-esque sexual hierarchy, you earn your manhood by destroying your reprehensible womanhood. The paradox here is that the assumed poles of sexual behavior (normal and not) are inextricably conjoined within the framework established by the patriarchy itself. In her 1973 essay "Vietnam and Sexual Violence," Adrienne Rich writes,

> Rape is a part of war; but it may be more
> accurate to say that the capacity for
> dehumanizing another which so corrodes male
> sexuality is carried over from sex into war.
> The chant of the basic training drill: ("This is
> my rifle, this is my gun; this is for killing, this
> is for fun") is not a piece of bizarre
> brainwashing invented by some infantry
> sergeant's fertile imagination; it is a
> recognition of the fact that when you strike
> the chord of sexuality in the patriarchal
> psyche, the chord of violence is likely to
> vibrate in response; and vice versa (115).

Kubrick's recognition of this link between sexuality and war has produced previous filmic examinations of the corruption of power (*Paths of Glory* [1957]) and the insanity of war (*Dr. Strangelove* [1964]).

In *Full Metal Jacket* we get the extreme end of the course charted in these earlier movies: in *Paths of Glory* Kirk Douglas still represented a moral stance against corruption, and in *Dr. Strangelove* the impending horror of nuclear warfare was couched in black comedy which sustained a slightly uncomfortable but morally defensible distance from George C. Scott fuming as the ultimate red-scared military man, Slim Pickens riding his giant bomb-phallus into the horizon, and Sterling Hayden ranting about his "precious bodily fluids."

In *Full Metal Jacket*, the humor is blunted by the moral void that was the reality. Sexuality and war collide in the out-of-control chain of command in Vietnam. Here is no coherent resolution and no summary mythology of the war. Here is memory and nightmare: a full range of possibilities and impossibilities, at once terrifyingly unrepresentable and relentlessly enacted. Paradox consumes the film, leaving no moral residue that might recoup its battering imagery, no tearful revelation to return to the rational. It's surely not the first time someone has pointed out the relation between sexuality and warfare--guns and penises are old bedfellows--but Kubrick interrogates the cultural forces that created institutional chaos out of this connection: in Vietnam there was no longer even a nominal delineation between war and sex or salvation and destruction. Self and Other was the only meaningful opposition, and "self" included fellow troops (the unified body-Corps) when the entire environment became Other.

Trained to fight a visible, definable enemy (named variously "Charlie," "slope," "gook"), American troops arrived in Southeast Asia to find that the South Vietnamese villagers didn't want them there, the North Vietnamese couldn't be found, that all the Vietnamese looked alike. It is this otherness of the experience that Kubrick, along with co-writers Gustav Hasford and Michael Herr, hit so exactly: at the heart of this war was a hardcore sexuality which defined male in opposition to female, manhood in opposition to death. Vietnam, according to *Full Metal Jacket*, was about fucking your enemy, and naming that enemy (and yourself) by the act of fucking.[6]

Basic training develops what the system calls the Marines' "natural" desire to kill the other, to rape the enemy. Sex signifies only violence. But the system itself is founded in paradox: the recruits learn to revere the Virgin Mary and to love their guns as precious females; however, they also learn to believe in their Beloved Corps, to assimilate an obsessive rage at an unfathomable opponent that is not of their "body," that is implicitly female. As Teresa de Lauretis has noted, "Sexuality is produced discursively (institutionally) by power, and power is produced institutionally (discursively) by the deployment of sexuality" (36). *Full Metal Jacket* underlines the discursive means by which the American military uses sexuality to establish and elaborate its power to name the other. The institutional equation of killing with rape declares both to be imperative military, masculine actions. But at the same time this collapse of terms inculcates a desperate contradiction between loyalties to self (body-gun) and other (gun-body). Power becomes imminently uncontrollable.

First, the rifleman's creed, recited while the men lie rigid in bed with their guns, weds them heart and soul to their weapons, while denigrating the other that the rifle represents. The opposition of "men" and "pussy" infuses this logic of loyalty. Hartman tells them: "Tonight you pukes will sleep with your rifles. You will give your rifle a girl's name. Because this is the only pussy you people are going to get....You are married to this piece, this weapon of iron and wood. And you will be faithful."

Second, the Marines accept their weapons as additional "tools," as extensions of themselves: one hand on their guns and the other on their genitals, they recite, "This is my rifle! This is my gun! This is for fighting! This is for fun!" This impossible contradiction, between gun as "girl" and gun as "self," stems from the patriarchal system's dread of the woman as representative of sexuality and potential loss of (male) self/control. Instead, "she" must be repressed, named unrepresentable. No more "Mary Jane Rottencrotch" for these recruits. Their sexual "energy" is channeled into grossly representable military action; that is, the destruction of the other.

The absurdity of this contradiction between self and other is evidenced by Leonard (Vincent D'Onforio). Originally soft, overweight, and almost comically timid, Leonard is a pathetic joke to Sergeant Hartman, who names him Gomer Pyle. Literally battered into shape, Leonard is the logical product of Marine Training: he is "born again hard," a perfect "killer," without fear, with a passion only for his gun/cock. He's possessed by the spirit of the American fighting and fucking machine. Unable to reconcile his marriage to "Charlene" (his female rifle) with his loyalty to a Corps that dictates murderous aggression against the other (female) body, Leonard shoots down Hartman in the barracks bathroom, splattering too red blood on the sheer white walls. Hartman, the repulsive representative body of the Corps, is surprisingly fragile in his regulation underwear and the illogical equation of self with gun collapses. After the murder, Leonard can only implode: Charlene in his mouth, he pulls the trigger, climaxing in the ultimate act of masturbation, a self-performed blow job.

The bizarre blue light and exceedingly clean isolation of this last scene in the Parris Island Head contrasts violently with the muggy filth of Da Nang. Our introduction to Vietnam is a lithe, mini-skirted prostitute sashaying away from the low-level camera while the soundtrack plays Nancy Sinatra's sexually threatening "These Boots Are Made for Walking." Immediately the film connects sex with violence: the whore is the enemy, the enemy is a woman. Ensuing battle scenes are counterpointed by the men's attempts to "get laid"; battle lines are drawn specifically between the sexes.

The Vietnamese prostitutes are thin and leggy, and long black hair or sunglasses hide their faces. The camera appraises them like a horny soldier's eye, like an enemy's eye. These "others" are frankly economically motivated, enigmatic by virtue of broken English and a simultaneous, seemingly paradoxical, availability and obscurity: "Gonna love you a long time," they say. Rape at only ten dollars a throw.

In front of a bombed out movie theater, a young woman in dark glasses arrives on the back of her pimp's motorbike, and is paraded before the Marines who sit in theater chairs lined up outside the theater--the show is out here now, the war is the movie. The men in the pointedly named "Lusthog Squad" fight over possession of the woman's body: for her "performance" Animal Mother (Adam Baldwin) takes her inside the theater itself, out of sight, a spectacle for no audience. In the obscenely violent landscape of Vietnam, sex, of all things, is pornographic and can't be shown. The woman is merely body ("Don't get between a dog and his meat," says Eightball), fought over and awarded like a prize, then discarded. The alien prostitute acts like the perfect (male) fantasy, paid for and delivered. But there is always the potentially fatal danger of otherness. There is always the promise: "Me suckee-suckee. Me love you too much."

"Too much" is right. All of Vietnam becomes Too Much. In *Full Metal Jacket* the male protagonists have been deconstructed within the text, fragmented by their experiences and the deaths around them. On his way into "the shit," Joker rides in a helicopter with a machine gunner who shoots off his gun/dick while shouting, "Get some! Get some!" Joker asks our (morally outraged) question, "How can you shoot women and children?" "It's easy," the gunner smiles, "Ya just don't lead 'em so much."

At first, our monotoned, dead-pan narrator Joker seems safely removed from the insanity of Vietnam, separated from the gunner even within the helicopter's confined space by a shot-reverse shot sequence. But Joker's distance soon becomes suspect: as a cynical reporter for the military mouthpiece *Stars and Stripes*, he is indeed a private joker. His sardonic responses to the War grow increasingly unfathomable. At Parris Island, Joker's parody of John Wayne signals his rebellion. Once he is in country, however, the routine is less a subversive performance than an encoding of his assimilation into the Corps. As death is more violently and more frequently represented, it becomes clear that Joker's survival depends on being "us" instead of "them." Though he begins as a glib observer who can "talk the talk," Joker learns to "walk the walk."

By the time Joker and the Squad reach Hue City after the Tet Offensive, the repercussions of the Americans' progressive alienation from their moral foundation have become absurd. As spectators of Kubrick's film, we are assaulted with the same impossibility of discursive reconciliation that faces the Marines. Our sense of narrative control and conventional processes of identification are thrown into question--we can't believe Joker. Here even the film's visual fabric begins to unravel: we are a doubled audience, watching and participating in the mayhem. To complicate this question of spectatorship, Kubrick shifts the focus in Hue, where a television crew probes the soldiers' reactions to the War. But their wan faces and perverse comments reveal only exhaustion and confusion. The doubled (television and movie) camera shoots the interviewees from a cool medium distance until for an instant the shot reverses and we see an awkward and expectant technical crew. While Joker's voice proclaims his intention to "meet interesting and stimulating people of an ancient culture and...kill them," the crew's stunned faces reflect our own. They wait for some answer to their and our impossible question.

In exploding the question--how to represent Vietnam--the film rejects any possible answer. Instead *Full Metal Jacket* plays across representational boundaries to show that "civilized" borders (of "us" and "them") can't hold. The enemy other that the Marines have tried so hard to extinguish is finally and ineradicably in themselves. The last encounter with the invisible Hue City sniper insists on the cultural construction of the violent, gender-based differentiation between self and other. (As Rich reminds us, "the capacity for dehumanizing another" is continuous in sex and war.) The female sniper is both enemy and victim and she is absolutely other. Initially she is represented only as a black hole in a burned out building; even her point of view shots reveal nothing but the gap through which she looks.

The long sequence depicting Joker's decision to kill the sniper leaves little doubt as to the American mission. The Marines' conference over the dying woman is constructed as a visual gang-rape: the camera hovers over her body as we gaze down from the men's perspective, shrouding her in shadow at the men's feet as she struggles to speak. The reverse shots show the men's dispassionate, spent faces, revealed by the flickering light of the hellishly burning building.

Up to this point, Joker's erratic irreverence and resistance to Vietnam's madness have marked him as the closest thing to a moral consciousness this film (this war?) will allow. But that's finally too easy.

Joker is essentially, supremely unreliable, a wild card representative of what he has called "the Jungian thing," the "duality of man," a paradox that eventually renders any assumed moral structure immaterial. Just as the film has dismantled binarism as a form of cogent social or intellectual organization, Joker's fragmentation finally repudiates the myth of subjective unity. He is disruptive, difficult to read or like, increasingly distant from us. Like the propaganda paper for which he writes, Joker represents the impossibility of frameworks in this war or in this movie. He represents the War's unrepresentability, so that when he kills the sniper, his individual wit and integrity are irrelevant. Rather, he joins the ranks of the Marines who are loyal to self over other.

But here again the movie slips its own definitional knot. The Marines want to leave the sniper to suffer: "No more boom-boom for this baby-san," says T.H.E. Rock, "She's dead meat"; "Fuck her," says Animal Mother. Surrounded by these men (who are named for their "hardness"), Joker's act of killing the sniper seems compassionate. Playing patriarchal God, he answers the sniper's prayer to die. Once more, the film turns the context around by rendering Joker's motive irrelevant: his benevolence and his comprehension of her Vietnamese prayer become insignificant--she speaks in plain (and sexually loaded) English: "Shoot me." Joker's "humane" acquiescence incongruously signals his induction into the War's inhumanity. He gets his "payback" for Cowboy's death (and his own, because he dies here metaphorically) with a "mercy killing" that makes him "hardcore," eligible for the Congressional Medal of Ugly. The camera never leaves his face during his fatal shot and the congratulatory comments of his Squad: the sniper's unrepresented death is his represented birth as a Marine.

Her body and language mangled, the solitary sniper is left to burn in the demolished city, now "saved" from the enemy. While the camera cranes in to track with the troops moving out and singing "The Mickey Mouse Club" theme, Joker's voice-over reprises the sexual/sexist language that defines the Marines' waking nightmare: "We have nailed our names in the pages of history," he says. "We hump down to the Perfume River to set in for the night." As the camera follows Joker singing about the "club that's made for you and me," his emotionless voice-over continues: "My thoughts drift back to erect nipple wet dreams about Mary Jane Rottencrotch and the Great Homecoming Fuck Fantasy. I am so happy that I am alive, in one piece, and short. I'm in a world of shit, yes. But I am alive. And I am not afraid."

Split between voice-over and singing, Joker is also divided in what he tells us. The "club" is indeed a "Mickey Mouse" operation; it is ludicrous and frightening in the simplicity of its objective--to survive. Its "you and me" are all Marines, part of a male Corps, their names "nailed" in the past yet erecting the future. Joker's hypocrisy is the hypocrisy of history; in this "world of shit" to be alive is to be afraid. "We can't just leave her here," he said before he killed the sniper. And he hasn't. Now "hard," a member of the club, Joker is also his own other--alive and dead. For it is Joker's own unrepresented death that paradoxically signals the end of the film and the continuation of the War. The final multiple transparent illusion of the "Homecoming" reveals that Joker will carry the legacy of sexual violence home from Vietnam. It serves as proper coda for this endless war.

Notes

1. The fact that degrees of "realism" have been used as a measure of worth for Vietnam movies seems to me to obscure that all movies reconstruct fictional or actual events, and "realism" is an effect just like any other; it is a set of cinematic conventions that denote "reality."

2. In "Sorties," Hélène Cixous writes, "...all these pairs of oppositions are *couples*. Does that mean something? Is the fact that Logocentrism subjects thought--all concepts, codes, and values--to a binary system, related to 'the' couple, man/woman?"

3. Rose's Lacanian framework is echoed by psychoanalytic feminist film theorists like Laura Mulvey, whose influential reckoning with female "otherness" in the movies set the agenda for subsequent feminist film theory. She writes, "Woman, then, stands in patriarchal culture as a signifier for the male other...bearer of meaning, not maker of meaning."

4. This plot bears more than a passing resemblance to Anatole Litvak's *Night of the Generals* (1967), a World War II movie starring Peter O'Toole as the Nazi murderer and Omar Sharif as the Nazi "cop" trying to stop him. The parallel between Nazis and Americans suggests that morality has become highly problematized in Vietnam. However, Crowe's film doesn't explore this idea, resorting instead to the cliché of a single psychotic killer.

5. All dialogue will be quoted from the soundtrack of *Full Metal Jacket* (Warner Bros., 1987); directed by Stanley Kubrick; written by Stanley Kubrick, Michael Herr, and Gustav Hasford.

6. Hasford, Herr, and Kubrick's screenplay is based on Hasford's novel *The Short-Timers* (New York: Bantam, 1979, 1983). The movie conflates the second and third parts of the novel in its second half; where the novel's Hue City sniper is a woman, this episode is followed by a confrontation with a second unseen sniper in the jungle, who picks off body parts of Marines trapped in a clearing. The film, though, ends in Hue, with the woman sniper performing this same grisly dismemberment. That the film ends with the death of the woman sniper indicates Kubrick's specific concern with sexual violence as it is inculcated by war and the military.

Works Cited

Cixous, Hélène. "The Laugh of the Medusa." *New French Feminisms: An Anthology*. Ed. Elaine Marks and Isabelle de Courtivron. New York: Schocken Books, 1981.

Cixous, Hélène. "Sorties." *The Newly Born Woman*. Ed. Hélène Cixous and Catherine Clement. Trans. Betsy Wing. Minneapolis: University of Minnesota Press, 1986.

de Lauretis, Teresa. *Technologies of Gender: Essays on Film, Theory, and Fiction*. Bloomington: Indiana University Press, 1987.

Mullvey, Laura. "Visual Pleasure and Narrative Cinema." *Screen* 16:3 (1975). Rep. in *Movies and Methods, Volume II*, Vol II. Ed. Bill Nichols. Berkeley: University of California Press, 1985.

Owens, Craig. "The Discourse of Others: Feminists and Postmodernism." *The Anti-Aesthetic: Essays on Postmodern Culture*. Ed. Hal Foster. Port Townsend, WA: Bay Press, 1983.

Rich, Adrienne. "Vietnam and Sexual Violence." In *On Lies, Secrets, and Silence: Selected Prose 1966-1978*. New York: W.W. Norton & Company, 1979.

Rose, Jacqueline. *Sexuality in the Field of Vision*. Norfolk: The Thetford Press, 1986.

Wood, Robin. *Hollywood from Vietnam to Reagan*. New York: Columbia University Press, 1986.

VOCABULARIES OF EXPERIENCE

J. T. Hansen

Writers of Vietnam narratives undertake the extraordinarily difficult task of communicating an essentially hermetic experience to an uninitiated readership. To those who did not serve in Vietnam, what happened to the soldiers who fought there has been as elusive to understand as it has been difficult to confront. Ambiguities permeate the aesthetic situation, especially questions about the war which remain unanswered to this day. Why were we in Vietnam? Did we win or lose the war? Did the soldiers sacrifice themselves in vain? It is not difficult to describe the horror of a firefight, but the soldiers discovered they returned home fundamentally changed. Like Krebs in Hemingway's "Soldier's Home," they cannot account for those changes to themselves or their countrymen. John Clark Pratt believes these problems arise from the fragmentary nature of the experience itself. While it is possible to define individual events with precision, there was no definable coherence in what Philip Caputo calls "the random violence of endless war" (126).

Pratt summed up the proceedings of the 1985 Asia Society Conference on "The Literature of the Vietnam War" by observing that a narrative "showers you with a whole bunch of fragments and lets you figure out what happens" (Lomperis 90). The aesthetic contract is that the writer will write, and the reader will draw conclusions. Superficially at least, the narratives are bewildering. Young Americans get off a plane into the blast of heat and humidity of Vietnam, shortly arrive at their line units, conduct bone-wearying patrols through exotic and alien terrain, experience the unpredictable terrors of firefights, gradually regress into a state of brute survival . . . and at the end of their year's tour they fly back to "the World." As Pratt suggests, the reader is put into the same situation as the characters. Vietnam narratives are mimetic. No one gave the soldiers an adequate rationale for what they experienced. As the soldiers had to figure it out for themselves, so must the reader. These acts of discovery were at the center of the experience of the war, and they have the same centrality for the contemporary reader.

The writers have one honor-bound intention in common--the desire to recreate the conditions of Vietnam so authentically that their readership will comprehend the enormity of contemporary warfare, particularly its impact upon the individual soldier. The authority for the realism and authenticity of the texts is what Michel Foucault would call

134

the soldiers' knowledge. Their knowledge is of the war they experienced it, as opposed to official (and presumably as more authoritative) analyses written by military and political leaders, academicians, and other recognized authorities. It is not enough to say that having served in Vietnam lends authority to anything a writer wishes to include. The participants in the Asia Society Conference, as well as veterans of my acquaintance, are resolutely and absolutely unforgiving about erroneous details. The survival code, the central theme in the narratives, leads repeatedly back to the proposition that the truth lies in the particular details, not abstract concepts and theories.

Understanding the narratives depends upon extraordinarily active reading. The reader must achieve an accurate knowledge of the facts, however fragmentary, then formulate descriptive generalizations which must be tested and modified in the light of each new fragment. There certainly are features which the narratives have in common, and they provide the starting point for framing generalizations. They have exciting and sometimes terrifying adventure plots, characters bonded spontaneously into Brotherhood groups, and individual Americans confronting the dimly perceived forces which determine their fates. The overriding question for the reader is how to formulate descriptive generalizations without distorting the narratives.

It is therefore appropriate for the commentator to define the perspective from which the narratives are being approached. I accept the literary conventions of Vietnam narratives. Since the writers are oblivious to conventional literary distinctions, I do not distinguish between autobiography and fiction. I approach them all as narratives. Secondly, the soldiers' vocabularies are more sharply differentiated in the more realistic books. I use Frederick Downs' *The Killing Zone*, Philip Caputo's *A Rumor of War*, James Webb's *Fields of Fire*, John Del Vecchio's *The 13th Valley*, and Gustav Hasford's *The Short-Timers* as primary evidence in my analysis. Thirdly, it is hazardous to approach the literature from the perspective of contemporary literary theory. Given the notorious ambiguity of our entire involvement in Vietnam, it is too easy to reify the theory in the texts. The danger is that the reader will inadvertently distort the books by selecting evidence from them according to an external standard, thereby treating the abstractions as if they either determine or are the relevant facts. The result, if I may make a political point, is to obscure the uniqueness and seriousness of the Vietnam experience. It seems only right to minimize this tendency by respecting the terrible specificity of the war. T. S. Eliot's early insights into these features of modern literature are as theoretical as one can be without eventually discovering that attention has been displaced from the literature to the theoretical issues.

The experience itself contains the resources required to bring the fragments together into coherent forms. As recruits proceed successively from civilian life through military training and into Vietnam, they are indoctrinated into a series of organizations and made fluent in their vocabularies. The narratives bring coherence to the experience by the elegantly simple expedient of using vocabularies to differentiate the roles, values, and feelings the men successively encounter. Concurrently, the reader develops fluency in the vocabularies and thus an increasingly sophisticated understanding of the experience. This control over language impresses me as evidence that Vietnam narratives have achieved a literary excellence far beyond conventional war stories. That they have done so in this unconventional manner reflects the unconventional nature of the war and the legitimate priority assigned to authenticity in the texts or an analysis of them.

The soldiers' knowledge is inchoate--tacit, incipient, metaphoric, and referential. In their Brotherhoods, it is bad form to be too explicit about the meaning of events. The characters must learn from their own experience--trial and error, imitating others, figuring it out for themselves, and plain luck. Writers rarely use authorial commentary to clarify complexities and ambiguities. Reading comprehension is not so much a matter of looking between and behind the facts as paying close attention to changes in language. Through this very complex process, the language from the experience itself becomes the basis for the reader to develop an informed, sensitive response to the texts.

For the purposes of this study, the vocabularies can be grouped into three broad categories: standard American English, military, and conversational. Standard American English predominates in descriptive sections, the characters' reflections on what is happening to them, and authorial commentary. This vocabulary has the advantages of being both a language actually used in Vietnam and one already known to the reader. Military language lends specificity and realism to events, especially the exigencies of combat. The conversational vocabulary is a delightful mish-mash of post-adolescent slang, the bluntness and obscenity of lifers, and the referential verbal code of the Brotherhood. Used in isolation, the vocabularies delimit the empirical features of the events and the characters' responses to them. Used in combination, they either clarify the internal dynamics of the experience or enable the reader to draw inferences and formulate conclusions. By these means the narratives communicate facts to the uninitiated reader, individuate the characters, describe the complex forms which their lives assume, and steadily lead the reader to an understanding of the qualitative aspects of the Vietnam experience.

Standard American English is the vocabulary of cultural institutions such as the family, schools, churches, and the media. As a generic language, its gains in clarity are balanced by losses in connotation and specificity. Though the vocabulary lacks vividness, it creates ironies by juxtaposing bland, generic words and the brutal chaos of contemporary warfare. It understates the soldiers' subjective responses to the events, and the resulting tension serves as an analogue to the psychological pressure the men were obliged to repress.

Frederick Downs uses this vocabulary extensively in *The Killing Zone*. His straightforward, objective descriptions simply report the sensations and thoughts he experienced. During a firefight he courageously rescues one of his men:

> After an eternity, I reached Bell. I grabbed him by the back of his fatigue jacket and literally jerked him out of the small depression he was in. As I was pulling him up, one of the machine gun bullets grazed across the back of my left hand, ripping off the skin. It didn't really hurt bad, but it burned like hell and surprised me. It was almost like I was in another world. The blood rushed from the back of my hand. I threw Bell's arm around me and put my body between him and the machine gun. I started back up the hill with bullets flying by us and ricocheting off everything around us. (186-7)

This calmly narrated scene is actually a bloody firefight in which he acted with astonishing competence and bravery, but his language has not changed from his descriptions of the countryside or the contents of his pack. Short, simple, informal words are constructed into relatively short, grammatically correct declarative sentences. The slangy verbs are the primary source of vividness, especially in contrast to the past tense used to describe his being shot. The acuity of consciousness which Caputo found so invigorating (218) is defined in such clear language that the interested reader has no difficulty following the action and drawing inferences from it. Because of the plainness of standard American English and the fact that it comprises sixty to eighty per cent of most texts, the narrative voice in Vietnam literature varies surprisingly little from book to book.

Basic training has several purposes, but acquiring the military vocabulary is unmistakably the most valuable. It consists of jargon, technical terms, numeric and verbal codes, and acronyms. Because it is rigidly denotative, it enables the military services to coordinate their functions efficiently in the heat of combat. It therefore contributes directly to the men's survival, but the narratives do not oblige the reader to figure out its cryptic meanings in passing. Technical terms are often defined parenthetically in the texts or in a glossary. The writers want there to be no barrier to the readers' learning it quickly. Then again, military terminology becomes a memory test; once a term has been defined, the narratives assume the reader's familiarity with it from that point on.

Because its terminology is so abstract, this vocabulary introduces major ironies into the texts. In *The 13th Valley*, John Del Vecchio faithfully imitates the conventions of battle summaries to emphasize the gulf between the official after action reports and the actual fighting in the Khe Ta Laou Valley in August, 1970:

> AT 1242 HOURS CO A WAS ATTACKED BY A LARGE WELL COORDINATED ENEMY FORCE WHILE THEY WERE EVACUATING PREVIOUSLY WOUNDED SOLDIERS. A MEDICAL HELICOPTER, HIT BY RPG FIRE, EXPLODED ON THE LZ KILLING THE PILOT AND COPILOT. CO A RETURNED ORGANIC WEAPONS FIRE AND ARA AND GUNSHIPS WERE EMPLOYED. WHILE STILL UNDER FIRE, CO A WAS EXTRACTED. ONE US SOLDIER WAS KILLED, SEVEN WOUNDED. KNOWN ENEMY CASUALTIES WERE 44 KIA, 30 BY ARA AND 14 BY SAF. (640)

The official summary sounds clinically accurate, but the brute facts have been glossed over. A cast of characters the reader has gotten to know over six-hundred and forty pages has completed a search and destroy operation in a North Vietnamese Army stronghold adjacent to the A Shau Valley. They found a command and supply center, and after a furious battle the survivors were evacuated by helicopter. Brooks, Egan, and Doc were roasted alive in the magnesium fire in the downed helicopter. Their bodies are irretrievable. They are considered missing in action and not even mentioned in the summary of American casualties.

The bitter ironies between official documents and the actual events are a major example of what Caputo calls "the ambivalent realities of the war"(xvi).   The soldiers were forever torn between pride in completing in a dangerous operation, grief over the loss of comrades, and despair over the chain of command's ignorance of their individual sacrifices. It is not difficult to draw inferences from such ironies. It is through this ironic mode that the authors emphasize their didactic purpose: to alert a naive electorate to the horribly traumatizing nature of contemporary warfare. The soldiers' greatest fear is that they will be killed or wounded gratuitously--without purpose or recognition. The net effect of official descriptions of events is to demonstrate the chain of command's callousness to their fates. Disparities such as these increase the reader's alertness to political points which the characters either do not dare or do not know how to phrase explicitly.

There are several components in the soldiers' conversational vocabulary. It is such an impenetrable mass of private meanings and multiple ironies that categorizing it is well beyond the scope of this essay. There are three sources of language, however, which can be traced quite clearly: the smart aleck posturing of post-adolescent males, the brutality and obscenity of enlisted men in time of war, and the metaphoric communication of the Brotherhood. By the late 1960s, the colorful expressions of Hippies and Blacks had been amalgamated into the mix. As a group, conversational vocabularies are referential, obscene, ironic, and often ungrammatical. They depend upon non-verbal signs for a large part of their meaning. Spontaneous combinations of these vocabularies enable the characters to communicate indirectly about the tacit, subjective, and personal dimensions of the experience. These combinations work because they have a concrete contexts in the characters' daily lives. Inexperienced replacements find understanding their comrades' conversations is quite as difficult as getting used to the heat and humidity, but learning the language is an essential survival skill. It is their means of expressing what little coherence they find in an otherwise utterly ambiguous situation.

Gustav Hasford's *The Short-Timers* captures a pure form of their nineteen-year-old kid vocabulary. The narrator, nicknamed Joker, meets a buddy from basic training. Because he is a combat correspondent out in the bush, the rest of Cowboy's squad is suspicious of him. Quick acceptance into the squad depends upon how effectively Joker's posturing impresses a tough audience, so he and Cowboy (a willing accomplice) drop easily into the mocking locker room behavior they all understand:

> Cowboy and I grab each other and wrestle and punch
> and pound each other on the back. We say, "Hey, you
> old motherfucker. How you been? What's
> happening? Been getting any? . . . " "Hey, Joker, I
> was hoping I'd never see you again, you piece of shit.
> I was hoping that Gunny Gerheim's ghost would keep
> you on Parris Island for-*ev*-er and that he would give
> you motivation." I laugh. "Cowboy, you shitbird. You
> look real mean. If I didn't know you were a poge I'd
> be scared." . . . Cowboy punches me in the chest. . .
> "We hitched down here this morning. We rate some
> slack 'cause our squad wasted beaucoup Victor
> Charlies. Man, we are life takers and heartbreakers.
> Just ask for the Lusthog Squad, first platoon. We
> shoot them full of holes, bro. We fill them full of
> lead." I grin. "Sergeant Gerheim would be proud to
> hear it." (40-41)

To win acceptance, Joker must prove that he is hard, and he does that
more by rough-housing with Cowboy than anything he says. The grin
takes on major meaning in Vietnam narratives, because it signifies
closure. Only when he feels confident that he has passed the test can
Joker grin.

One of the more obvious functions of the Brotherhood is that it
enables men to communicate their private feelings. It is not difficult to
realize Joker and Cowboy feel immense affection as they pummel and
shout at each other when they meet. They simply invert their language
and behavior. They trade insults, meaning genuine delight in seeing
each other again, and they hit each other instead of embracing.
Veterans of all wars have formed Brotherhoods for this precise
purpose. No one really knows what they are going through except their
comrades. This defense mechanism was even more important in
Vietnam. In previous American wars, there were compelling reasons
to fight, there were well-established measures of victory and defeat, and
there was widespread national support for the soldiers. In Vietnam the
men are further distanced from their superior officers by the
meaninglessness of a strategy of attrition and the disparity between
official optimism and the war they knew they were fighting. They felt
especially alienated because of the anti-war attitudes of many of their
fellow citizens. The survival of the Brotherhood was the only
motivation which kept them going. This part of their war was indeed

hermetic--cloistered, severely individuated, and requiring direct experience to comprehend.

In the sudden violence and compressed time of a firefight, even this vocabulary proves inadequate to the task. The characters are commonly reduced to yelling inarticulately to embolden each other and taunt the enemy. The limits of language are well illustrated in *The 13th Valley*:

> To the left, Egan is screaming, charging into fire coming down from above. He fires and charges, quick, agile. He is everywhere at once, firing rounds like walls of lead. He whirls. He kills. He does not linger on the sight of enemy death. He swings firing right left. "For Minh," he screams. He does not know he has yelled it. Marko and Jackson advance with him. Sachel charges explode before them. The concussion dissipates. Their ears ring. They do not know it. "Let um know they fuckin' with the O-Deuce," Egan screams. Marko shouts his battle cry. No sound leaves his throat. (607)

In this frantic effort to survive, they act below the level of verbal consciousness. Language proves inadequate because the men are reduced to too instinctual a level for words to express more than hostility and fear. Intensified by the presence of death, silence is itself articulate. It is not that there is nothing to be said; it is that nothing can be said. Events happen too quickly and are too destructive. As D. H. Lawrence so cryptically put it, the experience of American soldiers in combat creates a man who is hard, isolate, stoic, and a killer. With this final revelation the reader has achieved the fullest understanding possible for the uninitiated citizenry. It is done by the simple expedient of accurately imitating the vocabularies of the real war.

Thus the disciplined use of language is the primary way the writers resolve the conflict between their concern for developing the reader's understanding and their obligation to dramatize the experience authentically. By carefully controlling language, they manage these polarities with often stunning effect. An odd pair of words can be used to demonstrate these intriguing uses of language: "motherfucker" and "it". In the process, the writers unconsciously adopt Eliot's assertion that a writer must at times "dislocate if necessary, language into his meaning" (248). To describe the viciousness and obscenity of warfare, as well as the comraderie of the Brotherhood, they dislocate "motherfucker" from its context in standard American English and redefine it with relation to their experience in Vietnam. "Motherfucker" has a distinct meaning in each vocabulary, so changes in its meaning help the reader differentiate and stratify the parts of the experience. "It" serves a multitude of purposes, especially within the Brotherhood. Recognizing the different usages of "it" enables the reader to identify moments of illumination, to correlate the parts of the experience, and to frame inferences about the impact of events on the characters.

In standard American English "motherfucker" signifies one of the strongest cultural taboos.   One of the more telling post-Vietnam experiences involves veterans asking family members to "pass the motherfucking spuds," then being jarred back to civilian reality by the astonished looks on their faces. The task for the writers is to show how the meaning of obscenity is altered by changes in the experience. If readers make those transitions, they both indicate a willingness to understand and begin that process under circumstances which approximate the experience of the war. Following these changes has the fortuitous effect of demonstrating yet another of Eliot's more famous insights: the objective correlative (125). As "motherfucker" changes meanings, the reader is given "a set of objects, a situation, a chain of events which shall be the formula for" the sympathies and affections, which could only be expressed and reciprocated within the Brotherhood.

The military vocabulary carefully avoids even the appearance of obscenity. Indeed, one of the grosser ironies of the war was the chain of command's genius for inventing ways to avoid acknowledging the brutally violent and, in that sense, truly obscene aspects of warfare. When he served as casualty reporting officer, Caputo objected to writing reports in:

> that clinical, euphemistic language the military prefers
> to simple English. . . . the phrase for dismemberment,
> one of my favorite phrases, was "traumatic
> amputation." . . . After I saw some of the victims, I
> began to question the accuracy of the phrase.
> *Traumatic* was precise, for losing a limb is definitely
> traumatic, but *amputation*, it seemed to me, suggested
> a surgical operation. (157-8)

Once again the disparity between official communications and the soldiers' experience alerts the reader to a political point: one way the chain of command cloistered itself from the realities of the battlefield was to redefine them. The soldiers' knowledge of death and maiming is perfectly existential. From their perspective, seeing a friend's decapitated body is truly obscene: it offends their sensibilities and violates their sensibilities; it is offensive to modesty and decency; it is disgusting and an incitement to violence. Anything which debases their lives is obscene, properly so-called.

There is an informal vocabulary within the military organization which provides language for the passion and violence missing from militarese. This is the field expedient, utterly uneuphemistic language of career military men. When the inexperienced Downs had to confront a man who refused to advance during a firefight, he knocked him down and then:

> Pointing my rifle within a few inches of his face, I told him (my face undoubtedly contorted in rage), "You move now, motherfucker, or I'll shoot you through the head." The shock of being hit plus the actual belief that I might kill him caused his muscles to force his body up and forward. (57-8)

Freedom to use obscenity indiscriminately is thus extremely useful to the soldiers once they arrive in the combat zone. In *Better Times Than These*, Winston Groom's Lt. Kahn observes, "The only thing that improved was the cursing, which seemed the only way the men could describe their condition" (226). It enables them to communicate effectively and enhances their chances of survival.

Macho soldier talk is also used to assert the significance of their individual selves and to provide defenses against the fear of dying. The motto some men write on their flack jackets serves these purposes:

> YEA, THOUGH I WALK THROUGH THE VALLEY OF THE SHADOW OF DEATH, I SHALL FEAR NO EVIL, BECAUSE I'M THE MEANEST MOTHERFUCKER IN THE VALLEY. (Herr 87)

Obviously, "motherfucker" no longer means incest. In the metaphoric vocabulary of the young soldiers, only certain qualities of incest are relevant: passion, violence, a complete lack of moral scruple, and an almost psychotic commitment. The parody of the 23rd Psalm enhances these connotations, the not too difficult irony being that this is the type of prayer which passes the field expedient test. As Eliot would put it, some of the meanings of "motherfucker" have been dislocated and transposed into a context, where they are redefined in relation to new circumstances. By recognizing this change, the reader has passed the obscenity test and is thereby drawn one step closer into an imaginative understanding of the actual experience of the war.

"Motherfucker" takes on yet another, and even more significant meaning in the Brotherhood. With his refined ear for the soldiers' language, Michael Herr reports:

> There were some Marines stretched out a few feet
> from us, passing around war comics and talking,
> calling each other Dude and Jive, Lifer and Shitkick
> and Motherfucker, touching on this last with a special
> grace, as though it were the tenderest word in their
> language. . . . (189-90)

Thus the meaning of "motherfucker" has changed completely, and the changes are an objective correlative for developing the extent and quality of the reader's understanding.

To recapitulate: In standard American English, "motherfucker" is so obscene that it is unspeakable. Its excessive use in the lifers' speech is a means of modifying behavior and intensifying other words. In the tough talk of the ground troops, "motherfucker" loses the incest denotation and becomes an assertion of masculinity and proclaims pure meanness. In combat, words are used to embolden and taunt, but even such instinctual screaming is inadequate to express the speed and violence of contemporary warfare. In the Brotherhood "motherfucker" is estranged completely from its conventional context and communicates tenderness and human sympathy, the opposite of its meaning in Standard American English. Significantly enough, veterans of my acquaintance report that in Vietnam the pronunciation changed from "motherfucker" to "muh-thuh-fuck-uh" to "muh-fuck."

Following the pronoun "it" through a Vietnam narrative is an absorbing exercise in close reading because "it" serves a multitude of purposes in the narratives. "It" appears most often as a conventional pronoun with a definite referent in the text. In this usage, "it" serves the normal function of making communication less repetitious. Especially within the Brotherhood, "it" adds the functions of sometimes emphasizing and sometimes obscuring its referents, which are themselves often obscure. In the major cliche of the war, "There "it" is." "It" is a means of confirming a sudden insight into the ambiguity and paradox of their experience. On the other hand, Robert Stone points out that "it" can be generalized to include to the mysterious forces in the war which could only be inferred from an accurate perception of their effects:

> "There it is," they used to say in Vietnam. It was as if an evil spirit were loose, one of the demons known to the Vietnamese as *ma*, weaving in and out of visible reality, a dancing ghost. It would appear suddenly out of [the] whirl, shimmer for an instant, and be lost. People came to recognize it. Recognizing it they would say without excitement, "There it is," with emphasis on the last word to let their friends know they had seen it and to be sure their friends had seen it too. It was without form itself, but it could assume a variety of forms. . . . It became events. It became things themselves. . . . It was at the heart of every irony, however innocuous, however hideously cruel. (8)

"It" enables the characters to confirm, just precisely enough, the tacit knowledge they share as soldiers and members of the Brotherhood. Finally, "it" can be used in more than one of these functions and have several possible referents. The ability to follow these tricky and sometimes only implicit references without becoming hopelessly confused is one of the most important means by which the writers test the quality of their readers' understanding.

In standard American English, "it" is a pronoun for referring to abstractions. The frequency of this usage accurately reflects the excessive abstractness of the strategies and tactics of the Vietnam War. Caputo's "Prologue" to *A Rumor of War* forcefully reminds us that the climate of belief in the early 1960s was based on Kennedy-like commitments to abstract values, such as assuring the survival of freedom and guaranteeing self-determination for Third World countries such as South Vietnam. The reality proved to be very different. Del Vecchio's Chelini soon learns this most basic lesson in the survival code. He, too, had been motivated by abstract causes and expected a war without mysteries. The morning after a murderously effective night ambush he prepares to join in the body count:

> Cherry rose slowly. He rose to full height and stretched. He threw his shoulders back, stretching out the night cramps. . . . He felt for his frags. They were in a pouch on his belt as was right. His rifle was in his left hand. He ran his fingers over it. He

> aimed the muzzle downward and slowly withdrew the
> bolt carrier halfway, draining any water which might
> have entered the barrel during the night. Noiselessly
> he let the bolt slide back closed and he shoved hard
> to insure it seated completely. Then he looked up
> again. They, it, was still there. (545)

The "it" Chelini finds is neither victory nor defeat. He finds the
imponderable mystery of death. His altruistic motives have been
reduced to killing as many of the enemy as he can. But then he has
also found a refuge in the ambiguity of language. The vocabularies he
has learned have one important characteristic in common. They are
obscure communication as well as clarify it. The generic "it" has the
advantage of not stating facts too explicitly. He has not violated the
major taboo of the Brotherhood; he has not used the word "death".

Those moments when the men know what something means, those
moments when their understanding converges, can be identified well
enough by saying "There it is." The most subtle understanding belongs
to the men who say "There it is" at exactly the right moment. In James
Webb's *Fields of Fire*, Lt. Robert E. Lee Hodges, just arrived as a
replacement, spent his first night at a base camp watching a firefight
several kilometers away. To his chagrin, he is assigned to that unit the
next day. As he and Flaky, his radio man, inspect the first dead body
Hodges ever saw, he is reminded of the disparities between the
platoon's experience and his own: "You all must have really been in
some shit last night." Flaky's reply is classic, and to be sure the New
Guy understands his perspective on the entire situation, he elaborates
in perhaps more detail than Hodges wanted:

> "There it is, Lieutenant. Been like this for ten days
> now. I'm the only one left from the CP. Me and
> Rabbit." Flaky was shrewdly sizing Hodges up. "Yup.
> I been a radioman for three months. Already had me
> three lieutenants." (72)

The attentive reader has been thoroughly prepared, both cognitively and
subjectively, to recognize the tacit meanings involved in this
conversation. In the fleeting moment, Flaky verbalizes their mutual
understanding just precisely enough to confirm his agreement with
Hodges' entire meaning. His elaboration is, of course, much less
important to Hodges' acceptance by the platoon than his non-verbally
expressed assessment of the new officer.

Combinations of these vocabularies can be used in the same context to communicate the subtler denotations and shades of meaning each best expresses. Del Vecchio utilizes the fullest resources of the soldiers' language to clarify the complex implications of a conversation on the causes of war between Egan (respectfully nicknamed The Boonierat) and Lt. Brooks:

> Egan's concentration on his thoughts deepened. "Each [technological] advance brings greater stability yet with a higher, more complex structure supporting it. Each period of stability brings a population explosion. That can be documented. If you plot the growth of human population before every major increase, you'll find a major technological advance. After each major increase you find population pressure and war. Pressure is conflict, L-T. Want to stop the pressure? After the next advance, stop people from fuckin each other."
>
> "Sew up all the cunts of the Third World, huh?" Brooks joked, laughed, trying to lessen Egan's last statement to the absurd because to Brooks [a Black] it smacked of racism.
>
> "The whole world," Egan said sharply, defensively. "Fuck it, Man. You listenin? There ain't no chance about this. There ain't no such thing as chance. Only ignorance of natural laws. . . . You can make just as good an argument for war being man's nature. If you want the truth all you gotta say is man's nature is intermittently warlike. War and peace. They have a continuous, maybe sine-like, maybe erratic, function. Did you know that on any given day there's an average of twelve wars goin on on earth? There's been over a hundred wars since World War Two. You don't gotta justify war. Fuck the pansyass politicians and the pantywaist left. War's its own justification."
>
> "That's sad," Brooks said.
>
> "Why?" Egan demanded.
>
> "We're here and that justifies our being here?"
>
> Brooks made it sound ridiculous.
>
> "The only justification you need for Nam is we're doin it. It is, thus it is right. That goes for everything. If it is, so it is." (535-7)

As college graduates, Brooks and Egan formulate their ideas in the academic variant of standard American English--using proper grammar and a mixture of plain terminology and technical terms. Equally importantly, they express their emotions and their mutual trust by selectively using the informal, tacitly defined conversational vocabularies. They thus express both their ideas and feelings by alternating vocabularies and the meanings each is best able to convey, augmented as always by non-verbal signals. The cumulative effect is to summarize what two very capable soldiers have learned after nearly completing their extended tours of duty. Egan's fatalism (as distinct from the cynicism of the chain of command) is unmistakable, while Brooks' response to both Egan's fatalism and implicit racism is softened by his respect and affection for the exemplary soldier.

Thus narratives triumph over the mysteries of the experience of the Vietnam War, and the soldiers' knowledge is not as hermetic as it at first appears. Learning to construe language is the reader's primary means of penetrating the texts. Some generalizations about the use of the vocabularies emerge rather quickly from their readers' active involvement in the texts. As is appropriate with mimetic literature, written to imitate human experience, the first effort must be to study how accurately the narratives reflect the Vietnam experience. The texts which have been analyzed have satisfied the unforgivingly critical examination of veterans. They might not agree what the American involvement meant or the extent to which a book represents the Vietnam experience, but they do agree on the authenticity of these texts.

Taken as a group, the language of the narratives represents an impressive achievement. Standard American English enables the writers to communicate the unadorned facts of life in the combat zone and forms the linguistic base of the narratives. Because it lacks vividness and sharply defined connotations, it understates the soldiers' subjective response to events that the reader finds terrifying. This act of interpretation by the reader begins the process of active involvement in the soldiers' knowledge of the war. Military language provides specificity lacking in Standard American English but is even less connotative. The stark contrasts between militarese and events force judgments by the reader as to the wisdom and compassion of the chain of command. The complex blend of informal, conversational vocabularies add the missing dimensions of vividness, connotation, and metaphor. Words such as "motherfucker" and "it" demonstrate how the language of the narratives is stratified into orderly components and how fragmentary knowledge converges into moments of insight and understanding.

In a larger sense, then, the language of the narratives is an objective correlative for the entire Vietnam experience. The structure of the language imitates the structure of the experience. By mastering the languages, the reader is drawn ever more deeply into the Vietnam experience. While there is no substitute for having served in Vietnam, the experience is not in the final analysis merely hermetic. There are degrees of understanding, and they can be extended by active reading and respect for the authenticity of the texts. The extent of the reader's understanding is constantly expanded, tested, and reinforced. This is particularly true of contexts in which the vocabularies are used in combination to dramatize the complexity of the more mysterious, ambiguous aspects of surviving a year in the combat zone.

Works Cited

Caputo, Philip. *A Rumor of War*. New York: Ballantine Books, 1978.

del Vecchio, John. *The 13th Valley*. New York: Bantam Books, 1982.

Downs, Frederick. *The Killing Zone*. New York: Berkley Books, 1983.

Eliot, T. S. *Selected Essays*. New York: Harcourt, Brace and Company, 1950.

Groom, Winston. *Better Times Than These*. New York: Berkley Books, 1979.

Hasford, Gustav. *The Short-Timers*. New York: Bantam Books, 1980.

Herr, Michael. *Dispatches*. New York: Avon Books, 1978.

Lomperis, Timothy J. *"Reading the Wind:" The Literature of the Vietnam War*. Durham: Duke University Press, 1987.

Stone, Robert. *Images of War*. Boston: Boston Publishing Company, 1986.

Webb, James. *Fields of Fire*. New York: Bantam Books, 1979.

THE HELICOPTER AND THE PUNJI STICK:
CENTRAL SYMBOLS OF THE VIETNAM WAR

H. Palmer Hall

After spending a few years reading hundreds of books and viewing dozens of films based on the experiences of soldiers in the Vietnam War, I must confess that images begin to blur. A helicopter in book number one hundred and three seems the reincarnation of a Huey I met back in books number two and seven and in numbers ten through seventeen and so on. A chopper flies out of *Platoon* and in a moment of bizarre discongruity lands in the midst of *The Green Berets*. Punji sticks that penetrate the boots of an ARVN officer in David Halberstam's *One Very Hot Day* come out the other side of the boots of a young soldier in *Go Tell the Spartans*. Lieutenant Anderson in the Halberstam novel marks off one more day on his short-timer's calendar and you see the pencil finishing its mark on the *Playboy* centerfold of the Anachronism in William Pelfrey's *The Big V*. A series of persistent images of violence, independent of the individual novels, yet central to each of them, begins to form.

Among the blurring images, the calendar flips from page to page, from year to year. The war as it was in 1963, in 1965, in 1968, in 1972. Each year a different kind of war. Each book a separate evocation of the same images fixed in its individual year. The books dealing with the war before 1965 are almost alien to those that portray events of the later war. *The Green Berets, One Very Hot Day, The Barking Deer*, and the other early novels bear only a remote kinship to *Going after Cacciato, The Big V, Fields of Fire*, and *The 13th Valley*. Just as the film versions of *The Green Berets* and *Go Tell the Spartans* resemble only slightly *Platoon, Apocalypse Now*, and *Hamburger Hill*.

What ties the works together is pure imagery. That helicopter flying John Wayne to a Green Beret attack outside of Saigon could be the same chopper that flies Charley Sheen away from that last devastating attack in *Platoon*. As he often does in *Dispatches*, Michael Herr puts it best:

> In the months after I got back the hundreds of helicopters I'd flown in began to draw together until they'd formed a collective meta-chopper, and in my mind it was the sexiest thing going; saver-destroyer, provider-waster, right hand-left hand, nimble, fluent, canny and human; hot-steel, grease, jungle-saturated

canvas webbing, sweat cooling and warming up again,
cassette rock and roll in one ear and door-gun fire in
the other, fuel, heat, vitality and death, death itself,
hardly an intruder. (9)

Helicopters were used for almost as many purposes as there were
missions in the war. They were observers, searching for the Viet Cong;
destroyers, raining bullets on the enemy from the sky; saviors,
transporting the wounded to military hospitals; hearses, carrying the
dead to morgues; status symbols, cadillacing for every field grade and
general officer. The helicopter is the great friend and the great enemy
of the American soldier in the novels and films of the war, a stable
image that spans the years of the war, having the same meanings in the
books and films of 1967 as it has in 1988.

As an active, rapid-moving war engine, hopping from place to place
quickly, quickly, back to its first location, out to a battle in the middle
of the jungle, zipping to a hospital in Pleiku, crashing into the
wilderness of the tri-border area--luxurious speed--the helicopter serves
well as a central symbol of the American Army and the American war
effort.

Its counterpart is more evasive, metamorphic, shifting from the
early years of the war into a new transformation after 1967. That punji
stick that partially disabled Lieutenant Thuong in *One Very Hot Day*
becomes much more effective as the land mind that destroys the
Anachronism in *The Big V*. The swinging punji trap that kills the good-
natured supply sergeant in *The Green Berets* is more effective as a
Bouncing Betty explosive mine in *The Boys in Company C*.

The transformation occurs after the build up of American troops
in 1965, but the explosive mine does not fully replace the punji stick as
a symbol until the 1968 Tet Offensive when the Viet Cong and the
North Vietnamese Army demonstrated their ability to attack in force
in many places in the country at the same time. From that point on,
the punji stick is effectively ended as a symbol. But its replacement
serves the same symbolic purpose. Just as the helicopter can be seen
to represent the American way of doing war, the speed with which the
country kept hoping to end the war, the punji stick and the explosive
mine may be seen to stand for the Viet Cong. A symbol of patience
and of the willingness to fight as long as necessary, the punji stick
points up waiting for its victims. The helicopter, on the other hand,
flies frantically, searching for an elusive and patient enemy, rarely
finding him, often becoming a victim itself.

In only a few of the novels do we actually see these two symbols of
the war in close conjunction, and in those cases the action occurs in the

earliest stages of the war. After the 1968 Tet Offensive, the punji sticks play such a small role that few of the writers even mention them.

Two of the novels published in 1967, John Sack's *M* and David Halberstam's *One Very Hot Day* focus in some detail on the punji sticks and place them in direct comparison to the American helicopter.

M is a black comedy played out on a battlefield that is uniquely its own among all of the Vietnam novels. There is no central character for reader identification as there is in most of the novels. M is a complete company of interchangeable men; Demirgian and the other soldiers in the novel are stick figures being led through the war by the book's author, John Sack. M Company arrives in Vietnam during the first year of the big buildup of American soldiers. In their first in-country briefing M learns that:

> "We have one of those I say critical situations with Charlie [the VC] here. Charlie now he could be watching us right now, Charlie could be at the concertina wire and watching now, Charlie could be there now--that he could. Out there Charlie got machine guns, machine guns, and Charlie got mortars, machine guns and mortars and Charlie got punji pits..."
> "Punji pits." A helpful Virginia lieutenant was at the briefing to interpret some of Allen's more problematic words. "Punji pits, and they're poisonous, and they're deadly poisonous..." (111)

Of all of the weapons of the VC, the punji pit receives the most attention from Sergeant Allen and from the lieutenant; that is undoubtedly because of the strange nature of the weapon. All other weapons mentioned are also held by the American forces; only the punji stick is uniquely the VC's.

In *M* the helicopter is placed in direct opposition to the punji stick. M is being flown in assault helicopters to an anticipated battle on the Michelin rubber plantation:

> With its whole silent battalion and three battalions more, M was in combat clothes and being lifted out towards the Michelin rubber plantation, a forest where the communists, all busy little beavers, had been whittling bamboo stakes for days, dipping them in buffalo dung, urinating on them, putting them in punji pits, in foot-traps, in mad little batman traps in

trees, *whiz*! out of the bushes, *pop*! out of ferns --
aargh! (143)

No one from M is injured by stepping into a punji pit. But no one from M lands at the Michelin rubber plantation. The helicopters set them down at the wrong location. No one from M sees a communist. The punji pits can be effective only if the American helicopters put the soldiers in a place where the VC have been located. *M* is a comedy of American errors, and even though many in M die, it is almost by accident rather than through the intent of war.

Although the punji pits injure no one in M, they remain a major symbol of the VC "whittling bamboo stakes." The helicopter continues to be the central symbol of the American forces, rushing soldiers to battle sites where no enemy can be located or to places where the VC wait in ambush.

David Halberstam also discusses the manufacture of punji sticks in *One Very Hot Day*. When ARVN Lieutenant Thuong steps into a pit, he examines the stick that pierced his boot. "He was sure this spike was infected, probably with buffalo turds, a VC favorite, they came cheap after all, and the more subtle forms of chemical warfare were not so readily available" (35). The punji wound continues to fester throughout the hot day. It is symbolic of the other side--the Viet Cong side--of the war, a side that fights as the Viet Minh had fought the French, with native weapons and guile. The wound becomes a symbol of the painful necessity Lieutenant Thuong feels to fight his own countrymen in a confusing war. For him, there will be no relief from pain and this very hot day will become simply another hot day.

As in *M*, *One Very Hot Day* waxes less than enthusiastic about the helicopter as a fighting instrument. The spokesman is Captain Beaupre, a veteran of Korea and Lieutenant Thuong's counterpart on the day's patrol. Captain Beaupre, sitting with a group of officers as plans are being made to move soldiers to potential battle site, resists being transported to war in a helicopter, even though he sees the heat and a long march as nearly deadly enemies:

> Beaupre sat in the briefing and waited, hoping he looked impassive. Perhaps, he thought, they will think I want it. He didn't want the helicopters and he didn't want the reserve force, which sat there by the CP and worked only when there was contact, and was dropped in, more often than not into a specially prepared second ambush; he wanted the ground troops. (9)

It is Beaupre's age, his experience in both the Korean and Vietnam wars, that makes him see and resist the danger of helicopter warfare. Beaupre is aware that the Viet Cong took special joy in shooting down helicopters and were, therefore, prepared to sacrifice more for a helicopter than for a squadron of ground troops.

> Perhaps the impassive ones, he thought, want the helicopters too but are too proud to show it. Beaupre was a little older and probably a little more frightened than most. He watched the Lieutenant next to him, *his* lieutenant, the most eager face there. The Lieutenant wanted the helicopters; he liked the assault. (9-10)

That the helicopter is an ambiguous weapon is reflected in most of the novels coming out of the Vietnam War, as well as in the non-fiction memoirs. Philip Caputo reports in *A Rumor of War*, his account of his experiences in Vietnam as a Marine lieutenant, that:

> On the ground, an infantryman has some control over his destiny, or at least the illusion of it. In a helicopter under fire, he hasn't even the illusion. Confronted by the indifferent forces of gravity, ballistics and machinery, he is himself pulled in several directions at once by a range of extreme, conflicting emotions. (293)

M and *One Very Hot Day* are early Vietnam War novels, both published prior to the Tet Offensive of 1968. They reflect the concerns and, to a certain extent, myths of those early days of the war when Green Berets worked with Montagnards and the regular army served as advisers to the ARVN. But as the war grew older and the Viet Cong prepared for the Tet Offensive, writers began to lose their fascination with the strange weapon that was whittled from bamboo stakes and coated with fecal matter. More and more of the books fail even to mention punji sticks, but concentrate on a more deadly waiting trap, the exploding mine.

The loss of the punji stick's stature as a weapon to be feared is clearly highlighted in a fine book dealing with the transitional period of the war--that period during the build up of American forces and the beginning of the Tet Offensive. William Pelfrey's *The Big V* covers, among many other events, a patrol in the Central Highlands and one soldier's stepping into a punji pit. Instead of worrying about the wound, the other soldiers assume the wounded man is a slacker, using a pit he had found to deliberately wound himself so that he could be sent back to the rear.

A more deadly form of booby trap is introduced at the end of *The Big V* and its effectiveness is directly related to the helicopter as an assault vehicle. Rather than merely wound, it kills one of Winsted's close friends--as he leaves a helicopter:

> Our bird hovered behind the other, our pilot watching the lead bird's insertion. Then we dove in like a Cobra, tree-top level, the nose jerking back up as it hovered over the LZ.
>
> Sam and I jumped together, almost choreographed, both hitting on our feet and running for the wood line. The explosion must have gone the instant we jumped. I heard nothing because of the shrill vibrating and grinding of turbine and rotors.
>
> The explosion was a second "chopper" carrying Winsted's friend "the Anachronism" into a booby trap. I remember smiling at first, feeling proud of my jump, hitting and immediately running with rifle at high port, like you're supposed to. I saw the Anachronism right off but didn't know it was him. He jerked his head and arms in spasm, three times. As I ran I didn't realize it was him, couldn't imagine it.
>
> But I did know something had happened. Gulping and squeezing the rifle's hand guards, handset flopping against the strap of my ruck.
>
> The lieutenant was spread on his back--chest and face solid red, *solid*, the bandoliers blown apart. His arms and legs were stretched at symmetrical angles. The Anachronism too was dead by the time Sam and I got there. (149)

We are given the results of the booby trap before we are actually shown the trap. When compared with the results of the punji trap earlier in the novel, the mine, made from a 105mm rocket shell, is much ghastlier. This is a new stage of the war, more terrible than the last.

The story of the helicopter tripping a booby trap as it lands recalls Beaupre's unwillingness to volunteer for helicopter duty during his day on patrol. The Anachronism was delivered to his death by a helicopter and was "the first one they carried away on the KIA bird" (150).

The helicopter makes three appearances in booby trap scenes in *The Big V*: first, in rescuing the soldiers wounded either by accident or deliberately in the punji pit--the saver bird; second, in delivering the Anachronism to his death in the 105 artillery shell trap--the assault bird, death bird; and third, in removing the Anachronism in a body bag--the hearse bird. As rapid and mobile as it is, the helicopter faces a patient enemy and cannot win.

Published in 1972, *The Big V* depicts military operations occuring just before the Tet Offensive of 1968. That offensive destroyed the image of the VC as a poorly supplied enemy relying primarily on tools that he would have to construct himself. In January and February of 1968 the Viet Cong demonstrated for the first time their ability to rise up in strength and attack in several locations at once throughout South Vietnam. Although they failed to achieve even one of their major objectives during Tet, the Viet Cong and the North Vietnamese Army managed to turn an obvious military failure into a major public relations victory. After the Tet Offensive demonstrated that the Viet Cong had large supplies of sophisticated weapons available to them, the punji stick lost its value as an appropriate symbol for them. The patience of the Viet Cong, the waiting game that would eventually lead to American withdrawal, continues to be represented by booby traps, but traps that are technologically superior to the punji pits, as demonstrated in *The Big V*.

The shift in use of the symbols is clearly evident in Tim O'Brien's *If I Die in a Combat Zone*. O'Brien got to Vietnam a year after the Tet Offensive and in this non-fiction memoir of his war year makes only a brief remark about the punji stakes:

> Eyes sweep the rice paddy. Don't walk there, too soft. Not there, dangerous mines. Step there and there and there, not there, step there and there and there, careful, careful, watch. Green ahead. Green lights, go. Eyes roll in the sockets. Protect the legs, no chances, watch for the fucking snipers, watch for ambushes and punji pits. (35)

The punji pits are only one minor part of a huge killing field made up of mines, mortars and snipers. But O'Brien goes into much greater detail in describing the more sophisticated traps. In "Step Lightly" he does not mention punji pits but does make an extensive catalogue of various types of Viet Cong mines:

> The Bouncing Betty is feared most. It is a common mine. It leaps out of its nest in the earth, and when it hits its apex, it explodes, reliable and deadly. If a fellow

is lucky and if the mine is in an old emplacement, having been exposed to the rains, he may notice its three prongs jutting out of the clay. The prongs serve as the Bouncing Betty's firing device. Step on them, and the unlucky soldier will hear a muffled explosion; that's the initial charge sending the mine on its one-yard leap into the sky. The fellow takes another step and begins the next and his backside is bleeding and he's dead. We call it "ol' step and a half." (125)

For six pages O'Brien catalogs and describes various types of mines, interspersing incidents of friends killed or maimed by them:

More destructive than the Bouncing Betty are the booby-trapped mortar and artillery rounds. They hang from trees [e.g. the trap in *The Big V*]. They nestle in shrubbery... Chip, my black buddy from Orlando, strayed into a hedgerow and triggered a rigged 105 artillery round. He died in such a way that, for once, you could never know his color... And there was Shorty, a volatile fellow so convinced that the mines would take him that he spent a month AWOL. In July he came back to the field, joking but still unsure of it all. One day, when it was very hot, he sat on a booby-trapped 155 round. (125-126)

O'Brien lists a great variety of mines: "the M-14 anti-personnel mine, designed to disable;" "the booby-trapped grenade," resting inside a tin can; "the Soviet TMB and the Chinese anti-tank mine," designed to take out tanks, but occasionally tripped by marching soldiers; "the directional-fragmentation mine," equivalent to the American claymore; "the corrosive-action car-killer," placed in the gas tank and causing a killing explosion weeks later. After the catalog is completed, O'Brien states that "In the three days I spent writing this, mines and men came together three more times. Seven more legs, one more arm" (125-126).

The mines succeed the punji pits, more dangerous, less obvious in appearance. Although they existed and were used prior to the Tet Offensive, they were not as important to the novelists as were the exotic punji pits. Most novels set after the Tet Offensive pay tribute to the mines with the exception of the novels of heroism. In those novels there is no room for the almost accidental maiming and killing that is inherent in accidentally tripping a mine. As Ben Compton of John Cassidy's *A Station in the Delta* puts it:

> "I think a war where you don't look the man in the
> eye when you kill him is not war. It's just a kind of
> butchery. The side that kills the most wins."
>   "I'd think it would be the other way around. To be
> able to look a man in the eye and then kill him..."
>   "If you have to kill him, you should honor him," said
> Ben. (321)

The idea of honor is central to the hero novels; the authors concentrate
on honorable, courageous acts, acts which cannot include "a question of
accidents," such as stepping on a mine.

The heroic novels give us the clearest, most unadulterated view of
the helicopter as an effective instrument in helping the United States'
effort in Vietnam. Most of the other novels are at best ambivalent and
at worst clearly disapproving of the machines. In *A Station in the Delta*
Jerry Burkholder and Dino Gallup make a truly heroic rescue of Ben
Compton after he is wounded. The detailed narrative of the helicopter
flying through enemy fire to lift the wounded soldier out of My Tho
reveals nothing but admiration for the men who fly the Hueys. But in
most of the other novels, there is as much contempt for pilots who
refuse to land to pick up wounded because of heavy firing as there is
admiration for those who do make the attempt. There is great
contempt for pilots and door gunners picking off suspected Viet Cong
from the safety of the air, much fear at the idea of helicopter assaulting
and disgust at the helicopter retrieval of bodies.

In William Eastlake's *The Bamboo Bed*, we have the ultimate
helicopter. For the only time in the Vietnam novels the helicopter
becomes the sex machine, as well as saver and destroyer. Before we
meet the helicopter named "The Bamboo Bed," we are treated to a
picture of the general ineffectiveness of helicopters in Vietnam:

> The choppers, having performed their no-mission,
> hurled themselves away only to rise ten metres and at
> once crash in a storm of hostile fire and scatter
> themselves down the slope in a twisted pyre of
> aluminum scrap with one enormous rotor blade pointing
> straight up skyward like some shining and final
> American erection. (17)

Eastlake has with this burning symbol of a downed helicopter made
a startling comment on the role of the helicopter as symbol that
underlines all other uses of the helicopter in the Vietnam War. While

ostensibly a potent symbol of American power, the helicopter comes to reflect the impotence of the American war effort in the face of an enemy that is prepared to wait until the Americans leave. The final erection is doomed to failure; the spurts are sterile.

It is after this image of sterility and impotence that we are introduced to "The Bamboo Bed," a helicopter used for meaningless love affairs and for rescue operations. "The woman and the man [inside the helicopter] were tangled in fantastic attitudes on the rear seat, lying beneath the silent, hard and black vanadium-steel M60 machine gun" (38). The sexual symbolism inherent in many machines of war is emphasized throughout Eastlake's book, from the M60 to the helicopter itself.

The relationship exists in other Vietnam war novels as well, most notably in Gustav Hasford's *The Short-Timers*, but not quite as prominently or as graphically as in *The Bamboo Bed*. Even the war itself is secondary to the sex that is facilitated by the helicopter:

> The helicopter slipped awfully to the starboard and in the same quick instant took four machine-gun bursts on the fleeing side so that the ground fire, hard and straight, rising from the sombre innocent steady jungle forest beneath flew harmlessly past the darting butterfly.
> "Shall I stop?"
> "No."
> "Not for the war?"
> "It's a dirty war."
> "But somebody has to do it."
> "More?"
> "Yes."
> "Somebody has to do it."
> And they did it in the helicopter, the Bamboo Bed, that sailed and jerked vivid and mothlike in the Vietnamese sun. (38-39)

The military purpose of "The Bamboo Bed" is to serve as a search and rescue helicopter, but in doing that job it is as useless and sterile as it is as a sex machine. The major search in the novel is for Captain Clancy whose platoon had been decimated in a fight early in the novel. Finally, "The Bamboo Bed" finds Clancy, nearly dead. The search is successful, but the rescue fails:

> The Bamboo Bed was entering the monsoon. It got black-dark. Clancy tried to hold the Bamboo Bed

together until it came out the other side. It took
everything he had left. When the Bamboo Bed came
out the other side there was nothing left.
     The copter soared up against the sun, aerial and light.
The Vietnamese sun bore down with such a sudden
magnitude in the abiding Asia forest that the butterfly,
the Bamboo Bed, the insect in the vastness, was for long
seconds visible until it once again came into the long
shadow of the monsoon and was forever lost,
disappeared, eaten by tigers, enveloped in the gentle,
tomb-like Asian night. (350)

It was upon the helicopter that the United States staked its chances
of winning the war in Vietnam--the helicopter and other instruments
of high technology. But the helicopter was not enough. The purported
mission of rapid assaults and swift rescues belies the actuality of the
war as depicted in the novels. Helicopters were, undoubtedly,
instrumental in saving the lives of thousands of wounded American
soldiers, but were unable to save the war.
     The very technology that the United States relied upon stands as
a major symbol for the novelists of the war--and it is a symbol that
more often hurts than helps the American cause. Ranged against the
punji sticks and land mines of the Viet Cong, ranged against the
patience of the National Front for the Liberation of South Vietnam,
high technology proved as ineffectual as the rescue attempts of "The
Bamboo Bed."

Works Cited

Cassidy, John. *A Station in the Delta*. New York: Charles
     Scribner's Sons, 1979.

Caputo, Philip J. *A Rumor of War*. New York: Holt, Rinehart
     and Winston, 1977.

Eastlake, William. *The Bamboo Bed*. New York: Simon and
     Schuster, 1969.

Halberstam, David. *One Very Hot Day*. Boston: Houghton Mifflin,
     1967.

Herr, Michael. *Dispatches*. New York: Knopf, 1977.

Pelfrey, William. *The Big V*. New York: Liveright, 1972.

Sack, John. *M*. 1967. New York: Avon, 1985

PART II

LOOKING GLASS TEXTS

REREADING *THE DEER HUNTER*: MICHAEL CIMINO'S DELIBERATE AMERICAN EPIC

Robert E. Bourdette, Jr.

The scene that succeeded was one of those, of which so many have occurred in our own times, in which neither age nor sex forms an exception to the lot of savage warfare.
James Fenimore Cooper, *The Deerslayer; or the First War-Path*, Chapter XXX.

Say that the hero is his nation, In him made one. . . .
Wallace Stevens, "An Examination of the Hero in a Time of War"

I

Of the American films of the 1970s, Michael Cimino's *The Deer Hunter* (1978) remains one of the most controversial[1]; certainly of those films that have attempted to engage the implications of the United States' involvement in Southeast Asia, Cimino's film has provoked the most acrimonious criticism and the harshest of reviews. Over a decade later, those critical comments--now divorced from their often perceptive contexts--have hardened into the generally received opinion on the film: jingoistic, racist, even fascist. When the film--one of the first to be concerned with Vietnam--was released, there were rigid expectations about what such a film that involved that conflict should convey. These demands, often contradictory, were reflected in the early criticism: such a film was expected to be single-minded in opposing our involvement in Vietnam; it was expected to portray a literal, even documentary-like, record of events; it should demonstrate overtly and with no ambiguity our moral failure as a nation. These demands, however politically and socially understandable, tended to run rough-shod over the nuances of the text and the implications of the images of *The Deer Hunter*. Despite the formalization of the hostile criticism of the film, the passage of time and changes in our political and historical perspective on that national watershed allow us to return to Cimino's film with more critical understanding, if not total objectivity. What Cimino has achieved in the film (as opposed to what viewers and critics wanted the film to achieve at the time of its release) may be clearer now than when the film was first encountered. The unveiling of the Vietnam Memorial in

Washington--itself attended by great controversy--and an explosion of more recent studies, histories, documentaries, and films--notably Kubrick's *Full Metal Jacket* and Stone's *Platoon*--have refocused our attention on the painful complexities of this critical moment in our national history. These more recent efforts to come to grips with the ambiguities of our involvement in Vietnam suggest that the time is right to give *The Deer Hunter* a rereading.

I use the term "rereading" deliberately. When *The Deer Hunter* first appeared, Cimino's film was "read" without much regard for the larger historical and literary contexts on which it so essentially depends. Though occasional references were made to the title's possible allusion to James Fenimore Cooper's *The Deerslayer* and to the hero's affinities with Hemingwayesque protagonists, only Arthur Schlesinger, Jr. briefly attempted to place the film in such historical and literary contexts. In this otherwise substantial critical vacuum, the various elements of the film--character, visual effects, language, and metaphoric details--were discussed in isolation; the whole, as a consequence, was attacked on moral, political, historical, and aesthetic grounds.

Pauline Kael, for instance, charged that the film has "no more moral intelligence than the [Clint] Eastwood action pictures" on which Cimino had previously worked (66). In the *Atlantic Monthly*, Arthur Lubow attacked the film's lack of political awareness; in *Harper's*, Tom Buckley condemned the film's utter lack of historical validity: "It is as though [Cimino] believed that the power of his genius could radically alter the outlines of a real event. . . . that is still fresh in the memory of a nation" (88). A similar, even more forceful, criticism was made by Peter Arnett who, like Buckley, served as a war correspondent in Vietnam: "Absent are the disillusion at home, the bitterness of those who served, the destruction of a country, and any other factors that might lessen the epic theme" (6). Finally, more than one critic questioned the aesthetics of the three-hour film as it moves from a Pennsylvania steeltown to Vietnam and back again. Particularly troubling to many critics has been the film's fusion of gritty realism with "unrealistic" details: the drab, industrial landscape of the steel town versus the majestic, even "Romantic," scenes of the deer hunt (purportedly set in the mountains of western Pennsylvania but actually filmed against the very different mountains of the Cascades); the sharp realism of the attack on the Vietnamese village versus the so-called "unhistorical" use of Russian roulette in Vietnam; these scenes of Russian roulette juxtaposed to actual film footage of the fall of Saigon.

These are potentially serious charges, all the more so when advanced by reputable critics and by correspondents who took some part in the events with which this film is concerned. It is clear that many such critics demanded, as I have noted earlier, that *this* film, which deals with so immediate and so emotionally charged a subject-- an event "still fresh in the memory of a nation"--should have *reproduced* their version of history rather than to have chanced the more daring task of illuminating the meaning of that history. This debate between historical verisimilitude and poetic truth is as old as Plato's *Republic* and as current as *The New Yorker*. In that journal Michael J. Arlen recapitulated the debate in discrediting the validity of the Russian roulette sequences and, hence, the historical validity of the entire film:

> "But *The Deer Hunter* didn't have to be true to facts.
> It showed the poetic truth of war," a young friend said
> to me as I was making these complaints the other day.
> "But how do you know, since you weren't there?" I
> asked.
> "Well, I know because of the movie," he said. (125-
> 26)

There is room, even a necessity, for the documentary approach that Arlen is here requiring, a requirement that has since begun to be fulfilled; at the same time there is a corresponding necessity for an imaginative realization of events that transcends a narrow reading of historical events. Aristotle claimed in the *Poetics* that poetry is more valuable than history because poetry--by which Aristotle meant epic and tragic poetry based on myth--could convey the enduring truths underlying a literal account of events. "The point is," Andrew Horton has argued in commenting on another epic film, "that we must not only be aware of events as events, but also of their wider personal and social significance at the deepest human level" (10).

Writing of a work that also emerged out of a long period of war and national travail, a critic of the *Aeneid* has argued that

> The time was ripe to see more clearly what war is and
> what it does to human nature. [It] is one of those works
> of literature that derive their artistic impetus from the
> fact that a stage has been reached in the history of
> ideas where a whole society can be brought through
> literature to the imaginative realization of a moral truth
> which a recent traumatic experience has equipped it to
> grasp. (Quinn 22)

The Deer Hunter obviously must suffer in comparison with Virgilian epic, but it is, I think, in exactly this context of an "imaginative realization of a moral truth" presented in epic form in which Cimino's film must be "read" and judged.

Iterated through even the most hostile criticism of the film is the clue to a more comprehensive reading of the film, a clue that reveals the artistic and moral unity of the so-called disparate details of the film. Peter Arnett referred without further elaboration to Cimino's "epic theme" (6); Pauline Kael had earlier called *The Deer Hunter* "a three-hour epic scaled to the spaciousness of America itself" (66). Al Auster and Leonard Quart referred to the film as an "epically conceived work" (6), and Schlesinger had described it, somewhat tautologically, as a "self-appointed American epic" (18)--as if all deliberate epics were not "self-appointed." In film criticism, unfortunately, the term "epic" tends to be loosely used, applied indiscriminately to describe any long, usually sprawling, film narrative, so it is hardly surprising that none of these critics developed the implications of their own characterization.

However inadequate, the literary definition of "epic" attempts slightly more precision. C. M. Bowra has written that "An epic is by common consent a narrative of some length and deals with events which have a certain grandeur and importance and come from a life of action, especially of violent action such as war. It gives a special pleasure because its events and persons enhance our belief in the worth of human achievement and in the dignity and nobility of man" (1).

In words that anticipate a more positive interpretation of Tom Buckley's charges against *The Deer Hunter*--"that [Cimino thought] the power of [his] genius could radically alter the outlines of a real event" --Lascelles Abercrombie sees the epic-maker as "accepting, and with his genius transfiguring, the general circumstances of his time. . . symbolizing, in some appropriate form, whatever sense of the significance of life he feels acting as the unconscious metaphysic of the time" (39).

The compulsion to create a specifically American epic has been superbly treated by Roy Harvey Pearce in *The Continuity of American Poetry* (59-136). Earlier, in "Toward an American Epic," Pearce had written that

> [T]o do it right, to invent. . . a genuinely American analogue of the traditional epic, the poet would have to break radically with the very tradition which he would be trying to carry on and invigorate. . . . Confronted with a society which supplied him with no authentically American epic material, he would yet have to find that material, to transubstantiate what his society gave him so that he could transform it" (362).

The problems inherent in fashioning a contemporary epic have been limned by M. M. Bakhtin; in distinguishing between the epic and the novel, he argues that

> the world of the epic is the national heroic past: it is a
> world of "beginnings" and "peak times" in the national
> history, a world of fathers and of founders of families,
> a world of "firsts" and "bests." . . . . The epic was never
> a poem about the present, about its own time. . . . (13)

He suggests that it is possible to conceive of the present as "heroic, epic time, when it is seen as historically significant"; if one can "distance it, look at it as if from afar". . . one can relate to the past in a familiar way. . . . But in so doing we ignore the presentness of the present and the pastness of the past; we are removing ourselves from the zone of "my time," from the zone of familiar contact with me" (14).

Such a reading of the formally constitutive features of epic underscores the way in which Cimino breaks radically with the tradition he invigorates; past and present are inextricably linked. Instead of distancing the present, he forces us to engage the present in order to understand how our myths have made present reality. The Vietnam war was exactly that traumatic national experience out of which an American epic might be fashioned, providing as it did the pressing occasion for the potential epic-maker to imagine the moral truths that need to be confronted by the society.[2] The literary epics of our past --the *Iliad*, the *Odyssey*, the *Aeneid*, *The Faerie Queene*, *Paradise Lost*, Joyce's *Ulysses*, Melville's *Moby-Dick*--perhaps the closest thing we have to an American epic--each embodied the "accepted unconscious metaphysics" of a specific time and place. Yet, even beyond the celebration of events "from a life of action," these epics share something else in common. Epic ultimately concerns the costly, problematic but essential struggle to assert the value of *community* in the face of forces hostile to that humanizing value. Indeed, the most intense expression of the epic impulse seems to emerge at exactly those moments in history when a particular sense of community is at the point of vanishing.

II

Cimino anchors his images of this struggle to assert the value of community inside a reading of contemporary history. As E. M. W. Tillyard has remarked, epic attains its fullest expression when "tragic intensity coexists with the group consciousness of an age, when the narrowly timeless is combined with the variegatedly temporal" (13), and our involvement in Vietnam is that recent traumatic experience that insists that we confront, once again and painfully, the fragility of our temporal hold on a sense of community.

The text and images of *The Deer Hunter* are rooted in this sense of community. In an interview, Christopher Walken ("Nick") remarked that

> When we started [the film] Cimino gave us all a small photo of very young children standing around. He didn't say anything about it, just handed it to us. And it was very useful; you looked at the picture and realized that the people you were about to play really did have their arms around each other and posed for this snapshot twenty years ago. It brought home the news to me that I was to be a member of a community. (Hodenfield 28)

From the first seconds of the film as a tank-truck blasts through the early dawn in Clairton, the viewer is plunged into this sense of place and community. The "Deer Hunter" of the title, Michael Vronsky (Robert De Niro), shares a trailer home with his closest friend, Nick Cevotarevich (Christopher Walken). Michael serves as the center of a group of friends, though he stands apart from that community. Nick, in contrast, expresses in his actions an intense awareness of the importance of community. Both Michael and Nick are in love with Linda (Meryl Streep), though Michael represses his love for her when Nick asks her to marry him when he returns from Vietnam. Steven (John Savage) is the innocent; he is about to marry Angela (Rutanya Alda), who is already pregnant, but not by Steven. Three other men serve as foils to Michael, Nick, and Steven. Stan (John Cazale) attempts to be like Michael; Michael's obvious strengths (macho as they are at the outset of the film) become merely ridiculous as expressed in Stan's displays of bravado, claims of sexual exploits, and fascination with guns. Nick's awareness of the importance of community is paralleled by John (George Dzundra), who owns Welsh's Lounge, the bar that is the hangout of the group of friends. Singing in the choir at the wedding of Steven and Angela, he smiles above the crowd like a presiding spirit, a genius of the place, for he is the affable archangel of sociability, delighted with life and intent that people be happy, well-supplied with food and drink. Paired with Steven's innocence is the rougher innocence of Axel (Chuck Aspergrin) who asserts in his one recurrent expression--"Fuckin' A"--that all is right with his world.

By setting the film in an ethnically unified community--with its ornate Russian Orthodox cathedral, the VFW in Lemko Hall, Welsh's Lounge, The Eagle Supermarket, the bowling alley--Cimino not only telescopes the Americanization process (the "past" planted firmly in the present), but also evokes our own mythic and nostalgic desire for that communal sense these images create. These images are also a powerful metaphor for that larger national community that was splintered by the conflicting attitudes engendered by the Vietnam War. This apparent communal unity is most powerfully conveyed by the film's specific images of individuals at one with their community: the male coterie of friends emerging arm-in-arm from the steel mill; the older women of the community bearing the wedding cake through the streets to the reception hall; the men of the community organizing the decorations of the hall, dominated by enlarged graduation pictures of Michael, Nick, and Steven; plump John Welsh doing an impromptu but graceful dance at the reception; an old couple asleep in one another's arms at the end of the reception. Perhaps the most elaborate evocation of this sense of community is the folk-dance that brings the reception festivities to a close--an image of the community dancing in consort. This image expresses the ideal of communal order and joy. It is the mark of this film that, by the end, we should recall this dance and the ideal that it expresses with new insight. The dance epitomizes our longing for order and community, but it is also an image that--for the younger members of the community, at least--embodies the rituals of a barely remembered, scarcely understood past.

Interlaced with these *communal* images, however, are absences that show us an opposing force--a fragmentation that has the potential of isolating the individual from that sense of community. At the heart of the "myth" of the American community is the family. In his review, Buckley observed as a negative criticism that "in this close-knit town, scarcely anyone has a family" (86). Buckley is right, but such an absence is deliberate. The family, which *might* be the bond to hold together our fragile sense of community, is either not present or impotent as a cohesive force. Only Steven's mother and Linda's father are sketched, but these brief scenes are pointed. On the day of the wedding, Steven's mother complains to the priest about her son's approaching wedding: "My own boy. . .with a strange girl." The family here is no longer unified, and the rituals of the church fail to provide either comfort or knowledge about a community that is changing and whose assumed values are collapsing. In the scene between Linda and her father, we are given another image of the breakdown of the family.

Linda, in a bridesmaid's gown, takes lunch upstairs to her drunken and nearly incoherent father. He has ransacked the bedroom and is holding a photograph, presumably of his wife who has deserted him. Through the window we see parked cars, and the father mutters that he will slash all the tires. As Linda attempts to help him, he strikes her, and the scene ends. As a consequence of this confrontation, Linda will move out of this broken home and into Mike and Nick's trailer while they are in Vietnam. The wedding itself, which ritualizes family life, is a kind of familiar fraud. The bride is already pregnant, but not by the man she is marrying. At the marriage ceremony itself, the participants are unsure of the ritual forms; Nick and Linda, as attendants, make halting uncertain gestures as they attempt to play out their roles in the elaborate ceremonials, and Michael humorously mocks Stan, who is going through the motions of the religious rituals.

The family, which in the American past had served to bind a society together, is replaced in *The Deer Hunter* by an intricate association of friends. The male members of the group leave their graveyard shift at the steel mill and head for their early-morning beer at Welsh's Lounge. The comraderie--adolescent horseplay and pleasant obscenities--is heightened by the approach that evening of Steven's wedding and the imminent departure of Michael, Steven, and Nick, who have volunteered for service in Vietnam. This small cohesive society is breaking up; yet it is already flawed from within. The flaws are natural but potentially destructive: adolescent braggadocchio, male exclusivity, homoeroticism. In such a society, there is a fear of expressing feelings and of thereby risking isolation. Stan, for instance, reacts to something Michael says during the first deer hunt by exclaiming, "There's times I swear you're a goddamn faggot." And in an earlier scene in which Michael and Nick prepare for the post-wedding deer hunt, Nick expresses this fear of just such isolation in giving voice to his deeper feelings:

> I don't know. I guess I'm thinking about the deer. . .
> or maybe going to 'Nam. I don't know. I think about
> it all. I like the way the trees are in the mountains. All
> the different ways the trees are. I sound like an
> asshole, right?

Rituals, whether of weddings or of friendships, serve to obscure that threat of isolation[3]; the reality of isolation, however, keeps breaking through. Cimino brackets the wedding itself with two brief images of such isolation: just before the wedding ceremony, we are given a glimpse of a man alone, swigging from a bottle, leaning against a building; just after the wedding, there is an image of a woman, again alone, watching from a window the departure of the wedding party. In the most powerful image of isolation in the first third--the Clairton section--of the film, a Green Beret enters silently into the raucous wedding reception in the VFW. At the bar, Michael and his cronies attempt to make friendly contact, to find out what Vietnam is really like: "Send us where the bullets are flying, and the fighting is the worst," Nick says, adopting his companions' macho values; the Green Beret is isolated by his experience, and remains silent--except for a muttered "Fuck it!"-- in the face of their ignorance. Cimino pairs this stark image of isolation with a more playful but no less telling scene. On the dawn trip to the deer hunt following the reception, the men stop to relieve themselves after the all-night excesses of the reception. Rushing back to the car, they drive off, leaving John behind; they come back and then drive off just as John attempts to get in the car, returning just when he thinks he has been abandoned. As preludes to the implications of isolation that will occur later in the Vietnam sequences, these two scenes provide proleptic images. It is on behalf of these contradictory values of a Pennsylvania community, given to us as metaphors of the larger American experience, that the hero of Cimino's American epic is forced to act.

III

In traditional epic, the most significant man performs the most significant act. The epic hero is made to embody the most intense expression of the conflicting values of his society. At the same time, this individual may himself be--indeed, he usually is--flawed and ignorant of the vital things that he must know. It is through the action that he undertakes--an action involving great tensions between the asserted values of the society and their exacting fulfillment--that the hero gains self-knowledge, a self-knowledge that the epic text passes on to its community of readers; through the hero's *agon*, the epicist requires us, as audience, to reexamine the values involved.

Michael Vronsky is that hero and the Vietnam war that *agon*. At the end of the wedding reception, Michael (whom Nick had earlier described as a "control freak") makes a wild, Dionysiac run through the streets of Clairton, stripping off his clothes as he goes. This naked run is both a logical outcome of the communal celebration, with its potent sexual subtext, and Michael's escape from that claustrophobic communal world. Nick pursues Michael, and in the conversation that follows, exacts a promise from him:

> You know something? The whole thing is right here.
> I love this fuckin' place. I know that sounds crazy, but
> if something happens, Mike, don't leave me. You gotta
> promise me, Mike. You gotta promise. You got to.
> Mike replies, "Hey, you got it, pal."

In making this apparently simple promise to Nick, Michael assumes--at once naturally, deliberately, and ignorantly--the whole burden of an action that will ultimately test his values and attitudes and those of the society for which he must act. In the *Aeneid*, Aeneas gazes ignorantly on the images on the shield given him by his goddess mother:

> Aeneas marvels at his mother's gift, the scenes on
> Vulcan's shield; and he is glad for all these images,
> *though he does not know what they mean.* Upon his
> shoulder he lifts up the fame and fate of his sons' sons.
> (VIII, 951-55; emphasis added)

Like Aeneas, Michael assumes the burden of the heroic undertaking with a fundamental ignorance of what values will be tested and what price will be exacted from him and his community on the way to their fulfillment.

As *The Deer Hunter* presents him, Michael *is* his nation. He embodies the American myth; he is, as Wallace Stevens has phrased it, "his nation made one" (279). Like that nation, he carries in himself the potential both for destructive ignorance and of saving wisdom. He is a version, first of all, of American industrial man. We see him first against the background of the fires of the steel mill. As Auster and Quart aptly point out, the steel mill here "is neither a monstrous polluter of a virginal landscape, nor a 'dark satanic mill' filled with alienated workers" (6). The mill in its force and fire celebrates industrial society; yet it is also evident, as we see in Michael's attitude toward the approaching deer hunt, that his authentic being is rooted in that "virginal landscape."

Michael is at once the essential touchstone of his community and an outsider. Throughout the film, Michael is imaged as such an outsider, shown standing at the edges of the scene, simply observing the action. As Stan says, "Mike, there's sometimes nobody but a doctor can understand you." As the solitary outsider, he is the hunter of the title and of the American myth. In his review, Schlesinger cites to advantage Richard Slotkin's *Regeneration through Violence: The Mythology of the American Frontier* (1973), relating Michael to the white hunter-heroes of the myth.[4] Although Schlesinger, like too many other critics, sees Michael only as an unchanging character in the film as he embodies that myth, it is a fact that, at least in the first half of the film, Michael is indeed the static embodiment of that potent myth. In the naked run after the wedding, Michael attempts to escape from the restrictions of the society; in his aloofness, Michael sets himself against the social order. "The white hunter-heroes of the myth," Slotkin argues,". . . are men of solitude, men whose intense privacy sets them temporarily or permanently against the social order. The wilderness for them is an alternative to the obligations/protections/restrictions of civilization" (559). And, like Slotkin's mythic hunter-figure, Michael ventures both backward and forward in our national history (see Slotkin 559-60). In the opening sequences of *The Deer Hunter*, Michael ventures unknowingly, even ignorantly, into the unfolding history of our war in Vietnam, strengthened yet burdened by the values inherent in American myth. And through Michael, we also make contact with those myths of the American past. Emerging from the steel mill, Steven glimpses a solar phenomenon. What he sees is a halo around the sun and, at four points on the rim of the halo, miniature replicas of the sun itself. It is Michael who interprets this solar image to his now urbanized industrial society: "Sun dogs," he says, "a sign. A blessing on the hunters sent by the Great Wolf to his children. . . . It's an old Indian thing." By setting the film in a distinct ethnic locale, Cimino, as I have suggested, has given us a condensed history of the "Americanization" process--from the "old Indian thing" through immigration to an industrial society--with all the ambiguities that that process entails; in the "sun dogs" episode, he reaches back to that Indian heritage. The immediate point of the scene is to establish Michael's mythic qualities and to emphasize his role as an interpreter of that past. As Kenneth Rexroth has said, "Our memory of the indians connects us with the soil and the waters and the non-human life about us. They take the place of nymphs and satyrs and dryads--the spirits of place"(35; cited in Slotkin 17). So the "sun dogs" scene connects Michael to these "spirits of place." At the same time, Michael's "memory" of this Indian past is made ironic by the urban setting: the community that Michael speaks to and for is cut off from any sense of that past, while he, the outsider, attempts to give voice to and, ultimately, to act on behalf of, the values of that dimly-remembered past. Michael's initial version of the values inherent in the "hunter" myth is stated in an early scene with Nick. Michael says, "A deer should be taken with one shot. One shot is what it's all about. You try to tell people. But they won't listen."

The "one-shot" ideal that Michael expresses has a dual function in the film. It embodies an absolute value--a sense of fair play, of discipline, of purity. In the first deer hunt, before Michael goes to Vietnam, he takes a buck with one clean shot, a scene contrasted to the deer hunt after Michael's return from Vietnam in which Stan sloppily wounds a deer. In the larger context of the film, however, the implicit link between the "one-shot" ideal and our involvement in Vietnam illustrates Cimino's more important point: our belief, rooted in our myths, that as a nation we could solve that complex historical situation by "one-shot."

Michael's wilderness values and his exclusivity and absolutes--the "one-shot" principle--will be modified by the *agon* of his Vietnam experience; however, these initial values are placed in relief by Nick even before those traumatic events. He provides the antidote to Michael's absolutes by his instinctive generosity of spirit. Nick embraces many of Michael's values but refines their macho, alienating aspects: "I don't think about one-shot that much anymore," Nick had said early in the film. "I like the way the trees are in the mountains. All the different ways the trees are." Nick, as the catastrophe will reveal, embodies and indeed is ultimately the victim of the paradoxes inherent in the "one-shot" ideal. Throughout the film, a visual link is made between Nick and the deer. In the scene in which Michael states his "one-shot" credo, Nick and a deer head are framed in the same image. Slotkin provides a passage that serves as an apt commentary on this scene:

> Yet the paradox is itself the essence of the myth of the hunter, in which each man kills the thing he loves, and the thing he loves is both his darker self and his necessary other half. . . . In the act of seeking and struggling with the other self, one's own identity is created and confirmed. (429)

Michael's absolute "one-shot" ideal is ultimately humanized by Nick, Michael's "necessary other half," but the enactment of the "one-shot" absolute within history--within the complexities of the Vietnam war-- reveals the "darker self" by which Michael's own identity is created and confirmed but in which Nick's identity tragically becomes cut off from humanity, a victim of Michael's initial "one-shot" value.

In a confrontation between Michael and Stan during the first deer hunt, it is Nick's responses that emphasize the potential flaws in Michael's values. Stan has--as usual--come off unprepared; Michael, in a tense scene, refuses to give Stan his own extra pair of hunting boots. When he is refused, Stan sarcastically asks, "What are you going to do, shoot me?" There is--for a split second--the implication that Michael may do just that. It is Nick who gives Stan his own boots, maintaining, through that action, at least an appearance of community. Nick looks disgustedly at Michael: "What's the matter with you?" It is Nick who makes the essential connection between community and the enduring spirit of place.

Associated with the potentially destructive aspects of the "one-shot" ideal is Michael's (and his community's) ignorance of the complexities of history. Just before the wedding, Michael looks at his reflection in a mirror. Nick asks, "You trying to look like a prince?" Just above Michael's head in this brief scene is a photograph of John F. Kennedy. Just as Michael's "sun dog" speech connects him to the American past, so this image connects Michael to a more immediate "heroic" past. Such a juxtaposition in a film that concerns our involvement in Vietnam recalls the stirring rhetoric of Kennedy's inaugural (1961), heroic rhetoric that was to be tested--and for many, discredited--by the actualities of Vietnam:

> Let every nation know, whether it wishes us good or ill,
> that we shall pay any price, bear any burden, meet any
> hardship, support any friend, oppose any foe, to assure
> the survival and success of liberty.

Michael and the community on behalf of which he acts are profoundly ignorant, at the outset, of the price that will be exacted by history in the attempted fulfillment of such a heroic pledge. It is with these inherent strengths and implicit weaknesses that, like Aeneas, the hero of *The Deer Hunter* takes up the burden of history. In epic terms, Nick's request to Michael evokes Elpenor's request to Odysseus: "I ask that you remember me, and do not go and leave me behind unwept, unburied when you leave" (XI, 71-73). Michael's promise is made out of friendship and love, but neither Michael nor Nick can comprehend what the request and promise will exact.

IV

The implied fissures in the sense of community, conveyed most powerfully in the first third of the film by images of isolation, become explicit in the central Vietnam sequence. War creates inhumanity; in *The Deer Hunter*, a sense of community metamorphosizes suddenly into the terrors of isolation. The friends return from the post-wedding deer hunt and gather in Welsh's Lounge. They sing a boozy rendition of "Drop Kick Me, Jesus, Through the Goal Posts of Life." The mood changes as John plays a moving version of a Chopin Nocturne. This is farewell; the camera lingers on all the characters but perhaps most poignantly on Stan, who is not going to Vietnam. He is in the shadows, isolated from the group. At the end of the sequence, as Nick raises a can of Rolling Rock Beer in silent toast, we hear the sound of helicopters. We are in Vietnam, plunged into an attack on a Vietnamese village. Thus, in one of the most skillful transitions in recent films, Cimino uses sound and track overlap to bring Vietnam into the bar, into the community itself.

Rituals that attempted to preserve the sense of community now give way to destructive, dehumanizing rituals. The three friends--Michael, Nick, and Steven--fortuitously are reunited in battle, are captured, and are forced by their North Vietnamese captors to play Russian roulette. Much has been made of this particular incident, especially its racist overtones and the way Russian roulette is used as a continuing metaphor in the film. Arlen argues that these scenes prove that "the movie maker has lost touch with his material and so has dipped into his grab bag of powerful visual effects" (125). It *is* a powerful visual effect--recalling as it does the famous photograph of a Vietnamese policeman executing another Vietnamese--but it is also organic, a deliberate extension and counter-point to the "one-shot" ideal. Russian roulette is the logical outcome of the darker elements of that mystique and conveys, in a way no set battle piece could do, the terribleness of *this* war and the utter randomness of death. One of the few critics who grasped the significance of the Russian roulette sequences has written that "[T]he roulette game becomes a metaphor for a war that blurred the lines between bravery and cruelty, friends and enemies, sanity and madness" (Rich 86).

Michael himself nearly falls victim to such a blurring. Forced to play Russian roulette in imprisonment with Michael and Nick, Steven is overwhelmed by its horror; he falters and, wounded and traumatized, is thrown into the river pit-cage by his captors. From the cage, Steven calls to Michael for help, but Michael tells Nick to forget him because Steven is not going to be able to make it. Once again, it is Nick who is the voice of humanity: "Who do you think you are? God?" Turning his gun on their captors, Michael pulls off the rescue of Nick and himself and then, without words being exchanged, rescues Steven from the pit-cage. Later, while Michael, Nick, and Steven are being plucked from the river by a rescuing helicopter, the weakened Steven drops from the ropes of the helicopter, and Michael deliberately drops into the river to save him. The image of Michael pulling the injured Steven from the river and putting him on his (Michael's) back is one of the clearest evocations of a specific epic episode: in the *Aeneid*, Aeneas lifts his father Anchises on his back as they escape from Troy:

> Come then, dear father, mount upon my neck; I'll bear
> you on my shoulders. That is not too much for me.
> Whatever waits for me, we both shall share one danger,
> one salvation. (II, 956-59)

Yet as Roy Harvey Pearce has pointed out, the American epicist has "to break radically with the very tradition which he would be trying to carry on and invigorate" (362). In Cimino's revision of the Virgilian episode, Michael bears on his shoulder a modern version of the "world of fathers and of founders of families, a world of 'firsts' and 'bests'," but that "world" has been seen as already fissured. and what Michael bears is a past nearly emptied of value and an uncertain future that may contain only a dubious promise of "salvation."

The terrors of isolation, touched on in the earlier Clairton section, now have become a terrible reality. Michael puts Steven on an American jeep that is--with hordes of refugees--fleeing toward Saigon, and Michael and Steven are separated. Nick, saved by the helicopter but separated from his comrades and overcome by guilt, has every reason to believe Michael and Steven are dead. From a seat in a Saigon military hospital, he looks out on rows and rows of caskets; when he does tell his name to a doctor, the doctor asks if his name--Cevotarevich--is a foreign name. "American," Nick answers. When he tries to make contact with that world of American innocence in a phone call to Linda, he is incapable of completing the call. He wanders in the chaotic streets of Saigon, rushes up to a figure that he mistakes for Michael, and then goes first into a brothel and then into a gambling den where Russian roulette is being played for sport. Stunned by the scene, Nick disrupts the game, pulling the trigger first against one of the participant's head and then against his own. The gun doesn't fire, but Nick's isolation is all but complete as he is propositioned by a Frenchman to join the insanity of the game of roulette. This last scene of this central section of the film shows Michael also isolated. Having put Steven on the Jeep, Michael has made his way back to Saigon and is in the same gambling den, coldly observing the roulette game, when he catches a glimpse of Nick; as Nick rushes into the crowded streets, Michael is unable to reach him and loses him in the confusion.

This theme of isolation is carried out in Michael's return to a hero's welcome in Clairton. He is unable to face the celebration prepared for him and hunkers down in a motel room, alone. He has lost track of both Nick and Steven. He finds out, eventually, that Nick is AWOL and that Steven is in a veterans' hospital. Reduced to a catatonic state by events, Angela (Steven's wife) scribbles a phone number on a scrap of paper for Michael. Like Nick earlier, Michael is unable to complete this call, and his own isolation is now complete. He has proven himself a hero in terms of American myth, the absolute values of which have enabled him to rescue both Nick and Steven from the prison camp; on his return, however, those heroic values have been emptied, by his experience, of their saving potential.

In a bowling alley scene, Michael now stands alone, watching Linda--who is wearing Nick's bowling shirt. Suddenly Axel pins himself beneath the pin-setting machine, and everyone instinctively looks to Michael. This parodic "heroic" rescue superficially restores Michael to the group and begins his re-entry into the community. Yet the ignorance of that community, now contrasted to Michael's greater knowledge, is also emphasized; at the end of the "rescue," the friends walk arm-in-arm once again, and Axel proposes a deer hunt: "Just like the old days; no women." For Michael--separated by Vietnam from Nick and Steven and from Linda by his devotion to Nick--the old macho ethic no longer has the power of truth or salvation.

Perhaps nowhere in the film is the fragility of community emphasized more intensely than in the second deer hunt and the scenes that follow. Michael, now alone, tracks a magnificent buck. He gets the deer in his sights, but at the very last second raises his gun as he fires. This action by the modern deerslayer emphasizes that the lessons of the past must be relearned in the present: "There may not be any cowardice, in overcoming a deer," Natty Bumppo says in *The Deerslayer*, "but sartain it is, there's no great valour" (499-500). But the modern Deer Hunter's unarticulated sense of what he has learned is not easily communicated to that community of friends who still live under the old values. When Michael returns to the hunting cabin, Axel has made a crack about Stan's "stupid little gun." Stan cocks the gun and aims it at Axel: "Say that one more time: one fucking more time! Go on, say it." The image and Stan's rhythm of speech evoke the North Vietnamese roulette sequence; Michael is enraged, and his outrage is aimed not only at Stan's stupid behavior but at the entire family of friends:

> You guys want to play games? Then I'm going to play
> your fuckin' games! I'm going to show you how it's
> really played.

Michael reenacts the roulette scenes, holding the gun against Stan's head. Stan's flippant question on the first deer hunt--"What are you going to do, shoot me?"--receives its answer. Michael shoots; only by chance does the gun click on a empty chamber. Michael's action is an act of intense love that is close to hate. He desperately needs to communicate the inadequacy of the old values and the meaning of his experiences in Vietnam to his community. The "one-shot" ideal has proven inadequate to the demands imposed upon it by history, and his actions leave the friends stunned and uncomprehending. Returning from the aborted deer hunt, Michael goes alone into the trailer he once shared with Nick. The friends slowly disperse, ignorant of the forces that have erupted to destroy the communal sense of "the old times."

This third section of the film, beginning with Michael's return to Clairton, is shaped by the hero's struggle to discover values that will now suffice. His recognition of the true significance of community is made all the more powerful by his own sense of alienation. Following his destruction of the community after the second deer hunt, it is Michael who acts to rebuild that communal sense. Throughout the film, Michael's intense but suppressed love for Linda has been visually expressed; his suppression of his feelings is made all the more poignant when, on his first meeting with Linda after his return, she says, "Oh, Michael, I was hoping. . . somehow that Nick would be with you." Yet it is Linda who attempts to comfort Michael by asking him to go to bed with her, an invitation that he at first rejects.

It is after this and the second deer hunt, with Michael's traumatic confrontation with Stan, that he now seeks out Linda and finally goes to bed with her. The scene is almost entirely visual; out of context, its images would be unremarkable, even banal; yet these images now have nearly three hours of allusion built into them: an image of Michael and Linda in bed; an image of Michael looking out of the window at the mills in Clairton; an image of a deer head. It is impossible, as someone has said, to imagine the truly heroic without love. Michael is able to embrace Linda, his sexual being now able to transcend the narrow limits of the male myth. This sexual fulfillment is linked with moral wisdom. Michael sees the community and comprehends the meaning of Nick's earlier words, "It's all here." The image of the deer head recalls the "one-shot" ideal and, through the association of Nick and the deer, Michael's promise to Nick. These images, without accompanying dialogue, suggest that the most complex moment of heroism is within, the inarticulate moment of decision and commitment and love. Michael goes forth to reestablish the necessary sense of community.

He goes out into the night to call Steven, now completing the connection that he had resisted earlier. In finding and rescuing Steven, now an amputee, Michael saves Steven from his self-imposed isolation and restores him to the community. In the conversation with Steven in the hospital, he discovers that Nick is still in Saigon. He makes, then, the heroic descent into the underworld, returning to Saigon at the moment of its fall to attempt the rescue of Nick.

What Michael encounters is a Nick shattered by his confrontation with an unnatural world. Nick was, to use Virgil's phrase, *insignis pietate*--remarkable for goodness--but now he has been brutally dehumanized by war and its consequences. Nick now plays the symbolic game of war--Russian roulette--for money. Except for an enigmatic thread of elephant heads and money that he has somehow sent on to Steven, Nick is totally isolated from the community that he loved. When Michael first reencounters him and speaks to him in that underworld, Nick has no memory of the past or of Michael. In a supreme act of devotion to Nick and the values that he embodied, Michael contrives to oppose Nick in the game of Russian roulette in the hopes of breaking through Nick's terrible isolation. He reminds Nick of the past that they once shared, first recalling Nick's love of the trees and then by recalling the "one-shot" mystique with which Michael had imbued Nick. At last, Michael says, "I love you, Nick." This scene contains a terrible paradox. Michael's statement of love begins to awaken Nick's memory, but it is the reference to the "one-shot" that has real effect. For a flickering moment, Nick recognizes Michael; in that second, Nick pulls the trigger and kills himself.

The chilling paradox is that it is Michael's initial ideals (expressing as they do the American myth) that have put us in Vietnam; Nick is there for other ideals--patriotism, belief in communal values, comradeship. His ideals cannot stand up to the intolerable burden put upon them. Michael has moved, as we have already seen in the second deer hunt sequence, far beyond the "one-shot" mystique; he has achieved and, by his descent into the underworld, has surpassed Nick's own earlier instinctive expression of civilizing, communal values. Yet the very value that Michael has now outgrown is the very value that results in the destruction of Nick, *insignis pietate*.

V

The *Iliad* closes with a funeral and a feast:

> They piled up the grave-barrow and went away, and thereafter assembled in a fair gathering, and held a glorious feast within the house of Priam, king under God's hand. Such was their burial of Hektor, breaker of horses. (XXIV, 801-804)

Like that other epic close, *The Deer Hunter* ends with a funeral and a feast: the funeral of Nick who, like Hektor, embodied the best of his society's values, and a feast of the mourners who survive. As in most of its epic predecessors, *The Deer Hunter*'s ending is a warring of intense emotions, a mixture of triumph and tragedy, of hope and despair. And, like most epics, the ending is elegiac, celebrating an order that no longer prevails.

This elegiac note in the film is sounded first on the larger historical canvas. A television set is on in Welsh's Lounge, and Hillary Brown of ABC is reporting the final collapse of South Vietnam and the chaotic attempts to rescue troops and civilians from the fall. We watch a helicopter being toppled from the deck of a carrier: "This seems to be the last chapter in the history of America's involvement in Vietnam," Brown reports. Such an attempt to write *finis* to the anguish engendered by our involvement there is a delusion, of course, one anticipated in a Clairton storekeeper's earlier remark to Michael, "We won over there, didn't we?" But the history of our involvement in Vietnam is imaged not only on the grand scale that the reporter describes but in the shattering of the lives of the Clairton community of friends, a metaphor for the nation itself.

From the scenes on television, the film cuts to Nick's funeral. Michael is one of the pallbearers, and, in an image that eerily anticipates the reflections of observers in the Vietnam Memorial, Michael sees himself reflected in the surface of Nick's casket. After the graveyard service, near one barren tree in an otherwise barren landscape ("I like," Nick had said, "all the different ways the trees are") the friends, awkward in their grief, gather in Welsh's Lounge. In his wheelchair, Steven is helped into the bar, but his wife and child stand apart. For Michael and Linda, the memory of Nick at once links and separates them. No one knows what to do; the friends fumble with cups, with silverware, with the rituals of grief. "It certainly is a grey day," Angela remarks. In a tentative act of reconciliation, Steven reaches out for Angela's hand and kisses it. Alone in the kitchen, John Welsh breaks into wrenching tears. "Who could have guessed," Linda had said even before the death of Nick, "that things would turn out like this?" Still alone in the kitchen, John begins first to hum and then to sing the words of "God Bless America." In the other room, the song is picked up, first by Michael and then by Linda and finally by the entire group as John comes in to join them.

No scene in the film, with the possible exception of the Russian roulette sequences, has engendered so much debate and harsh criticism as the intentions of this final scene. Frank Rich wondered whether one was meant to laugh or cry (26); Lance Morrow felt that it had "the effect of being an absolution, a subtle exoneration of the American role in Vietnam" (24); Buckley, in perhaps the harshest comment, felt that in this scene "the political and moral issues of the Vietnam war. . .are

entirely ignored" (88). These criticisms mistake the true moral concern
of *The Deer Hunter*. If I am right in suggesting the film's epic intent
and Cimino's efforts to underscore the fragile sense of community, then
there is a profound morality in this controversial scene. Cimino intends
to communicate not only what the individual characters are feeling in
this ambiguous moment, but intends to force us, its audience, to
confront the "realization of a moral truth."

Though gathered as a tenuously reassembled community in Welsh's
Lounge, each of the characters comes to the moment with complex and
private feelings about the meaning of Nick's death, a death that is the
audience's most potent symbol for the implications of our Vietnam
adventure.   Steven, now restored to the community, has made an
attempt to rescue Angela from her catatonic state; Axel and Stan, who
did not go to Vietnam, come to the gathering with their own guilt and
the knowledge that their world of innocent camaraderie has been
altered forever; Linda, mourning Nick and loving Michael, must
reconcile loss and love; John, who only ever wanted all his friends to
have a good time, now must weep. Of all the characters, it is Michael
alone who comprehends fully the price that has been paid. He had
tried, in the hunting lodge scene, to communicate that knowledge to his
friends and has, inevitably, failed. In this final scene, he still wears his
Green Beret uniform--recalling as it does the burdened silent soldier at
the wedding reception--and emphasizing Michael's own unwillingness
or inability to shed that emblem of his burden. John, alone in the
kitchen, now reaches after something that may give comfort. What he
reaches after is a sense of order, a sense of the past, reaching back to
that sustaining spirit of place, the "land that I love," that Nick had
celebrated in his statement, "It's all here." At the end of the song,
Michael proposes a toast--echoing Nick's earlier silent toast at the end
of the first deer hunt--"To Nick." Coming at the conclusion of the song,
this commemoration of Nick represents all the ideals that--as a result
of the Vietnam war---we have begun to doubt. Nick symbolizes that
innocence that we perhaps now can no longer believe and, by his loss,
all the values of community that seem at the point of vanishing as we
move toward an doubtful and demystified future.

In the same issue of *Harper's* in which Tom Buckley's comments on
The Deer Hunter appeared, John Lahr wrote of "The new barbarianism
--a nation that has no faith in the peace it seeks or the pleasures it
finds" (28). The comment is now over a decade old, and interpretation
of American "faith" and "pleasures" has gone through much political
and social revision. Yet, in Cimino's film, understood as an American
epic, the hero, at once embodying the American myth and moving from
parochial ignorance to a more communal vision, struggles to reconstruct

that essential sense of community. In that heroic action, he epitomizes our attempt, imperfect and incomplete as it must be, to find faith in the peace we seek and the pleasures we find.

Notes

1. *The Deer Hunter*. Universal Pictures and EMI Films. Story by Michael Cimino and Deric Washburn and Louis Garfinkle & Quinn K. Redeker. Screenplay by Deric Washburn; dir. Michael Cimino. I have quoted directly from the film, with reference to "Location Draft" (28 January 1973), property of EMI Films, Inc., Lost Angeles, California, and to *The Deer Hunter* [a novelization based on the screenplay] (New York: Jove Publications [Harcourt Brace Jovanovich], 1978).

2. The significance of rituals in *The Deer Hunter* is perceptively discussed in Robert T. Eberwein's "Ceremonies of Survival: The Structure of *The Deer Hunter*," *The Journal of Popular Film and Television* 7 (1979): 352-364.

3. After I had completed this essay, I encountered John Hellmann's excellent *American Myth and the Legacy of Vietnam* (New York: Columbia University Press, 1986). He considers *The Deer Hunter* in his chapter, "Epic Return" (pp. 171-204); our approach to the film coincides in some ways, but Hellmann treats *The Deer Hunter* not so much as epic but as a film "whose inspiration is obviously the western's frontier mythos" (173).

4. "The white hunter-heroes of the myth," Slotkin argues, "who are identified as men of solitude, men whose intense privacy sets them temporarily or permanently against the social order. The wilderness for them is an alternative to the obligation/protections/restrictions of civilization. They are, as [D. H.] Lawrence says, integral souls venturing outward in space and backward or forward in history; or, as Melville puts it, '*Isolatoes*,' 'fleeing from all havens astern.' The image of the solitary hunter is, however, an imposition of a colonial vision of social conflict on the indian. For the tribesman, wilderness life, notwithstanding its requirement of hunting, was one of community rather than solitude. For the indian the wilderness was home, the locus of the tribe that was the center of his metaphysical universe as well as his social existence. Even in moments of physical solitude, on a long hunt or a vision quest, the world community about him remained intact,

for the gods and the wild animals were his fellows and his kin. The border of tribal solidarity extended out from the village center to the edges of creation. The white hunter was an alien, *paradoxically achieving a sense of profound physical, moral, and psychological isolation* [emphasis added]. His destiny was personal rather than tribal; his moral obligation was to himself, his 'gifts,' and his racial character, rather than to his fellows and his environment" (559-560). It is notable that Cimino's "hunter-hero" starts out by fulfilling these characteristics; however, in the process of the epic *agon*, Michael moves from a destiny that is "personal" to one in which he comprehends that his "moral obligation" is indeed to the larger community, "to his fellows and to his environment."

Works Cited

Abercrobie, Lascelles. *The Epic*. London, 1914; rpt. Freeport, New York: Books for Libraries Press, 1969

Arlen, Michael J. "The Tyranny of the Visual." *The New Yorker*. 23 April 1979: 125-26.

Arnett, Peter. "War Reporter Compares Deer Hunter to Reality." Special to the *Los Angeles Times*; rpt. in *The Times-Picyune* (New Orleans, Louisiana). 13 April 1979: *Fanfare*, 6-7.

Auster, Al and Leonard Quart. "Hollywood and Vietnam: The Triumph of the Will." *Cineaste* 9, No. 3 (Spring, 1979): 4-9.

Bakhtin, M. M. *The Dialogic Imagination. Four Essays by M. M. Bakhtin*. Ed. Michael Holquist. Translated by Caryl Emerson and Michael Holquist. Austin and London: University of Texas Press, 1981.

Bowra, C. M. *From Virgil to Milton*. London: Macmillan & Co., 1948.

Buckley, Tom. "Hollywood's War." *Harper's*. April, 1979: 84-88.

Cooper, James Fenimore. *The Deerslayer; or the First War-Path*. In *The Leatherstocking Tales*. Vol II. Ed. Blake Nevius. New York: Literary Classics of the United States [The Library of America], 1985.

Eberwein, Robert T. "Ceremonies of Survival: The Structure of *The Deer Hunter*," *The Journal of Popular Film and Television* 7 (1979): 352- 364.

Hodenfield, Chris. "Point-blank: *The Deer Hunter's* Christopher Walken." *Rolling Stone*. 8 March 1979: 27-28.

Homer. *Iliad*. Trans. with an Introduction by Richmond Lattimore. Chicago: University of Chicago Press, 1962.

---. *Odyssey*. Trans. Robert Fitzgerald. Garden City, N. Y.: Anchor, 1963.

Horton, Andrew. "Film as History and Myth in Bertolucci's *1900*" *Film and History* 10 (Spring, 1980): 9-16.

Kael, Pauline. "The God-Bless America Symphony." *The New Yorker*. 18 Dec., 1978: 66-79.

Lahr, John. "Sondheim's Little Deaths: The Ironic Mode and its Discontents." *Harper's*. Apr. 1979: 71-78.

Lubow, Arthur. "Natty Bumppo Goes to War." *Atlantic Monthly*. Apr. 1979: 95-98.

Morrow, Lance. "Viet Nam Comes Home: Two Winning Films Signal the Struggle to Learn from a Lost War." *Time*. 27 Apr. 1979:22-28.

Pearce, Roy Harvey. *The Continuity of American Poetry*. Princeton: Princeton University Press, 1961.

---. "Toward an American Epic." *Hudson Review* 13 (1959):362-377; rpt. in *Parnassus Revisited: Modern Critical Essays on the Epic Tradition*. Ed. Anthony C. Yu. Chicago: American Library Association, 1973: 342-353.

Quinn, Kenneth. *Virgil's* Aeneid: *A Critical Description*. Ann Arbor: University of Michigan Press, 1969.

Rexroth, Kenneth. "Classics Revisited LXI: Parkman's History. *Saturday Review of Literature*. February 24, 1968: 35.

Rich, Frank. "In Hell without a Map." *Time*. 18 Dec. 1978:
    86.

Schlesinger, Arthur, Jr. "Deer Hunter, Man Slayer." *Saturday
    Review*. 17 February 1979: 50-51.

Slotkin, Richard. *Regeneration through Violence: The Mythology of the
    American Frontier 1600-1800*. Middletown, Conn.: W e s l e y a n
    University Press, 1973.

Stevens, Wallace. *The Collected Poems of Wallace Stevens*. New York:
    Alfred A. Knopf, 1964.

Tillyard, E. M. W. *The English Epic and its Background*. New York:
    Oxford University Press, 1966.

Virgil. *The Aeneid of Virgil*. Trans. Allan Mandelbaum. New York:
    Bantam Books, 1972.

STYLE IN *DISPATCHES*: HETEROGLOSSIA AND MICHAEL HERR'S BREAK WITH CONVENTIONAL JOURNALISM

Matthew C. Stewart

When *Dispatches* appeared in 1977, Michael Herr's nonfiction account of his days in Vietnam was quickly recognized by several reviewers as one of the finest works about the Vietnam War. Since then it has become one of a handful of books consistently to receive critical attention when Vietnam War literature is the topic. Much of this recognition stems from the work's distinctive, highly crafted style, its obvious desire to couple an overt sense of literariness with nonfiction reporting on Vietnam. Typically, even those who chide Herr praise his stylistic virtuosity.[1]

One does not read far into *Dispatches* without realizing that it is intent on breaking the rules of ordinary journalism. Indeed, this work is not the usual collection of essays strictly arranged in either chronological order or according to discreet, well-marked-out topics and written in an objective, reportorial style. In the process of departing from conventional practices, Herr periodically alludes to the failures of mainstream journalism without ever elaborating on them at length in any one section. The reader must piece together his scattered statements and draw inferences from the countertraditional nature of Herr's work itself to make any catalogue of the exact nature of these failures. But there is no mistaking his belief in the inadequacy of status-quo journalistic practices and style. "Conventional journalism could no more reveal this war," he writes, "than conventional firepower could win it, all it could do was take the most profound event of the American decade and turn it into a communications pudding . . ." (232). We learn that Herr abandons many of the precepts of journalistic practice and transcends the ordinary or expected journalistic style of writing partly because traditional reporting is impossible under the circumstances and partly because his own interests and involvement in the war necessitate a new journalism.

In his search for a suitable form, Herr frequently crosses into novelistic territory. One need not have a rigidly narrow conception of what a novel is to decide that *Dispatches* is not, in the end, a novel in any traditional conception of the genre. However, much of its newness, and consequently its literary effectiveness, is grounded in novelistic techniques. By *novelistic* I mean to invoke not only a traditional, mainstream conception of the literary genre, but also and especially M. M. Bakhtin's conception of "novelness" as a heteroglossia of dialogized voices, as propounded in his essay "Discourse in the Novel."

Dispatches is a demanding book in that it requires not so much the traditional reader of history or memoirs, one who is ready to sit back and soak up facts, opinions and interpretations of Vietnam, perhaps periodically pausing to quibble or disagree with the writer's conclusions; rather, it requires a reader willing to collaborate in a truth revealed more often than not in pieces, by fits and starts, by accumulation and repetition, by variations on theme. Herr's style itself asserts that whole truths--unadulterated, unambiguous truths--may be in short supply even when they are assiduously striven for. In *Dispatches* Herr's truths about Vietnam are inextricably linked with self-discovery, and the foregrounding not only of these truths but of the methods and means by which Herr and, thus, the reader gain access to them is as much a part of his story as the truths themselves.

As for the circumstances which necessitated unorthodox coverage, Herr suggests that very few reporters were able to surmount or circumvent standard procedures to establish the truth of the war "because they worked in the news media, for organizations that were ultimately reverential toward the institutions involved: the Office of the President, the Military, America at war and, most of all, the empty technology that characterized Vietnam" (228). Yet, Herr is not interested in blaming his more conventional colleagues. They are largely seen to be victims of an ineluctable system which seems to have taken on a life of its own, controlling input and output about America's involvement in Southeast Asia. In addition to this monolithic system set up to "handle" the media, most correspondents (and soldiers) suffered from a framework of consciousness almost indelibly stamped with various impressions, with mental and emotional constructs, shaped by long-term and repeated exposure to media versions of reality.

Herr testifies to the insidious potency of the media for all those who went to cover Vietnam:

> We'd all seen too many movies, stayed too long in Television City, years of media glut had made certain connections difficult. The first few times that I got fired at or saw combat deaths, nothing really happened, all the responses got locked in my head. It was the same familiar violence, only moved over to another medium; some kind of jungle play with giant helicopters and fantastic special effects, actors lying out there in canvas body bags waiting for the scene to end so they could get up again and walk it off. But

that was some scene (you found out), there was no
cutting it. (223)

So those who hope to depict Vietnam are apt to find themselves
trapped within pre-packaged images and programmed responses which
nullify or detract from their ability to engage their experiences as
unmediated, authentic versions of reality. The journalist's first task,
then, was to overcome obstacles so well integrated into the self that he
or she was not even initially aware of their existence ("a lot of things
had to be unlearned before you could learn anything at all" [224]). As
John Hellmann has said, "even the most terrible facts will not provide
sufficient information for one to grasp truth unless the structures of
consciousness organizing them are changed as well" (150). In his
stylistic ground breaking and his departures from the journalistic norm,
we see Herr in the very process of reorganizing these structures.

The Vietnam reporter had to face still other problems, problems
created by and inherent in the system responsible for the transfer,
dispersal, and--although those within the system would not have cared
to admit it--very often the creation of "information."[2] Herr periodically
makes manifest his disdain for the information passed on to the press
by government and military liaisons, as in the following example:

> Rounding Le Loi there was a large group of
> correspondents coming back from the briefing,
> standard diurnal informational freak-o-rama, Five
> O'Clock Follies, Jive at Five, war stories; at the
> corner they broke formation and went to their offices
> to file, we watched them, the wasted clocking the
> wasted. (37)[3]

Of course the sarcastic diction carries most of the meaning here, but it
is also interesting to note the play on words involved in the coinage
"*information*al freak-o-rama," a reference to the fundamental falseness
and ludicrous uselessness of the briefing, and the "formation" of duty-
bound, blinkered journalists about to pass on what they have "learned."
In one of his most damning statements, Herr in fact concludes that "in
Saigon it never mattered what they told you, even less when they
actually seemed to believe it" (44). The writer in pursuit of truth in
Vietnam, then, not only had to free his mind, but had to develop ways
of freeing himself from the system's "war stories" and finding his own.

For Herr this escape to freedom, which resulted in both self-
discovery and fine reportage, seems to have entailed a happy

combination of necessity and personal proclivity. He shows himself as being most interested in getting a "grunt's eye" view of Vietnam, evidently believing that the most important aspects of the war resided in the lower echelon, in the mundane fright and grind of the combat GI, and most of all in the ever-presence of death. "The press got all the facts (more or less), it got too many of them," Herr believes. "But it never found a way to report meaningfully about death, which of course was really what it was all about" (229). Not a few people have tried to explain that "it" was "about" many things beside (or alongside) death: political struggle, nationalism, imperialism, centuries of history, race relations, economic struggle. But for Herr the import of the clashes of these fundamental, global forces is to be found in the conduct and suffering of the United States soldier. This is a book in which an interview with General Westmoreland is relegated to five sentences enclosed carefully within parentheses, but in which slang-filled, obscenity-riddled conversations with ungrammatical, anonymous grunts are given center stage. By the end of the section entitled "Colleagues," Herr has made it overtly clear that his sense of writerly mission is inextricably bound together with the belief that he must serve as prolocutor for the grunts: "And always, they would ask you with an emotion whose intensity would shock you to please tell it, because they really did have the feeling that it wasn't being told for them, that they were going through all of this and that somehow no one back in the World knew about it" (220).

Throughout Herr shows his allegiance to the grunts not only with such overt pronouncements but in the very diction he uses, a language replete with both the historically charged slang of the late sixties and the special lingo of the men in the field: "cool," "cooled things out," "uptight," "digging it," "cream you," "scarfed," "spaced," "fucked up," "going down," "bad," "freak," "get stoned," "get laid," "get straight," "groove," "strung out," "chop," "grease," "wired," "wasted," "thousand-yard stare," "candy-assed," "zapped." This is not an exhaustive list of words and phrases found in Herr's own narration--not in quotation of others (although quoted speech is also full of such slang), but as his own language, adopted for the project of delivering the reality of Vietnam.[4]

Consistent with Bakhtin's conception of jostling languages, Herr's adoption of his generation's language is not only a positive act, willed to give voice to the voiceless; it must also be seen as reacting in opposition to the language of those in authority.[5] It is both action and reaction. Herr has little use for those who wish to give official versions of reality, who would turn the war into a centrally controlled monologue.

> In this war they called it "acute environmental reac-
> tion," but Vietnam has spawned a jargon of such
> delicate locutions that it's often impossible to know
> even remotely the things being described. Most
> Americans would rather be told that their son is
> undergoing acute environmental reaction than to hear
> that he is suffering from shell shock, because they
> could no more cope with the fact of shell shock than
> they could with the reality of what had happened to
> this boy during his five months at Khe Sanh. (97)

And lest the example Herr chooses be shrugged off as unfortunate,
possibly benign, paternalism rather than be recognized for the self-
serving falsification that it is, Herr later gives us more examples of what
he scathingly refers to as "the really mindless optimism" and falsifying
powers of "Mission diction" (154, 236):

> like "discreet burst" (one of those tore an old grand-
> father and two children to bits as they ran along a
> paddy wall one day . . .), "friendly casualties" (not
> warm, not fun), "meeting engagement" (ambush),
> concluding usually with 17 or 117 or 317 enemy dead
> and American losses "described as light." (237)

Throughout *Dispatches* we see that the grunts' language is much closer
to the core of Vietnam than that of those responsible for explaining the
United States' presence and activities there. Grunt lingo is much closer
to the reality of death, for example, which is what this body-bag war
was all about, Herr has told us--as in the image-provoking "greased" of
the ordinary GI set in opposition to the euphemistic "killed by friendly
fire" favored by officials.

In a self-revelatory scene, Herr tells us that on his very first
afternoon of the war he had responded to a sergeant that he was not
a "reporter" but a "writer." And although he chastises himself in
retrospect for being "dumbass and pompous" in giving such a reply, we
see that he has, in fact, succeeded in describing the essential nature of
his project in Vietnam by simultaneously declaring what he is and
implying all that he is not (178). We have seen that his role involves
being a mouthpiece for the grunts, but it transcends even this partial
description. In speaking of his colleagues in the press corps, Herr
makes much in the book's penultimate section of his own marginal
status within the contingent:

> I never had to frequent JUSPAO unless I wanted to.
> . . . I could skip the daily briefings, I never had to
> cultivate Sources. In fact, *my concerns were so rarefied*
> that I had to ask other correspondents what they ever
> found to ask Westmoreland, Bunker, Komer and
> Zorthian. (231, my italics)

Herr uses this passage to emphasize the futility of seeking the truth through official sources and by conventional means, but I wish to draw special attention to his own estimation of his concerns because he himself never overtly states the final aspect of his writerly purpose (though he hints at it here). This is because that aspect is to be found in the very shaping of his unconventional methods; it is to be found in his style.

Learning to avoid falsehood and to get at the truth is not one and the same as developing methods to reveal or embody this truth, although it would be impossible to accomplish the latter without realizing the former. Indeed, Herr's style is so distinctive, his departures from conventional journalism so dramatic (which is not to say that he does not borrow from proven literary methods), that his style deserves further elaboration.[6] Early on the text itself makes clear that Herr is in Vietnam to report, to find and write "stories" (like *information*, a key word for Herr, one he begins to weave into the text from the outset). Everything we read will be colored by our expectations of what a journalistic account of war entails. It is toward this set of presuppositions which we shall next turn our attention.

Indeed, *Dispatches* is likely to call on its readers to suspend certain kinds of judgment until its cumulative effect can be apprehended. It is certainly not written in the straightforward, expository style long associated with conventional journalism. *Dispatches* assumes a readership familiar with the basic facts about Vietnam, about dates and places, events and geography (or at least readers willing to suspend any discomfort occasioned by ignorance). Such information is supplied only when and insofar as it is relevant to Herr's project, and when it is supplied it is very likely to be done haphazardly, without any traditional sort of ordering of facts. As Roger Sale writes, "Herr at his best hurls one into his experience, insists an uninitiated reader be comforted with no politics, no certain morality, no clear outline of history" (35).

Our set of expectations regarding journalism is probably as much a part of our predisposed readerly consciousness as the previously discussed images and modes of perception implanted in us by the media. As such, it is another obstacle to be overthrown by Herr's style.

The journalistic tradition, of course, has as one of its tenets that writers must search out the facts and not print anything which cannot be supported by hard evidence. This tradition would include such typical activities as verifying rumors and checking the authenticity and authority of sources and statements. Yet these are rules which Herr often flouts in his reportage. "I'd heard that the GVN Department of Labor had nine American advisors for every Vietnamese," he writes (40), drawing attention not only to the amazing ratio he has cited, but also to the fact that he is willing to report what is an unsubstantiated assertion. He had "heard" but he had not verified. Yet verification of a matter like this should have caused an experienced reporter such as Herr few pains indeed in a country rife with statistic-gathering agencies, offices and bureaucrats eager to divulge their findings. But Vietnam was also a place where "the uses of most information were flexible," and we begin to conclude that the manner of gathering and reporting them (and later reading about them) might require flexibility as well (1).

From time to time, particularly in the first section, "Illumination Rounds," Herr demonstrates his comfort with mixing rumor and fact in order to portray the experience of Vietnam: "People close to Special Forces *had heard* upsetting stories about the A Camps down there, falling apart from inside, mercenary mutinies and triple cross, until only a few were still effective" (50, my italics). Perhaps by reporting rumors, Herr best describes the fact of rumor and its impact on the American war effort (indeed, the word rumor is scattered liberally through the text, sometimes as the dominant or controlling word of an entire paragraph).

But Herr is not parodying traditional journalism--though the occasional foregrounding of his disregard for journalistic practices may make it seem so--as much as he is inventing a new journalism capable of allowing him to cover the war (cover being another of the text's key words), or perhaps, since much of what he writes is written after the lapse of several years, recover the war. The fact is that some rules simply became irrelevant in Vietnam. Rules and procedures that were intended to establish standard methods for obtaining and ensuring the truth in fact became more than irrelevant; at times they were active forces for falsification, as we have seen, and as we see here:

> All in-country briefings, at whatever level, came to
> sound like a Naming of the Parts, and the language
> was used as a cosmetic, but one that diminished
> beauty. Since most of the journalism from the war
> was framed in that language or proceeded from the

> view of the war which those terms implied, it would be
> as impossible to know what Vietnam looked like from
> reading most newspaper stories as it would be to know
> how it smelled. (98)

With his allusion to Henry Reed's famous antimilitary poem, Herr reminds us that the use of language to convey truth has long been among the major casualties of war. In this passage (especially in its framing context which is too long to quote here) we are reminded of the astonishing degree to which "information" was withheld, shaped, distorted and manipulated by those in charge of releasing it. Not only did the authorities fail to play square, but those in the know, including large segments of the general population, including many journalists, knew very well that briefings and press conferences were a sham--"the five o'clock follies." What is more in this passage, Herr implies that his own writing may have as its goal not only truth, but beauty as well, an unusual notion for all except those ready to apply Keats quite literally to the mundane world of journalism and, indeed, to war itself.

The journalist is expected not only to verify sources, but to maintain (or at least always strive to achieve) objectivity. Part and parcel with this objectivity is the necessity of not becoming overly involved with one's subject, of maintaining a proper distance in the hope of gaining perspective. Many writers, critics, and theorists have recently cast serious doubt as to whether objectivity, even used in the broadly defined sense of journalistic fairness and even-handedness, can be achieved. However this may be, for the general public journalistic objectivity is still the hoped-for and expected norm; it is still taught in schools of journalism as one of the bases of journalistic ethics, and, whether achieved or not, is still the stated aim of mainstream journalists.[7] But Herr shows that those who "cultivate sources" and attend briefings to obtain supposedly verified information from the authorities may be fulfilling the dictates of journalistic objectivity but not telling the truth. Herr knew his project was different. He wanted to capture the reality of Vietnam, not hand on authorized but inauthentic versions of it. John Hellmann has pointed out that, far from trying to maintain the distance from his material necessary to achieve supposed objectivity, Herr's "method of communicating and achieving 'penetration' or insight was to empathize so completely with any and all situations and characters he encountered that he could gain understanding relatively undistorted by personal attitudes or preconceptions" (Hellmann 147).

Herr's break with conventional journalism includes the adoption of techniques traditionally associated with the novel, such as an emphasis on elaborating and typifying even minor characters through their dialogue. More interestingly, this break enables *Dispatches* to participate in the sort of multivocality ("heteroglossia") which Bakhtin has described as the hallmark of the novel. To truly appreciate the fullness of dialogue in *Dispatches*, it is necessary to expand the traditional notion of this term to include the socio-verbal interplay described by Bakhtin, for much of the meaningful dialogue occurs in passages not actually set off with quotation marks. For example, many times the speaker is unknown or is an amalgam of possible speakers, what Bakhtin has termed a "hybridization," that is, "the mixing, within a single concrete utterance, of two or more different linguistic consciousnesses, often widely separated in time and social space" (429).[8]

The detailed characterization of Mayhew and Day Tripper in the Khe Sanh section is very much novelistic in that the emphasis on elaborating their characters transcends any possible confinement of them to a journalistic role as mere representatives of a typical GI in a historically important phase of the Vietnam war. (Even the role of subjects for "human interest" stories is far surpassed here.) Novelistic characterization through a hybrid form is exemplified in the passage describing the personal problems of Mayhew's Tennessee-hill friend, Orrin. The exact nature of Orrin's predicament is revealed by an amalgam of Herr's own voice and that of Orrin's wife, who is herself characterized to an extent in this excerpt:

> Orrin received a letter from his wife. It told him straight off that her pregnancy was not seven months along, as he had believed, but only five. It made all the difference in the world to Orrin. She had felt so awful all the time (she wrote) that she went to see the minister, and the minister had finally convinced her that the Truth was God's one sure key to a beautiful conscience. She would not tell him who the father was (and Honey, don't you never, never try and make me tell), except to mention that it was someone Orrin knew well. (134)

Several times we hear the intrusion of Orrin's wife's "voice" with her own verbal idiosyncrasies intact, and even the minister is characterized by the capitalized *T* in *Truth*. Here the focus is far removed from Khe Sanh and its historical significance, and it is equally far removed in the subsequent paragraph which is devoted largely to describing Orrin's face. Both the concentration on the characterizing capacity of the various voices and the sheer verbal virtuosity in these paragraphs outstrip any traditional journalistic aims or accomplishments in them, and they reflect Herr's practice of intertwining his project with the lives of the grunts.

Just as Herr's narrative voice intermixes with that of the GIs in order to characterize them, sometimes it mixes with that of authorities and leaders. Often the effect is satirical, as in the following passage where Herr adopts the voice of an officer conducting a briefing:

> What if [enemy soldiers] want it so badly that they are willing to maneuver . . . over barricades formed by their own dead (a tactic, Colonel, favored by your gook in Korea) . . . What if they are still coming . . . as the first MIG's and IL-28's ever seen in this war bomb out the TOC and the strip, the med tent and control tower (People's Army my ass, right, Colonel?). . . . (121)

Herr mimics the Colonel in order to expose the ethnocentrism and lack of intelligent vision which Herr apparently grew weary of encountering in so many United States military leaders. His anger is also directed at the staged press conferences characteristic of Vietnam, typified by the "cross-fertilization of ignorance" inherent in a system which ensures that reporters will not ask any probing questions because military officers will not seriously entertain prospects potentially detrimental to public relations.

Much of *Dispatches'* unmarked dialogue may appear in the normal flow of the narrative, but probably its most provocative presence is within the parenthetical remarks with which Herr's narrative is replete. Indeed, Herr is a master of parentheses to the degree that his copious use of them might be thought of as his idiosyncratic signature. Many times the speaking voice within parentheses is Herr's own; sometimes it is another's voice readily identifiable from the context; other times it is a hybrid voice. When other voices are parenthetically inserted into the narrative, whether they are enclosed in quotation marks or not, they have the effect of elaborating character, of demonstrating different responses to a given situation, of corroborating Herr's viewpoint, of modifying it, of showing the existence of an alternative viewpoint which Herr has been forced to counter or expose for its falseness. This multiplicity of effects and uses of Herr's parentheses is impossible to reconstruct with any sort of brevity, but the multivocality which they both mirror and perpetuate demonstrates that "both object and language are revealed to the novelist in their historical dimension, in the process of social and heteroglot becoming" (Bakhtin 330).

When Herr speaks in his own voice, he sometimes uses parentheses to fill in general or background information relevant to a specific story or incident he is telling, or the parenthetical material may not be so much background as supportive or elaborating information. Sometimes such parentheses may last for several sentences, filling up a large portion, perhaps even the lion's share, of a paragraph or page. In such cases as these, the parentheses serve to draw attention to the material in a fashion paradoxical to the reader's expectations. Far from being secondary material that one might skip without losing the thread of the text, far from carrying any air of off-handedness, digression, trivial embellishment or involuted subtlety, such material is actually the most important aspect of the sentence or paragraph in which it appears. In the following triad of sentences, for example, the non-enclosed sentences have less impact than the parenthetical sentence they sandwich, and not the other way around, as in ordinary use:

> If the war in I Corps was a matter for specialization among correspondents, it was not because it was inherently different as war, but because it was fought almost exclusively by the Marines, whose idiosyncracies most reporters found intolerable and even criminal. (There was a week in the war, one week, when the Army lost more men killed, proportionally, than the Marines, and Army spokesmen had a rough time hiding their pride, their absolute glee.) And in the face of some new variation on old Marine disasters, it didn't much matter that you knew dozens of fine, fine officers. (108)

Such unusual uses of parentheses, examined on an individual, appearance-by-appearance basis, demonstrate Herr's desire to find new methods of drawing and sustaining attention for his reportage of the horrors of war. Moreover, the effect of dialogue, as Bakhtin has asserted, is to undercut any monologic, authoritarian tendencies of language and of the society which shapes and reveals its perception of reality through that language. In this way Herr's style is most consistent with the theme and tone (the text's "project") of undercutting authoritarian discourse and revealing the callous and cynical falsities such discourse contained during the Vietnam era.

Once they are viewed in a larger sense, as a frequently recurring, centrally important element of the text, these parentheses take on a more general significance which speaks to two major elements of *Dispatches*--dialogue and consciousness. So profuse and lengthy are these parenthetical expressions, that they have the effect of carrying on a dialogue with the nonparenthetical elements of the text. Through them, Herr as narrator talks to himself, juxtaposing generality and specificity, background and incident, history and anecdote, any one of which may be one time inside parentheses, another time outside. Such stylistic effects tend toward demonstrating that truth is best revealed through dialogue and toward motivating the reader to collaborate in this project by breaking up or defamiliarizing the expected method of transcribing (hi)stories. At the same time, this narration as dialogue with the self, points to another of the text's central strands of meaning, and that is Herr's struggle with handling and shaping the raw materials of his experience. This struggle to find conscious expression is an element of the text which I shall discuss at more length shortly.

Along with the use of parentheses, one of Herr's most refined stocks-in-trade as verbal craftsman is his repetition of key words, sometimes in close proximity so that they dominate a paragraph, a page, or in some cases the entire book.[9] One such key word, which is particularly profuse in the opening section, "Breathing In," is *information*, the use of which illustrates Bakhtin's idea that "any . . . (utterance) finds the object at which it was directed already as it were overlain with qualifications, open to dispute, charged with value, already enveloped in an obscuring mist . . . " (276). *Information* is a good word to examine in this light because of the ambiguity and multiple meanings it displays in the text, and because of the struggle for possession of this word between Herr, who needs it as a writer, and the authorities, who have their own uses for it. In his reportage of a war wherein "the uses of most information were flexible," Herr has decided that his own uses of that word must infuse it with the many shades of meaning and use it had in the war. To do so is more than a simple matter of separating "proper" from "improper" uses of the word, though we have seen how information could be used to falsify or could be false in itself.

Indeed, one of the questions upon which the word *information* pivots in its various appearances has to do with utility. Sometimes information is missing, as in the instance when Herr conflates a contemplation of the horrors of Vietnam with a recollection of looking at magazine pictures of the dead in his youth: "Even when the picture was sharp and clearly defined, something wasn't clear at all, something repressed that monitored the images and withheld their essential information" (18). Here Herr feels acutely his inability to penetrate the heart of darkness because of some difficult-to-define missing ingredient, an ingredient that the use of the word *essential* (to modify information) suggests is somehow bound up with an inability to truly realize the actuality, the very real existence of death. Yet at other times, as Herr humorously tells us, information can be taken in so quickly and in such superabundance that it overwhelms, as it occasionally did his friend, Sean Flynn, who would return from an assignment "overloaded on the information, the input! the input!" (6).

The usefulness of information is not necessarily tethered to questions of factuality or the lack thereof. In Saigon and at the various press "facilities" (a word Herr uses with sardonic amusement), information is likely to be in the form of numbers, statistics, intelligence reports--forms of information whose very factuality as well as uses were flexible, but almost always linked to the maintenance of power. And in the end the mountains of reports and reams of statistics were ineffective: "We were backgrounded deep, but when the background started sliding forward not a single life was saved by the information" (51). So Herr learns that information can be both dangerous and necessary, useless and indispensable, and because information itself is flexible so must be anyone who would manage it. This is a daunting, uncertain, physically and psychically dangerous task:

> There was the terrible possibility that a search for information there could become so exhausting that the exhaustion itself became the information. Overload was such a real danger, not as obvious as shrapnel or blunt like a 2,000-foot drop, maybe it couldn't kill you or smash you, but it could bend your aerial for you and land you on your hip. Levels of information were levels of dread. . . .
> Cover the war, what a gig to frame yourself, going out after one kind of information and getting another. . . . There were times when your fear would take directions so wild that you had to stop and watch the spin. (68-69)

In his realization and depiction of the slipperiness of both history and the language that is used to convey it, Herr introduces a metafictional strain into *Dispatches*. Near the end, he speaks directly to the writer's difficulties and to the gap between experience and the act of writing, realizing after he has been home for some time: "I hadn't been anywhere, I'd performed half an act" (268). And though I would not wish to diminish or downplay the central role of Vietnam as an experienced presence in *Dispatches* (a mistaken tendency that even perceptive critics fall into), one can see the strong strain of truth in Philip Beidler's assertion that the "terrain of *Dispatches* . . . of necessity becomes the terrain of consciousness itself" (142). Throughout the book, Herr has played with the word *cover*, using it frequently, letting it both signify ordinary, dictionary meanings and accumulate special nuances of its own. Yet his real task has been to recover the war, to combine history and imagination.

In one of the book's most frequently cited passages, Herr attests to one of the dangers of his emotionally involved style of journalism, the difficulty he had redistancing himself from the war's phenomena sufficiently to give shape to what he has seen: "I went to cover the war," he writes, "and the war covered me. . . . The problem is that you didn't always know what you were seeing until later, maybe years later . . . The information isn't frozen, you are" (20). It is in this final act of recovering the war that Herr takes the concluding step which frees him from the traps and constraints of phenomenal experience, the step that allows him to transform experience into language. The writing of his text has necessitated an arduous process which has demanded that he surmount or see past the mundane circumstances and status-quo journalistic practices of Vietnam; that he strip away years of media-produced versions of reality and media-induced modes of perception; that he not only reject traditional journalistic style and rules of writing but also actively formulate his own new style. A new reality requires a new frame of mind requires a new style. In this formula the reader must play his or her part too, must be ready to forego a steady emphasis on recounting well-ordered facts for an emphasis on being informed in a new way. As Philip Beidler has said, the reader must collaborate by entering into "the complex function of creative consciousness in *Dispatches*. It is the ground on which 'information,' . . . in some cases searches out and in others actually contrives new paths of connection, forges the link between personal witness and larger visions of history and culture" (143). If we are not willing to engage Herr's provocative style, to involve ourselves in his process of recovery, then it is quite likely that *Dispatches* will simply "cover" us.

Notes

1. James Wilson is probably representative of those who object to *Dispatches* when he states that it is "just a personal narrative" and accuses it of failing "to go beyond a surface description," of the war; just as typically, he also acknowledges "its stylistic brilliance" (Wilson 45, 46, 45).

2. I use the word *information* self-consciously partly because *Dispatches* is itself shot through with the word. Herr has made sure to include it often, letting it accumulate nuances and shades of meaning for us as it must have for him. The quotation marks are also meant to signify that what passed for information frequently could only be received as such by those with a fine sense of irony, a too capacious sense of humor, or a state of mind numbed to what was really occurring. Later we shall explore more fully the multiple meanings and uses of the word *information*.

3. The first *wasted* refers to the fact that Herr and his friends have been drinking in a nearby hotel.

4. This reality also includes quotations transcribed from flak jackets and helmets, from latrine graffiti. We are reminded here of Bakhtin's insistence on the "diversity of languages" within novelistic discourse. More than once he uses the example of "languages of generations and age groups" as an important example of a dialogized voice (262-63). Such a voice is most appropriate not only for Herr's mission as mouthpiece for the GI, but also as a part of his Voice (in the largest possible sense) speaking of and out of the Vietnam era, an era when confrontation between generations was so keen as to spawn the term "generation gap."

5. In fact Bakhtin lists as other examples of voices in novelistic discourse "professional jargons," "languages of the authorities" and "languages that serve the specific sociopolitical purposes of the day," all of which are a part of *Dispatches'* verbal network (262-63).

6. Bakhtin has said that a central aspect of style is the "distancing of the posited author or teller . . . from conventional literary expectations" (312).

7. Even with the impact of New Journalism during the Vietnam era, mainstream journalism and the expectations of its readers remain much the same now as in 1960. John Hellmann has noted the differences between Herr and two of New Journalism's most famous practitioners, Norman Mailer and Hunter S. Thompson, in his very insightful article "The New Journalism and Vietnam" (146-47).

8. This succinct definition of hybridization is actually found in the glossary of the cited edition and was presumably written by the editor in conjunction with his fellow translator.

9. To discuss each of these examples would be an exhaustive undertaking, but even the first-time reader will recollect certain words which appear and reappear, for example: cover, waste, face, smile, ground, mobility/motion, spook, Mission, story. For an example of a word dominating a short stretch of writing, one can study the uses of the word *spook* on pages 52-53, where it appears ten times as one part of speech or another.

Works Cited

Bakhtin, M. M. *The Dialogic Imagination*. Ed. Michael Holquist. Trans. Caryl Emerson and Michael Holquist. Austin: University of Texas, 1981.

Beidler, Philip. *American Literature and the Experience of Vietnam*. Athens: University of Georgia, 1982.

Hellmann, John. "The New Journalism and Vietnam: Memory as Structure in Michael Herr's *Dispatches*." *The South Atlantic Quarterly* 79 (1980) : 141-51.

Herr, Michael. *Dispatches*. 1977. New York: Avon-Discus, 1980.

Sale, Roger. "Hurled into Vietnam." Rev. of *Dispatches*, by Michael Herr. *New York Review of Books*. 8 Dec. 1977: 34-35.

Wilson, James C. *Vietnam in Prose and Film*. Jefferson, NC: McFarland, 1982.

GOING AFTER CACCIATO: TIM O'BRIEN'S "SEPARATE PEACE"

Robert M. Slabey

"It was the best of times, it was the worst of times"--
Charles Dickens

"I remember. . .the fine times and the bad times" -- Ernest
Hemingway

"It was a bad time" --Tim O'Brien

While the war novel has been an established genre in American
letters since the Civil War, each war has had its own meaning, requiring
its own aesthetic. For Ernest Hemingway and Norman Mailer war was
a metaphor for the way in which a man engages life. More recently,
Norman Mailer has declared that if World War II was like Joseph
Heller's absurdist *Catch-22*, a Vietnam book will have to be surreal like
William Burroughs' *Naked Lunch* (85). But for Vietnam both
Burroughs' technique and the styles used to depict earlier wars have
proven inadequate or inappropriate. In reviewing Michael Herr's
Vietnam journal *Dispatches* C.D.B. Bryan noted that "Vietnam required
not only new techniques of warfare, but new techniques in writing as
well. Newscameramen and photographers could show us sometimes
what the war looked like, but an entirely new language, imagery and
style were needed so that we could understand and feel" (1). Since
much Vietnam literature mixes facts and fictions, realities and
imaginings, Philip Beidler has observed that the great theme has
become the process of meaning-making itself. Among the many
impressive works that have appeared in reportage, memoir, poetry,
drama, film, and fiction, I have selected for discussion Tim O'Brien's
novel, *Going After Cacciato* (1978).

Vietnam has been the matrix for O'Brien's work, though his first
novel, the realistic homecoming story *Northern Lights* (1974), is only
tangentially about the war. His personal narrative *If I Die in a Combat
Zone* (1973) conveys the feelings of many veterans who did their
traditional duty in a war they privately despised. O'Brien's wartime
contemplations of desertion are imaginatively realized in his second
novel, *Going After Cacciato*. While the Vietnam era is within the
parameters of *The Nuclear Age* (1985), O'Brien has returned to the war
itself in his recent story "The Things They Carried" and in the
metafictive "How to Tell a True War Story." His treatments of the war

are, respectively, realistic fiction, memoir, and finally a form of fictive irrealism. Vietnam was a war like all wars but, unlike others, e.g. World War II, the issues were not clear and the battle lines were not regular. Vietnam, lacking the traditional progress, logical structure, beginning-middle-end, required an innovative form rather than the conventional chronological narrative.

O'Brien, moreover, as a war novelist, writes knowingly in a tradition developed by Crane, Dos Passos, Hemingway, Mailer, Heller and Vonnegut in which a young soldier considers fear and bravery. He, however, modifies the repeated situation of a soldier's making a "separate peace." While Hemingway's Lt. Henry deserts the army and Heller's Yossarian embarks for Sweden, O'Brien's Paul Berlin goes AWOL only in his mind. As his attempt to depict the meaning of Vietnam O'Brien combines realistic war scenes, absurdist events, along with fantasy in an original and aesthetically convincing manner. Several critics have applied the term "Magical Realism" (associated with Borges and Garcia Marquez) to *Cacciato*. Such forms combine the verifiable aspects of realism with the magical effects of fairy tale and folklore, often beginning with a fantastic premise from which everything then follows logically (Young 1-8).

First, O'Brien gives his readers gritty combat scenes, the stark facts of death and destruction, and the debilitating experience of war on the individual soldier. In addition, he presents absurdist incidents, e.g. Paul's inability to tell if his promotion board's questions are serious, and a corporal's lecture on survival consisting of one hour of silence. Doc describes the whole war situation: "a bunch of kids trying to pin the tail on the Asian donkey. But no fuckin tail. No fuckin donkey" (131). As counterpoint to the grim realism and black humor, O'Brien's third style is lyrical: beautiful descriptions of landscape and the whole dreamlike state of the imaginary journey in which "Money was never a problem, passports were never required. There were always new places to dance."

Three styles but two ways of seeing: external fact versus subjective truth. O'Brien thus contrasts war and peace: Vietnam, the nightmare wasteland and public disaster, and Paris, goal of the quest-journey, the dream paradise. *Going After Cacciato* begins where *Catch-22* ended, with a desertion, Cacciato's departure from Vietnam to walk 8000 miles over the mountains to Paris. Like Orr in Heller's novel, Cacciato offers the vision of a better life in another country. In O'Brien's geography the mountains are untouched by the war, clean and unpolluted (as in Hemingway); the ascent is to the region of spirit (Montsalvat) or to the world of imagination (Parnassus). Paul's actual location during the entire narrative (except the first and last chapters), the Observation Post, becomes for him the ivory tower of art where "possibilities" are realized. During the six night-hours the six-months trip to Paris is accomplished. This, the first time-level in the novel (the nine "Observation Post" chapters) is the actual present in Quang Ngai. A second time level is Paul's remembered past--his childhood, youth, and his earlier bleak experiences in Vietnam. The third is the imagined quest following Cacciato to Paris. While the memories of what happened are random and fragmentary, the might-have-been journey is orderly and chronological.

The search for the runaway becomes an odyssey, a pilgrimage, the language gradually shifting from military jargon to quasi-religious imagery. In a chance to escape the stranglehold of a real world Paul and the squad become a community experiencing love and responsibility. In contrast with destruction and pointless wandering around in Vietnam, they have a positive and meaningful destination. Running away becomes running towards something; the impossible becomes the possible. Moreover, the external mission is internalized, into learning important things about the Self. Paul began worrying about "how to act wisely in spite of fear." But courage becomes not facing the enemy but confronting reality and pushing it closer to one's dreams and ideals. "The real issue was the power of the will to defeat fear." The choice becomes either to surrender freedom to a totalitarian war machine or to the imagination. O'Brien's epigraph from Siegfried Sassoon suggests Paul's choice: "Soldiers are dreamers."

Going After Cacciato celebrates the imagination's way of resisting the destructive powers of immediate experience, but it also questions the imagination. Paul Berlin creates in his head a fiction in order to displace his fear. His dream journey, however, finally brings him face-to-face with reality, thus helping him meet the challenges of life. O'Brien then is dealing not only with the traditional themes of war fiction--fear and courage and freedom--but also with the imagination. The "real issue" for Paul was "figuring a way to do it. Somehow working his way into that secret chamber of the human heart, where, in the tangle, lay the circuitry for all that was possible."

Paul Berlin's name, linking him with World War II, his father's "good" war, may also invoke Remarque's young soldier of the Great War, Paul Baumer. His background of small town Midwest values made overt resistance to the war impossible. Paul went to war "Not because of strong convictions, but because he didn't know . . . . If the war was right or wrong. . . . So he went. . . . Because he believed in law. . . . because it was expected. . . . Because he loved his country and, more than that, because he trusted it" (313). Sensitive and confused, he is not a disaffiliated youth, but he is still a postmodernist protagonist for whom the lines blur between dream and reality. For Paul a soldier's dream of escape is enacted by Cacciato, a man who had always distanced himself from the war by indulging in simple pleasures--whistling, smiling, or eating candy. Cacciato, nonetheless, was the only one brave enough to retrieve Buff's gory helmet from the ditch.

In the midst of the wasteland of war Cacciato had quixotically gone fishing in a bomb crater. For Hemingway fishing had been a true alternate to the war. And Orr hoped to catch fish in waters where no codfish had ever been caught before (Heller 326). For O'Brien, in contrast, there is neither stream nor fish, only a bomb crater. But Cacciato, having the capacity to imagine an alternate to death unavailable in actuality, believes that the impossible is possible. Associated with the moon, Cacciato follows the lunar way of intuition and imagination. And his dream of peace becomes the dream of Paul during his own moonlit meditation.

Pursuing Cacciato the fugitive becomes following Cacciato the guide who, described with religious imagery, becomes "the light of the world" (37). Paul identifies with the man not afraid to live out his imagination, and the hunters come to share the vision of the hunted, verbally associating themselves with him. As Doc says, "Cacciato runs. We chase" (270). (Cacciato's name in Italian means "hunter" from *caccia* "hunt" or "chase.") O'Brien is not the first to apply the hunt metaphor to Vietnam; Mailer's *Why Are We in Vietnam?* and Michael Cimino's *The Deer Hunter* both use it as a central image. It is appropriate that Vietnam, a hunter's war, should be associated with the prototypical American figure, the isolated hunter in the wilderness. Peter Aichinger has already proposed that warfare, as treated in American fiction, is an avatar of the frontier spirit, with the soldier replacing his progenitors, the cowboy and the frontiersman (ix). Not accidentally, Stephen Crane's Civil War novel which appeared just at the closing of the frontier, describes the "advance of the enemy . . . like a ruthless hunting" (78) and in *The Naked and the Dead* Mailer labels Sam Croft "The Hunter." With the widespread use of imagery from the hunt and Indian warfare Vietnam becomes an extension of the American Westward movement.

Paul's trip is partially a projection of his reality. In Vietnam the men were ordered to search the tunnels. (Paul's "double" *Bernie Lynn* dies in a tunnel Paul refused to enter.) On the road to Paris the group falls into a labyrinthine tunnel but one that (unlike the endless war) has "a light at its end." The tunnel, a principal metaphor for American involvement in Southeast Asia, just as to Paul the land itself was a "great maze" (300), is playfully extended into the legendary "road to Mandalay." A young Vietnamese woman, Sarkin Aung Wan, joins Paul as he enters the mirror world of art, and they, like Alice, fall into a hole in the ground. Sarkin, a refugee from the war, a dreamer who never gives up hope, lures Paul away from reality, but, unlike the femme fatale, not to his destruction. Superficially resembling a movie-cliché oriental, Sarkin is the Anima, the female personification of the unconscious, the woman within man who conveys vital messages to the Self (Jung). Like Dante's Beatrice, she is the guide--and not only out of the tunnel but on to Paris. As Anima she helps Paul discover truths hidden within and puts his mind in touch with right values as she articulates Paul's desire to escape the war.[1]

Paul's relationship with Sarkin is chaste, unlike that of Hemingway's lovers in *A Farewell to Arms*, because O'Brien is also drawing on the American tradition of the hunt where the white man's companion is a dark-skinned male (e.g. Chingachook, Queequeg, Sam Fathers). Paul and Sarkin's journey takes them not through the American wilderness but through an Old World civilization which has been physically devastated and vulgarized (Cf. Jolly Chand's forty bottles of ketsup in Delhi). O'Brien utilizes the mythic form that Richard Chase has identified as a major strategy for encountering the contradictions of American experience.

Having reached Paris, Paul and Sarkin hold a debate in the Majestic Hotel, site of the contemporary Peace Negotiations. Here Sarkin urges Paul to live the dream and opt for personal happiness. But Paul argues that he cannot live in exile from life: "Even in imagination we must be true to our obligations. . . . Imagination like reality has its limits" (378). His sense of public obligation requires that he embrace the organizing principles of duty and the American cause. Unlike Hemingway's Lt. Henry, he does not select desertion and exile, and unlike Heller's Yossarian, he does not openly rebel or physically leave the war zone, and unlike Vonnegut's Billy Pilgrim, he does not retreat into subjective fantasy. During the journey Paul has been guided by Sarkin, but after their climactic debate, she leaves him to face "the facts" alone.

During his night in the Observation Post Paul has undergone a change in perception, experiencing an imaginary external journey to Paris and a real internal journey into the self. Through his power of the will he has been able to imagine an alternate that will then allow him to face reality, the fact of death, and his own fear. In the narrative as a whole O'Brien dramatizes both men in action and one man escaping the war. He does not argue the issues of the war, but he does include an implicit judgment. Paul's choice of chauvinism over pacificism is undercut by his quotation of patriotic clichés. Paul accepts the rhetoric of politicians, but, remember, the scene takes place in his mind. The counter argument is also Paul's since Sarkin is part of his psyche. Paul has searched for peace and comes to accept his share of responsibility and will summon the courage to face reality. Imagining an alternate to death during the dark night of Vietnam, Paul finds a key to survival not in physical escape but in spiritual inscape.

Tim O'Brien, admitting that while in Vietnam, he had lived "in his head a great deal," has said that "We live in our heads a lot, but especially during situations of stress and great peril. It's a means of escape in part, but it's also a means of dealing in the real world--not just escaping it, but dealing with it" (Schroeder 138). In addition he writes fiction "to alert readers to the complexity and ambiguity of a set of moral issues--but without preaching a moral lesson" (McCaffery 149).

In 1976 Peter Jones predicted that "Because of its length and the degree to which all Americans have been compelled to assume moral attitudes towards it, there is a strong probability that the Vietnam War will eventually produce a novel of intellectual and artistic scope sufficient to place the experience in perspective" (186). *Going After Cacciato*, I feel, is one such book, significant in an original use of traditional materials and the literary mythologizing of war as well as an innovative combination of styles and strategies--realistic, absurdist, fabulous. O'Brien's deviations from the conventional novel are especially appropriate to Vietnam, a chaotic and morally ambiguous war, in which the soldiers, whether captives or not, were all "prisoners of war," with no discernable purpose except "to keep from getting killed."[3]

Notes

1. Paul "dreams" two Vietnamese, Sarkin and Li Van Hgoc, who have a background in the Toaist-Buddhist-Confusian matrix of Asian thought. They tell Paul that *Xa* the Land, with the tunnels as the mysteries contained within, was the true enemy (107-108) and that only by giving himself up to the *Xa* can he escape the labyrinth: "The way in is the way out." *Xa* ("village community") had its roots in the old ideograph signifying "land," "people," and "sacred," and the Vietminh and NLF translated "Socialism" as "*Xa Hoi*," thus identifying the revolution with

the past (Fitzgerald 192-193). O'Brien implies that the *Xa*-archetype exists on the unconscious level of Paul's psyche. Incidentally "Sarkin" is an ersatz Oriental name, but Li Van Hgoc, the first VC actually seen, bears an authentic Vietnamese name.

2. This essay is based on a paper read at the Popular Culture Association Convention, Toronto, March 29, 1984.

Works Cited

Aichinger, Peter. *The American Soldier in Fiction, 1880-1963*. Ames: Iowa State U P, 1975.

Beidler, Philip D. *American Literature and the Experience of Vietnam*. Athens: U of Georgia P, 1982.

Bryan, C.D.B. Rev. of *Dispatches* by Michael Herr. New York *Times Book Review* Nov. 20, 1977: 1, 54.

Chase, Richard. *The American Novel and Its Tradition*. New York: Anchor, 1957.

Crane, Stephen. *The Red Badge of Courage*. 1895. Ed. Sculley Bradley et al. 2nd ed. New York: Norton, 1962.

Fitzgerald, Frances. *Fire in the Lake: The Vietnamese and the Americans in Vietnam*. 1972. New York: Vintage, 1973.

Heller, Joseph. *Catch-22*. 1961. New York: Dell, 1979.

Jones, Peter G. *War and the American Novelist: Appraising the American War Novel*. Columbia: U of Missouri P, 1976.

Jung, Carl G. *Man and His Symbols*. Ed. M.-L. von Franz. Garden City: Doubleday, 1964. 177-188.

Mailer, Norman. *Cannibals and Christians*. New York: Dial, 1966.

McCaffery, Larry. "An Interview with Tim O'Brien." *Chicago Review* 33 (1982):129-149.

O'Brien, Tim. *Going After Cacciato*. 1978. New York: Dell, 1979.

_____. "The Things They Carried." *Esquire* August 1986: 76-81.

_____. "How to Tell a True War Story." *Esquire* October 1987: 209-215.

Schroeder, Eric James. "Two Interviews: Talks with Tim O'Brien and Robert Stone." *Modern Fiction Studies* 30 (1984): 135-151.

Young, David. Introduction. *Magical Realist Fiction*. New York: Longman,1984. 1-8.

PLURALITIES OF VISION: *GOING AFTER CACCIATO* AND TIM O'BRIEN'S SHORT FICTION

Catherine Calloway

Tim O'Brien's second novel, the critically acclaimed *Going After Cacciato*, has long been considered one of the best works to have emerged from the canon of Vietnam War literature, due in part to its emphasis on the subjective nature of perception. Like other postmodernist writers, O'Brien questions the problematic nature of reality itself, a process that engages both the protagonist and the reader. Can there be any definite objective reality in the war? Does absolute truth really exist? Like the elusive Cacciato, the soldier on whom the imaginary journey from Vietnam to Paris is centered, *Going After Cacciato* taunts us with many faces and angles of vision. The protagonist Paul Berlin cannot distinguish between what is real and what is imagined in the war just as the reader cannot differentiate between what is real and what is imagined in the novel. As O'Brien writes, "It was a matter of hard observation. Separating illusion from reality. What happened, and what might have happened" (*GAC* 247). Paul Berlin is forced, as is the reader, into an attempt to distinguish between illusion and reality and in doing so creates a continuous critical dialogue between himself and the world around him.

The impossibility of simplistic judgments--of knowing the reality of the war in absolute terms--is further illustrated in a number of short stories that O'Brien published shortly before *Going After Cacciato*. These stories contain many of the same events and characters as the novel, but differ somewhat from the novelistic versions. While some stories reveal only minor stylistic changes, others contain major differences that serve to provide another perceptual dimension to *Going After Cacciato*, another window on the ever-elusive reality of war or war of reality.

That reality is an on-going process is first illustrated by seemingly minor details that O'Brien changes between the publication of the short fiction and the novel. For example, in the short story entitled "Going After Cacciato," the mileage from Vietnam to Paris is noted as being exactly 6,800 miles, but in the novel by the same name the distance is precisely 8,600 miles. O'Brien further mocks the reader with mathematical discrepancies in the story "Where Have You Gone, Charming Billy?" There only 26 soldiers go on a night march, while 32 go in the novel, and Paul Berlin counts to 3,485 to keep his mind off of the war, not to 8,060 as in the later version. Similarly, in "The Way It

Mostly Was," the soliders number 58, in the novel only 38. Such shifts in detail include characters as well as figures. Whereas in the novel *Going After Cacciato* only Lieutenant Sidney Martin is mentioned as having died in a tunnel, in the short story "Going After Cacciato," a Lieutenant Walter Gleason dies as well. Also, when Paul Berlin thinks of the death of Billy Boy of a heart attack on the battlefield, he is comforted in the story "Where Have You Gone, Charming Billy?" by a character named Buff. However, in the novel, Buff is mentioned as having died face-down while in a praying position in a ditch, and it is Cacciato, not Buff, who comforts Paul Berlin while on the night march the evening after Billy Boy's death. O'Brien even adds details to Billy Boy's accident. "Where Have You Gone, Charming Billy?" reveals not only that Billy Boy dies of a heart attack when his foot is blown off by a mine, but also that his body suffers further abuse when it falls out of a helicopter removing it from the combat zone:

> the helicopter pulled up and Billy Boy came tumbling out, falling slowly and then faster, and the paddy water sprayed up as if Billy Boy had just executed a long and dangerous dive, as if trying to escape Graves Registration, where he would be tagged and sent home under a flag, dead of a heart attack. . . Later they waded in after him, probing for Billy Boy with their rifle butts, elegantly and delicately probing for Billy Boy in the stinking paddy, singing--some of them-- *Where have you gone, Billy Boy, Billy Boy, Oh, where have you gone, charming Billy?* Then they found him. Green and covered with algae, his eyes still wide-open and scared stiff, dead of a heart attack. . . (132)[1]

Such differences in versions draw the reader into the text, leading him to question the ambiguous nature of reality. What really is the exact distance between Vietnam and Paris? How many soldiers actually go on the march? Who was Lieutenant Gleason, and what was his story? Which soldier comforts Paul Berlin when he thinks of the dead Billy, and did Billy's body really fall out of the helicopter? The questions posed are, of course, far more important than any definite answers or resolutions.

    Even more significantly, O'Brien's denial of a fixed, objective reality in *Going After Cacciato* and the short fiction is revealed through inconsistencies in characterization. Many of O'Brien's characters are ambiguous, and he heightens this ambiguity by changing details about the characters from the short fiction to the novel. A good illustration is Lieutenant Sidney Martin whose view of soldiering differs considerably from that of Paul Berlin. Through Sidney Martin's observation of Paul Berlin, O'Brien makes the point that no two people may know what goes on in the mind of the other, especially in warfare. In *Going After Cacciato*, Lieutenant Martin is a professional soldier who believes in mission and in war. War, he feels, was invented "so that through repetition men might try to do better, so that lessons might be savored and applied the next time, so that men might not be robbed of their own deaths" (*GAC* 201). Lieutenant Martin watches Paul Berlin march on the way to battle, seeing Paul Berlin "as a soldier. Maybe not yet a good soldier, but still a soldier" (*GAC* 200). From his perspective, Sidney Martin admires Paul Berlin with pride, thinking that the youth is steady and persistent:

> Lieutenant Sidney Martin watched him come. He admired the oxen persistence with which the last soldier in the column of thirty-nine marched, thinking that the boy represented so much good-fortitude, discipline, loyalty, self-control, courage, toughness. The greatest gift of God, thought the lieutenant in admiration of Private First Class Paul Berlin's climb, is freedom of will. Sidney Martin, not a man of emotion, felt pride. He raised a hand to hail the boy. (*GAC* 203-04)

However, O'Brien points out that Paul Berlin does "not have the lieutenant's advantage of perspective and overview and height" (*GAC* 201). Paul Berlin is not thinking of mission or of winnning battles; instead, "He knew he would not fight well. He had no love of mission, no love strong enough to make himself fight well" (*GAC* 202). It is ironic that Paul Berlin lacks the very qualities that Lieutenant Sidney Martin thinks he possesses: "He marched up the road with no exercise of will, no desire and no determination, no pride. . . moving, climbing, but without thought and without will and without the force of purpose" (*GAC* 203). What O'Brien states in this passage is that the reality in a person's mind, his own subjectivity, may have no connection with what is happening in the external world. People project their own pesonal misunderstandings onto the world at large, just as the pragmatic Lieutenant Sidney Martin projects his heroic attitudes about war onto the unsuspecting Paul Berlin, who really has no will, no heroic goals. In fact, long before this passage, the reader is told that Paul Berlin's "only goal was to live long enough to establish goals worth living for still longer" (*GAC* 43). He is more interested in survival than in a military victory.

This concern with the problematic nature of reality is revealed even further in O'Brien's short story version of the same march. "The Way It Mostly Was" contains the same ironic contrast between Sidney Martin and Paul Berlin as *Going After Cacciato*, but adds details that make Sidney Martin a more ambiguous figure. In the novel, Sidney Martin is portrayed as being so unprofessional that he lacks a human element. He makes his men undertake dangerous tasks such as searching Vietnamese tunnels, and he marches his men "fast and hard" (*GAC* 194). According to a paragraph included in the novel but omitted in the short story, Sidney Martin advises his men prior to the march that "if a man fell out he would be left where he fell" (*GAC* 194). "The Way It Mostly Was" also reveals that the men must suffer hardships; for instance, they must carry "forty-pound rucksacks" and march until "Their legs and feet were heavy with blood" (35). Sidney Martin, though, is never directly blamed for placing the men under these adverse conditions, and they demonstrate no hostility toward him. The beginning of "The Way It Mostly Was" chapter in the novel indicates that the soldiers are not happy with their lieutenant. There, one character comments that Lieutenant Martin "'always looks for more trouble. He want it? Is that the story--do the man *want* trouble?'" (*GAC* 194). Sidney Martin also hopes that someday his men will understand why he believes "in mission first...that in war it is necessary to make hard sacrifices" (*GAC* 197-98). In contrast to the novel's soldiers, the short story's characters seem more understanding of Sidney Martin's view about mission and do not complain about their leader or hint of threatening him.

Thus, in spite of his strict view of soldiering, Captain Sidney Martin of "The Way It Mostly Was" is presented as being somewhat more humanistic than the Lieutenant Sidney Martin of *Going After Cacciato*. Certain passages in the story add a new dimension to the character and challenge the reader to try to determine which version, if either, is accurate. We are told in O'Brien's novel that Sidney Martin is "*not* [emphasis added] a man of emotion" (*GAC* 204), yet in the story we are told just the opposite--that the captain is "a man of emotion" ("The Way" 45). He is so emotional, in fact, that watching Paul Berlin march makes him want "to cry" ("The Way" 45). There is no mention of the extremely dangerous tunnel searches. This Captain Sidney Martin believes, "in human beings deeply" and feels "sad and defeated when one of the human beings in his company of soldiers died or got maimed" ("The Way" 40).

Another character whose nature O'Brien leads us to question is Jim Pederson, a Texan who appears in two short stories as well as in *Going After Cacciato*. Paradoxically, Pederson is described as both a good missionary and a "fine" soldier, and he seems to inspire both good works and evil deeds in his fellow soldiers. In *Going After Cacciato* and the short story "Landing Zone Bravo," Pederson is perhaps best remembered as the soldier who is shot and killed by American helicopter gunners who fire into the same rice paddy where they have dropped the soldiers. The gunners become annoyed when Pederson, who has a real fear of helicopters, is too frightened to exit the aircraft. After throwing Pederson out and then shooting him in the legs, the gunners do not stop but continue to fire methodically until Pederson collapses. Pederson's reaction to being gunned down by his own countrymen is to take careful aim and return fire at the gunship in an effort to make it crash and kill the pilots on board.[2]

This incident demonstrates well the moral ambiguity that confronts Pederson and his fellow squad members in the war. O'Brien uses the characters' recognition of the problematic nature of evil to exemplify problems in the nature of reality itself. Eleven chapters after Pederson's death, the novel presents an image of him that totally denies an inherently violent nature. In Chapter Twenty-two, Pederson is portrayed as a peaceful figure, one whom the other soldiers see as having a "Moral Stance" (*GAC* 174). Pederson "gave first aid to a dying VC woman" (*GAC* 174) and wrote a letter of condolence to the parents of a dead soldier. He also treated the Vietnamese villagers kindly. Yet Pederson's death at the hands of his fellow American soldiers serves only to incite Paul Berlin's squad to violence. After Pederson's body is removed, the soldiers reduce a Vietnamese village to rubble. Ironically, while Pederson had previously prevented the squad from burning a village, they now channel their frustrations over his death into emotionlessly doing just that. They are, in fact, not content with just burning it, but must savagely fire into it as well:

> They lined up and fired into the burning village. Harold Murphy used the machine gun. The tracers could be seen through the smoke, bright red streamers, and the Willie Peter and HE kept falling, and the men fired until they were exhausted. The village was a hole. (*GAC* 100)

The duality of Pederson's own nature is demonstrated further in a short story "Keeping Watch by Night" that develops Pederson's character much more fully than does the novel. O'Brien tells us that "Jim Pederson had been a missionary in Kenya before he was drafted, and was fond of witnessing to the powers of Christ as Healer" (Keeping Watch" 65). Pederson ironically narrates a story about his involvement in religious faith and healing to Doc Peret and Paul Berlin as he plants Claymore mines on a road and sets up an ambush against the Viet Cong. Therefore, as he is telling the story of the saving of the life of an Indandis woman, he is constructing an L-shaped ambush, "a reliable killing zone" ("Keeping Watch" 66) designed to take a number of lives. Pederson is also portrayed as being trustworthy, yet possibly untruthful. The story reveals that Pederson has been selected to prepare such a difficult ambush because he is particularly trustworthy, and the comment that "no one had better eyesight in the dark" ("Keeping Watch" 66-67) than Pederson implies that he can see both physically and spiritually better than the other soldiers. However, the soldiers to whom Pederson tells his supposedly true story of faith healing, his miracle of vision, question its validity: "there were too many uncertainties, too many spots for misinterpretation..." ("Keeping Watch" 68).

Perhaps the most significant textual changes deal with the characters of Cacciato and Paul Berlin. In *Going After Cacciato*, O'Brien offers only a segmented portrait of Cacciato, the character in the imaginary journey who is described frequently, yet who is not really described fully. Cacciato is as elusive in description as he is in action. O'Brien deliberately omits any fine detail about Cacciato in order to keep him from being too familiar (Schroeder 150). We know only that he is "A smudged, lonely-looking figure" with a "broad back" and "a shiny pink spot at the crown of the skull" (*GAC* 20). He has "big and even and white" teeth (*GAC* 256), "short, fat little fingers with chewed-down nails" (*GAC* 284), and a "pulpy" face "like wax, or like wet paper. Parts of the face, it seemed, could be scraped off and pressed to other parts" (*GAC* 284). Cacciato is "curiously unfinished," lacking "fine detail" (*GAC* 21), and the images surrounding him are always fuzzy. Most frequently, Cacciato is described in negative terms. As "Dumb as a month-old oyster fart" (*GAC* 14), he "'missed Mongolian idiocy by the breadth of a genetic hair'" (*GAC* 21). Furthermore, he is a "'dumb slob'" (*GAC* 53), as "Dumb as milk" (*GAC* 147), "a dumb kid" (*GAC* 79), a "'sleazy little creep'" (*GAC* 93), and a "'gremlin'" (*GAC* 112). "But who was he?" (*GAC* 147) asks Paul Berlin.

The short story entitled "Going After Cacciato" continues the same segmented portrait as the novel. Cacciato is a "'rockhead'" (*GAC* 47) and a "'blockhead'" (*GAC* 50) who is "tolerated" by the other soldiers

"The way men will sometimes tolerate a pesky dog" (*GAC* 49). He is not only going bald, but is as "'Bald as an eagle's ass'" (*GAC* 48) and as "'Bald as Friar Tuck'" (*GAC* 48). Whereas we learn little, if anything, about how the novelistic Cacciato feels about himself, in the short story version we learn of another side to this problematical character, one that is somewhat sensitive to his own ugliness. O'Brien tells us that "Cacciato always took great care to cover the pink bald spot at the crown of his skull" (*GAC* 47).

Ambiguous images of Cacciato permeate O'Brien's fiction. For example, in Chapter One of *Going After Cacciato* when the squad begin their pursuit of the real Cacciato, he waves to them from the summit of a mountain, flapping his arms with "wide spanning winging motions" (*GAC* 25). Cacciato's flying motions have been interpreted as Christ-like (Roundy 188), although Cacciato also exhibits the traits of an anti-Christ. His actions can be compared to those of Satan, the great tempter, who must beat his wings in Canto 34 of Dante's *Inferno* while crunching traitors in his mouth. And, in a sense, Cacciato is a Satanic figure. While he guides the squad and rescues them from perils on their imaginary journey, he also serves as the temptation which leads them further into their possible desertion of the war, an act that would condemn them as traitors to their country. Consequently, Cacciato can be viewed as both a symbol of good and evil. How does one distinguish between the two polarities? Such ambiguities draw the reader into the search for Cacciato along with the characters. As Cacciato's face appears, only to metamorphosize into the moon or a Halloween jack-o-lantern, the reader creates his own version of the mythical soldier, the same process of constituting reality that is undertaken by the individual members of Paul Berlin's squad.

Cacciato's ambivalence is complicated even further by the appearance of different details in the short story. Whereas in the novel Cacciato's palms are down when he flaps his arms to signal the squad, in the short story his palms are up (Gaspar 327, fn 27), another reinforcement of a Christ-like image. Yet the reader of both the novel and the short stories learns that Cacciato is both compassionate *and* unfeeling. On one hand, he is kind to Paul Berlin in the novel, offering him gum and talking to him after Billy Boy's death. He is also the one soldier in the squad in both the novel and the short story "The Fisherman" who does not want to see Lieutenant Sidney Martin die, stating that Martin is "'not all that bad'" (*GAC* 286). However, O'Brien makes Cacciato even more problematical by showing us a horrific side of him that coexists along with the compassionate part. While Cacciato does not want to participate in the fragging of Lieutenant Sidney

Martin, evidence indicates that he is certainly not adverse to atrocity. His perverse nature is revealed in the photograph of "Cacciato squatting beside the corpse of a shot-dead VC in green pajamas, Cacciato holding up the dead boy's head by a shock of brilliant black hair, Cacciato smiling" (*GAC* 147).

Paul Berlin's attitude toward Cacciato also varies somewhat between the novel and the short story. In the novel we are told that Paul Berlin has "nothing" against Cacciato, but in the short story we are told that he has "nothing *special* [emphasis added] against him" (*GAC* 48), implying that he does indeed have something against Cacciato. Some readers of the novel have concluded that Paul Berlin would like to harm Cacciato. Peter Roundy, for instance, suggests that Paul Berlin wishes to kill Cacciato, his double, in "an act of symbolic suicide," because he feels guilty that he himself has not left the war, a war in which he has never believed (211-12). Katherine Kearns advocates that the novel implies that Paul Berlin really kills Cacciato (78). Certainly the novel contains statements that could be interpreted that way. In Chapter One, Paul Berlin experiences "a vision of murder. Butchery, no less: Cacciato's right temple caving inward, silence, then an enormous explosion of outward-going brains" (*GAC* 29). Then in Chapter Two, an observation post chapter, Paul Berlin thinks of the possibilities, the many ways in which the pursuit of Cacciato could have ended. At one point, he questions, "Had it ended in tragedy" (*GAC* 44)? Yet, at the same time, he posits, "Had it ever ended" (*GAC* 44)?

The ambiguity is heightened even further in the short story when Paul Berlin elaborates on his "vision of murder." "It was no metaphor; he didn't think in metaphors" (*GAC* 55-56), he states, indicating that the murder is real and not imagined. However, he also adds, "it was a simple scary vision...Nothing to justify such a bloody image, no origins....Where, he thought, was all this taking him, and where would it end" (*GAC* 56)? He further thinks that Cacciato does deserve to die:

> Murder was the logical circuit-stopper, of course; it was Cacciato's rightful, maybe inevitable due. Nobody can get away with stupidity forever, and in war the final price for it is always paid in purely biological currency, hunks of toe or pieces of femur or bits of exploded brain. And it *was* still a war, wasn't it? (*GAC* 56)

Is Paul Berlin suggesting that he wishes to kill Cacciato or merely that Cacciato may take so many risks that he will be killed in the war? This ambiguity is important because such a technique potentially involves the reader in the process of creation. The "deep, jagged, complex country" (*GAC* 58) in which the squad travels as Paul Berlin has these thoughts perhaps suggests that Vietnam contains no simple answers or resolutions. [3]

The fate of Paul Berlin is left as uncertain as that of Cacciato. At the end of the novel, Paul Berlin is still in Vietnam, and we never learn whether or not he survives his tour of duty, just as we never learn whether or not certain events in the novel actually take place. O'Brien, however, has written a story, "Speaking of Courage," which focuses on Paul Berlin after his return home from the war. While the story is not included in *Going After Cacciato*, it plays off of Chapter Fourteen, "Upon Almost Winning the Silver Star," where Lieutenant Sidney Martin orders someone to search a Vietnamese tunnel. None of the men, including Paul Berlin, will volunteer for the dangerous task, so Lieutenant Martin forces Frenchie Tucker to search the tunnel by threatening him with court martial. Frenchie Tucker enters the tunnel only to die of a gunshot wound. In "Speaking of Courage," Paul Berlin is thinking about how he might have won the Silver Star for bravery in Vietnam had he managed to rescue Frenchie Tucker himself. [4]

Although the story begins by stating that the war is over, we have no way of knowing whether Paul Berlin's return to the United States really takes place or whether it is conceived in the mind of Paul Berlin as he "pretends." In fact, Paul Berlin makes it clear that he is "pretending" in certain parts of the story. He imagines a conversation with his father:

> "How many medals did you win?" his father might have asked.
> "Seven," he would have said, "though none of them were for valor."
> "That's all right," his father would have answered, knowing full well that many brave men did not win medals for their bravery, and that others won medals for doing nothing. "What are the medals you won?"
> And he would have listed them, as a kind of starting place for talking about the war. . . ("Speaking of Courage" 245)

The use of indefinite verb forms such as "might" and "would" in specific passages provides a clue that Paul Berlin is more than likely fantasizing once more, even though the story itself is told as if Paul is really at home and only thinking about the war in his past. Again, though, we are left with no definite answers or resolutions. While "Speaking of Courage," supposedly takes place after Vietnam, it by no means answers the question of whether or not Paul Berlin survived the war.

It is O'Brien's refusal to allow us final knowledge, the suspension of final judgment through all of his works, that contributes to his fiction's distinction. Both *Going After Cacciato* and the short fiction are arguments against viewing reality in terms of fixed perceptions. How in life and in literature can one distinguish between what is real and what is not? By raising issues and by still not resolving them, O'Brien continues to resist simplistic answers while portraying the complex tangles and nuances of actual experience. Even more importantly, he demonstrates the need of American culture to reject any oversimplifications of the Vietnam War's inconsistencies and discrepancies and shows us the dangers of imposing final definitions on this elusive and on-going chapter of our American history. *Going After Cacciato* and the short fiction are significant in that they are postmodernist works that carry their readers far beyond a one-dimensional view of reality or the war. Not only do they project the war's pluralities of vision, its moral complexities, and its unsolvable oppositions, but they also prove that there is no one definite way in which to tell a war story. In both theme and technique, Tim O'Brien allows for what he terms "a million possibilities."

Notes

1. Other textual changes in the short story paint the war in slightly more ominous tones. In "Where Have You Gone, Charming Billy?" Paul Berlin's first experience with death is treated less sympathetically than in *Going After Cacciato*. When Paul Berlin closes his eyes, rests, and pretends that he did not witness Billy Boy's death, he is abruptly forced to open his eyes by another soldier who threatens to shoot him if he is even suspected of sleeping while on duty. In contrast, the soldier in the novel who tells Paul Berlin to get up is rather pleasant. His reaction to Paul Berlin's resting is to whisper that it is "'No problem'" (*GAC* 251).

2. Jim Pederson's death is also revealed in more intensity in "Landing Zone Bravo." He is shot by his fellow American gunners as in *Going After Cacciato*, but O'Brien repeats the words "the gunners kept firing and firing" more frequently. Pederson is shot an additional time, in the stomach as well as in the legs and the groin, and we see the effect that his blood has on the rice paddy: "The blades stirred creamy whitecaps that lapped over Pederson so that the colors mixed and blended, paddy-yellow and brown and green and red" and "boiled green and hot red" ("Landing Zone Bravo" 76-77).

3. In the novel the wilderness is "jagged" but not "deep" and "complex;" instead, it is "beautiful, lasting country. Things grew as they grew, unchanging" (*GAC* 31). The difference between the two versions perhaps suggests the difficulty of really knowing the ambiguous Vietnamese landscape.

4. As Gaspar points outs, in this version of the episode O'Brien omits the character of Bernie Lynn and has Paul Berlin unsuccessfully attempt to rescue Frenchie Tucker (325-26, fn 13).

Works Cited

Gaspar, Charles Jamieson, Jr. "Reconnecting: Time and History in Narratives of the Vietnam War." Diss. University of Connecticut, 1983.

Kearns, Katherine Sue. "Some Versions of Violence in Three Contemporary Novels: John Irving's *The World According to Garp*, Tim O'Brien's *Going After Cacciato*, and Alice Walker's *The Color Purple*." Diss. University of North Carolina at Chapel Hill, 1982.

O'Brien, Tim. "The Fisherman." *Esquire* October 1977: 92, 130, 134.

---. *Going After Cacciato*. New York: Dell, 1978.

---. "Going After Cacciato." *Ploughshares* 3.1 (n.d.): 42-65.

---. "Keeping Watch by Night." *Redbook* December 1976: 65-68.

---. "Speaking of Courage." *Massachusetts Review* 17 (1976): 243-53.

---. "The Way It Mostly Was." *Shenandoah* Winter 1976: 35-45.

---. "Where Have You Gone, Charming Billy?" *Redbook* May 1975: 81, 127-28, 130, 132.

Roundy, Peter Edward. "Images of Vietnam: 'Catch-22,' New Journalism, and the Postmodern Imagination." Diss. Florida State University, 1981.

Schroeder, Eric James. "Two Interviews: Talks with Tim O'Brien and Robert Stone." *Modern Fiction Studies* 30 (1984): 135-64.

NARRATIVE STRUCTURE IN *APOCALYPSE NOW*

David Everett Whillock

> I love the smell of napalm in the morning.
> It smells like victory.
> > Major Kilgore in *Apocalypse Now*

When Francis Ford Coppola made public his decision to produce and direct *Apocalypse Now* in 1975, there were only a few films that depicted the Vietnam conflict in any direct way. While *The Boys of Company C* and *Go Tell the Spartans* were released before *Apocalypse Now*, *The Green Berets* was the only film in release that directly treated America's involvement in combat during the Vietnam conflict. Because of Coppola's past cinematic success in *The Godfather* (1972) and *The Godfather Part II* (1974), anticipation for a definitive film about the Vietnam war was high in both cinematic and historical circles. However, because of the film's lengthy production process (four years), *Apocalypse Now* was the last of several films released in the middle and late 1970's.

Films that focused on Vietnam in the 1970's for the most part investigated how the conflict affected the returning veteran and his placement or displacement in American society. Only two films released in the 1970's, *Go Tell the Spartans* and *The Boys of Company C*, placed their characters in combat situations. Gilbert Adair in his book *Vietnam on Film* considers these two films as opportunistic in the wake of the pre-release publicity of *Apocalypse Now*:

> While neither *The Boys of Company C* nor *Go Tell the Spartans* is absolutely devoid of interest, they are what one might call "quickies;" if not B movies then resolutely A minus, whose existence seem motivated solely by opportunism... inspired by the hope of cashing in on the much delayed *Apocalypse Now*.[1]

Apocalypse Now made its public debut at the 1979 International Cannes Film Festival in France. The film entered as a "work in progress," and shared the top picture honor, the *Palme d' Or*, with the West German film *The Tin Drum*. John Simon wrote in the *National Review* that one reason Coppola's film was so long in production was that an ending to the film was not easily conceived.[2] At Cannes, Coppola had hoped to resolve the indecision which had led him to film three different endings. Yet Coppola presented an ending at Cannes that he later dropped for the American release.[3] On October 3, 1979, the decision was made by United Artists to release the film nationwide after a two month marketing trial in Los Angeles, Toronto, and New York. *Apocalypse Now* met with mixed critical response but was nominated for eight Academy Awards including best picture, direction, adapted screenplay, supporting actor, cinematography, art direction, and sound. The film won two Oscars: sound and cinematography. *Apocalypse Now* remains a controversial film in two regards: its adaptation of Joseph Conrad's novella *Heart of Darkness* and its surrealistic depiction of the Vietnam war.

THREE POINTS OF ANALYSIS

Methodological foundations for critical analysis have become commonplace in contemporary academic criticism. The importance of any method is underscored by film scholar Bill Nichols when he writes that "methodologies are a tool to aid the writer and reader in understanding the world: [that is] how things relate, or better, how relationships function."[4] In the following investigation of *Apocalypse Now,* a narrative structural analysis based on the theories of Lévi-Strauss will focus on these functional relationships.[5] This analysis will be developed through three narrative elements: 1) the environment portrayed in the film; 2) the characters; and 3) the story motifs. The environment of the film consists of the physical setting and the cultural background of the opposing societies caught in the conflict: Vietnam and the United States. The analysis of the characters is concerned with both major and minor characters and their relationships to each other as well as their function(s) within the story. In contrast, the story-motifs will investigate those elements of the plot that underscore binary demarcations that are found not only in dialogue and narration, but in action as well.

The analysis of each element is achieved through the identification and discussion of each "constituent unit" (which Lévi-Strauss has termed "binary bundles of relations") and how such binary opposition within the story are resolved. The resolution, according to Lévi-Strauss, is dependent upon a mediator.[6] A mediator is any element within the story that facilitates the resolution of the binary opposition.

The resolution, achieved through the mediating device, is the transformation of the opposing binary units into a closer relationship. As the mediating device "permutates" (transforms) the binary opposition toward a more middle position, the characteristics of each binary unit will become less distinctive. The resolution of the narrative takes place once the transformation of opposition is complete.

Using this method Lévi-Strauss allows the film scholar to view the Vietnam war film as an entity in itself and separate from the American war films of the past. The justification and method of war found in World War II films, for example, are clearly seen as righteous. However, the Vietnam war film does not present these elements in such a biased manner. In fact, the justification for the war is at issue in these films. By using Lévi-Strauss we are compelled to explore both sides of the equation. By resolving the contradictions found in the narratives through the mediator, the viewer comes closer to his/her own resolution of the war.

ENVIRONMENT

In *Apocalypse Now*, the basic constituent unit found in the environment is that of the binary opposition between controlled/uncontrolled. Lévi-Strauss defines such binary opposition as Culture/Nature. By extension of Lévi-Strauss' formula for the structure of myth, the relationship of the oppositions would thus be: nature is to culture as uncontrolled environment is to controlled environment. The opposition between the uncontrolled environment and controlled environment in *Apocalypse Now* is more specifically exemplified as city/jungle.

The environmental conflict is introduced in the first sequence of *Apocalypse Now*. Willard's alcoholic opening nightmare is of a peaceful lush green jungle immediately bursting into an apocalyptic red explosion of napalm as an air attack is in progress. He awakes from this nightmare only to be confronted with the realization that he is "only in Saigon." As he approaches the window, the camera reveals Saigon as an ordered and modern city. Concrete buildings, modern domestic vehicles, and paved streets assure Willard that he is not in the jungles of Vietnam. Willard laments his position by expressing his knowledge that every day he remains in the city he gets "weaker," while every day that "Charlie squats in the jungle," Charlie gets stronger. (This strong/weak opposition becomes a significant point later with the confrontation between Kurtz and Willard.)

There are five separate physical settings that deserve attention in this analysis. They are: 1) the combination of Saigon and intelligence headquarters at Nha Trang; 2) the battle for the Vietcong village at Vin Drin Drop; 3) the episodic experiences of the journey up the Nung

River; 4) the last American outpost at Do Lung Bridge; and 5) Kurtz's fortress near Nu Mong Ba in Cambodia.

These environments represent permutations (transformations) between the binary oppositions of controlled and uncontrolled. As Willard's mission up the Nung River takes him through these environments, the opposition between controlled and uncontrolled moves closer to resolution. An analysis of each environment will clarify their function in the transformation.

Saigon and Nha Trang. Saigon and intelligence headquarters at Nha Trang are the most controlled environments in *Apocalypse Now*. The Mayor's request over the radio that off-base American soldiers not hang their laundry in the street windows informs the audience that the city government of Saigon has a strong control of the city's internal affairs while there exists a force of United States soldiers to control "outside" problems that might come into the city from the jungle. The COMSAC headquarters at Nha Trang is also a highly controlled environment because of its need for security from "outside" intruders. As Willard enters the perimeter of the headquarters, he is carefully checked and signs a security sheet to be allowed to enter. Once inside the headquarters, the controlled environment is maintained through Army regularity as he is met by a Major who informs Willard that he may "stand at ease." (This maintenance of discipline within the Army system begins to dissolve as Willard moves further away from Saigon and Nha Trang.)

Battle for Vin Drin Drop. Once Willard receives his mission, he is taken to Major Kilgore who is currently involved with "mopping up" an attack on a Vietcong strong hold. The contrast between the ordered life of both Saigon and Nha Trang, and the chaos of battle is evident in this sequence. (The oppositions between Culture and Nature are particularly exemplified by buildings: a burned out French church standing among the bamboo structures of the village huts.)

The next morning Kilgore and his Air Ninth Cavalry attack the village at Vin Drin Drop. This Vietcong village also underscores the differences between the controlled environment of a "hot" society (culture) as compared to a "cold" society (nature). The village is physically in opposition to Saigon. There are no concrete buildings in this village and the streets are dirt paths into the surrounding jungle. However, there is an internal order in this village. As the attack begins, a grade school is in session. The guard on duty sounds the alarm and the children are removed in an orderly fashion. The soldiers that defend this village are trying to protect themselves against "outsiders" from the air, not the jungle. Indeed, the jungle for this village is friendly as its density protects the defending soldiers.

The war machines in these separate environments are also indicative of the binary oppositions between the film's presentation of nature and culture. The American war machine, which depends upon the notion of "replaceable parts," is in direct opposition to the village war machine, which is made up of old machine guns and vehicles that are for the most part not replaceable. In light of such a differential, the Vietcong village is quickly destroyed, as the village war machine is no match for the American. The Vietcong run into the jungle to be protected by its dense cover, while Major Kilgore radios in a napalm strike from Air Force jets. Militarily, there is no equality within the binary opposition of modern war machines/antiquated war machines.

Nung River. The Nung River is the mediating environment between the opposition of controlled/uncontrolled environment. The importance of the river as a linking device is echoed by Willard when he states that the Nung River "snaked through the war like a main circuit cable plugged straight into Kurtz." The river touches both the controlled environment of the city (culture) and the uncontrolled environment of the jungle (nature). The river remains a kind of fulcrum that balances the extremes of culture and nature (controlled/uncontrolled environments). This is exemplified when Chef, one of the characters in the boat, wants to go ashore into the jungle to gather mangos. While in the jungle, he and Willard are surprised by a tiger. After the incident Chef exerts his preference for a more controlled environment by expressing that he must remember never to "get off the boat." This preference is echoed by Willard who suggests that one should never get off the boat unless he is willing to go "all of the way." In fact, he reminds us that Kurtz got off the boat and is now fully indoctrinated into the uncontrolled environment of the nature opposition. Willard's point becomes important to the narrative when he leaves the boat to assassinate Kurtz.

The river as mediator can be illustrated by comparing the city (culture) to the jungle (nature). As discussed earlier, the opposition found in the environments of *Apocalypse Now* is Saigon (city) and Kurtz's compound (jungle). The Nung River, because of its relation between that of Saigon and Kurtz's compound, is a mediator between the two. The Nung River carries Willard's boat from Saigon, yet it also carries the boat back. Thus the river is both of Saigon (culture) and of Kurtz's compound (nature). As a result, the river's function in *Apocalypse Now* is that of a mediating device.

Aptly, the closer the river gets to Kurtz and the further from Saigon, the less control there is over the environment. While Willard is on the river, the opposition between nature and culture becomes pronounced when a Vietnamese sampan is stopped by the American boat to search for smuggled weapons. The orderly search is suddenly ripped apart by an over-anxious crew member who kills the family on board because of a sudden movement by one of the family members to protect a hidden puppy. The death of the members aboard the junk is a turning point on the river. From that point on, the river is no longer a symbol for safety. This is underscored by the events at Do Lung Bridge on the Nung River.

Do Lung Bridge. This bridge, we are told, is the last American outpost before Cambodia. Willard and his crew arrive during a phantasmagoric night battle to destroy the bridge. A controlled environment does not exist here. As the boat arrives, American soldiers at the bridge jump into the river begging the crew to take them back to civilization. Willard is met by a dispatcher who is also anxious to leave, telling Willard he is in the "armpit of the world." When Willard tries to locate the commanding officer at the outpost, he is met with remarkably unstructured methods of warfare. There is neither order nor a commanding officer; there is only chaos and death.

As the crew leaves the bridge and gets closer to Kurtz, the environment has transformed from culture to nature. The boat passes burned villages and wrecked war machines as they move upstream. Half of a fuselage and stabilizer of a crashed B-52 stick out of the river, symbolizing the loss of control that the American war machine has over the jungle. In fact, the symbolic fulcrum represented by the river slowly dissolves as the boat goes deeper into the jungle. With the death of two crew members (one by a Vietcong bullet, and one by a native spear), the boat itself is no longer safe.

Kurtz's fortress. Willard and the remaining two crew members arrive at Kurtz's fortress to find that the Colonel has gone insane. The bodies of dead North Vietnamese, Vietcong, and Cambodians are left decaying in the jungle heat. In contrast to the environment in Saigon, cultural control is missing. There is no rank among Kurtz's army, no distinction between the native Montagnards and the invading Americans with Kurtz. In the fortress there are no streets nor buildings. Only the Buddhist temple serves as a protection from the jungle. Kurtz's army sleeps in the open leaving the jungle to control the outer perimeters of the compound.

The resolution between controlled environment and uncontrolled environment is represented by the Nung River. The "balance" of the story begins to shift toward the jungle and its uncontrolled environment after the Do Lung Bridge. Equilibrium is restored only after the death of Kurtz when Willard leaves the uncontrolled environment and makes his way back down the river toward Saigon.

In this fashion, the river connects both the controlled and uncontrolled environments of the narrative. Willard uses the river to travel to and from both environments. The extreme end of the uncontrolled environment in the binary relationship no longer exists at the end of the film; however, neither does the controlled environment. Willard's experience has led him (and the audience) to conclude that there is no controlled environment. Recall how the battle of Vin Drin Drop revealed a madness of a distinct method without real control. At the Do Lung Bridge, both method and control are absent.

The resolution of the binary environments is one of several within the story. Lévi-Strauss argued that to analyze a myth all such bundles of relations must be investigated before stating whether there is a resolution within the myth (narrative) or not. The oppositions between characters may give further insight into the question of resolution within *Apocalypse Now*.

CHARACTERS

While there are several constituent units found among the characters of *Apocalypse Now*, two units in particular deserve attention in this analysis: first, the binary opposition between the Generals of the United States Army and Colonel Kurtz, and second, the binary opposition between two minor characters, Lance and Chef.

Generals/Kurtz. The central binary opposition in *Apocalypse Now* is that between the Generals of the United States Army and Colonel Kurtz. The generals have decided that Kurtz's methods are unsound and his command must be terminated. In an intercepted taped message, Kurtz says that the Vietcong are animals that are not threatened by the orderly, methodical form of combat orchestrated by the controlled environment of the generals. Thus, Kurtz must be annihilated. The Generals tell Willard that Kurtz has taken the war into his own hands and is operating in an unorderly, non-methodical war "without any human decency at all."

Kurtz is full of contradictions himself. He views the war through the binary oppositions of purity of will versus corruption of will. The answer for Kurtz lies in the dialectic existence of life and death (also to be discussed as a thematic opposition under story-motif). Kurtz's view of the war is in direct contrast with the Generals' view. The Generals want a war with rules and moral decency, while Kurtz feels that the war cannot be fought without the strength of the primordial instincts of survival, no matter what the moral cost. The opposition between the Generals and Kurtz is placed in the dichotomy of method/no method of war. Willard is sent by the Generals to resolve the conflict that exists between them. The conflict is resolved for the Generals by the assassination of Kurtz.

Willard serves as a distinct function in this conflict. Like the Nung River in the constituent unit of controlled/uncontrolled environment, Willard plays a mediator in the opposition between the characters of Kurtz and the Generals. The character of Willard is the mediator because of his centered position in the continuum between the Generals and Kurtz. Lévi-Strauss would see Willard as mediator because of his "position halfway between two polar terms, he must retain something of that duality--namely an ambiguous and equivocal character." This is exemplified by Willard's indecision about the mission. While he agrees to take the mission, Willard describes his concern over killing an American and fellow officer. However, Willard also recalls killing "six people close enough to blow their last breath in [his] face." The audience realizes that he is not necessarily of the "orderly decent humanitarian world" that was described by the General at Nha Trang. The experience of the Vietnam war has changed him. He is no longer a cultural being, yet his resistance to killing Kurtz implies that he is equally not of the "evil" world that the Generals have proclaimed Kurtz to be a part of. Thus, Willard is ideologically in the middle, binding the two points of view together.

As a true mediator, Willard resolves the conflict between the Generals and Kurtz. He solves the Generals' problem by killing Kurtz. However, he also resolves a problem for Kurtz. Kurtz wanted his view of the war presented to his son. After killing Kurtz, Willard takes the position paper written by Kurtz to give to Kurtz's son. With the paper in hand, Willard exits the compound leaving both Kurtz and the Generals behind. After his mission is complete, his orders are to call in an air strike to destroy Kurtz's headquarters. Instead, he shuts off the radio, the only representative of culture left in the film, and begins his journey back down the river. Even in one ending of the film when an airstrike does destroy the compound, the viewer is left with the impression that it was not Willard who called it in.

Chef/Lance. A particular relationship between two crew members of the boat is also indicative of the binary oppositions between nature and culture in *Apocalypse Now*. The crew members Chef and Lance are representatives of culture and nature respectively. Chef is a New Orleans Saucier who represents, through his profession, a high cultural role. Chef was raised to become a professional chef. He has, in essence, a pedigree. He was trained through his early life to become a specialist in sauces and was preparing to study in France when he was drafted. The cultural side of Chef is also underscored by his desire not to kill. This is illustrated when the boat detains the Sampan on the river to search for weapons. When a sudden move on board the junk begins the carnage, it is Chef who does not shoot his weapon even though he is directly in danger.

At the other end of the continuum is Lance, a secondary character who represents nature. He is a professional surfer. Instead of transforming a raw material into something for use, as Chef does, Lance becomes part of that which he uses. The natural wave of the ocean is his tool and it remains untransformed for Lance's use. His name alone underscores a natural image (a lance is a native weapon used by Kurtz's warriors). Another strong indication of Lance's function in this opposition is found in Lance's behavior going up the river. The closer the boat gets to Kurtz's compound the more Lance takes on the look of a native. By the time the crew reaches the compound, Lance has adopted their dress. Because Lance has accepted this existence, he is spared the cruel death that awaits Chef.

The function for Willard as secondary-character mediator is a simple one. He is neither a part of Lance's nature nor of Chef's culture. Willard's mediating role between Lance and Chef is developed early in the journey up the river. It is Willard who goes with Chef to gather mangos, and it is Lance who accompanies Willard at Do Lung Bridge. More important, after the other crew members are killed, the three remaining characters become representatives of the binary oppositions that exist in the narrative. The boat thus becomes a microcosm for the larger conflict.

In this structural analysis, the binary oppositions of the characters as represented by the Generals and Kurtz exemplify the extreme binary opposition of the continuum between nature and culture, and other characters (Chef and Lance) represent a closer relationship between nature and culture. The permutation between the binary characters occurs through the continuum of relations between other "closer" characters. With Willard as mediator, the two extreme oppositions between Nature and Culture come closer together. Resolution occurs when Willard kills Kurtz and takes Kurtz's position paper back with him. Neither extreme triumphs over the other as Willard mediates a compromise in this element of the narrative.

The resolution of character and environmental conflicts has, overall, a direct influence on the outcome of the story. However, more subtle conflicts also give the story a depth of meaning. These subtle recurrences of binary oppositions, the story-motifs, give the narrative an internal structure which allows the more obvious conflicts of characters and environment a progression toward resolution through their mediating devices. It is these subtle conflicts within the story that support the major "spine" or focus of the story.

STORY-MOTIFS

One binary opposition is foremost between two elements of the story-motif that supports the characters and environment of *Apocalypse Now*. This conflict is found in the story-motif of method of war/no method of war.

The underlying theme of *Apocalypse Now* is Kurtz's unsound method of warfare versus the General's sound method of war. Kurtz finds war an immoral event that should be fought without judgment and with moral terror. Kurtz's method has in essence become unsound because the war for Kurtz is not the "conventional war" fought by the Generals of a cultured nation.

Kurtz emphasizes this lack of morality in the Vietnam war when he tells Willard of his experience in the Special Forces. Kurtz was assigned to inoculate the children of a village for polio. After the forces inoculated the children and left, the Vietcong chopped the inoculated arms off of the children to stop the infestation of the American serum (cultural medicine). What Kurtz found so ingenious is the purity of will that it took to achieve such an act. He says, "it was as though a diamond bullet went into the center of my forehead and I realized that it was this kind of purity of will that would win the war. If I had ten divisions of men with that kind of will, I knew I could win." For Kurtz, an Army of men without human compassion would win the war. To the Generals this was no method for fighting a "humanitarian war." While *Apocalypse Now* does not exemplify the type of war the generals or Kurtz embrace, a permutation (transformation) of the story-motif between the binary oppositions of the General's method of war and Kurtz's no-method of war is represented in the film's presentation of the battles of Vin Drin Drop and Do Lung Bridge.

The battle of Vin Drin Drop and the Do Lung Bridge are permutations that are indicative of the developing resolution between the two extremes of Culture (method) and Nature (no-method). In *Apocalypse Now* the permutations of the story-motif, represented as method/no-method of war, resolve the conflict between binary oppositions. By bringing together both binary oppositions in the two battles (Vin Drin Drop and Do Lung Bridge) the extreme oppositions are placed closer together in the continuum. Thus, resolution takes place between the two extremes in the story-motif of *Apocalypse Now*.

CONCLUSIONS

To discuss the resolutions found in *Apocalypse Now*, we must break the narrative into three specific elements: transformation, opposition, and mediation. The transformation that occurs in *Apocalypse Now* is Willard's decision to bring Kurtz's story back with him after he has killed Kurtz. Willard's decision metaphorically offers the audience a way out of Vietnam. Through the process of the film the audience has an opportunity to view the war as a confusing conflict between the General's ideal method of war and Kurtz's non-method. Through Willard's mission up the Nung River, the horror of war is presented as the insanity of both methods. The audience becomes a witness to war and will hopefully understand its futility.

The binary opposition between the Generals and Kurtz is one of many in *Apocalypse Now*. While that particular constituent unit is the focus of the narrative, there are other binary units that have an indirect relationship to the General's/Kurtz opposition and which affect the outcome of the resolution that occurs between the central characters. Using the three levels of analysis (environment, characters, and story-motif) and the major binary opposition of nature/culture, we can chart several examples of constituent units found in the narrative within each level. These binary demarcations can be illustrated through the following series of antinomies.

CULTURE	NATURE
ENVIRONMENT	
The United States	Vietnam
"Hot Society"	"Cold Society"
Saigon	Kurtz's Compound
CHARACTERS	
Generals	Kurtz
Chef	Lance
STORY-MOTIF	
Method of War	No-method of war
Humanity	Savagery

Modern Machinery	Antiquated Machinery
of War	of War
Corruption of Will	Purity of Will

With this list there is evidence that *Apocalypse Now* is structured by binary oppositions. However, according to Lévi-Strauss the function of the narrative is to resolve the binary oppositions. In *Apocalypse Now* there are several oppositions resolved through the permutations achieved by the mediators. As developed through the preceding analysis of environment, characters, and story motifs, the constituent units of Saigon/Kurtz's compound, the Generals/Kurtz, and method of war/no-method of war are transformed and resolved through mediating devices. The binary opposition between the major characters of the Generals/Kurtz is resolved through Willard; the environment opposition is resolved by the Nung River; and through the mediating device of the events on the Nung River (battles of Vin Drin Drop and Do Lung Bridge), the binary opposition in the story motif of method/no method of war is resolved.

The permutations leading to the resolution of method/no method of the war and between that of culture/nature in the analysis of environment are dependent upon Vin Drin Drop and Do Lung Bridge. As battles, these locations are a midpoint between the General's idealistic viewpoint of the war and Kurtz's lack of "sound method" for waging war. As geographical locations they are of special importance in the transformation from the ordered city of Saigon and the unordered jungles of Kurtz's compound. Whereas the permutations and resolution between culture/nature in the analysis of characters is developed through the mediating device of Willard, Willard remains a fulcrum between the major character opposition of Chef/Lance.

One of the most important underlying story-motifs, as expressed by method/no-method, is exemplified as corruption of will/purity of will. This "theme" in *Apocalypse Now* is the "unpronounced" conflict in the method/no method opposition. This binary opposition is finally resolved through Willard's assassination of Kurtz.

What special insights, then, does this analysis give us? The development of the Vietnam war in our culture has taken on mythic proportions. Media representations of the Vietnam war give us an opportunity to investigate our social fabric and help understand the war and its effects on our culture. These representations also allow our culture to articulate interpretations of a historical event through narrative forms to new members of our society. Through the narrative structure of *Apocalypse Now* our cultural contradictions may be played out on the screen and through a cinematic resolution we may come to terms with our own doubts and confusion about the war America lost.

Notes

1. Gilbert Adair, *Vietnam on Film* (London: Proteus Publishers, 1981): 114.

2. John Simon, "Apocalypse Without End," in *Mass Media and the Popular Arts*, Fredric Rissover and David Birch, eds., (New York: McGraw-Hill, 1981). p. 444. There were three separate versions of the ending in *Apocalypse Now*. For this analysis the ending used in the theatrical release 35 millimeter version will be used. This ending portrays Willard leaving Kurtz's headquarters safely with a subsequent airstrike on the headquarters after Willard departs.

3. Eleanor Coppola chronicles the development and the production of *Apocalypse Now* in her book *Notes* (New York: Simon and Schuster, 1979).

4. Bill Nichols, ed., *Movies and Methods: An Anthology* (Berkeley: University of California Press, 1976): 1.

5. Using Lévi-Strauss' formula, the application of the opposition between nature/culture and uncontrolled environment/controlled environment is possible. Claude Lévi-Strauss, *Structural Anthropology, Volume I*, Trans. Claire Jacobson and Brooke Schoepf (New York: Basic Books, 1963): 228.

6. Lévi-Strauss, *Structural Anthropology, Volume I*: 226-228.

BOTTLES OF VIOLENCE: FRAGMENTS OF VIETNAM IN EMILY MANN'S *STILL LIFE*

Kate Beaird Meyers

Emily Mann's *Still Life* is important to the canon of literature about the Vietnam War not only because it dramatizes the plight of the veteran and his family, who are also "veterans" of the war, but because it examines the basic dichotomies of American culture: "American Myths" are brought into direct confrontation with the realities of the aftermath of Vietnam. The unusual structure of *Still Life* makes it a classic example of a form Philip Beidler finds characteristic of Vietnam literature written since 1975, in which the age's "need to examine the nature of its own myth-making processes" is the central focus. According to Beidler, "even as the shapes of art begin to transform experience into a new medium of signification, experience itself begins to generate new shapes of art in its own image as well" (141). The play, somewhat reminiscent of Jean Paul Sartre's *No Exit*, consists of a long conversation between three characters, each of whom is a metonymic representation of some aspect of the Vietnam generation. Although they are not literally confined together, as are Sartre's, Mann's characters are figuratively bound by their involvement with each other and with the Vietnam War. The characters analyze their own interrelationships, but only superficially. They talk about the war but do not analyze it in terms of its being "right" or "wrong." The real question they address is how to recover from a war that brought an entire nation into conflict with itself and exposed some of the basic conflicts found in American culture: America is both a nation of peace, love, and freedom and a nation with an inherent tendency toward what Richard Slotkin has called "regeneration through violence"; America is a nation in which both sexes are conditioned to accept the phallocentric myths of the "American Adam" and the "angel of the house" but where the reality of Sartrean "facticity"[1] makes belief in such myths both foolish and dangerous. It is the dialogue between these dichotomies that creates the tension of Mann's play.

The story of *Still Life* is deceptively simple. Mark is a Vietnam veteran, a former Marine. Haunted by the guilt of having killed a Vietnamese family (mother, father, children), angry at the contradictions of the war itself and at the treatment of returning veterans, Mark has difficulty communicating with anyone. He was convicted of selling drugs and served a term in prison; he became an alcoholic but has not had a drink for nearly a year. He has started a career as an artist, creating scenes inside bottles and jars using fragments of memorabilia from Vietnam; he is also an amateur photographer. Cheryl, Mark's wife, is a former "flower child" who spent much of the sixties on drugs. She is now aged beyond her years by her struggles with Mark. She has a young son and is noticeably pregnant again. Mark has beaten her severely several times, for which they both blame the war and Mark's inability to recover from it. Cheryl will not discuss the war; she prefers to think of it as a past event, refusing to acknowledge the fact that Mark still fights it every day. The third character is Nadine, a woman ten years older than Mark and Cheryl. She has several children and is divorced from an alcoholic husband. She has befriended Mark, who has confided in her some of his feelings about the war, which she professes to understand. Nadine was involved in the anti-war movement during the sixties and is now completely disillusioned with the American Dream.

These simple characterizations are in actuality highly complex. Each of them functions as a metonym for a large portion of the generation of Americans to which they belong. Mark represents Vietnam veterans who are confused and angry about the war and its aftermath:

> My unit got blown up. It was a high contact. We got hit very, very hard. [. . .] What can I say? I am still alive-my friends aren't. [2]

Cheryl is both the wife/victim and the voice of a nation that does not want to know about the unpleasantness of the war. If it is not discussed, perhaps it will go away:

> I can't deal with that at all. But I find that if I can at least put it out of my mind it's easier. If I had to think about what he's done to me, I'd have been gone a long time ago. (SL 296)

And Nadine speaks for those members of the sixties generation who no longer believe that "all you need is love":

> God, we hated those vets. [. . .] All that nonsense about long hair, flowers and love. [. . .] I think I knew then what I know now. [. . .] The problem now is knowing what to do with what we know. (SL 303, 305)

Although she is disillusioned, Nadine remains hopeful that if America remembers the lessons of Vietnam, "maybe we can protect ourselves and come out on the other side" (SL 321). Like the larger groups of which they are emblematic, the three characters do not communicate well with each other. During their conversation, they never really connect with each other; in fact, the last words of the script, before "END OF PLAY," are: *"The WOMEN's eyes meet for the first time as lights go down"* (SL 325). They talk about themselves and about each other but always to the audience, which serves as a therapist, watching and listening as Mark, Cheryl, and Nadine work through their problems. The characters do have one concern in common, however--concern for their own futures in an American society that remains unable to come to terms with the Vietnam War.

I

America's involvement in the Vietnam War may be a natural result of a dichotomy that has long existed in the American psyche between two epistemologies Richard Slotkin equates with the mythical archetypes "hunter" or "warrior" and "shaman." The (masculine) hunter follows a code of "war and killing"; the (feminine) shaman follows a moral code of "self-abnegation, kindness, and peace." The law of the hunter clearly resembles the "entrepreneurial spirit" of the colonists and frontiersmen, and of their modern counterpart the "military-industrial complex," while the laws of the shaman are closely akin to those of Christianity, especially the Quakers (Slotkin 44). Among the Puritan settlers of America,

> the lifeway represented by the shaman came to be thought
> of as the way of the victim, the sufferer, the captive. In
> situations of extreme fear and insecurity . . . the balance
> between the shaman and hunter as equal symbols of value
> is destroyed. The shaman then becomes symbolic of
> weakness in man, the hunter symbolic of strength. . . . The
> consequences of such a dichotomy are severe: the natures
> of shaman and hunter become intensified, and the warrior
> feels driven to prove his strength and power through acts
> of incredible cruelty, which is exacerbated by his fear of
> being at one with the totally helpless victim he destroys.
> (Slotkin 50)

The Puritans synthesized the hunter and the shaman as a means of rationalizing their violence toward the Indians, even though such a rationalization is in direct conflict with the Christian ethics on which the colonies were founded. They created the "errand into the wilderness" as a means of making their followers believe that destroying the Indians and taking their land was a religious duty. Through this synthesis, the voice of the shaman, the peace-maker who spoke against murdering Indians and usurping their land, was silenced.

The Puritans believed that they were the "Chosen People," sent to the New World to build a "City upon a Hill" from which God's light would shine perpetually, a "light whose radiance would keep Christian voyagers from crashing on the rocks, a light that could brighten the world" (Baritz ll). However, creating that city presented the Puritans with major problems. In order to "civilize" the wilderness, it was necessary to make violence a corollary to their "Christian" mission. The Indian was an obstacle that had to be removed. The Indian wars were an "acceptable metaphor for the American experience," since the Puritans "could pit their own philosophy, doctrine, culture, and race against their cultural opposites and could illustrate God's favor to their way of life in recounting their triumph and the discomfiture of both the heathen enemy and those of their own people who had been less than rigorous in their faith" (Slotkin 68). The Indian was transformed into evil incarnate, an emissary of the Devil, sent to torment and to test the Puritans.

But this acceptance of violence brought the Puritans face to face with their fear of the wilderness, as represented by the "savage." In his likeness to "primitive inner man" the Indian "was a threat to the Puritan's soul," and many feared that too much contact with Indians might cause even the best of Christians to revert to savage ways (Slotkin 55). The Puritans were frightened by the fact that their own soldiers "behaved precisely like their Indian enemies--burning the villages of their enemies, slaughtering not only the warriors but also the wounded, the women, and the children." Ministers and historians, attempting to ease the situation, told their listeners and readers that such violence was "divinely sanctioned" (Slotkin 55). Three centuries later, the American government used the same rhetoric to justify sending troops on another "errand." As Frances FitzGerald explains:

> American officers liked to call the area outside GVN control "Indian country." It was a joke, of course, but it put the Vietnam War into a definite historical and mythological perspective: the Americans were once again embarked upon a heroic and (for themselves) almost painless conquest of an inferior race. (491-92)

It was an American soldier's moral duty to go to Vietnam to kill the "godless Communists," and, as in earlier times, the reversion of some soldiers to a "savage state" was an issue of much concern to the military and to the nation at large. Soldiers in Vietnam created "fantasies of exactly the same sort that the Americans had created about the Indians"; they "stripped the Vietnamese of their humanity in order to deliver themselves of their guilty desires," and, ultimately, the war "brought out their latent sadism, as perhaps all wars between races . . . have brought it out of all armies" (FitzGerald 496). One important aspect of the hunter/shaman dichotomy that cannot be ignored is the role of gender. Originally, both the hunter and the shaman were male, but, as the myths became Europeanized, the hunter became associated with qualities traditionally seen as "male" and the shaman with those qualities seen as "female."[3] The active male/hunter figure was valued by society far more than the passive female/shaman. As European civilization increased its territorial holdings, the male/hunter came to see his divine task as settlement of the frontier, penetrating as deeply as possible into the "virgin" wilderness. Through violence against the land and its native population (a figurative rape), he could regenerate himself and his people. The violence he perpetrated against the wilderness, stripping the land in order to plant his seed, provided him, and the society that lived vicariously through his exploits, with a kind of sexual release. The female land, and the females of the land, were there to receive his assaults and provide relief for his pent-up energies. Because Indians were not considered "human," violation of Indian women was not considered criminal behavior. At least indirectly, this same "macho" ideology may be to blame for the rape and murder of Vietnamese women and children during the war and for much of the domestic violence still suffered by American women and children.

II

In Vietnam Mark was forced to confront his own desire for "regeneration through violence," as well as the Puritan fear of the effects of the wilderness on "civilized" man. He was intoxicated by the violence he found in the jungle, by the power it gave him: "At night, you could do anything . . . It was free-fire zones. It was dark, then all of a sudden, everything would just burn loose. It was beautiful. . . . You were given all this power to work outside the law. We all dug it" (SL 280). His gun became a figurative penis; each time he killed, he experienced a pleasure akin to orgasm: "It's like the best dope you ever had, the best sex you've ever had" (SL 273). When he returned home, Mark could not control the savage impulses unleashed by his experience in Vietnam. Now, he is unable to resolve the contradictions he finds in a society that tells him to kill one day, then expects him to be "civilized" the next: "This country had all these rules and regulations and then all of a sudden they removed these things. Then you came back and try to make your life in that society where you had to deal with them. You find that if you violate them, which I found, you go to jail, which I did" (SL 316). He went through a period of needing inordinately frequent sexual orgasm as a means of reaching the same "high" he got from killing Vietnamese: "I wanted to fuck my brains out" (SL 306). Finally, Mark's anger and guilt exploded into violence against his wife and son.

When he first returned from Vietnam, Mark tried to communicate with his family but found it impossible. Even while he was in Vietnam, he tried to convey to his parents and brother the horror of his experience. He sent them a bone from the body of someone he killed-- as a warning not to let his brother go to war. But they refused to acknowledge the gesture. Mark's mother was "upset," and his father, a veteran of World War II, had no comment. On his first day home, when he hoped to talk to his parents about the war, they preferred to act as though he had not been gone rather than listening to his pain: "I came home from a war, walked in the door, they don't say anything. I asked for a cup of coffee, and my mother starts bitching at me about drinking coffee" (SL 266); "I still want to tell my folks. I need to tell them what I did" (SL 317). Initially, Mark saw Cheryl as a means of re-connecting with "the world": "Cheryl is amazing. Cheryl has always been like chief surgeon. When the shrapnel came out of my head, she would be the one to take it out" (SL 267). But Cheryl, too, refused to listen. Finally, Mark turned to alcohol and the violence it released as a form of consolation. Unfortunately, most of the violence was released on Cheryl. After one especially violent episode in which Mark severely injured her (he pushed her down a flight of stairs), he began to see Cheryl as a comrade, a fellow casualty of Vietnam: "See, I see the war now through my wife. She's a casualty too. She doesn't get benefits for combat duties. The war busted me up, I busted up my wife" (SL 276).

Mark has quit drinking and turned to art as a means of expressing his guilt and anger. He collects gruesome photographs of the war dead, some of which he shows as slides during Act II: "(*Snaps on pictures of mass graves, people half blown apart, gruesome pictures of this particular war) [. . .] (Five slides. Last picture comes on of a man, eyes towards us, the bones of his arm exposed, the flesh torn, eaten away. It is too horrible to look at)*" (SL 287-88). He uses other photographs to make his "jars." Mark puts little pieces of Vietnam into bottles--photographs, bullets, broken glass, jagged pieces of metal. He bottles up pieces of violence, just as the fragments of war are bottled up inside him.

Cheryl represents certain aspects of the "shaman." She does not understand Mark's violence or his inability to put the war out of his

mind. Cheryl "did a lot of speed" in the sixties (SL 276), but now she
wants to put all that behind her. She sees the sixties and the war as
part of a past she can only dimly recall: "[T]here's a lot of things, weird
things, that happened to us, and I just generally put them under the
title of weird things . . . and try to forget it. And to be specific, I'm real
vague on a lot of things" (SL 267). She would prefer to shut her eyes to
the past, especially Mark's past: it's over, so why remember it? Cheryl
is ready for the future. She is concerned about her own and her
children's futures. She wants to move on with her life, and Mark's
problems are holding her back: "I got a kid and another one on the
way. And I'm thinking of climbing the social ladder. I've got to start
thinking about schools for them, and I mean this, it's a completely
different life, and I've had to . . . I've WANTED to change anyway" (SL
267). Most of all, she wants to return to the Catholic Church: "I mean,
when there's no father around, the Church shows some order, you
know" (SL 315). She is at a turning point in her life but does not know
which way to turn.

Nadine is a personification of the modern shaman/hunter
dichotomy. In the sixties, she was totally opposed to the war, abhorred
violence, and hated the men who fought in Vietnam. She believed that
the violence was not only wrong but could be avoided; then she became
a victim of domestic violence. Her ex-husband, an alcoholic, abused her
frequently, until one day her own suppressed violence erupted and she
fought back: "Okay--I really was drunk, really mad. And I beat him up
and do you know what he said to me? He turned to me after he took
it and he said: I didn't know you cared that much" (SL 277). Suddenly
Nadine understood that everyone is capable of violence; that everyone
can feel hatred; and, worst of all, that it is possible to enjoy the kind of
release violence can bring: "I was 'anti-war', I marched, I was 'non-
violent'. (Laughs) [. . .] But I'm capable of it. [. . .] We all are" (SL
278). She considers herself Mark's "best friend." She does not flinch
when Mark tells her about his experience in Vietnam or when she looks
at his photographs of mutilated bodies; she wants to hear the stories
Cheryl will not listen to: "I'm not moved by anything he tells me. I'm
not changed. I'm not shocked. I'm not offended. And he must see that"
(SL 274).

Like Cheryl, Nadine also fears for the future, but her reasons are
quite different--and more alarming. Nadine's fears are not just personal;
they are fears for the future of America:

> You know, all Mark did was--he brought the war back
> home and none of us could look at it. [. . .] We couldn't
> look at ourselves. We still can't. [. . .] Oh, God. I'm

worried about us. I keep this quiet little knowledge with
me every day. I don't tell my husband about it. I don't
tell my kids, or Mark. Or anyone. But something has
fallen apart. [. . .] I worry I have these three beautiful
daughters (pieces of life) who I have devoted my whole
life to, who I've put all my energy into [. . .] then
somebody up there goes crazy one day and pushes the
"go" button and phew! bang, finished, the end.(SL 306-07)

She sees the shallowness, or naivete, of those protestors of the
sixties who did not understand the tendency toward violence they
shared with the soldiers they condemned. Many anti-war
demonstrations ended in violence. Whether the police or the protestors
instigated the violence is not so important as the fact that violence, used
as force or as resistance, existed on both sides of the confrontation. The
point is not that those who protested the war were wrong, but that they
did not recognize the potential for violence inherent in all Americans--
even themselves: "I only hope I would have done exactly what Mark did.
[. . .] I think he survived because he became an animal. I hope I would
have wanted to live that bad. [. . .] We just can't face that in ourselves"
(SL 304). It is this knowledge that frightens Nadine: even the peaceful
shaman is susceptible to the intoxicating effects of violence.

III

In American culture, gender relations have operated traditionally
on the basis of two equally phallocentric myths: the male myth of the
American Adam--the existential hero who is responsible for the security
and preservation of the "promised land," during peace and war, and the
equally male-centered myth of the "angel of the house"--woman as
mother, homemaker, and stoker of home fires. Mark and Cheryl's
wrecked marriage is the result of their failure to recognize and deal
with the conflicts those myths create for both men and women living in
post-Vietnam America. The situation is further complicated by Mark's
use of violence as a means of preserving his role as dominant partner
and by Cheryl's acceptance, early in their relationship, of Mark's
behavior. Mark has been trained to believe that "real men" are
obligated to fight wars, to be the sole support their families, to protect
and control their women. He has read Hemingway; he has seen John
Wayne movies. He is a victim of Americans' tendency to ignore what
Sartre called the "facticity" of their lives and create a living history in
accordance with what they want to believe about themselves and the
past. Rather than dying a quiet death at the end of the nineteenth

century, the frontier mentality that created the myth of the existential hero has been perpetuated in American culture in books and movies, especially Westerns, in which the "hero commits murder, usually multiple murders, in the name of making his town/ranch/mining claim safe for women and children" (Tompkins 373). Movie characters like those played by John Wayne have kept the image of the hunter/warrior alive in American culture, and boys like Mark are still taught to idolize "the cowboy," "the gunfighter," and "the soldier." Lloyd B. Lewis, in a section of *The Tainted War: Culture and Identity in Vietnam War Narratives* called "The 'John Wayne Wet Dream'," discusses the extent to which "The Vietnam War was, at least for some of the soldiers who fought it, *The Vietnam War Movie*, replete with a cast of characters that miraculously included them" (23). War, according to the John Wayne mythos,

> is a test of manhood. It is the ultimate test of the capacity to endure not just fear but also any form of travail from minor irritation to imminent death and disfigurement. Moreover, one is not only required to submit to hardship but also actively to seek it in order that certification be made . . . . As a proving ground for this kind of endurance, Vietnam offered ample opportunity to display "manhood." War, in this view, had been romanticized for Americans into a kind of "placement test," the results of which determined who would wear the social identity of "man" and who would be stigmatized by the label "coward." (Lewis 36)

Movies like John Wayne's *The Green Berets*, to name only the most glaring example, depicted war as a means of determining who was a *real* man (Lewis 37).

At one point in *Still Life* Mark wonders why the soldiers in Vietnam, who knew that the war was out of control, did not just stop fighting: "I could have got out. Everybody could've. If EVERYBODY had said no, it couldn't have happened. There were times we'd say: let's pack up and go, let's quit. But jokingly. We knew we were there. But I think I knew then we could have got out of it" (SL 280-81). They could not go because the myth is too deeply engrained. Like Huck Finn, the quintessential American Adam, they were forced to choose between the evil of killing and the evil of seeming to be un-American. But Huck Finn was not in a firefight; he had not seen fellow soldiers castrated or decapitated. For Mark and his comrades there was no new territory to "light out" to. They stayed and fought knowing that turning their backs would be suicidal. When they came home, however, the same country whose myths they were fighting to preserve turned against them, on the one hand calling them murderers and on the other completely ignoring them. They were "social outcasts to be ignored or reviled":

> The world's initial response serving to confirm this identity was a deafening silence--the absence of recognitions with which the warriors were met. . . . The Vietnam warriors, returning one by one or in shifts over the span of almost a dozen years, drew no dramatic public acclaim to mark the end of sacrifice for God and country. The most wrenching experience of their young lives went un-remarked, a rite-of-passage aborted. (Lewis 151)

The reality is not the myth; the reality is that America does not like to face unpleasantness, particularly if it requires an admission of guilt or recognition of the potential for violence among its own native sons and daughters.

Cheryl is a product of the myth of the "angel of the house" --a myth that continues to influence the upbringing of both boys and girls in America. The woman's role is to be the homemaker and mother; the man's is to be a good provider and devoted father. The woman cooks and cleans; the man works outside the home. But Cheryl's marriage to Mark does not go according to the myth, because the myth fails to take into account the realities of life lived in the aftermath of the Vietnam War, realities that Cheryl did not anticipate: "It was my naiveté. I was so naive to the whole thing, that his craziness had anything to do with where he'd been. [. . .] I was naive to the whole world let alone some body who had just come back from there" (SL 265). Mark is abusive, unfaithful, a poor provider. Not only has he has forced Cheryl to have sexual relations with him ("I've exploited Cheryl as a person, sexually . . . it wasn't exactly rape, but . . . " [SL 296]) but with other couples and other women as well: "[He] brought this woman into our room. He wanted me to play with her. He wanted me to get it on with her, too. It just blew my mind" (SL 299). He has made her pose for obscene photographs:

> Mark's got this series of blood photographs. He made me pose for them. There's a kitchen knife sticking into me, but all you can see is reddish-purplish blood. It's

about five feet high. He had it hanging in the shop! In
the street! Boy, did I make him take it out of there.
[. . .] You just don't show people those things. (SL 287)

Worst of all, at least from Cheryl's perspective, is the fact that
Mark makes so little money, and what money he does make goes to his
dog first and his family second: "I run out of dogfood, Mark sends me
right up to the store. But I run out of milk I can always give [my son]
Kool-Aid for two or three days. [. . .] We haven't been to the grocery
store in six months for anything over ten dollars worth of groceries at
a time" (SL 295).

Cheryl was raised to believe that marriage is the solution to life's
problems; her Catholic upbringing has taught her that divorce is not an
option: "Divorce means a lot of nasty things like it's over. It says a lot
like Oh yeah. I been there. I'm a divorcee. . . . Geez. You could go on
forever about that thing. I gave up on it" (SL 259). Rather than the
"angel in the house," Cheryl is a captive in one of Mark's jars--a
photograph placed amid scraps of violence:

> I came across this jar . . . [. . .] He had a naked picture
> of me in there, cut out to the form, tied to a stake with
> a string. And there was all this broken glass, and I know
> Mark. Broken glass is a symbol of fire. [. . .] there was a
> razor blade in there and some old negatives of the blood
> stuff, I think. I mean that was so violent. That jar to me,
> scared me. That jar to me said: Mark wants to kill me.
> Literally kill me. [. . .] He's burning me at the stake like
> Joan of Arc. (SL 262)

Cheryl knows she should leave Mark, but to do so would be to
admit the failure of her own American Dream. So she stays, living in
fear of the very person who should make her feel safe:

> If I ever told him I was scared for my life, he'd freak out.
> [. . .] I got too much to lose. [. . .] I have a little boy here.
> And if I ever caught Mark hurting me or that little boy
> again, I'd kill him. And I don't wanna be up for
> manslaughter. [. . .] God, I'm scared. I don't wanna be
> alone for the rest of my life with two kids. And I can't rob
> my children of what little father they could have. (SL 279)

Once again, Nadine provides a synthesis between Mark and Cheryl.
She also shared the idea of traditional roles. She believed that her

husband would provide money, love, and security, and she would be the homemaker. But her husband began to drink, to hit her, to gamble away large amounts of money, eventually leaving her $45,000 in debt. She would be a mother, but she had difficulty with childbearing: "When the labor started, we merrily got in the car and went to the hospital. They put me immediately into an operating room. I didn't even know what dilation meant. And I couldn't. I could not dilate. [. . .] I was in agony, they knocked me out. [. . .] They gave me a C-section. I don't remember anything else" (SL 265-66).

Although she loves her children, Nadine dislikes the duties of mothering, and sometimes her frustration shows: "Just to keep my kids going. I don't sleep at all. When my kids complain about supper. I just say: I know it's crappy food. Well, go upstairs and throw it up" (SL 268). Still, she does not hate men. In fact, she understands the pressures many men feel:

> What's a man? Where's the model? All they had left was being Provider. And now with the economics they're losing it all. [. . .] We don't want them to be the Provider, because we want to do that ourselves. We don't want them to be heroes, and we don't want them to be knights in shining armor, John Wayne--so what's left for them to be, huh? Oh, I'm worried about men. They're not coming through. [. . .] They were programmed to fuck, now they have to make love. And they can't do it. It all comes down to fucking versus loving. We don't like them in the old way anymore. And I don't think they like us, much. (SL 281-82)

Placed in the position of "head of household," Nadine can empathize with Mark's frustration (and his bursts of violence) as well as with Cheryl's disappointments and fears. She sees all three of them as victims of America: "Christ, I hate this country. I can remember everything. Back to being two years old, and all these terrible things they taught us. I can't believe we obeyed them all" (SL 297-98). When the two women finally acknowledge one another at the end of the play, there is an unspoken link between them, as casualties of violence, that resembles the link Mark describes between himself and another veteran, his cousin who also served in Vietnam: "He and I never talked. Ever. Someone else communicated his story to me, and I know he knows my story. [. . .] I saw my cousin at his dad's funeral last December. [. . .] Wherever we moved, we knew where the other was.

Something radiates between us. [. . .] Our eyes will meet, but we can't touch" (SL 298-99).

IV

Two aspects of the narrative strategy Mann uses in *Still Life* enhance the viewer/reader's understanding of the subject (the human cost of the Vietnam War) and intensify the emotional impact of the play. First, the flow of the dialogue imitates the chaotic pattern of the veteran's experience during and after the war. Act I, like the war itself, is fast-paced, confused. Act II is slower, more thoughtful, a little like the first relief of coming home, when the combat veteran tries to describe his experience to friends and family. Act III is filled with confessions, with soul-searching by each character, similar to the kind of analysis many veterans and their families must go through in order to deal with PTSD. And, second, Mann skillfully uses the motif of "still life" throughout the play as both a play on words to illustrate the misery of her characters' lives and as a means of replicating Mark's fragmented artistic vision of the war. The first act of *Still Life* is intentionally fragmented, confused. The characters talk but not to each other. They speak randomly to themselves and to the audience:

> Cheryl: He keeps telling me: He's a murderer. I gotta believe he can be a husband. Mark: The truth of it is, it's different from what we've heard about war before. Nadine: He's just more angry than any of us. He's been fighting for years. Fighting the priests, fighting all of them. Mark: I don't want this to come off as a combat story. Cheryl: Well, a lot of things happened that I couldn't handle. Mark: It's a tragedy is what it is. It happened to a lot of people. (SL 263)

Fragments of their stories pour out but without background or apparent order. Mark rages about the war; Cheryl complains about Mark; Nadine rambles about her relationship with Mark and criticizes Cheryl. Occasionally, the characters interrupt one another to make statements totally unrelated to the subject at hand. At other times, one of them picks up a topic that another brought up and dropped several pages before. At one point, Nadine and Cheryl speak simultaneously (SL 268-69). The tempo of the act is rapid, much of it resembling a firefight. The characters are engaged in battle with each other and with the memory of the Vietnam War. Their words are like bullets fired across the stage; a few hit their targets but most miss. Like soldiers in battle, each of them has a position to defend and little sympathy for the enemy.

In Act Two the pace slows. The tiny fragments of stories mentioned in the first act are filled out. Some evolve into whole stories; some remain fragmented but with enough additional detail to allow the audience better insight into the characters. Mark's anger is more focused, and it becomes clear that a dark secret exists at the root of his anguish: "I did a really bad number . . . It went contrary, I think, to everything I knew. I'm not ready to talk about that yet" (SL 287). Cheryl explains her feelings about Mark. She is both afraid of him and extremely angry with him. She was first attracted by the "power" of Mark's "imagination" (SL 283) but came to fear it when she discovered his "art," the gruesome photographs and frightening jars, and realized that his imagination is "usually sexually orientated" (SL 284). In fact, she says, "Everything he's done, everything is sexually orientated in some way. Whether it's nakedness or violence--it's all sexually orientated" (SL 286). Still buying into the American Dream, she is furious about Mark's inability, or perhaps unwillingness, to provide a real home for his family. Mostly, she wants a house of their own: "Now, if [the rental house] were mine I'd be busy at work. [. . .] I'd be painting the walls, I would be wallpapering the bedroom. I would be making improvements. [. . .] I can't do it because it's not mine. [. . .] And Mark will never be ready to have the responsibility of his own home. Never. Never" (SL 290-91). Nadine tries to sort out Mark's and Cheryl's problems while sorting out her own. She encourages Mark to keep working at his marriage: "I tried to explain to Mark that Cheryl may not always want from him what she wants right now: looking for him to provide, looking for status" (SL 290). But, though she appreciates Cheryl's position, she cannot understand why a woman living in America in the 1980's does not take control of her own life:

> [B]etween us, I can't understand why a woman her age,
> an intelligent woman, who's lived through the sixties and
> the seventies, who's living now in a society where women
> have finally been given permission to drive and progress
> and do what they're entitled to do . . . I mean, how can
> she think that way? (SL 291)

She is especially upset by Cheryl's decision to become pregnant a second time, knowing how troubled her marriage is: "She decided to have that child. [. . .] It's madness. Everyone was against it" (SL 294). Toward the end of the act, Nadine begins to repeat the phrase, "Christ,

I hate this country!" like a refrain. It is not really the country she hates as much as the refusal of people to learn from the mistakes of the past.

The final act mirrors the aftermath of the war for many veterans. The voices are calmer, the comments more pointed and coherent. Mark discusses his father, his anger over the treatment of returning veterans, and his own fears about the future, with or without Cheryl. He confesses the truth about his "war crime" and worries about the extent to which it has affected his relationship with his own son:

> I killed three children, a mother and father in cold blood. (Crying) [. . .] I killed them with a pistol in front of a lot of people. [. . .] I have a son . . . He's going to die for what I've done. This is what I'm carrying around; that's what this logic is about with my children. A friend hit a booby-trap. And these people knew about it. I knew they knew. I knew that they were working with the VC infrastructure. I demanded that they tell me. They wouldn't say anything. I just wanted them to confess before I killed them. And they wouldn't. So I killed their children and then I killed them. (SL 317-l8)

His guilt has not been lessened by the fact that the military knew what he did and did not punish him:

> It was all rationalized, that there was a logic behind it. But they knew. And everybody who knew had a part in it. There was enough evidence, but it wasn't a very good image to put out in terms of . . . the marines overseas, so nothing happened. [. . .] All that a person can do is try and find words to try and excuse me, but I know it's the same damn thing as lining Jews up. It's no different than what the Nazis did. It's the same thing. I know that I'm not alone. I know that other people did it, too. (SL 319)

Most of all, Mark is confused by the anger he cannot control. Like other veterans suffering the effects of PTSD, Mark is both a victim of the war and of a society that has stereotyped him as potentially dangerous. In many cases, the veteran's "'unprovoked' anger" is actually a result of "justifiable outrage at historical events" rather than a "psychological aberration." Asking the returnees to "bottle up" their anger is the easy answer for society, but it has been devastating for veterans who have no outlet for their rage. Some internalize their distress, harming themselves; some externalize it, harming others (Lewis 164-65). Many, like Mark, do both.

In the penultimate scene, Mark reads a roll call of his friends who died in the war or as a result of it. Nadine fades into the background, but Cheryl continues to talk. Her sermon about male/female relationships, the futility of discussing the war, and the necessity of a future in which everything goes "back the way it was" before the war is interrupted every few lines by the name of a dead soldier. This scene effectively mirrors the veteran's position in post-Vietnam America. The voices of protest have faded, and the nation struggles to forget--to pretend that Vietnam did not happen or that it is best left in the past. But the voice of the veteran remains loud, a constant reminder of those who died and those who are living a "still life":

> Mark: Spaulding, Henry. Cheryl: You'll look, you'll go in college campuses now and it's completely back the way it was . . . and it should stay there. Mark: Stanton, Ray. Cheryl: I don't wanna see that shit come back. I didn't even get that involved in it. I got involved in it in my own little niche. [. . .] Mark: Vechhio, Michael. Cheryl: I'm a happy-go-lucky person. I used to be anyway, before I met Mark, where you couldn't depress me on the worst day. And I had a good day every day of my life. Mark: Walker, (Pause) Cheryl: And that is the way life was gonna be for me. Mark: R. J. (SL 324)

Throughout *Still Life*, Mark shows slides, placing a second narrative layer on top of the drama itself. The first slide is a picture of Cheryl as she used to be; the next is a photo of a Marine boot and leg below the knee (Mark wanted to remember his foot in case he lost it). He shows a slide of himself in full Marine dress, wearing his Purple Heart. This is followed by pictures of children, American and Vietnamese. The slideshow turns ugly as Mark begins to show pictures of the war, "mass graves, people half blown apart." As the second act ends, Mark turns off the slide machine and turns on a tape recording of Holly Near's "No More Genocide," adding a musical component to his already multi-media presentation. Act Three opens with a slide of Mark and his best friend R. J., followed by a picture of a boy whose head was blown off by a rocket. Mark starts to cry and exits the stage. He returns with slides of wounded Vietnamese children, the discussion of which leads to his "confession."

The last slide is a photograph of "two grapefruits, an orange, a broken egg, with a grenade in the center on a dark background"; there is also "some fresh bread, a fly on the fruit." From far away, however, it appears to be an "ordinary still life" (SL 324). The double entendre of the title becomes clear. Mark is "still alive" while his friends are dead. He now leads a "still life," suspended forever in these fragments of war--momentary glimpses of children and mutilated bodies, bits and pieces of glass and bullets and metal. In the photographic "still life" lies Mann's final comment on America: those people who prefer not to look too closely will continue to see America as a nation of plenty, filled with bread and fruit; but up close the picture is not so pretty. At the center of American culture is a penchant for violence, a grenade ready to explode, or perhaps implode, a nation that refuses to look into its own heart of darkness.

Notes

1. Frederic Jameson explains Sartre's idea of "facticity": "[The] past can be described in two different ways: it is that which can no longer be changed, which has passed out of reach . . . fixed forever; and yet at the same time it is constantly subject to change and renewal at our hands; its meaning is as fluid as our freedom" (4). For example, when the frontier closed at the end of the nineteenth century, ending America's horizontal expansion, rather than face the end of the frontier and shape their future accordingly, Americans found ways to expand the nation vertically, upward into the land of imagination. By creating a mythical frontier inhabited by mythical heroes, they could ignore the dead past and invent a living history in accordance with what they chose to believe. Instead of allowing the frontier to remain past, fixed forever, Americans reshaped it in images of their own desire.

2. *Still Life* 324-25. Subsequent references are cited parenthetically in the text as SL followed by page number. Bracketed ellipses within quotations from *Still Life* are mine. All other ellipses actually appear in the text of the play.

3. See Slotkin 49-56. For an excellent discussion of the way the male warrior/female shaman dichotomy currently operates in American culture, see Susan Jeffords, "Debriding Vietnam: The Resurrection of the White American Male," *Feminist Studies* 14.3 (Fall 1988): 525-43.

Works Cited

Baritz, Loren. *Backfire: A History of How American Culture Led Us into Vietnam and Made Us Fight the Way We Did*. New York: Ballantine Books, 1985.

Beidler, Philip. *American Literature and the Experience of Vietnam*. Athens, GA: University of Georgia Press, 1986.

FitzGerald, Frances. *Fire in the Lake: The Vietnamese and the Americans in Vietnam*. New York: Vintage, 1972.

Jameson, Frederic. *Sartre: The Origins of a Style*. New Haven: Yale University Press, 1961.

Jeffords, Susan. "Debriding Vietnam: The Resurrection of the White American Male," *Feminist Studies* 14.3 (Fall 1988): 525-43.

Lewis, Lloyd B. *The Tainted War: Culture and Identity in Vietnam War Narratives*. Westport, CT: Greenwood Press, 1985.

Mann, Emily. *Still Life. Coming to Terms: American Plays and the Vietnam War*. New York: Theatre Communications Group, 1985. 253-326.

Slotkin, Richard. *Regeneration Through Violence: The Mythology of the American Frontier*, 1600-1860. Middletown, CT: Wesleyan University Press, 1973.

Tompkins, Jane. "West of Everything." *South Atlantic Quarterly* 86.4 (Fall 1987): 357-77.

SYMBOLIC NIHILISM IN *PLATOON*

William J. Palmer

In the late seventies, Vietnam War films, specifically *Coming Home, The Deer Hunter, Go Tell the Spartans* and *Apocalypse Now*, served as barometers which measured the submerged public opinion toward that war and toward the soldiers who fought in that war. These movies indicated that beneath the surface of American society, a society paralyzed by the disasters of that decade (particularly the defeat in Vietnam and the embarrassment of Watergate), there was a real and thoughtful sympathy, emanating both from the left (*Coming Home*) and from the right (*The Deer Hunter*), for understanding the situations of the veterans who fought and survived that war as well as a historical curiosity (as represented in both *Go Tell the Spartans* and *Apocalypse Now*) as to how that war was fought and what that war meant. In other words, in the seventies the Vietnam War, both in society and in movies, was still an issue, something either happening in itself (being fought by Americans and American allies all the way through the fall of Saigon in 1975), or affecting society and those who had returned from the war.

In the eighties, however, social interest in the Vietnam War lost its immediacy with increased assimilation of Vietnam veterans into American society after an eight-year denial of their existence. A number of particularly eighties events kept the Vietnam War alive, not as a social issue but as a meta-issue, a cautionary metaphor from the seventies for other eighties issues. That unique set of events which kept both America and the eighties cold war world attuned to the lessons of the Vietnam War were the Russian invasion of Afghanistan in late 1979, the failure of the hostage rescue mission into Iran due to the inability of American planes and helicopters to cope with blowing sand (another failure of American technology), the increasing American presence in Central America, particularly in El Salvador and Nicaragua, the loss of life and the withdrawal of troops from Beirut. In all of these cases, the Vietnam War was repeatedly cited as a test case, a text for contemporary comparison, a precedent for American failure. Political voices (once again, both on the right and on the left concerning both Nicaragua and El Salvador) began using the Vietnam War to make points about the political choices open to the Reagan administration in its action in Central America and around the world. In the eighties, Vietnam veterans themselves used the war to gain political leverage and push a number of issues relevant to their reinstated voices and new-found political clout. The issues of MIA/POW accountability, of Agent

Orange contamination and treatment, of Amerasian children, and of Post Traumatic Stress Disorders (PTSD) all kept very much alive the American social consciousness of the nature, the legacy, and the continuing quest for meaning of the Vietnam War. Vietnam became a warning, a political albatross, a symbol of defeat and loss, but, most of all, it became a text. Whether it was the movies or the literature or the political theory or the history of the Vietnam War that was being studied, whether the Vietnam War was being used to buttress political arguments concerning Afghanistan, Central America, Grenada, Beirut, or the Persian Gulf, whether the Vietnam War was being used as an emotional focal point for the arguing of veterans' issues, it was an extremely complex text which was constantly being interpreted, reinterpreted, deconstructed, and exploited all through the eighties.

The literary concept of story has found diverse form in a large and growing body of Vietnam War literature. Simultaneously, a whole body of Vietnam War films has accumulated into a rather full sub-genre in the last eleven years. Beginning in 1976, the Vietnam War film has progressed through three rather clearly delineated phases: 1) the Epic Phase, 2) the Comic Book Phase, and 3) the Symbolic Nihilist Phase. Folded or layered into these three phases are the three major themes which dominate the Vietnam War films: 1) life in the war itself (adaptation, survival, loss of innocence, change, morality); 2) the meaning of the war; 3) coming home from the war. These three themes are present in all three phases of the Vietnam War movie timeline, but different themes are much more prominent in some phases than in others.

By far the most often explored of these three themes is the third, "Coming Home." Thus, the Vietnam War films are both a text of the war as well as of the post-war re-entry of the soldier into American society, "the World" as he called it when he was in the war. Prior to 1987-88, with very few exceptions (such as *Go Tell The Spartans*), these films have proven to be a rather muddled and inaccurate text. The first phase of that text, the Epic Phase (1976-79), was a traditional, story-oriented text, a war text aligned with the traditions of twentieth-century American Modernist literary and film war texts. In one sense, the films of the Epic Phase were all, in one way or another, clichés. How different, for example, is the journey through the Vietnam War of Captain Willard (Martin Sheen) in *Apocalypse Now* from that of Henry Fleming in Stephen Crane's *The Red Badge of Courage*? How different, for example, are the training camp to combat films like *The Boys In Company C* from the dozens of movies from *Sergeant York* to *To Hell and Back* to *The Sands of Iwo Jima* to *Darby's Rangers* to *The Devil's Brigade* to *The Dirty Dozen* to *The Big Red One*? It is no coincidence that two of the earliest and most powerful books about the Vietnam War, Philip Caputo's *A Rumor of War* and Gustav Hasford's *The Short Timers*, both choose this conventional Modernist psycho-realistic generative structure, really the education, growing up to self-consciousness, *bildungsroman* structure of James Joyce's *The Portrait of the Artist as a Young Man*, to present their versions of the evolution of the Vietnam War Everyman soldier. Thus, the Epic Phase, with its story orientation, its generative linearity of character development, its traditional structures and themes, is the Classical/Modernist phase of the Vietnam War film history.

Phase Two, the Comic Book Phase, is a text corrupted mainly by 1980s Reagan administration chauvinistic rhetoric. In speeches throughout the eighties, President Ronald Reagan often valorized the idea that America didn't really lose the Vietnam War and that, in fact, that war could be refought and re-won in places such as Grenada and Central and South America and/or the Middle East. This valorization by an extremely popular President cleared the way to profitability for a whole series of "return to Vietnam and do it right this time" propagandist fantasies in the period 1980-1986. John Rambo was, of course, the Sergeant Rock of this Reagan administration war comic. In 1986, as his Comic Book image, more often than not draped in the American flag, appeared on the covers of Time and Newsweek and in the pages of every newspaper and magazine in America, John Rambo nee Sylvester Stallone was invited to the White House and treated as if he were a real Congressional Medal of Honor winner. This was a propagandist valorization of an actor who, during the Vietnam War, had both taught in a girls' school in Switzerland and made porno and B-movies until in 1976 he got lucky with *Rocky*, another comic book character based on Joe Palooka. Perhaps this Comic Book Phase of the Vietnam War films is one of the best examples of the manner in which American film and orchestrated (propagandist) social history can complement one another.

From 1980 to 1986 the Vietnam War entered its Comic Book Phase. The two Rambo sequels and the stupid POW rescue movies such as *Uncommon Valor* and Chuck Norris' three *Missing in Action* shoot-em-ups are the best examples of the mindless exploitation of the war and of Vietnam veterans that was so rampant in American society and the American media during the late seventies and early eighties. Ironically, *Apocalypse Now*, generally considered the Vietnam War epic, was originally conceived, in its first script version by John Milius, as a sort of G.I. Joe comic book set in Vietnam. In describing that first script of *Apocalypse Now*, Francis Coppola said:

the script as I remember it, took a more comic-strip Vietnam War and moved it through a series of events that were also comic strip: a political comic strip. The events had points to them -- I don't say comic strip to denigrate them. The film continued through comic strip episode and comic strip episode until it came to a comic strip resolution: Attila the Hun (i.e. Kurtz) with two bands of machine-gun bullets around him, taking the hero (Willard) by the hand, saying, 'Yes, yes, here! I have the power in my loins!' Willard converts to Kurtz' side; in the end, he's firing up at the helicopters that are coming to get him, crying out crazily. A movie comic strip . . . That was the tone and the resolution. The first thing that happened after my involvement was the psychologization of Willard.

In those early stages of the history of the Vietnam war film, it is encouraging that Coppola's vision of the war was more expansive, psychological, and literary than was Milius' shallow, pop culture, comic book approach.

Not all of the comic book characters of this second phase of the Vietnam War film history are action figures out of *Marvel Comics*, however. Richard Pryor played a Vietnam POW as a black Bugs Bunny in the coming home movie *Some Kind of Hero* (1981) and the sequel to *American Graffiti* (1973), *More American Graffiti* (1979) portrayed the Vietnam generation as if they were the characters in *Archie* comic books. *The Stunt Man* (1980), however, is one movie from this period which is worth noting. It is possibly the most artful and sophisticated of all the veteran-coming-home Vietnam films. In *The Stunt Man*, life and the Vietnam War are metaphorically represented as movie. An anonymous Vietnam veteran joins the crew of a movie company making a World War I movie and, suddenly, all of his experiences, his insecurities, his sense of never knowing what was going on, of what was real and what was just an illusion, of who he is and why he is there on this insane movie set come flooding back to him as a strange sort of variation on a Vietnam War flashback. *The Stunt Man* is the only comic movie of this Comic Book Phase to actually strive for any symbolic or characterizational depth. In portraying the issues of the Vietnam War as movie, *The Stunt Man* shares its central metaphor with Julian Smith who in *Looking Away: Hollywood and Vietnam*, published in 1975 before there really were any Vietnam War movies, wrote:

Vietnam was like a movie that had gotten out of hand: gigantic cost overruns, a shooting schedule run amuck,

> squabbles on the set, and back in the studio, the first
> auteur dying with most of the script in his head, the
> second quitting in disgust, and the last swearing it was
> finally in the can, but sneaking back to shoot some extra scenes
> (103).

and the same metaphor would guide the ensemble TV company of
Saturday Night Live in 1983 who did a series of sketches in which the
Reagan Presidency was represented as simply the making of a movie
with Ed Meese as the director and Ronald Reagan as the actor who
always asks "when do I get to ride the horsey?"

This whole series of Comic Book passes at the issues and themes of
the Vietnam War focused almost exclusively upon the theme of "coming
home" and then somehow going back, either psychologically as in *Some
Kind of Hero* or *The Stunt Man* or *Cease Fire* (1986) or *Firefox* (1985)
or actually (though in almost every case ridiculously, unbelievably)
physically returning to rescue those who were originally left behind as
in *The Deer Hunter, Uncommon Valor* (1983), *Rambo II* and the *Missing
In Action* (1984-87) films. This wishful survivor guilt fantasy best fit the
Comic Book commando hero type and throughout the early eighties,
culminating in *Rambo II* in 1986, it was the essential plot of the
majority of the movies dealing with the legacy of Vietnam. What none
of the movies was really dealing with was the Vietnam War itself, how
it worked and what it meant.

And then came 1987-88, the year of Vietnam at the movies, the
second coming of 1977-79 when *Coming Home, The Deer Hunter* and
Apocalypse Now all appeared. In the short space of 16 months from
December, 1986, when *Platoon* was released to April, 1988, when *Off
Limits* hit the theaters, no less than 6 major Vietnam War movies were
released. Of these six, only *Platoon, Full Metal Jacket, Off Limits* and
Hamburger Hill are really about the Vietnam War. *Gardens of Stone*
and *Good Morning Vietnam* are not really about the war itself. Of
these six movies, *Good Morning Vietnam* is the least of the lot, totally
lacking in substance or even interest in the Vietnam War. Of the six,
Full Metal Jacket presents the greatest categorization, interpretation
and implication problems. *Full Metal Jacket* is the most important of
these six films of the year of Vietnam at the movies because it does
what *Platoon* makes a valiant attempt to do. It gives a full definition to
the nihilism that all the soldiers in the Vietnam War movies of this year
feel. In John Del Vecchio's novel *The 13th Valley* the recurring grunt
expression of the nature of the infantryman's situation in Vietnam is "It
don't mean nothin'." *Full Metal Jacket* also underscores that phrase and
then, in a series of striking images, presents a full, highly symbolic view

of that nihilistic approach to life in the Vietnam War. Thus, because the recurring conclusion that each movie in its own way draws is that "It don't mean nothin'," the third phase of the history of the Vietnam War film can be called the Symbolic Nihilist Phase.

Only this Third Symbolic Nihilist Phase of the Vietnam War Film History makes an honest attempt to portray the Vietnam War in ways that film as medium best deals with human experience, history, and idea. These films are a significant advance in the American perception of the Vietnam War. In general, they eschew story and, while focused upon stereotypical characterization, attempt to capture the moments, the confusion and chaos, the temper of the war in the same way that the "illumination rounds" of Michael Herr's *Dispatches* did through his remarkable postmodernist style. These movies of the third phase do not generally attempt to impose order upon a primary text which had no order. In the case of *Platoon*, such an attempt to impose the order of story, to construct an order out of something as unstructured as the war fails in the face of the consistently deconstructing text. When these third phase movies succeed, they capture the existential feel of disorder, confusion, utter meaninglessness, which came to be this war's essential character. Thus, the 1987-88 phase of Vietnam War film history is its postmodernist phase, containing a series of films which consciously deconstruct the war which was consistently deconstructing itself even as it was going on.

What is important about this third Symbolic Nihilist Phase of Vietnam War films is that, except for *Gardens of Stone*, all of the films are all or in part set in Vietnam, in the war, and are really about, or attempt to be about, what it was actually like to be there in the midst of the war. The consensus which all of these movies seems to arrive at is that being in the Vietnam War occasioned an almost complete annihilation of a former, civilized, moral self just as the circumstances of the war itself had accomplished a complete annihilation of the participant's grasp of reality, morality, or sanity. As Conrad wrote about another desperate place in *Heart of Darkness*, Vietnam was a world where everyone had been "kicked loose of the earth" and was operating "without restraint." Symbolic Nihilism is the representation or dramatization of an individual's or a group of individuals' gradual movement into a void in which all positive aspects of the self, all powers of self-determination and control are not simply temporarily lost, but rather are so totally annihilated that the self no longer believes in any contexts, no longer hopes for any progress toward any of the ideals, moral designs, social relationships that it held before entering that void. In literary/filmic terms, each of the major Vietnam War films of 1987-88 -- *Platoon, Full Metal Jacket, Hamburger Hill, Off Limits* -- works on two levels of symbolic interpretation. Each is a film of the initiation of the protagonists into nothingness, emptiness, the annihilation of the self, the realization of helplessness in the face of evil so all-encompassing that their past lives become nothing more than sentimental dreams, illusions bearing no relevance to their present realities in Vietnam. Simultaneously, however, each is also a film about what Vietnam did to America, how it subverted the Kennedy idealism of the early sixties, took what had been the most powerful society in the world's positive (even arrogant) sense of itself and humiliated that sense of itself into emptiness, loss and complete moral breakdown.

The release of Oliver Stone's *Platoon* in December of 1986 opened the year of Vietnam at the movies. When *Platoon* appeared, the professional movie critics were unanimous in their praise for it as a movie.[2] What was more interesting about *Platoon's* critical reception, however, was the number of essays by non-professional critics in major newspapers and magazines. These commentaries on the film, written almost always by Vietnam veterans, are also almost unanimously positive toward the film while going a number of steps further than the professional film critics who had praised and analyzed the film as art, had unanimously stressed the film's realism, had praised its representation of the life (and death) of an infantryman in the Vietnam War. The non-professional critics analyze the aesthetic realism of the scenes, the characters, the themes of *Platoon* much more carefully and complexly than do many of the professional film critics. These non-professional critics make a clearer distinction between realism in art and the realism of life. It is a textual distinction which sets the inevitable differentation between combatant textuality and non-combatatant textuality. For the Vietnam War, the credential of having "been there" seems to override any other credential that is ever raised by the critics of film, books, political strategies. Unfortunately, the combatant textuality of some non-professional film critics tends to reach for personal emotional reasons for making critical judgments rather than artistic or historical or social reasons. However, some of these non-professional critics also examine the film from the perspective of social history. They attempt to analyze why, more than fifteen years after the fact, a film on the Vietnam War could still frag the American cultural imagination.

David Halberstam, writing in *The New York Times* (8 March 1987), argues:

> By nature the movie industry has been a notorious cheat when it comes to confronting serious subjects, and on Vietnam in particular there was a rare schizophrenic attitude

on the part of the industry's leaders . . . . Of the serious postwar films that have preceded *Platoon*, none to me ever passed the test of being a true Vietnam War movie . . . . By contrast, *Platoon* is about Vietnam. It exists only, as they say, in-country. It has no other objective, no other agenda. To me it is both a great American movie and a great War movie. Its combat scenes are as good as any I have ever seen . . . . It is painfully realistic . . . . Real it is. This is the ultimate work of witness, something which has the authenticity of documentary and yet the vibrancy and originality of art.

General Bernard E. Trainor of the Marine Corps, writing in that same issue of *The New York Times*, echoes Halberstam's evaluation:

As a career Marine, I had seen my share of war, both on the silver screen and in real life. Needless to say, they are different, but *Platoon* does succeed in narrowing some of the differences. A filmgoer does not experience Vietnam by seeing *Platoon*, but he will see those who did. It is less a war movie than a movie of men at war . . . . A film can never replicate those experiences although this one makes an honest attempt to do so . . . what does come through in *Platoon*, to make it a notable war movie, is its authentic portrayal of infantrymen.

As *Platoon*'s title intimates, and as both Halberstam and Trainor stress, the film is not really about just its young protagonist or the conflict between its two symbolic sergeants, it is about the whole platoon, the group, this microcosm of America sentenced to the jungles of Vietnam.

Both the professional film critics intuitively and the non-professional Vietnam veteran film critics speaking from experience stress the manner in which *Platoon* attempts through art to represent realistically, the feel of Vietnam and its effects on the psyches of the infantrymen fighting there. The dynamism, the fluidity, the non-linear, almost vortextual, motion of that aesthetic realism in *Platoon* is the film's major contribution to the sub-genre of the Vietnam War film. But *Platoon* is a schizoid movie in terms of story and intention, much as was Coppola's *Apocalypse Now*. David Halberstam writes of *Apocalypse Now* (*The Washington Post*, 8 March 1987) that it "was two films, an occasionally brilliant Vietnam movie mixed together with Coppola's version of *Heart of Darkness*." A similar doubleness exists in two of the major Vietnam War films of 1987-1988. *Full Metal Jacket* is without question two movies, one about Parris Island, one about in-country Vietnam. *Platoon*, like *Apocalypse Now*, doesn't really split as does *Full Metal Jacket* , but rather is layered into a double structure, one conventional and linear, the other fluid and postmodernist. *Platoon* attempts to tell the linear story of a group of allegorical *bildungsroman* characters. On a second plane, that for which it has been most highly praised, it offers, in unstructured bursts of imagery, language, emotion, and realistic detail (like automatic weapons fire or like what Michael Herr in *Dispatches* calls "illumination rounds") the feel, the sense, of what it was like to be there in Vietnam in 1968.

Story and intention -- those are the two sides of *Platoon*'s split personality. In terms of story, *Platoon* is a conventional, utterly predictable, flatly characterized, simplistic, clichéd narrative. In other words, its story of a young man coming of age in a world peopled with, as Pauline Kael has noted (*New Yorker*, 12 January 1987), "medieval morality play" characters who are flat personifications of Good and Evil, Life and Death, is of little concern in any analysis of *Platoon*'s success, its tremendous impact upon its Eighties audiences. *Platoon* does not succeed as a film experience in terms of its story.[3]

In terms of representational narrative, the story told in *Platoon* is a worn-out, cumbersome Manichean myth of good and evil, the light side and the dark side. It attempts the same sort of dialectical narrative tension that the symbolic myth of "the Force" in the *Star Wars* trilogy posited. Chris Taylor (Charlie Sheen) serves as the synthesis character in the Manichean dialectic of *Platoon* as does Luke Skywalker serve as mediator between the Light side of "the Force" as represented by Obi Wan Kenobe/Yoda and the Dark side as embodied in Darth Vader. *Platoon*'s "medieval morality play" story also carries all sorts of mythic, literary baggage. As did Francis Coppola's *Apocalypse Now*, *Platoon* offers simultaneous representations of the Christ myth and the mad intensity of Ahab's quest for Moby Dick.[4] The Christ imagery, as unmistakeable in the slow-motion death of Elias (Willem DaFoe), and the Ahab parallel, as intoned in Chris Taylor's voice-over, are as obvious, as artificial, as pretentious as was Coppola's ponderous panning over the books in Kurtz's selective library in *Apocalypse Now* -- Fraser's *The Golden Bough*, Jessie Weston's *From Ritual to Romance*, T. S. Eliot's *The Hollow Men* -- which comprises a sort of pedantry which turns a movie theater into a lecture hall and violates what the film media is best equipped to do. In other words, *Platoon* is not about the story of Chris Taylor and Sergeants Elias and Barnes (Tom Berenger). It is not a movie about growing up. It is not a movie about Good and Evil. It is not a movie about Life and Death. It is certainly not a movie about Christ or Captain Ahab. It is a movie about fear, about death in the lower case, about anger, about pain, about love, about honesty and dishonesty, about stupidity and cowardice and courage, about drugs and booze and blacks and whites and rich and poor and hippies and red necks, about smells and tastes and how the jungle feels and sounds, about snakes and bugs and rain and blood and fire, about screams and terrible silences, about darkness shattered by bright light, about calm erupting into frenzied flight, about tracer bullets and invisible trip wires, about helicopters and tunnels, about sexual depravity, mindless brutality and instinctual sympathy, about atrocity and survival, about children caught in war and warriors who are still children, about green and red and brown and black, about flesh and metal and wind and water, about how people feel in war, the Vietnam War. Story in *Platoon* is of little concern. Waste the story and concentrate on the imagery, the action, the words when they are not pretentious or story-directed, but when they are psychological or inner-directed. *Platoon*, better than any other Vietnam War movie, tries to present to the audience visceral ways of understanding what the Vietnam War was like.

More than anything else, however, *Platoon* is a movie about confusion.[5] In Chris's first letter he writes, "I don't even know what I'm doin' . . . . Nobody cares about the new guys. They don't even wanna know my name." Only moments later in the movie, Taylor's perception is confirmed as two battle-hardened veterans, Elias and O'Neil (John C. McGinley) argue about whose fireteam should go out on ambush. "Whaddaya want me to do?" O'Neil whines, "Send some of my guys out? You got the new meat, Elias." Only short screen minutes later, after a "cherry' or "FNG" who came in with Taylor is killed in his first night in the bush, Elias zips him into a body bag and, almost noncommittally, notes, "He'd still be alive if he had a few more days to learn somethin'." Learning the war is an absolute necessity for survival, yet none of the veterans who know the war is willing to teach it to the nameless "new meat." Mere confusion turns into ultimate chaos, and takes on the immediacy and thematic impact necessary to make the audience actually feel what the unique confusion of a grunt in Vietnam must have been like.

Platoon has a three-part dramatic structure which overlays its linear plot and bursts of imagistic realism. Each of the three parts contains an apocalyptic scene(s) in which ultimate chaos reigns. All builds toward the ultimate rejection of all identity, morality and humanity in the midst of the utter nihilism of chaos. In *Platoon* the ultimate symbol of this nihilistic chaos is the firefight. In part one of *Platoon*, a night ambush, the searching of a booby-trapped bunker complex and, finally, a village atrocity right off the CBS News, a near My Lai 4, begins the gradual escalation of firefight chaos.   In each succeeding scene, the violence gets heavier, the corpses get bloodier, the humanity of the infantrymen gets raggeder.   Step by step, scene by scene, Stone is chronicling the wearing away of the existence, the morality, the social class, the civilization, the whole being of his grunt characters. In part two of *Platoon* the morality play is resolved in the confrontation between Elias and Barnes in the jungle and the firefight crucifixion of Elias as his fellow grunts watch helplessly from on high. Part three of *Platoon* is composed almost exclusively of the ultimate firefight, the culmination of the film's recurring symbol of nihilistic chaos.

Part one of *Platoon* is an extended "naming of parts." It fulfills the purpose that the basic training sequences in most conventional World War II movies and in *Full Metal Jacket* serve. As the audience goes out on patrol with the platoon to which Chris Taylor has been assigned, it is oriented to the Vietnam War right along with Taylor, the "FNG," which stands for "fucking new guy." But this orientation is much more direct and graphic and real than any basic training simulation could ever be. *Platoon* is absolutely at its best when it is presenting even the tiniest visceral details of what life in the Vietnam War is all about. In the very first dramatic firefight scene, Chris Taylor's first guard duty on a night ambush, the tiny detail of the condensation on his wristwatch is simultaneously very real and highly symbolic. This is the first instance of time being blurred and meaningless, a sub-theme which will recur throughout the film and contribute to the universal meaninglessness which is *Platoon*'s central theme. In this first night scene, Chris's sense of time breaks down, then his defenses break down, then the perimeter of the platoon breaks down, and the result is chaos as, suddenly, the firefight erupts.   When the shooting stops, all that is left is the unintelligible screams of the wounded, followed by the hopeless, scared -- "Take the pain! Take the pain!" -- orders of the survivors. Those frantic screams are the first indication of the utter unintelligibility of this war.

This simultaneously realistic and symbolic "naming of parts" continues in the next scene in the Heads Bunker as Elias teaches Chris Taylor to shotgun dope. Though it seems just an exotic foray into drug lore, it too carries a symbolic irony.   Taylor, in volunteering for Vietnam, has put a gun to his own head just as surely as he is accepting the double barrels of Elias's shotgun in this scene. Each visual detail upon which Stone's camera lingers in this opening "naming of parts" section carries this real/symbolic irony duality. Echoing Jake Gittes in *Chinatown* (1974), when a booby trap explodes killing one of his men, Barnes screams "nothing is ever what it seems."[6] The platoon's entry into the *Chinatown* world of the bunker complex, which Stone offers in a series of subjective point-of-view shots from a hand-held camera, identifies the audience with the cautious, scared, yet still unsuspecting members of the platoon. Their immediate self-explosion of the booby trap on the box of NVA maps and documents points to the building sense of confusion of this whole first part of the film. You can name the parts, but you can never understand them. You are your own worst enemy. The tension of living within this constant duality of the war builds all through part one of *Platoon* until it finally snaps.

Part one of *Platoon*, this symbolic "naming of parts," ends with the burning of a Vietnamese village by the enraged platoon. It is a scene which draws heavily upon the earlier Vietnam War literature. It is not My Lai at all, but rather a scene directly out of Caputo's *A Rumor of War*. Taylor's intensive, portentous voice-over introduces the scene badly: "Barnes was the eye of our rage. Our Captain Ahab. We would set things right again. That day we loved him." It is hard to believe that he is really writing this sort of thing to his grandma. As soon as the platoon enters the village, madness confronts them and they cannot deal with it. Chaos reasserts its control over them as it has earlier in the night ambush and in the bunker complex. The madness of the war confronts them in the dead eyes of a Vietnamese boy. In *Dispatches*, Michael Herr wrote:

> A little boy of about ten came up to a bunch of Marines from Charlie Company. He was laughing and moving his head from side to side in a funny way. The fierceness in his eyes should have told everyone what it was but it had never occurred to most of the grunts that a Vietnamese child could be driven mad too, and by the time they understood it the boy had begun to go for their eyes and tear at their fatigues, spooking everyone, putting everyone really uptight, until a black grunt grabbed him from behind and held his arm. "C'mon, pore lil' baby, 'fore one of these grunt mothers shoots you . . . (75).

The first atrocity of this village burning scene is an instant replay of Herr's descriptions. First, Taylor makes the mad boy dance with machine gun fire, then another young American, unable to stand the madness in the Vietnamese's staring eyes, beats the mad boy to death with the butt of his rifle. Ironically, the Americans strike out at the madness of the war with their own form of madness as they kill, rape, and burn the village and its inhabitants then walk away from the holocaust like missionaries, carrying the children of their victims.

This is a pivotal scene in *Platoon*. In earlier scenes, the chaos, the annihilation of normality and reason, was engineered by the enemy, the NVA soldiers or the invisible Viet Cong, but in this village scene at the very end of part one it is the Americans who are accepting the chaos of the war, who are annihilating their own moral images of themselves. It is they, not the barbarian enemy, who have given up all pretension to civilization, all claim to humanity. As Taylor breaks up the gang rape of a Vietnamese child, he screams, "She's a fuckin' human being, man. You're all animals." Philip Caputo, in a speech on the war and the books and films about the war (Purdue University, March 1988), defines the schizoid nature of the American soldier and, by extension, the whole American psyche in Vietnam, as a dialectical tension between "the outlaw and the missionary." The final scene of part one of *Platoon*, the burning of the village, captures this frightening duality within both Chris Taylor and the others in the platoon. The parallel to a very similar scene in Philip Caputo's *A Rumor of War* is obvious.[7] First, Chris Taylor screams unintelligibly at the mad-eyed Vietnamese boy and shoots his M-16 to make him dance, but when a mad-eyed, dead-eyed American boy (Kevin Dillon) beats the Vietnamese to death with the butt of his rifle, Taylor quickly sobers and changes from temporary "outlaw" back to his original "missionary." Earlier in the movie, when Chris was telling two other grunts about his past life and why he enlisted, he generated this reaction: "What we got here is a Crusader," one of his fellow grunts comments sarcastically.

As the Americans snap in the village scene -- "Let's do the whole fuckin' village," one proposes -- Chris realizes that the "crusader," the "missionary," must always contend with the "outlaw" in Vietnam or every act will result in madness, atrocity, massacre and the total annihilation of all that is human. When he screams, "You're all animals! You just don't fuckin' get it," as he breaks up the gang rape, he is commenting directly upon the nihilism which has caught the Americans in its grip. First, Taylor fights with himself, then he fights with his fellow grunts, then Elias and Barnes (the physical embodiments of the psychological outlaw and missionary impulses which are contending for Chris Taylor's soul) fight with each other over the methods of dealing with the village.

Part two of *Platoon* is the least interesting part of the film. It is the morality play, dominated by the symbolic, allegorical opposition between Sergeants Elias and Barnes. Ultimately, these two, Light and Dark, Good and Evil, Life and Death, Christ and Satan face off alone in the bush to fight their own symbolic war, orchestrate the dialectic clash of their contending philosophies. They confront each other. Elias smiles in conciliation. Barnes draws a bead on Elias and shoots him in cold blood. Nihilism -- expressionless, empty, dead -- murders reason, morality, idealism. But who cares? Elias and Barnes are not the central concern of this scene. Only one aspect of the whole acting out of this morality playlet in part two has any significant and symbolic meaning for the central thematics of the film. The only important thing about the private morality play war between Elias and Barnes is the fact that Chris Taylor stands as witness to it. His role as witness in this part two of *Platoon* is the same role Joker (Matthew Modine) plays all through the somewhat similar three parts of *Full Metal Jacket*.

Waiting in the LZ for the choppers to evacuate them from the firefight, the platoon learns that Barnes and Elias are still in the bush. Taylor goes back to help them. In doing so, Chris Taylor, All-American Boy, though he doesn't see the attempted murder, becomes a witness to American naivete being shot down, to American betrayal by fellow Americans, to American ruthlessness, to American opportunism, to American rejection of all that is right and fair and real, to American murderousness, to the ultimate nihilism which the Vietnam War has dropped over the American character like a bell jar.

The choppers arrive. In the chaos of the chopper wind, in the panicky rush to get on, Barnes tells Taylor that Elias is dead. The choppers rise off the hot LZ and suddenly the whole film goes maudlin, sentimental, embarrassingly obviously symbolic, cloyingly artificial. The action goes to romanticized slow-motion. The orchestral "Adagio for Strings" rises out of the gunfire and the gunship wind like a dirge. Elias appears running and being shot repeatedly in slow-motion by a uniformed, rack-focus-blurred mob. In slow-motion to orchestral strings he stretches his arms out to the sky, to the choppers hovering overhead, in the classic death pose of the Christus. It is all a contrived, mannered, artificial, sentimental set piece, an embarrassing crucifixion, and, in the context of what *Platoon* is about (Chris Taylor's confusion, America's confusion in Vietnam), it means nothing.

Part three of *Platoon* is what the film is really about. In this section, the confusion escalates out of control and Taylor's role as observer and witness changes to that of participant and focus of the film's symbolic nihilism. Back in the base camp after the death of Elias, the platoon talks of fragging Barnes. Drunk, taking long pulls from his bottle of Kentucky bourbon as if it were a moonshine jug, Barnes intrudes upon their guilty conspiring and, in one speech, defines the whole "reality versus humanism" dialectic of the war. He synthesizes that dialectic into a mechanistic, dehumanized nihilism which offers no solution, no hope, no salvation, no progress, no existential selfhood, only endurance, survival, continuation on a general not a personal basis. What Stanley Kauffman (*The New Republic*, 19 January 1987) says about Taylor's voice-over narration is exactly what Barnes is telling the platoon about the war. Kauffman writes, the "voice-over comments. . . . shunt the film momentarily into the shape of an object lesson, when the real point is that there is no lesson. . . . "

"I am reality," Barnes growls. "Here's the way it oughta be. Here's the way it is. Elias is full of shit. Elias was a Crusader. Now I got no fight with anyone does what he's told. But when he don't the machine breaks down. And when the machine breaks down, we break down, and I ain't gonna allow that." Barnes' speech echoes the earlier sarcastic characterization of Taylor as a "Crusader" and goes on to characterize the platoon as simply a machine with interchangeable human parts. Barnes' declaration, "I am reality," is a statement of the nihilism, the scarred, empty, dehumanized, brutal, survivalist, mad nihilism that they all must accept and embrace if they are to exist as cogs in the machine of the war. What Barnes is saying is that all must become like him if they are to survive. In affirmation of Barnes' speech, in the last major scene of the film, Chris Taylor, who earlier was a "Crusader," becomes exactly like Barnes, participates in an instant replay of Barnes' murder of Elias in the bush. Taylor accepts and acts upon the nihilism of Barnes' speech. Taylor rejects his own naive humanism, accepts the realism of Barnes, then goes beyond that mere realism into the utter nihilism of his own heart of darkness. Proving once again that the Americans are their own worst enemies, that the nihilism of the Vietnam War lies within the American psyche not in the war itself, Taylor murders Barnes in cold blood as Barnes had earlier murdered Elias.

Platoon, however, ultimately is not at all about Elias or Barnes or Chris Taylor or Americans killing each other in Vietnam. *Platoon* is a film about confusion, confusion on every level of human perception, confusion on every level of national intention, confusion swirling and popping and exploding and spurting and twisting and turning and rising and falling so fast that nothingness, total void, is the only resting place. Moral confusion, existential confusion, confusion of time, of place, of reality, of sanity, confusion of intention, confusion of direction, ultimately just the utter confusion of meaningless action is the fuel that moves the movie. All that is imaged and happens in *Platoon*, all of its "naming of parts" and "morality playlets," simply leads to the ultimate symbol of nihilistic confusion in part three of the film, the Ur-firefight, chaos personified and extended.

By the time the final firefight begins, Chris Taylor has learned the Vietnam War, has become proficient in death-dealing, has moved from the innocence of the Crusader to the realism of the grunt. He has learned to read the bush and see the attacking NVA in the night as he couldn't in the opening night ambush scene. He can find his claymore switches right away as he couldn't in the opening night ambush scene. He knows by instinct exactly when to get out of his foxhole as he didn't earlier. He has become a part of the machine of fighting the war and he knows how to do it right. When the final firefight starts, Chris Taylor goes on automatic, gives himself over to the confusion of the moment, becomes one with the chaotic, whirling, flux-focused action. He chooses to exist within the nullity of the moment, the only possible truth available to him. He literally forgets himself, forgets everything. Insanely, he charges the enemy.

The firefight begins slowly with shadows darting in the jungle and frightened screams piercing the terrified silence. A basketball flare floats down on its fragile Cracker Jack box parachute throwing surreal Caligari light over the dark and cluttered movie set. As the firefight begins, Chris has time to make a few rational decisions -- to stay not run, to set off the mines, to get out of the foxhole at the right moment -- but immediately the firefight explodes into what Vietnam was really all about. It explodes into madness and chaos. It explodes into the annihilation of all time, space, reason and sanity. Once the enemy gets inside the perimeter the real Vietnam, the nihilist place where utter confusion reigns, asserts itself. Images and actions rip by faster than automatic weapons fire. Oliver Stone empties clip after clip at the theater audience. Chris Taylor rushes face first into the firefight in a mad suicidal charge. The phones, the machines, don't work. The American commander drops napalm inside his own perimeter. All is confusion. Americans shoot the enemy, each other, no difference. The scene turns into a drawn-out nihilistic nightmare. For a few brief seconds a movie actually captures the mad minute pace of the Vietnam War.

The final scene of *Platoon*, in which Taylor confronts and murders Barnes, is anti-climactic. *Platoon* is a straightforward, slice-of-life parable of the descent of American optimism into the black hole of utter nihilism and the destruction of the self. In this coda scene, an American kills an American, stressing once again that in Vietnam America was its own worst enemy. Chris Taylor literally kills the self he has followed and become. He repeats Barnes' act of killing Elias. He becomes Barnes even as he kills Barnes. He refuses to accept any meaning in either Elias or Barnes. He kills meaning, opts for nothing. At the end of *Platoon*, all Chris Taylor can do is walk away utterly confused as did Jake Gittes from another oriental neighborhood in the most symbolic Vietnam allegory of the seventies, *Chinatown*.

Chris Taylor's final speech in voice-over as he is airlifted out of Vietnam is about teaching the war -- "I think now, looking back, we did not fight the enemy but ourselves, and the war was in us . . . but be that as it may, those of us who did make it have an obligation to build again, to teach to others what we know, and to try with what's left of our lives to find a goodness and meaning to this life." But the vets like Chris Taylor have not been able to find that meaning and if the very men who were in the war weren't able to teach it then how can any other medium -- books, movies, academic classes -- really hope to find meaning in it? The ultimate deconstruction of the Vietnam War, the ultimate example of the war's nihilistic meaninglessness, is the continuing confused mobility in the eighties of every text, be it film or novel or history or oral history or analytic study or classroom discussion in the attempt to find meaning in that war. The meaning of the Vietnam War is not, like the Viet Cong, merely elusive; in almost every extant text, it seems to be utterly non-existent.

Notes

1. Greil Marcus, "Journey Up The River: An Interview With Francis Coppola," *Rolling Stone* (11/1/79).

2. Peter Blauner in *New York* (8 December 1986) writes that in *Platoon* Oliver Stone "has gone after a lean, terrifyingly real vision of war, one that audiences will find hard to shake." Stanley Kauffman (*The New Republic*, 19 January 1987) writes: "Stone has written and directed a war film so strikingly genuine that we never bother to think that it's better than most war films." Pauline Kael, whose mixed review in *The New Yorker* (12 January 1987) rightly sees the *Platoon* script as a heavy handed morality play, also acknowledges that while the film "doesn't deal with what the war was about -- it's conceived strictly in terms of what these American infantrymen go through." David Denby in *New York* (15 December 1986) praises *Platoon* because "it captures, with an enduring power, and from the inside, what the commonplace horror of the conflict felt like. Those of us who opposed the war may not have wanted to experience the fighting man's emotions so directly. But we do experience them, and for us the war has lost some of its comforting remoteness, perhaps for good."

3. Stanley Kauffman in "An American Tragedy" in *The New Republic* (19 January 1987) makes this same point as he writes: "The action is not used as a ground for a story, conventional or otherwise. It is the experience of the war that this film wants primarily to give us, not drama" (24).

4. In *The Films of the Seventies: A Social History*, an extended comparison of Coppola's *Apocalypse Now* to Melville's *Moby Dick* was made.

5. Pauline Kael (The New Yorker, 12 January 1987) notes how the protagonist of *Platoon*, Chris Taylor, "arrives in the confusion of Vietnam" and suffers from "initial disorientation," but she quickly drops this theme for a more political and equally valid theme: "The film is about victimizing ourselves as well as others; it's about shame. That's the only way in which it's political." Please compare Kael's definition of this theme of shame with the discussion of the final scene of Platoon herein which deals with the irony of Americans killing each other rather than the enemy. David Denby (*New York*, 15 December 1986) also notes that "Stone has told the familiar young soldier's story without copping out on the ineradicable betterness and confusion of the Vietnam War."

6. In *The Films of the Seventies: A Social History* the long discussion of Roman Polanski's *Chinatown* contains a reading of that brilliant film as metaphoric Vietnam War film.

7. Philip Caputo, *A Rumor of War* (New York: Ballantine, 1978), writes: "A phosphorus grenade bursts in a cloud of thick, white smoke, and a hut begins to burn. Another goes up. In minutes, the entire hamlet is in flames, the thatch and bamboo crackling like small arms fire. The marines are letting out high-pitched yells, like the old rebel yell, and throwing grenades and firing rifles into bomb shelters and dugouts. Women are screaming, children crying. Panic-stricken, the villagers run out of the flame and smoke as if from a natural disaster. The livestock goes mad, and the squawking of chickens, the squeal of pigs, and the bawling of water buffalo are added to the screams and yells and the loud popping of the flaming huts.

'They've gone nuts, skipper,' Tester says. 'They're shooting the whole place up. Christ, they're killing the animals.'

He and Peterson try to stop the destruction, but it is no use: 3rd Platoon seems to have gone crazy. They destroy with uncontrolled fury. At last it is over. The hamlet which is marked on our maps as Giao-Tri 3 no longer exists. All that remains are piles or smoldering ash and a few charred poles still standing. . . . We are learning to hate" (103-4).

Works Cited

Caputo, Philip. *A Rumor of War*. New York: Ballantine, 1978.

Conrad, Joseph. *Heart of Darkness*. New York: Norton, 1963.

Del Vecchio, John. *The 13th Valley*. New York: Bantam, 1982.

Herr, Michael. *Dispatches*. New York: Avon, 1978.

New York. 15 December 1986.

New Yorker. 12 January 1987.

The New York Times. 8 March 1987.

The New Republic. 19 January 1987.

Palmer, William J. *The Films of the Seventies: A Social History*. Metuchen, N.J.: The Scarecrow Press, Inc., 1987.

Rolling Stone. 1 November 1979.

Smith, Julian. *Looking Away: Hollywood and Vietnam*. New York: Charles Scribner's Sons, 1975.

AFTER THE APOCALYPSE: NARRATIVE MOVEMENT IN LARRY HEINEMANN'S *PACO'S STORY*

Nancy Anisfield

At the 1985 Asia Society conference on "The Vietnam Experience in American Literature," author Tim O'Brien talked about the discovery of truth in a work of fiction. He said when a story or poem offers clarity, "It informs our souls or our spirits..." (Lomperis 54). Political science professor Timothy Lomperis elaborated on this idea, writing: "Fiction reveals emotions and can examine motives. It is in laying bare motives that we find out why things happen. And these are the real facts: the information that is put in an insightful pattern that allows us to understand" (62). O'Brien's and Lomperis's words defend the usefulness of fiction in establishing and recording an understanding of the world's history, and they emphasize the critical nature of the patterning of information presented in fiction. In most novels of the Vietnam War, a distinct pattern has predominated, but this pattern may impede readers' assimilation of much of the novels' information. The problem with this pattern is the location of the climax and its dependence on intensified violence to realize each work's teleological expectations.

In brief, the pattern begins conventionally by securing a focused location and minimal tension. The characters are introduced, then the conflict simmers and the action builds. Finally, the story explodes with an apocalyptic event designed to ensure the reader's awareness of the horror and alienation the characters have endured and how profoundly those characters have been altered by their experience. This apocalyptic event is not necessary, but it is impressive. Despite the ongoing ambiguity, confusion and terror of the American soldiers' experience in Vietnam, many writers seem to think it's necessary to go one better, make sure their readers feel the protagonist's desensitization and psychic wounds are justified. Even though throughout his tour of duty the poor grunt has been plunged into a baptismal bath of bullets, mortars, mines, leeches, heat, and bureaucratic absurdity, the demands of plot are too strong.

In Gustave Hasford's *The Short-Timers*, Joker must kill his closest friend to save the rest of the squad from a sniper. In the end of *The 13th Valley* by John Del Vecchio, the central characters face the final cataclysmic battle of their operation. Robert Stone's *Dog Soldiers* winds up with a big shoot out; William Pelfrey's *The Big V* concludes with Henry Winsted watching his friend and teacher, the Anachronism, get blown up by a booby trap. The list goes on: Spec 4 Paul Berlin's literal and imaginary journey culminates when he storms the grassy hill (and/or apartment) at the end of Tim O'Brien's *Going After Cacciato*, and in Donald Tate's *Bravo Burning*, once again the NVA overrun the hill and the central character is permanently maimed.

In an article in *Harpers*, C.D.B. Bryan, author of *Friendly Fire*, describes what he terms a "Generic Vietnam War Narrative" (63). His description includes a young white male who is slowly introduced to a platoon of diversified soldiers, his first patrol, an atrocity, some dope, a few helicopter assaults, a visit to Susie the bar-girl, and various battle scenes. Bryan goes on to say, "The Generic Vietnam War Narrative charts the gradual deterioration of order, the disintegration of idealism, the breakdown of character, the alienation from those at home, and finally, the loss of all sensibility save the will to survive" (69). What Bryan fails to include is that final gut-wrenching climactic event that pushes the character over the top, just in case everything else wasn't quite enough to turn him into an emotional void, a psychotic, an addict, or simply a young man who'd been scared and horrified once too often to be able to resurrect a believable standard of morals or values.

Both readers and writers acknowledge that something has to happen in a novel. Suspense, rising action, climax and resolution contribute to the pattern that not only is anticipated most often in stories and novels, but also forms the most dependable skeletal structure and circulatory system of any body of fiction. And certainly happy endings are inappropriate when writing about a morally ambiguous war that was America's first major conflict without a decisive victory. Given these parameters, most writers would find a devastating climax suitable.

However, the effectiveness of this pattern is called into question when the arguments begin that the Vietnam War was different and that it requires a different literature to tell its story. Perhaps the sense of closure inherent in the Aristotelean notion of plot -- a beginning, middle and end -- cannot represent the lack of closure still evident in our attempts to understand this war. Furthermore, plot depends on anagnorisis or recognition, and it's reasonable to say that with the Vietnam War, "recognition" (of purpose, enemy, status, results) has never been fully attained.

In her article, "Novelists and Vietnam: The War Goes On," Michiko Kakutani writes, "With Vietnam, however, the classic scenario of a boy going off to war and returning home a man (if he returns at all) suffers a dark revision. There are few opportunities for old-fashioned heroics -- or any of the other conventional tests of manhood -- in the cynical landscape of Vietnam. In Vietnam, simple physical and psychological survival is difficult enough" (39). If simple survival is difficult enough, why then do these characters have to finish their tour of duty with an apocalyptic event that demands even more: watching their best friend die or witnessing a surreal battle of theretofore unparalleled destruction? Isn't the normal everyday fear, pain, isolation and absurdity enough? An alternative consideration is the fact that these climactic, apocalyptic events happened every day or night, so the fiction of this war need not give them special designation as the final cause to the final effect. Perhaps these novelists were afraid that the American public was still too desensitized by the war's overbearing media coverage, that only extremes could cut through the bored familiarity of the war. Perhaps there is no need for extremes, just a presentation of the paradoxical balance: horrors happened daily in this war and daily life was a horror.

Even the novels focusing on veterans after the war seem to rely on the apocalyptic ending to make their point. Stephen Wright's *Meditations in Green* offers two climactic, shattering events -- the night when Griffin's base was overrun and he was wounded, and the tragic fight between Griffin and Trips during Trips' assault on the alleged Sergeant Anstin. *Walking Wounded* by Stephen J. Thorpe builds tension until it explodes in a bar room fight and a confrontation with a .22 caliber pistol. R. Lanny Hunter and Victor L. Hunter's novel, *Living Dogs and Dead Lions* is yet another example, climaxing with a brutal brawl between the veteran (and his dead buddy's wife and son) and several sleazy locals.

The frequency with which this narrative pattern is found is not what invalidates its effectiveness. As Bryan notes, "I do not mean to diminish the importance of Vietnam War literature by suggesting it is all 'of a type'" (69). The issue is simply that a fiction whose primary virtue and desire is to tell it like it was seems too often dependent upon a convention which uses emotional extremes to affect the reader.

Furthermore, because the representation of an intense experience (good or bad) is stimulating to a reader, a novel's anti-war message may be contradicted by the pleasure of stimulation. Narrative representation is not the same as actual experience, so deriving pleasure from evoked excitement or tension is not the same as wanting the actual experience -- enjoying combat narratives does not imply a desire for combat. Nevertheless, if a novel hopes to show its readers the tragedy of war, it may find its themes subverted by powerful action sequences.

Larry Heinemann, however, is one writer who has avoided this conventional narrative structure. His first Vietnam War novel, *Close Quarters*, is a book of rising combat action, but it doesn't depend on immediate violence for its climactic event. Throughout the novel the central character, Philip Dosier, speaks with a voice emanating from a post-war state of embitterment. **Within** a conventional tour of duty framework, the narrative chronicles the growth of this embitterment. The most violent combat sequence occurs four-fifths of the way through the book, yet the culminating event of the novel occurs approximately eight pages from the end. Obviously, the apocalyptic violence of "The Great Truce Day Body Count" is not intended as the climax. Instead, the narrative peaks when Dosier reads a letter telling him that his best friend, still in-country, has been killed. The moment is one of passive physical action even though it generates a strong internal response.

Heinemann's second Vietnam War novel, *Paco's Story*, refines the passive climax and develops the unconventional narrative structure even further. Again rejecting the generic pattern, Heinemann now reverses the structure completely, placing the apocalypse at the beginning of the novel and entirely eliminating combat-associated violence from the climax. In *Paco's Story*, the combat experience is encapsulated in one chapter -- the first chapter, noting that the devastation affected both Americans and Vietnamese, and idea frequently overlooked when the climactic action focuses only on American protagonists.

> ...the air came alive and crawled and yammered and whizzed and hummed with the roar and buzz of a thousand incoming rounds. It was hard to see for all the gunpowder smoke and dust kicked up by all the muzzle flashes, but everyone looked up -- GIs *and* zips -- and knew it was every incoming round left in Creation, a wild and bloody shitstorm, a ball busting cataclysm. We knew that the dirt under our bellies (and the woods and the villes and us with it) was going to be pulverized to ash...knew by the overwhelming, ear-piercing whine we swore was splitting our heads wide open that those rounds were the size of houses. (14)

The intensity of this experience is acknowledged and vividly portrayed, but the high-pitched action does not last. As a result, the reader concentrates on the terrifying aftereffects of the event, and stimulation is soon overshadowed by thought-provoking narrative.

The rest of the novel follows Paco, the only survivor, as he settles in a quiet town, working as a dishwasher. There is no tense build-up, no progression of initiate experiences, and no apocalyptic final event. This story takes place long after the apocalypse, yet what is left is probably more disturbing than the immediate horror of the climactic event.

Paco is the nuclear age, atomic nightmare survivor. He is the only one left. Unlike the last man on earth so often imagined in fiction, however, he is only the last man of a set few who were there. His past evaporated with most everything on Fire Base Harriette; the present Paco was born out of the ashes of that firestorm. The ingenious booby trap artist and the graceful soldier are repressed, alluded to only in the novel's final episode. And the boy from before the war has vanished. When questioned about his background, Paco's story never goes back before Harriette.

> "Where *you from*?" Jesse repeats; louder, sitting up. "What?" Paco says, unhooking his belt from the rim of the washtub and coming out from behind the high counter at the back. Ernest stops his work...standing ready to listen, surprised that Paco is going to any trouble -- thinking he's finally going to hear something. "From?" Paco repeats. "Not around here. Wounded in war..." (151-2)

After the apocalypse, his apocalypse, the world is still populated, but Paco lives in a separate place, haunted by the ghosts of those who died around him.

And Paco has told his brief story too many times: "He has dwelt on it with trivial thoroughness, condensed it, told it as an ugly fucking joke..." (72). Now someone else has to tell it for him. The reader learns of Paco though the observations of the medic who found him, the bus driver who takes him west, his boss, and, above all, the narrative voice which belongs to one of those ghosts from Fire Base Harriette. These figures are witness to Paco's experience -- from the moment of its eruption though the aftershocks that followed. Rather than relying on the emotional draw of a violent climax, Heinemann absorbs his reader with shifting perspectives, forcing the reader to become one of Paco's witnesses too.

Slowly the reader becomes accustomed to Paco. He is introspective, yet seems to accept his fate. He lives in physical pain yet depends on hard work to confirm his existence.

At the end of the novel, rather than a conventional climax, a passive, tightly focused internal event draws the narrative to its close. Paco reads the diary of Cathy, the young woman who lives next to him, and the reader sees him from a final, new perspective. The only action is within Paco's mind and that of the reader. Paco sits passively, languidly, on her couch and reads:

> Aunt Myrna says he has a way of stiffening up and
> staring right through you. As if he's a ghost. Or you're
> the ghost...And he's all pasty. And crippled. And
> honest to God, ugly. Curled up on his bed like death
> warmed over. Like he was someone back from the
> dead. . . (206-207)

Here the true quality of Paco's existence becomes apparent. In this passive moment, Paco and the reader (who is thrust into involvement by the shift in perspective) become aware that despite Paco's efforts to make a life -- however small -- after the war, he is an embarrassing oddity to those around him, and a half-man, half-ghost to himself. The moment is startling, disturbing, and quite effective in providing direction for the plot without relying on cataclysmic violence.

Here, both Paco and the reader realize that he'll never be part of the living. Though alive, he'll remain with the ghosts from Harriette, who cluster about his bed each night to haunt and torment him with the maddening question: Why him? They "bestir and descend...hover around him like an aura" (137), but the ghosts are also his only friends. "We reach out as one man and begin to massage the top of his head" (138). They are the only ones who comfort or soothe him. Cathy, on the other hand, is in the realm of the living, the pre-Harriette, pre-apocalypse world, and can't see the ghosts. Instead, she sees Paco moan and slam back and forth on his bed, rubbing his own back, crying out from his nightmares. Undoubtedly, Cathy and the other townspeople know nothing of Post Traumatic Stress Disorder. Her repulsion towards Paco's scars suggests hometown America's embarrassed rejection of the Vietnam veterans. She, like many others, is locked into her own vanity, desires, and narrow-minded view of the world.

Perhaps even worse is that after reading the diary Paco sees himself as lifeless. He thinks to himself, "Man, you ain't just a brick in the fucking wall, you're just a piece of meat on the slab" (209). Besides discovering his detachment from others, Paco discovers he is detached from his own goals and dreams as well.

Although both Philip Dosier and Paco Sullivan are out of the war, texts which bear witness to the war's effects still control their lives. The text Paco reads, however, wasn't even written for him, which underscores Paco's alienation from the forces that determine the state of his existence. Furthermore, the introspective nature of his discovery pushes the reader far from any action-generated stimulation. Instead, the reader probes deeply into the bilevel text to find truths about the war and its aftermath, not to find moments of consummate action and closure.

In the end of Stephen Crane's *The Red Badge of Courage*, Henry Fleming, having "rid himself of the red sickness of battle" (131) walks off, with a golden ray of sun shining through the hosts of leaden rain clouds. That was when men matured in war despite the horrors. At the end of *Paco's Story*, after reading Cathy's diary, Paco just leaves. No sunset, no clouds -- no horizon. Just a Texaco station and a bus Westward (where our story teller says "there's less bullshit") is traditionally the new frontier. But the closing images of the novel don't seem to offer much hope, only "the long incline of the entrance ramp," and Paco "is soon gone" (210).

Like the decreasing intensity of the novel's action, the figure of Paco diminishes at the end. The reader now views Paco as the subject of a text within a text, further removed from the rest of the world. He survives, but his existence shows no signs of regeneration or new life, and any idea of a new frontier has faded as well. The final event signals prolongation rather than end; the closing implies continuation rather than change.

To write about how Vietnam was different from other wars, to understand what it really did to the men and women who were there without enhancing their experience to the point of glorification, novelists have to go beyond the climactic event. It isn't necessary to jolt the reader with cataclysmic devastation. It is necessary, though, to find a new narrative structure that rejects apocalyptic closure and encourages careful examination of not only the Vietnam War, but also the aftermath of that war and the texts that will hold that war in America's collective memory.

Works Cited

Bryan, C.D.B. "Barely Suppressed Screams." *Harpers*. June, 1984.

Crane, Stephen. *The Red Badge of Courage*. 1895. New York: Bantam, 1983.

Heinemann, Larry. *Paco's Story*. New York: Farrar, Straus, and Giroux, 1986.

Kakutani, Michiko. "Novelists and Vietnam: The War Goes On." *The New York Times Book Review*. April 15, 1984.

Lomperis, Timothy. *"Reading the Wind": The Literature of the Vietnam War*. Durham, NC: Duke University Press, 1987.

"DEPENDING ON THE LIGHT":
YUSEF KOMUNYAKAA'S *DIEN CAI DAU*

Vicente F. Gotera

One of the dominant impulses informing war literature is the documentary urge: the drive to make the horrors, the senselessness of war concrete to the uninitiated. Not surprisingly, in the course of this documentation, the writer often discovers the self, grappling with the realities of war; Jeffrey Walsh has pointed to "uniquely American visions of self-renewal and discovery through the exigencies of warfare, and [how] most of them draw upon the literary reworking of the writer's own experience" (5). Typical examples are Whitman, Dos Passos, cummings, Mailer, Jarrell--writers who were close to the fighting, if not literally combat veterans themselves.

American involvement in Vietnam, however, has fostered a consciousness of war which is radically different from our visions of earlier wars, especially because the Vietnam War has dramatized the moral ambivalence of American military power and the shortcomings of military technology. The use by the military of what writers on Vietnam have called the "jargon stream"--such terms as "pacification," "kill ratio," and "defoliation"--has become a specific challenge to the writer, since this use of semantics is a deliberate obfuscation. In addition, the cultural and geographical remoteness of Vietnam (as brought home by television), the public backlash and national controversy, the rejection of the returning soldier--all these have contributed to what Philip Caputo has labelled the"ethical wilderness" of the Vietnam War. A wilderness in which the soldier-poet is lost.

Traditionally, poetry has been a source of solace to the beleaguered poet. The *locus classicus*, of course, is the elegy; we do not doubt that Shelley, for example, in writing "Adonais," sought and found surcease for his sorrow at Keats' death. The important question here is whether the "self-renewal" to which Walsh points in war literature implies that the Vietnam-veteran poet finds solace in lyric poetry. Since the anthologies of the early 1970s, veteran poets--Receveur, Paquet, Casey, Berry, Ehrhart, Weigl, among others--have been assiduously documenting the war: depicting the strangeness of Vietnam, recording the language of that war, and reporting the alienation of the returning soldier. The optimist would suggest that these poems result not only in personal growth but also in the opportunity for national renewal. In a 1987 essay, however, W. D. Ehrhart (one of the most outspoken veteran poets) writes:

> [O]ne might venture to say that the act of writing these
> poems--even the worst of them--is an act of cleansing.
> One would like to think that the soul of the nation
> might somehow be cleansed thereby, but that is hardly
> likely. More realistically, one hopes that in writing
> these poems, the poets might at least have begun to
> cleanse their own souls of the torment that was and is
> Vietnam. ("Soldier-Poets" 265)

Clearly, Ehrhart's language reveals his reluctance to believe that the
Vietnam-veteran poet has been consoled by his own lyric impulse and
the writing of poetry. I propose that Yusef Komunyakaa's *Dien Cai
Dau*, through its devotion to a lyric rapaciousness, through its insistence
on human connections, offers hope for such consolation.

Literary critics have cited the difficulty of depicting Vietnam and
the war in poetry; Jeffrey Walsh, for example, has echoed John
Felstiner in arguing that "poetry of a traditional kind has proved
inappropriate to communicate the character of the Vietnam war, its
remoteness, its jargonised recapitulations, its seeming imperviousness
to aesthetics" (Walsh 204). As the Vietnam War wound down, the first
poems to be published by veterans relied on violent imagery coupled
with the absurdity of Vietnam in the eyes of youthful Americans. Don
Receveur's "night fear" is typical:

> i heard my meatless bones
> clunk together
> saw the ants drink
> from my eyes
> like red ponies
> at brown pools of water
> and the worms in my belly
> moved sluggishly
> delighted.
>   (*Winning Hearts & Minds* 15)

This poem teeters on the verge of triteness and overstatement, but what
rescues it is the projection in the reader's mind of the *actual* experience
which certainly lies behind this poem, prompted by Receveur's insistent
concreteness. One critic has noted that in Receveur's work "the war
seem[s] actualized, made urgent through its particularity" (Walsh 204).

Even when an early Vietnam-veteran poem is more cerebral, there is still a strong flavor of the unbelievability of Vietnam. A good example is Basil T. Paquet's "They Do Not Go Gentle":

> The half-dead comatose
> Paw the air like cats do when they dream,
> They perform isometrics tirelessly.
> They flail the air with a vengeance
> You know they cannot have.
> After all, their multiplication tables,
> Memories of momma, and half their id
> Lies in some shell hole
> Or plop! splatter! on your jungle boots.
> It must be some atavistic angst
> Of their muscle and bones,
> Some ancient ritual of their sea water self,
> Some blood stream monsoon,
> Some sinew storm that makes
> Their bodies rage on tastelessly
> Without their shattered brains.
>
> (*Winning Hearts & Minds* 3)

Of course, the title is a reference to Dylan Thomas' famous exhortation affirming life and the pursuit of it. In Paquet's Vietnam, however, this primal urge is reduced to the body's momentary life after a shell hits, mere corporeal inertia. Diction here implies an intellectualized rationality: "comatose," "isometrics," "id," "atavistic angst." But the lasting impression is of "multiplication tables, / Memories of Momma" smeared "pop! splatter!"--American intangibles concretized by onomatopoeia. The point is that Paquet, whom Ehrhart has called "[l]iterate without being literary" ("Soldier-Poets" 248), sets up a tension between the quotidian realities of "the world" (everywhere outside Vietnam) with the incredible commonplaces of "the Nam."

Another preoccupation of Vietnam-veteran poetry has been language--both the jargonized as well as the colloquial. Michael Casey, whose collection *Obscenities* won the Yale Younger Poets Prize in 1972, "works exclusively with the truncated matter-of-fact speech rhythms [of the] Vietnamese grunt[s]" or infantrymen, as Ehrhart has noted ("Soldier-Poets" 248). Casey's "The LZ Gator Body Collector" is a revelatory example:

> See
> Her back is arched

Like something's under it
That's why I thought
It was booby trapped
But it's not
It just must have been
Over this rock here
And somebody moved it
After corpus morta stiffened it
I didn't know it was
A woman at first
I couldn't tell
But then I grabbed
Down there
It's a woman or was
It's all right
I didn't mind
I had gloves on then (56)

According to Casey's book, the "language is so simple and open, so plausible, that one scarcely notices the artfulness of the compression, the understatement" (xii). Gracefully ensconced within the clipped language of this poem is a parody of romance *and* pornography: "Her back is arched," "stiffened," "I grabbed / Down there"; the neologism "corpus morta" not only replaces "rigor mortis" but also emphasizes the connotations of *body* here. John Felstiner asserts that Casey, in "merely reassuring us that his death encounter was sanitary, . . . lets the war's full insanity come in on us with everything he does not say" (11). Such artful omission is what allows Casey's delimited language, finally, to carry a charged eloquence.

D. C. Berry, whose *saigon cemetery* was also published in 1972, creatively uses the unique military language of the Vietnam War. Casey uses Army slang for plausibility, to make his characters' speech sound genuine. Berry, in contrast, orchestrates language to oppose the "jargon stream" which Walsh suggests "can hide the reality of moral outrage" (206). Felstiner proposes that "Washington's need was to sanitize reality and quarantine the fact from the word--precisely what much poetry avoids" (10); Berry's poetry is an deliberate act against such linguistic conditioning. Note Berry's meticulous attention to language in this untitled poem:

The way popcorn   pops   is
the way punji sticks snap
into your skin and stab

pricking urine
into cardiovascular
systems and apparatus
apparently
unorganizing then demonstrating
it.

      then you die
either from the spike,
the   p,
or the

sun gone to grain
expanding

in your eye.   (41)

Berry uses sound adroitly in this poem: the onomatopoeic "pop" and the labial explosion of the plosive consonant "p." And the "p" sounds are not only initial or terminal (as in "snap"), but also medial ("apparatus," "spike," and "expanding"). In fact, Berry is even more clever when he uses the letter "p" separated from the rest of the line by white space rather than the slang "pee" which a poet more concerned with reportage might have used. The "jargon-stream"-like lines-"cardiovascular / systems and apparatus / apparently / unorganizing then demonstrating"--are deflated by the next line, a hard monosyllable, "it." As does Paquet, Berry contrasts "the Nam" and "the world" in this poem through the conflict between militaristic jargon and basic Anglo-Saxon language.

    A third focus of this body of poetry has been the veteran's return to America, dramatizing political activism and personal commitment within the poems themselves. W. D. Ehrhart's 1984 volume *To Those Who Have Gone Home Tired*, as Lorrie Smith has pointed out, "traces one representative veteran's growth from naiveté to disillusionment, anger, and political activism" (24). The title poem dramatizes the interlacing of Vietnam with myriad political and humanitarian issues:

After the streets fall silent
After the bruises and the tear-gassed eyes are healed
After the consensus has returned
After the memories of Kent and My Lai and Hiroshima
lose their power

and their connections with each other
and the sweaters labeled Made in Taiwan
After the last American dies in Canada
and the last Korean in prison
and the last Indian at Pine Ridge
After the last whale is emptied from the sea
and the last leopard emptied from its skin
and the last drop of blood refined by Exxon
After the last iron door clangs shut
behind the last conscience
and the last loaf of bread is hammered into bullets
and the bullets
scattered among the hungry

What answers will you find
What armor will protect you
when your children ask you
Why?

(*Carrying the Darkness* 97-98)

Again the ubiquitous contrast of America and Vietnam, but here it has
come home to roost *in* the home, in the child's question "Why?"
Ultimately, Vietnam becomes only one of many fronts for the political
activist: American aggression, the environment, animal rights, the
depatriation of Native Americans, and more. And the discovery of this
range of political issues is both mirrored and complemented by the
poet's own recovery of self; "Ehrhart," asserts Smith, "connects two
converging continuums: his personal coming of age and the destructive
flow of history" (24).

For Bruce Weigl, the commitment is not so much to historical or
political concerns as to personal responsibility; the poems in his 1985
collection *The Monkey Wars* chart a private rather than a public
landscape. It is this personal testimony, however, that gives these
poems their immediacy and, in our inevitable identification and
participation, their social and collective force. The book opens with
"Amnesia," an unrhymed sonnet whose octave and sestet contrast
Vietnam and America:

If there was a world more disturbing than this
Where black clouds bowed down and swallowed you whole
And overgrown tropical plants
Rotted, effervescent in the muggy twilight and monkeys
Screamed something

That came to sound like words to each other
Across the triple-canopy jungle you shared,
You don't remember it.

You tell yourself no and cry a thousand days.
You imagine the crows calling autumn into place
Are your brothers and you could
If only the strength and will were there
Fly up to them to be black
And useful to the wind.
                              (*Carrying the Darkness* 274-75)

In this poem, Vietnam is depicted concretely but not with explicit violence; instead, a paralyzing ambivalence dramatizes the speaker's wish to forget. But at the same time, there is a drive to remember, to become "useful to the wind," and *The Monkey Wars* is Weigl's heroic attempt to gather "strength and will," in order to resurrect and finally confront Vietnam, that "world more disturbing."

In these six poets, the documentary urge comes to encompass more than mere telling; the last three poems are set in second person, reflecting the polemical bent of much Vietnam-veteran poetry. Using "you" as the voice of a poem, however, also enforces the immediate and personal participation of the audience. Clearly, the implication, especially in a poem such as Weigl's "Amnesia," is that Vietnam can only be understood and appreciated by the civilian through a direct, if only imagined, taking part. But this device does not enjoin the "self-renewal" of the poet. In Weigl's "Amnesia," the speaker is enervated--he wants to transcend Vietnam, but "strength and will" are only imagined, not actual at the moment. Smith has argued that, in the work of Ehrhart and Weigl, "the lyric imagination utterly fails to ameliorate or transform the memory of Vietnam" (17). I propose that Yusef Komunyakaa's welding of an idiosyncratic ferocity to what we usually envision as "lyric imagination" in *Dien Cai Dau* affords the opportunity for such transformation and eventual amelioration.

Dien Cai Dau is Komunyakaa's fourth book of poems. In his earlier three books, he has not included a single poem on Vietnam, because he has been waiting for emotional distance--objective and journalistic-from his 1969-70 Army tour there. George Garrett, in his introduction to Berry's *saigon cemetery*, proposes that "ordinary judgment [of Berry's poems] must be suspended. We are too close, and the wounds and scars, literal and metaphorical, are too fresh" (viii). It is just such a suspension of judgment that Komunyakaa does *not* want; he wishes his work to be tested with the full rigor applied to all serious poetry.

The fact that Komunyakaa has waited almost two decades to publish poems on Vietnam differentiates his work significantly from that of other veteran poets, especially those who published in the early 70s. The difference is not so much that he has achieved a distance from his Vietnam experience but rather that the development of his craft has not been inextricably bound up with Vietnam, as Ehrhart's, for example, has been. Komunyakaa comes to the material with an academic grounding in modernist and contemporary poetics as well as classic surrealism, and his work registers an esthetic advance not only of poetry about the Vietnam War but also of war literature in general.

From his first chapbook, *Dedications and Other Darkhorses* (1977), through his most recent book, *I Apologize for the Eyes in My Head* (1986), Komunyakaa's forte has been the counterbalancing of seeming oppositions and incongruities. Critics of Surrealism have pointed to "The poet Isidore Ducasse, the 'comte de Lautréamont,' who . . . had provided the classic example in writing of 'the chance encounter of a sewing machine and an umbrella on a dissection table'" (Rubin 19), a serendipitous yoking in whose interstices an immanent, wholly startling signification can well. Komunyakaa has inherited this mode of juxtaposition from the Surrealists, specifically through the poet Aimé Cesaire. A typical example is "2527th Birthday of the Buddha":

> When the motorcade rolled to a halt, Quang Duc
> climbed out & sat down in the street.
> He crossed his legs,
> & the other monks & nuns grew around him like petals.
> He challenged the morning sun,
> debating with the air
> he leafed through-visions brought down to earth.
> Could his eyes burn the devil out of men?
> A breath of peppermint oil
> soothed someone's cry. Beyond terror made flesh-
> he burned like a bundle of black joss sticks.
> A high wind that started in California
> fanned flames, turned each blue page,
> leaving only his heart intact.
> Waves of saffron robes bowed to the gasoline can. (18)

This poem takes as its base a kind of journalistic language, and of course the seed of the piece is the rumor that the heart of a self-immolated monk literally had not burned, a rumor perhaps gleaned from an actual news story. But the poem quickly moves into the contrapuntal surrealistic plane with "the other monks & nuns . . . like petals," setting up a group of images: petals, leaves, and finally pages, reminding us of Holy Writ. (And the phrase "terror made flesh" of course vibrates for Christian readers.) But the Komunyakaa wrinkle here is how the political situation is mystically manifested--American collusion made evident by the "high wind that started in California." The astonishing final image juxtaposes "saffron robes" with "the gasoline can," succinctly summing up the Vietnam War which arises from this volatile situation: "the gasoline can," a harbinger of technology which emblemizes violence and death, becomes a new deity, and all the saffron robes will be ultimately consumed.

Komunyakaa's surrealism varies from that of the other veteran poets because he does not depict Vietnam itself or the Vietnam experience as *literally* surreal, as do many of the other poets. Surrealism has been defined as "the attempt to actualize *le merveilleux*, the wonderland of revelation and dream, and by so doing to permit chance to run rampant in a wasteland of bleak reality" (Gershman 1); in other words, the exploration of the strange, through fortuitous juxtaposition, allows revelation to occur in the midst of the real. Through surrealism, Komunyakaa *discovers*--or perhaps more appropriately, *reveals*--Vietnam and does not only document its apparent surreality for an incredulous audience. "Camouflaging the Chimera" enacts this process of revelation:

> We tied branches to our helmets.
> We painted our faces & rifles
> with mud from a riverbank,
>
> blades of grass hung from the pockets
> of our tiger suits. We wove
> ourselves into the terrain,
> content to be a hummingbird's target.
>
> We hugged grass & leaned
> against a breeze off the river,
> slowdragging with ghosts
>
> from Saigon to Bangkok,
> with women left in doorways
> reaching in from America.
> We aimed at dark-hearted songbirds.

> In our way station of shadows
> rock apes tried to blow our cover,
> throwing stones at the sunset. Chameleons
>
> crawled our spines, changing from day
> to night: green to gold,
> gold to black. But we waited
> till the moon touched metal,
>
> till something almost broke
> inside us. VC struggled
> with the hillside, like black silk
>
> wrestling iron through grass.
> We weren't there. The river ran
> through our bones. Small animals took refuge
> against our bodies: we held our breath,
>
> ready to spring the L-shaped
> ambush, as a world revolved
> under each man's eyelid. (3-4)

Surrealism in this poem does not function to present Vietnam to the reader as exotica, but rather to underline the existential reality of ambush: the internal psychic state of each combatant. The wish-fulfillment of camouflage involves *becoming* the landscape, abdicating one's memories and anything else which might disrupt the illusion. The angst of the situation, the impending firefight, is focused by "a world revolved / under each man's eyelid," a revamping of the cliché "my life passed before my eyes." Of course, the phrase also refers to "the world" or everything not Vietnam, delineating each soldier's acute realization that he does not *belong* in this place, that his death here would be literally senseless. The dramatic situation of this poem also acts certainly as a signifier for the entire war, and thus the word "Chimera" in the title serves as a political statement.

The poem "'You and I Are Disappearing'" (a quote from Björn Håkansson) is a bravura performance highlighting Komunyakaa's technique of juxtaposed images:

> The cry I bring down from the hills
> belongs to a girl still burning
> inside my head. At daybreak
>   she burns like a piece of paper.

She burns like foxfire
in a thigh-shaped valley.
A skirt of flames
dances around her
at dusk.
                We stand with our hands
hanging at our sides,
while she burns
                like a sack of dry ice.
She burns like oil on water.
She burns like a cattail torch
dipped in gasoline.
She glows like the fat tip
of a banker's cigar,
                silent as quicksilver.
A tiger under a rainbow
        at nightfall.
She burns like a shot glass of vodka.
She burns like a field of poppies
at the edge of a rain forest.
She rises like dragonsmoke
        to my nostrils.
She burns like a burning bush
driven by a godawful wind. (17)

In this poem, Komunyakaa is performing "the kind of intellectual wrestling that moves and weaves us through human language," as he told me in an interview. According to Komunyakaa, "language is what can liberate or imprison the human psyche," and this poem dramatizes a speaker who is simultaneously liberated and imprisoned. The speaker here is at a loss to describe this scene fittingly. The charged language grapples with a view that is both unimaginably beautiful and incredibly horrible, all at the same time. The speaker, again and again, tries to find a metaphor that will convey both the beauty and the horror--the dilemma of speaking the Sublime, in Edmund Burke's terms. And the speaker comes enticingly, asymptotically close without finding the ideal phrase. Finally, he simply has to stop. And the final image points a biblical finger: the girl will always burn in the speaker's mind in the same way that the burning bush could have burned forever unconsumed. What really nails this image is the phrase "godawful wind" which puns on "awful God," straight out of the Old Testament, while it resurrects the root meaning full of awe, or more properly here, filling with awe.

"'You and I Are Disappearing'" also demonstrates Komunyakaa's poetic ancestry in English, specifically William Carlos Williams and his use of the image. Just as Komunyakaa has been influenced by the Surrealists, Williams has been influenced by Cubist art; Marjorie Perloff notes that Williams' "*Spring and All* lyrics . . . provide verbal analogues of . . . Cubist fragmentation and superposition of ambiguously located planes" (182). In many of these poems, Williams' "images do not carry symbolic weight; they point to no external sphere of reality outside themselves," writes Perloff. "Rather, items are related along the axis of contiguity. . . . In a larger sense, the whole book constitutes just such a field of contiguities. Williams' recurrent images--wind, flower, star, white, dark--are perfectly ordinary, but it is their *relationships* that matter" (186-87). If we ignore for a moment that the signified is "she"-- a human being--Komunyakaa's images here are similarly ordinary: "a piece of paper," "oil on water," a "cigar," "a shot glass of vodka," "a field of poppies"; others are lexically more interesting but still reasonably innocent: "foxfire," "a sack of dry ice," "a rainbow," "dragonsmoke." What drives this poem is the anaphoric repetition of "she burns"--the accretion of which underlines the intrinsic horror of the poem and, by extension, the war itself. The ultimate focus is on humanity and on humaneness.

Many of the poems in *Dien Cai Dau* deal with human response and connection in combat. "Nude Pictures" begins at the end, only implying the story which comes before:

> I slapped him a third time.
> The song caught in his throat
> for a second, & the morning
> came back together like after
> a stone has been dropped
> through a man's reflection
> hiding in a river. I slapped him
> again, but he wouldn't stop
>
> laughing. As we searched
> for the squad, he drew us
> to him like a marsh loon
> tied to its half-gone song
> echoing over rice fields
> & through wet elephant grass
> smelling of gunpowder & fear.
> I slapped him once more.

Booby-trapped pages floated
through dust. His laughter
broke off into a silence
early insects touched
with a tinge of lost music.
He grabbed my hand & wouldn't
let go. Lifted by a breeze,
a face danced in the treetops. (25)

In "2527th Birthday of the Buddha," the typical Komunyakaa opposition
is the documentary vs. the figurative; here the conflict is between nature
and human intrusion. The morning shattered by a firefight "came back
together like after / a stone has been dropped through a man's
reflection / hiding in a river." The "stone," a semaphore for gunfire,
intrudes upon the harmony between humans and nature--here, the
squad and the morning. Now the hysterical soldier intrudes upon the
reassembled morning, "like a marsh loon / tied to its half- gone song"
(i.e., nature gone mad).

The final human intrusion occurs in the arresting close: "Lifted by
a breeze, / a face danced in the treetops." Literally, of course, this is
a wafting scrap of girlie magazine, with the face coincidentally framed.
On a figurative level, however, the image finally rescues humanity: the
lexical territory of "Lifted" and "danced" argues for an upbeat ending
here. Just as the speaker and the sole surviving soldier hold hands
("only connect," as Forster tells us) so too are humans and nature
harmoniously reunited, if only metaphorically.

Komunyakaa's devotion to a highly textured language is clearly
evident in the poems already discussed. There are arresting turns of
phrase throughout *Dien Cai Dau*: a tunnel rat moves "Through silver /
lice, shit, maggots, & vapor of pestilence" (5); the Viet Cong are "lords
over loneliness / winding like coralvine through / sandalwood & lotus"
(8); conspirators plan a fragging, "their bowed heads / filled with
splintered starlight" (16); an armored personnel carrier is "droning like
a constellation / of locusts eating through bamboo" (19). For the most
part, however, the language of *Dien Cai Dau* is a spoken language, in
the Wordsworthian sense--it is the extraordinary way in which these
everyday words are combined which makes the poems significant.

As Casey does in *Obscenities*, Komunyakaa uses the "grunt's"
language and speech for credibility. In "Hanoi Hannah," however, he
places the argot in the mouth of the enemy, to demonstrate the
ambivalent ambience of Vietnam:

Ray Charles! His voice
calls from waist-high grass,
& we duck behind gray sandbags.
"Hello, Soul Brothers. Yeah,
Georgia's also on my mind."
Flares bloom over the trees.
"Here's Hannah again.
Let's see if we can't
light her goddamn fuse
this time." Artillery
shells carve a white arc
against dusk. Her voice rises
from a hedgerow on our left.
"It's Saturday night in the States.
Guess what your woman's doing tonight.
I think I'll let Tina Turner
tell you, you homesick GIs."
Howitzers buck like a herd
of horses behind concertina.
"You know you're dead men
don't you? You're dead
as King today in Memphis.
Boys, you're surrounded by
General Tran Do's division."
Her knife-edge song cuts
deep as a sniper's bullet.
"Soul Brothers, what you dying for?"
We lay down a white-klieg
trail of tracers. Phantom jets
fan out over the trees.
Artillery fire zeros in.
Her voice grows flesh
& we can see her falling
into words, a bleeding flower
no one knows the true name for.
"You're lousy shots, GIs."
Her laughter floats up
as though the airways are
buried under our feet. (13-14)

It is interesting to note here that Hannah speaks not just colloquial
English, but fluent black English; her speech is so well tuned as to be
virtually indistinguishable from the American voice who says "Let's see

if we can't / light her goddamn fuse / this time." That Komunyakaa is
black generally makes no difference in many of the poems in *Dien Cai
Dau*, but here it is significant because blacks (and hence the poet) are
being directly addressed here by the Viet Cong; Hannah plays Ray
Charles and Tina Turner, speaks to "Soul Brothers," and taunts them
with Martin Luther King's assassination--it may well be the speaker's
first realization of that event. As this poem shuttles between reported
speech and narrative passages, it displays a seamlessness of diction,
unlike that of earlier Vietnam--veteran poets like Paquet, who
deliberately embattles one set of connotations against another for
tension. Here, the everyday diction--"duck behind," "light her . . . fuse,"
"buck like a herd / of horses"--is allowed to rest easy with slightly more
elevated phrases-"carve a white arc," "knife-edge song," "white-klieg /
trail of tracers." But the salient point here is Hannah's intimate
command of English and the social nuances conveyed by language.

The plight of the "grunt" home from the war is handled by
Komunyakaa differently from other veteran poets, and this variance
arises partly from questions of race. The black soldier remembers a
different Vietnam: Viet Cong leaflets saying, "*VC didn't kill / Dr. Martin
Luther King*"(47); the white bars and the black bars on "Tu Do Street"
in Saigon (29); the black POW remembering "those rednecks" in
Georgia, "'Bama," and Mississippi to help him through VC torture (42).
But other poems focus more universally on the generic returnee. The
poem "Combat Pay for Jody" focuses on a soldier and his inevitable
encounter with Jody, the folkloric figure back home who steals every
combat soldier's wife or girlfriend:

> I counted tripflares
> the first night at Cam Ranh Bay,
> & the molten whistle of a rocket
> made me sing her name into my hands.
> I needed to forget the sea
> between us, the other men.
> Her perfume still crawled
> my brain like a fire moth,
> & it took closing a dead man's eyes
> to bring the war's real smell
> into my head. The quick fire
> danced with her nude reflection,
> & I licked an envelope each month
> to send blood money,
> kissing her lipstick mouthprints
> clustering the perfumed paper,

as men's voices collected
in the gray weather I inhaled.
Her lies saved me that year.
I rushed to the word
Love at the bottom of a page.
One day, knowing a letter waited,
I took the last chopper back to Chu Lai,
an hour before the firebase was overrun
by NVA. Satchel charges
blew away the commander's bunker,
& his men tried to swim the air.
A week later when I returned
to Phoenix, the city hid her
shadow & I couldn't face myself
in the mirror. I asked her used-to-be
if it was just my imagination,
since I'd heard a man
could be boiled down to his deeds.
He smiled over his wine glass
& said, "It's more, man.
Your money bought my new Chevy." (49-50)

This poem literally brings clichés to life. The testimony of a "grunt" for
whom the thought of his lover functioned as a chivalric favor preserving
him from harm is so common that it becomes apocryphal. Ditto for the
stories of Jody's legendary exploits.   In "Combat Pay for Jody,"
Komunyakaa has composed a vividly lyrical narrative which
encompasses the thousand days of the speaker's Vietnam tour and his
eventual return to "the world." More importantly, he has created a
realistic voice which re-enlivens the overworked clichés of military life
and which points up the returning soldier's inability to navigate in what
used to be his personal landscape.

The Vietnam Veterans Memorial has become an emblem of the
difficulties of the Vietnam veteran, and Komunyakaa's poem "Facing It"
(the closing poem in the book) does exactly what its title says--face the
monument and what it signifies:

My black face fades,
hiding inside the black granite.
I said I wouldn't,
dammit: No tears.
I'm stone. I'm flesh.
My clouded reflection eyes me

like a bird of prey, the profile of night
slanted against morning. I turn
this way--the stone lets me go.
I turn this way--I'm inside
the Vietnam Veterans Memorial
again, depending on the light
to make a difference.
I go down the 58,022 names,
half-expecting to find
my own in letters like smoke.
I touch the name Andrew Johnson;
I see the booby trap's white flash.
Names shimmer on a woman's blouse
but when she walks away
the names stay on the wall.
Brushstrokes flash, a red bird's
wings cutting across my stare.
The sky. A plane in the sky.
A white vet's image floats
closer to me, then his pale eyes
look through mine. I'm a window.
He's lost his right arm
inside the stone. In the black mirror
a woman's trying to erase names:
No, she's brushing a boy's hair. (63)

This poem is literally a reflection about reflections; it is a "facing" of the dualities that govern this everyday life: there and here, America and Vietnam, living and dead, night and day, old and young, white and black (i.e., Caucasian and Negro). Komunyakaa does not declaim, does not decry; instead he presents, practically unmediated, a series of images. Like the speaker of "'You and I Are Disappearing'"--the poem about the burning girl--the poet here is faced with an ineffable scene, but instead of searching for apt metaphors to voice his feeling, he reverts to a reportorial mode. Everything ultimately is point of view, and we are always "depending on the light / to make a difference." This is what Vietnam poetry (and all poetry in essence) *must* do--enlighten, give light, illuminate, the better for all to see and see well.

   Dien Cai Dau is a breathtakingly original work of art because of the believable, down-to-earth language which speaks the thoughts and feelings of authentic characters, filtered through Komunyakaa's atypical vision. In the last line of *Dien Cai Dau*--a book whose title, after all, means "crazy"--a woman is "brushing a boy's hair," an action which affirms sanity and life in the face of the insanity of the war: the love between a mother and child, between two human beings. Writing about Weigl's *The Monkey Wars*, Smith proposes the potential of a "salvific poetic vision which might unify past and present, anguish and affirmation" (17); Komunyakaa fulfills this promise in *Dien Cai Dau*.

Komunyakaa's achievement points to the possibility and actuality of self-renewal and solace in poetry by Vietnam veterans. As the body of poetry by veterans moves from mere documentary to self-discovery and personal commitment, from a gratuitous surrealism to a conscientious use of French surrealistic technique, future work by Vietnam-veteran poets becomes increasingly able to transcend the paralyzing horror of the Vietnam War. Bruce Weigl's new book, *Song of Napalm*, which collects his previous Vietnam poetry and showcases new work, already demonstrates this potential; the new poems begin to ameliorate Weigl's despair in *The Monkey Wars*. The transcendental possibilities in poetry by Vietnam veterans, therefore, can make possible a more accurate national vision of the Vietnam War--both in documentary and spiritual terms-allowing us, as a nation, to confront fully the moral consequences of our presence in Vietnam. Perhaps, in some near future, it may not be too optimistic to wish, with Ehrhart, that "the soul of the nation might somehow be cleansed" by poetry.

Works Cited

Berry, D. C. *saigon cemetery*. Athens: U of Georgia P, 1972.

Casey, Michael. *Obscenities*. Yale Series of Younger Poets, v. 67. New Haven: Yale UP, 1972.

Ehrhart, W. D., ed. *To Those Who Have Gone Home Tired.* New York: Thunder's Mouth Press, 1984.

-----. "Soldier-Poets of the Vietnam War." *Virginia Quarterly Review* 63.2 (Spring 1987): 246-265.

Felstiner, John. "American Poetry and the War in Vietnam." *Stand*, 19.2 (1978): 4-11.

Gershman, Herbert S. *The Surrealist Revolution in France.* Ann Arbor: U of Michigan P, 1969.

Komunyakaa, Yusef. *Dien Cai Dau*. Middletown, CT: Wesleyan UP, 1988.

-----. Personal interview. 21 Feb. 1986.

Perloff, Marjorie. "William Carlos Williams." *In Voices and Visions: The Poet in America*. Ed. Helen Vendler. New York: Random, 1987.

Rottmann, Larry, Jan Barry, and Basil T. Paquet, eds. *Winning Hearts and Minds: War Poems by Vietnam Veterans*. Brooklyn: First Casualty Press, 1972.

Rubin, William S. *Dada, Surrealism, and Their Heritage*. New York: Museum of Modern Art, [1968].

Smith, Lorrie. "A Sense-Making Perspective in Recent Poetry by Vietnam Veterans." *American Poetry Review* 15.6 (Nov./Dec. 1986): 13-18.

Walsh, Jeffrey. *American War Literature: 1914 to Vietnam*. New York: St. Martin's, 1982.

Weigh, Bruce. *The Monkey Wars*. Athens: University of Georgia Press, 1985.

PART III

GENRE OVERVIEWS

THE FICTIVE AMERICAN VIETNAM WAR FILM:
A FILMOGRAPHY[1]

David Everett Whillock

One of the major obstacles in defining the discourse of the American Vietnam war film is the problem of defining a generic formula. What constitutes an American Vietnam war film? Are there any conventions that agglutinate this corpus of work? Before these questions of generic bonding can be addressed, we must first identify the Vietnam war film by its definition and scope.

This effort is impeded unless a structure is provided to the narrative elements which comprise the Vietnam war film. The binary extremes found in examining this problem are underscored by film critic Gilbert Adair in his book *Vietnam on Film*:

> . . . the two opposing axes of received wisdom concerning the subject [Vietnam war films]...--(1) that there are too few Vietnam movies to warrant a full-length study and (2) that every American feature film made during the decade of 1965-75 must directly or indirectly reflect some aspect of its political makeup and therefore be relevant to the debate--both may be said to contain elements of truth. [2]

Adair's first concern is justified if the definition of the Vietnam war film is a story that depicts combat. Until just a few years ago there were too few films to warrant categorization. With the new era of films ushered in by *Platoon* (1986) and *Full Metal Jacket* (1987), this concern has possibly been eradicated. Adair's second concern, however, still remains a viable issue. When we consider the number of movies distributed between *The Green Berets* in 1968 and *The Boys of Company C* in 1977 there is no doubt that the films were under the influence of Hollywood's institutional ideology. Because of the negative public reaction to *The Green Berets* for its overtly political approach in depicting the war, films released in this period either used a variety of subjects metaphorically in presenting Vietnam, or avoided Vietnam altogether. Indeed, if all the films which metaphorically present the Vietnam war are included for analysis, the task of codifying these films in a distinct genre would be overwhelming. Perhaps because of the ideological dichotomy of the American public over the war, Hollywood decided not to alienate either group and consequently cinematically avoided a direct presentation of the Vietnam conflict.[3] This ideological decision is reflected in Hollywood's "mainline" films from this era. During this time the American Cinema is more represented by *The Sound of Music* and *Oliver!* than it is by *Easy Rider* or *Medium Cool*.

Another problem that emerges in the development of a distinct genre is the task of cataloging the films that discussed the war. The problem is compounded given the fact that so many of the movies of this era were produced by independent filmmakers who rose to challenge the predominant ideology nurtured by the major studios. While the independent movement in American cinema began to gain strength and respect, the cultural significance of these films was restricted by the enormous problems of financing and distribution. If there were too few combat films and the body of films made between 1965-1975 did not carry a united ideological message, then how are the films about Vietnam to be defined?

We must begin the process of definition or standardization by investigating generic conventions found throughout the films that depict the war and/or its effects. However, no such set of conventions presently exists. It is argued by Hoberman, Basinger, Auster, and Quart that indeed these films are part of a generic formula that extends into the overall war film genre.[4] Yet, in their discussion of the material, they do not define or standardize the American Vietnam War film.

While generic conventions do not provide clear classification for Vietnam war films, five narrative structures do.[5] The commonality of these films rests in their direct referent to Vietnam as a major source for their narrative structure. These five types include: Pre-*The Green Berets*, The Vietnam Veteran/Coming Home, The Effects film, Incountry Films, and The Revenge Film, each of which will be defined subsequently. Using these five narrative formulas, this filmography will attempt classification of the large corpus of work that represents the American Fictive Vietnam war film.[6]

Pre-*The Green Berets*. In the late 1950's and early 1960's, films about Vietnam reflected the French point of view or depicted American involvement in the diplomatic or covert action aspect of the war. The characters of their narratives were French soldiers, ambassadors, state department employees, CIA operatives, or American mercenaries working for the French cause. One film, *Saigon* (Leslie Fenton, dir., P. J. Wolfson and Arthur Sheekman, screenplay, Paramount, 1947), used Vietnam as a background for a Veronica Lake and Alan Ladd film noir. However, most of the films that used the setting and conflict of Vietnam in their narrative development were more specific to the conflict. *Jump into Hell* (David Butler, dir., Irving

Wallace, screenplay, Warner Bros, 1955); *China Gate* (Samuel Fuller, dir./screenplay, 20th Century Fox/Globe Enterprises, 1957); *Five Gates to Hell* (James Clavell, dir./screenplay 20th Century Fox, 1959); and *The Lost Command* (Mark Robson, dir., Nelson Gidding, screenplay, Columbia/Red Lion, 1965) all depicted combat from the French or American mercenary point of view. With a rather clear political intent, these films attempted to produce a positive image of involvement in Southeast Asia to the American public.

Films that used diplomatic or covert narratives to focus on the problem included *A Yank in Indochina* (Wallace Grissell, dir., Samuel Newman, screenplay, Columbia, 1952); *The Quiet American* (Joseph Mankiewicz, dir./screenplay, United Artists/Figaro Inc., 1957); and *The Ugly American* (George Englud, dir., Stewart Stern, screenplay, Universal-International, 1962); *A Yank in Viet-nam* (Marshall Thompson, dir., Jane Wardell and Jack Lewis, screenplay, Allied Artists, 1963); *Operation CIA* (Christian Nyby, dir., Bill Balinger and Peer J. Oppenheimer, screenplay, Allied Artists/Warner-Pathe/Hei Ra Matt, 1965). Like the films that portrayed the French and American mercenaries fighting for a just cause, these films underscored the need for American involvement to stop the dreaded fall of nation-state dominos in the communist determination for world dominance. These films set the political agenda that climaxed in the 1968 combat film *The Green Berets*.

The Vietnam Veteran/Coming Home Film. The Vietnam veteran/coming home film investigates the plight of the veteran and his attempt to re-enter society. These films resolve their characters' conflicts either through a slow integration of the veteran back into society or through a violent attempt to rebel against society's laws. The veteran in these films feels a sense of betrayal and is physically or emotionally changed by his experience in Vietnam. In these films the individual must come to terms with a society that, for the most part, refuses to accept the war and blames the veteran for the negative feelings that occurred because of the war. The veteran in these films does not accept society's ridicule or rules.

In *Tracks* (Henry Jaglom, dir./screenplay, Rainbow pictures, 1975) and *Gardens of Stone*, (Francis Coppola, dir., Ronald Bass, screenplay, Tri-Star, 1987) the veteran comes to term with self and country by burying the Vietnam dead. These films underscore the cost in human life as it affected the veteran outside of his role in combat. This contradiction is important to juxtapose the violent death of America's youth with the seemingly serene and safe environment of home.

Several films have depicted the veteran coming to terms with his mental and/or physical wounds, at the same time adding the burden of coming home to an ambivalent or cynical culture. In these films the veteran is handicapped and must learn to negotiate a society that is not interested in his plight. *Heroes* (Jeremy Paul Kegan, dir., John Carabatos, screenplay, Universal/Turman-Foster, 1977); *Coming Home* (Hal Ashby, dir., Waldo Salt and Robert Jones, screenplay, United Artists/Jane Productions, Inc., 1978); *The Deer Hunter* (Michael Cimino, dir., Michael Cimino, Deric Washburn, Louis Garfinkle, and Quinn Redeker, screenplay, Columbia/EMI/Warner, 1978); and *Birdy* (Alan Parker, dir., Sandy Kroopf and Jack Behr, screenplay, Tri-Star, 1984) are representative American films that portray veterans in this fashion.

Some Kind of Hero (Michael Pressman, dir., James Kirkwood and Robert Boris, screenplay, Paramount, 1982) investigates the way a former POW reintegrates himself into society after his wife leaves him and the Army disowns him. Unlike most of the other films with narratives that reflect a homecoming experience, the protagonist beats the system through nonviolent methods.

After the critical failure of *The Green Berets*, Hollywood felt narratives about the war were poison. American films began to "look away" and to discuss the war through other methods of discourse. Most of these films represented the veteran as violent antisocial individuals who rebelled against an uncaring and accusing society. This violence was focused against corruption of authority figures or the invasion by outside forces into a seemingly peaceful existence. Several of these films used the nation's paranoia about motorcycle gangs (particularly such groups as Hell's Angels) as a catalyst. *Angels From Hell* (Bruce Kessler, dir., Jerome Wish, screenplay, Independent International/Kennis-Frazer, American International, 1968); *Satan's Sadists* (Al Adamson, dir., Dennis Wayne, screenplay, Independent Int/Kennis-Frazer, 1969); *The Hard Ride* (Burt Topper, dir./screenplay, MGM-EMI, 1971); *The Losers* (Jack Starrett, dir., Alan Caillou, screenplay, MGM-EMI, 1971); *Chrome and Hot Leather* (Lee Frost, dir., Michael Haynes, David Neibel, and Don Tait, screenplay, American International, 1971); and *The Black Six* (Matt Cimber, dir., George Theakos, screenplay, Cinemation, 1974) are representatives of the motorcycle/Vietnam veteran film.

However, motorcycle gangs were not the only films to represent violent reaction to social alienation and betrayal. Other films depicted their veterans as violent antiheroes who stand up to a corrupt system of authority. Many of these corrupt systems are found in a small town and the antihero is harassed until he violently protests the action. *Billy Jack* (Tom Laughlin dir., Tom Laughlin and Delores Taylor, screenplay, Warner/National Student Film Corporation, 1971); *Welcome Home*

Soldier Boys (Richard Compton, dir., Gordon Trueblood, screenwriter, 20th Century Fox, 1972); *The Visitors* (Elia Kazan, dir., Chris Kazan, screenplay, Associated Artists, 1972); *Gordon's War* (Ossie David, dir., Howard Friedlander, screenplay, 20th Century Fox, 1973); and *First Blood* (Ted Kotcheff, dir., Michael Kozoll, William Sackheim, and Q. Moonblood, screenplay, Orion, 1982) all contain veterans who attempt, through violence, to stop a corrupt system working in a small town.

Who'll Stop the Rain, based on Robert Stone's novel *Dog Soldiers*, (Karel Reisz, dir., Judith Rascoe, screenplay, United Artists, 1978) investigates corrupting influences of drug smuggling. This film indicts the authoritative "system" by representing the Narcotics Bureau Agent as corrupt. The "veteran" in this film is a friend of a war correspondent who picks up the drugs after the correspondent smuggles them into the United States.

The Edge (Robert Kramer, dir., Robert Dozier, screenplay, Blue Van Productions/Alpha 60, 1968); *Black Sunday* (John Frankenheimer, dir., Ernest Lehman, Ivan Moffat, and Kenneth Ross, screenplay, Paramount, 1976); and *Twilight's Last Gleaming* (Robert Aldrich, dir., Ronald Cohen and Edward Huebsch, screenplay, Lorimar/Bavaria Studios, 1977) place their veteran in a position for revenge on the system that sent them to Vietnam. These veterans become part of a terrorist plot to kill or blackmail the President in an effort to reveal political corruption.

Other films depict their veterans turning to violence because of violent acts against them. *Taxi Driver* (Martin Scorcese, dir., Paul Schrader, screenplay, Columbia/Warner/Bill Phillips, 1976) places its veteran in the night life of the underbelly of society. The veteran becomes a hero in the process of protecting a child prostitute. However, the decision to kill her pimp is made only after a failed attempt to kill a politician earlier in the evening. As in most of the films of this vein, *Taxi Driver's* veteran is not heroic in stature, but is a victim of chance and circumstance. *Rolling Thunder* (John Flynn dir., Paul Schrader and Heyward Gould, screenplay, American International Pictures, 1977) is an example of a Vietnam veteran who returns home after surviving a POW camp and is confronted with a violence that kills his wife and child. He systematically searches and destroys the gang who killed his family.

The Effects Films. The effects film confronts the struggle of ideological confrontation at home. As a ripple effect reaching into the social fabric of American life, these films depict the internal dichotomy that occurred in the United States during the war and the effects of the war on society. Two popular themes found in this type of film are protest and the draft. The protest films are focused on the college campus and the unrest that occurred in the late 60's and early 70's. These films include *Medium Cool* (Haskell Wexler, dir./screenplay, Paramount/S and J Pictures, 1969); *The Strawberry Statement* (Stuart Hagmann, dir., Isreal Horovitz, screenplay, MGM, 1970); and *Getting Straight* (Richard Rush, dir., Robert Kaufman, screenplay, Columbia/The Organization, 1970).

The films that used the draft for their narrative vehicle looked at individuals who are attempting to avoid the draft or who are in the process of waiting for induction into the armed forces. *Greetings* (Brian Di Palma, dir., Charles Hirsch and Brian Di Palma, screenplay, Eagle/West End Films, 1968); *Alice's Restaurant* (Arthur Penn, dir., Venable Herndon and Arthur Penn, screenplay, United Artists/Florin, 1969); *The Model Shop* (Jacques Demy, dir./screenplay, Columbia, 1969); *Summertree* (Anthony Newly, dir., Edward Hume and Stephen Yafa, screenplay, Columbia/Warner/Bryna, 1971); *Big Wednesday* (John Milius, dir., John Milius and Dennis Aaberg, screenplay, Warner Bros/A-Team Production, 1978); and *Hair* (Milos Forman, dir., Michael Weller, screenplay, United Artists/CIP Productions, 1978) represent this type of film.

Cowards (Simon Nuchtern, dir./screenplay, Jaylo International, 1970) and *Two People* (Robert Wise dir., Richard De Roy, screenplay, Universal/Filmakers Group, 1973) used deserters and how their action affected relationships back home.

Another type of film investigates the political ideologies in a more violent way. In these films the dichotomy between life styles is resolved through the use of violence, and the peaceful usually fall victim to a senseless murder. *Easy Rider* (Dennis Hopper, dir., Peter Fonda, Dennis Hopper, and Terry Southern, screenplay, Columbia/Pando/Raybert, 1969) and *Joe* (John Avildson, dir., Norman Wexler, screenplay, British Lion/Cannon Productions, 1970) illustrate the liberal/conservative split in a violent way. The liberal ideology is literally blown away through the use of conscienceless violence.

Films that investigate personal relationships and how the period affected them are found in *Zabriskie Point* (Michelangelo Antonioni, dir., Michelangelo Antonioni, Fred Garner, Sam Shepard, Tonio Guerra, and Clare Peploe, screenplay, MGM, 1969); *A Small Circle of Friends* (Rob Cohen, dir., Ezra Sacks, screenplay, United Artists/Small Circle of Friends, 1980); *The Return of the Secaucus Seven* (John Sayles, dir./screenplay, Salsipuedes/Libra, 1980); *Four Friends* (Arthur Penn, dir., Steven Tesich, screenplay, Filmways Pictures, 1981); *The Big Chill* (Lawrence Kasdan, dir., Lawrence Kasdan and Barbara Benedek, screenwriter, Columbia Pictures, 1983); *Running on Empty* (Sidney

Lumet, dir., Naomi Foner, screenplay, Warner Bros, 1988); and *1969* (Ernest Thompson, dir./screenplay, Atlantic, 1988).

Incountry Films. Incountry films place their characters in the midst of the conflict during the years of American military involvement. The narratives found in these films use combat in Vietnam as either a backdrop for their characters in a more personal story (romantic or human struggle) or as the major catalyst for their characters in their effort to overcome the adversity found in the day-to-day existence of war. The combat films usually carry an ideological message to its audience. Films such as *Apocalypse Now* and *Full Metal Jacket* present the war as a national nightmare or as insane, while *The Green Berets* and *Soldier's Revenge* present the war as a simple Manichean equation of good versus evil.

Films that use Vietnam as a backdrop for other more focused storylines include *Don't Cry It's Only Thunder* (Peter Werner, dir., Paul Hensler, screenplay, Sanrio Communications, 1982); *The Killing Fields* (Roland Jaffe, dir., Bruce Robinson, screenplay, Warner Bros, 1983); *Purple Hearts* (Sidney J Furie, dir., Sidney J Furie and Rick Natkin, screenplay, Warner Bros, 1984); *Good Morning, Vietnam* (Barry Levinson, dir., Larry Brezner and Mitch Markowitz, screenplay, Touchstone Pictures, 1987); *Off Limits* (Christopher Crowe, dir., Christopher Crowe and Jack Thibeau, screenplay, 20th Century Fox, 1988); and *Bat 21* (Peter Markle, dir., William C. Anderson and George Gorden, screenplay, Tri-Star, 1988).

Films that focus on combat as the narrative focus include *The Green Berets* (Ray Kellog and John Wayne, dirs., James Lee Barrett, screenplay, Warner/Bat Jac, 1968); *The Boys of Company C* (Sidney Furie, dir., Rick Natkin, screenplay, EMI/Raymond Chow, 1977); *Go Tell The Spartans* (Ted Post, dir., Wendell Mayes, screenplay, United Artists/Mar Vista, 1978); *Apocalypse Now* (Francis Ford Coppola, dir., John Milius and Francis Coppola, screenplay, Columbia/Warner/EMI/Zeotrope, 1979); *Platoon* (Oliver Stone, dir./screenplay, Hemdale/Orion, 1986); *Soldier's Revenge* (David Worth, dir., Lee Stull, screenplay, Trans World Entertainment, 1986); *Full Metal Jacket* (Stanley Kubrick, dir., Stanley Kubrick, Michael Herr, and Gustav Hasford, screenplay, Warner Bros, 1987); *Hamburger Hill* (John Irvin, dir., John Carabatsos, screenplay, RKO/Paramount, 1987); *Platoon Leader* (Aaron Norris, dir., Rich Marx, Andrew Deutsch, David Walker, screenplay, Cannon, 1988); and *84 Charlie MoPic* (Patrick Duncan, dir./screenplay, New Century/Vista, 1989).

Instead of using Vietnam as a setting, *M*A*S*H* (Robert Altman, dir., Ring Lardner, Jr., screenplay, 20th Century Fox/Aspen, Inc., 1969) places its characters in a combat hospital in Korea. As a parody,

Altman uses Richard Hooker's novel about a MASH unit in Korea to investigate the American involvement in Vietnam.

Revenge Films. The revenge film is important to the Vietnam war film. The films represented by this type underscore an attempt by Hollywood for a closure on the Vietnam war that was not possible before. The closure comes with the usual victory of a mission within the borders of Vietnam or Laos. The victorious mission by a small group of dedicated men (usually veterans) on POW camps is underscored by speeches on the righteousness of their mission and the inability of American bureaucracy to successfully win a war. In these films a small group will succeed where a nation failed. These films give the illusion of understanding and concern for the Vietnam veteran, while at the same time indicting the American way of war. By going into Southeast Asia and rescuing MIA's, these films resolve the last contradiction of the war. The films include *Good Guys Wear Black* (Ted Post, dir., Bruce Cohn and Mark Medoff, screenplay, Enterprise Pictures, Ltd., 1977);[7] *Uncommon Valor* (Ted Kotcheff, dir., Joe Gayton, screenplay, Paramount, 1983); *Missing in Action* (Joseph Zito, dir., James Bruner, screenplay, Cannon, 1984); *Missing in Action II: The Beginning* (Lance Hool, dir., Arthur Silver, Larry Levinson, and Steve Bing, screenplay, Cannon, 1985); *Rambo: First Blood II* (George P. Cosmatos, dir., Sylvester Stallone and James Cameron, screenplay, Columbia/EMI, 1985); *POW: The Escape* (Gideon Amir, dir., Jeremy Lipp, James Bruner, Malcomb Barbour, John Langley, screenplay, Cannon, 1986); and *Braddock: Missing in Action III* (Arron Norris, dir., James Brunner and Chuck Norris, screenplay, Cannon, 1988).

What, after separating the American Vietnam war film into five types, does this suggest for future films about the war in one form or another? As in many of our historical experiences, the further we move away from the event of Vietnam, the more diversified the presentations of that event will become. On the immediate horizon, these categories seem to adequately encompass the films currently in release or production. For example, Oliver Stone's film based on Ron Kovic's book *Born on the Fourth of July* investigates how the war affected a veteran handicapped from the war and the loss of the American dream; Bobby Ann Mason's *In Country* looks at the war's effect on a veteran's daughter as she tries to find some answers to her father's death in the Vietnam war. New productions of Incountry films include *The Iron Triangle*, whose characters feature both an American and a Vietcong protagonist, and *American Son*, which investigates the dichotomous issues of the war through two American soldiers in combat. As future films are produced and released, however, variations on the five types of Vietnam film will inevitably occur.

Even though the Vietnam war ended nearly fifteen years ago, the media presentations of Vietnam are still relatively new. Indeed it was four years after the American involvement ended that our first in-depth investigation of the war, *Apocalypse Now*, was released. With the current new wave of movies in the theater and at the video store, the Vietnam war film is still evolving. And yet, as time passes the issues and the film presentations of this complex war will become clearer in their direction. This is underscored by Warren Bayless in Julian Smith's book *Looking Away: Hollywood and Vietnam* when he states that "motion picture interest in a fiction drama on a war theme is best received some time after the actual conflict, and the reception by film people and then by audiences is a retrospective look."[8]

Notes

1. While the war was the subject for many excellent documentaries, the fictive mainline Hollywood film reflects more powerfully how a society looks at itself. The documentaries deserve careful attention and should be considered in another work. *The Anderson Platoon* (Pierre Schoendoerffer, dir., Films Inc., 1967); *A Face of War* (E. S. Jones, dir., Kit Parker, 1967); *The Bloods of Nam* (The Documentary Consortium, PBS Video, 1986); *Dear America* (Bill Couturie, dir., HBO, 1988); *Hearts and Minds* (Peter Davis, dir., Embassy Home Entertainment, 1974); *In the Year of the Pig* (Emile De Antonio, dir., New Yorker Films, 1969); *Vietnam: A Television History* (Richard Ellison, Prod., Films Inc., 1983); *Vietnam: An American Journey* (Films Inc., 1980); *Vietnam Requiem* (Jonas McCord and Bill Couturie, dirs., Direct Cinema Ltd, 1982) are a few examples of quality documentaries on the subject of Vietnam.

2. Gilbert Adair, *Vietnam on Film: From The Green Berets to Apocalypse Now* (New York: Proteus Publishing, 1981), p.11.

3. This is the main thesis for Julian Smith's excellent book on this issue, *Looking Away: Hollywood and Vietnam* (New York: Charles Scribner's Sons, 1975).

4. Albert Auster and Leonard Quart, *How the War was Remembered: Hollywood and Vietnam* (New York: Praeger Publishers, 1988); Jeanine Basinger, *The World War II Combat Film: An Anatomy of a Genre* (New York: Columbia University Press, 1986); and "America Dearest," in *American Film*, 13 (May 1988), pp. 39-44.

5. David E. Whillock, "Defining the American Vietnam War Film: In Search of a Genre," in *Literature and Film Quarterly* 16 (1988), Pp. 244-250.

6.   While an attempt has been made to be thorough, there will undoubtedly be some omission or disagreement in the selections. My selection of films reflect a timely search for as many obscure and direct films that represent the war and its effects.

7.   While the narrative of *Good Guys Wear Black* takes place in Vietnam, this film pioneered the conventions found in the later revenge films. These conventions include a small rescue team, cynicism about the government, racist portrayals of the Asians, and criticism of the American way of war. For more details discussing the MIA film, see Louis Kern, "MIAs, Myth, and Macho Magic: Post-Apocalyptic Cinematic Visions of Vietnam," unpublished paper presented to the Popular Culture Association Conference, April 2-6, 1987.

8.   Julian Smith, *Looking Away: Hollywood and Vietnam* (New York: Charles Scribner's Sons, 1975), p. 10.

SOLDIER-POETS OF THE VIETNAM WAR

By W.D. Ehrhart

I

In the spring of 1972, a slim volume of poems appeared called *Winning Hearts and Minds,* its title taken from one of the many official slogans used at various times to describe the American pacification and relocation program in South Vietnam. Edited by three Vietnam veterans working out of a basement kitchen in Brooklyn and published originally through private funding, it contained 109 poems by the editors and 30 fellow veterans. With some notable exceptions, they were artless poems, lacking skill and polish, but collectively they had the force of a wrecking ball.

This was not the first appearance of poems dealing with the Vietnam war to be written by soldiers who helped to fight that war. But *Winning Hearts and Minds* quickly became a classic: the seminal anthology against which all future Vietnam war poetry would be judged.

"[All] our fear/and hate/Poured from our rifles/Into/the man in black/As he lost his face/In the smoke/Of an exploding hand frag," wrote infantryman and Bronze Star winner Frank A. Cross, Jr. "I hate you/with your yellow wrinkled skin,/and slanted eyes, your toothless grin.../Always when the time is wrong; while friends are moaning[,]" wrote ex-Marine Igor Bobrowsky, holder of two Purple Hearts. "I'm afraid to hold a gun now," wrote Charles M. Purcell, holder of the Vietnamese Cross of Gallantry, "What if I were to run amuck [sic] here in suburbia/And rush out into the street screaming/'Airborne all the way!'/And shoot the milkman."

Most of the poems in *Winning Hearts and Minds* are carried by raw emotion alone, and most of the soldier-poets were not really poets at all but rather soldiers so hurt and bitter that they could not maintain their silence any longer. Some, however, stand out more sharply than others. Bobrowsky, Cross, and Purcell contribute powerful poems. Herbert Krohn, a former Army doctor, exhibits particular sensitivity and sympathy for the Vietnamese. In "Farmer's Song at Can Tho," he writes:

> What is a man but a farmer
> Bowels and a heart that sings
> Who plants his rice in season
> Bowing then to the river.

> I am a farmer and I know what I know.
> This month's harvest is tall green rice.
> Next month's harvest is hordes of hungry beetles.
> How can peace be in a green country?

Co-editor Jan Barry (the other two editors were Basil T. Paquet and Larry Rottmann), who had served in Vietnam back in the days when U.S. troops were still called advisors, speaks of earlier occupations by the French, Japanese, Chinese, and Mongols "In the Footsteps of Ghenghis Khan," but concludes:

> Unencumbered by history
> our own or that of 13th-century Mongol armies
> long since fled or buried
> by the Vietnamese
> in Nhatrang, in 1962, we just did our jobs[.]

Barry is perhaps the single most important figure in the emergence of Vietnam veterans' poetry, not only for his own pioneering poems but especially for his tireless efforts to encourage and promote the work of others.

But the two most noteworthy poets in the collection are Paquet and Michael Casey. Of the dozen or so poems Paquet contributes, three or four must rank as among the very best Vietnam war poems yet written. Literate without being literary, Paquet was, at the time, far and away the most skillful and practiced of the soldier-poets. His "Morning--A Death" is a masterpiece, capturing at once the new, sophisticated battlefield medicine of Vietnam and the ancient, ageless human misery and futility of all wars:

> You are dead just as finally
> As your mucosity dries on my lips
> In this morning sun.
> I have thumped and blown into your kind too often.
> I grow tired of kissing the dead.

Casey, a former military policeman, works exclusively with the truncated matter-of-fact speech rhythms that mirror the Vietnam grunts' favorite phrase: "There it is"--no further explanation offered. "School children walk by," he writes in "On Death":

> Some stare
> Some keep on walking

> Some adults stare too
> With handkerchiefs
> Over their nose
>
>   ***
>
> No jaw
> Intestines poured
> Out of the stomach
> The penis in the air
>   It won't matter then to me   but now
> I don't want in death to be a
> Public obscenity like this[.]

With the passage of time, Casey's poems seem less substantial than former medic Paquet's, but back then they were deemed good enough to earn him the Yale Younger Poets Award, and his collection *Obscenities* appeared almost simultaneously with *Winning Hearts and Minds*.

Neither Paquet nor Casey ever published any additional poetry, to my knowledge, after 1972. But for others in the volume, and for Vietnam-related poetry in general, *Winning Hearts and Minds* proved to be only the forerunner for a body of poetry that, 18 years later, is still growing. Many of the poets, like Paquet and Casey, surfaced briefly, then disappeared. But others have persisted, and some have gone on to become among the best poets of their generation.

Even before 1972 ended, D.C. Berry's *saigon cemetery* appeared from the University of Georgia Press. Another former medic, Berry offers a vision of the war in which "hope" (and almost everything else) appears in lower case:

> the boy's ma said may
> be he's one of the Lord's
> pretty flowers'll rise
> resurrection day--
>   "God woman ain't
> no dead bulb gonna rise this May
> never! God
>   pity you Martha!"

In many of Berry's poems, lines, pieces of lines and words are scattered across the page like dismembered body parts, mimicking that all-too-frequent reality of the war.

Equally significant is ex-Marine MacAvoy Layne's novel-in-verse, *How Audie Murphy Died in Vietnam*. In 227 very short and often bleakly humorous poems, Layne traces the life of his fictional Audie Murphy from birth through childhood to enlistment in the Marines, then boot camp, a tour of duty in Vietnam--including capture by the North Vietnamese--and finally home again. Some of the poems are as short as "Guns":

> When the M-16 rifle had a stoppage,
> One could feel enemy eyes
> Climbing
> His
> Bones
> Like
> Ivy.

None is longer than a single page. Though few, if any, could stand up alone without the support of all the others, their cumulative effect is remarkable and convincing.

More durable a poet--indeed, one of the very best--is John Balaban. His first book-length collection, *After Our War*, deservedly won the Lamont Award from the Academy of American Poets. Balaban is an anomaly: a soldier-poet who was not a soldier; indeed, he opposed the war and became a conscientious objector. But he chose to do his alternative service in Vietnam, first as a teacher of linguistics at the University of Can Tho, then as field representative for the Committee of Responsibility to Save War-Injured Children. Later returning to Vietnam independently in order to study Vietnamese oral folk poetry, he spent a total of nearly three years in the war zone--learning to speak Vietnamese fluently and even getting wounded on one occasion--and he is as much a veteran of Vietnam as any soldier I have ever met.

Because of his unique situation, however, Balaban brings to his poetry a perspective unlike any other. "A poet had better keep his mouth shut," he writes in "Saying Good-by to Mr. and Mrs. My, Saigon, 1972":

> unless he's found words to comfort and teach.
> Today, comfort and teaching themselves deceive
> and it takes cruelty to make any friends
> when it is a lie to speak, a lie to keep silent.

While Balaban's poems offer little comfort, they have much to teach. Years before Agent Orange was widely acknowledged for the silent killer it is--the deadly seed sewn in Asia only to take root at home among those who thought they'd survived--Balaban wrote in "Along the Mekong":

> With a scientific turn of mind I can understand
> that malformation in lab mice may not occur in children
> but when, last week, I ushered hare-lipped, tusk-toothed kids
> to surgery in Saigon, I wondered, what had they drunk
> that I have drunk.

And his "The Guard at the Binh Thuy Bridge" is a frightening exercise in quiet tension--the way it was; the war always a hair-trigger away, just waiting to happen:

> How still he stands as mists begin to move,
> as morning, curling, billows creep across
> his cooplike, concrete sentry perched mid-bridge
> over mid-muddy river.
>
>   ***
>
> Anchored in red morning mist a narrow junk
> rocks its weight. A woman kneels on deck
> staring at lapping water. Wets her face.
> Idly the thick Rach Binh Thuy slides by.
> He aims. At her. Then drops his aim. Idly.

Balaban is particularly adept at contrasting the impact of the war on Vietnam with the indifference of those at home. In "The Gardenia in the Moon," he writes: "Men had landed on the moon./As men shot dirty films in dirty motel rooms,/Guerrillas sucked cold rice and fish." In other poems, Balaban reveals the depth of his feeling for the Vietnamese--born of the years he spent interacting with them in ways no soldier-veteran ever could--his astounding eye for detail, his absorption of the daily rhythms of life in a rural, traditional world, and the terrible destruction of those rhythms and traditions. In "Orpheus in the Upper World," he offers perhaps an explanation for the hundreds and even thousands of poems written by those who fought the war:

> For when his order had burst his head,
> like sillowy seeds of milkweed pod,
> he learned to pay much closer watch
> to all things, even small things,

as if to discover his errors.

Not all the poems in *After Our War* deal with Vietnam. But if some of the non-Vietnam poems occasionally reveal the graduate student laboring to flex his intellectual muscle, they also reveal the poet's ability to transcend Vietnam and reach out to the wider world around him.

II

America's bicentennial year brought the publication of Bryan Alec Floyd's *The Long War Dead*, a collection of 47 poems, each given the name of a fictitious member of "1st Platoon, U.S.M.C." Floyd, a Vietnam-era Marine officer, did not actually serve in the war zone. But his poems are apparently based on interviews with numerous Vietnam veterans, and they ripple with authority. "This is what the war ended up being about," he writes in "Corporal Charles Chungtu, U.S.M.C.":

> we would find a V.C. village,
> and if we could not capture it
> or clear it of Cong,
> we called for jets.

> ***

> Then the village
> that was not a village any more
> was our village.

Floyd's poems have marvelous range, giving voice to those who supported the war and those who detested it, lashing out with equal vehemence at American generals and North Vietnamese diplomats, the anti-war movement and the failed war. He succeeds, like no other poet I know of, in offering the full breadth of feelings and emotions of those who fought the war.

Equally important in 1976 was a new anthology, *Demilitarized Zones*, which I co-edited with Jan Barry. Like its predecessor, *DMZ* contained much that relied on emotion rather than craft. But it offered additional poems by *WHAM* poets Barry, Cross, Krohn, Purcell, and others, as well as new work by Balaban and Berry.

It also introduced a handful of good newcomers. Ex-infantryman Steve Hassett contributed a half dozen poems, including his eerily ironic

"Christmas," in which "The Hessian in his last letter home/said in part/'they are all rebels here/who will not stand to fight/but each time fade before us/as water into sand[.]'" Former Airman Horace Coleman writes of his "Saigon daughter" in "A Black Soldier Remembers":

> She does not offer me one of the
> silly hats she sells Americans and
> I have nothing she needs but
> the sad smile she already has.

In "Death of a Friend," ex-artilleryman Doug Rawlings writes, "his death/begs me to follow/pulls me toward him/my hands grow weak/ and/cannot break/the string[.]" There are also excellent poems by Gerald McCarthy and Bruce Weigl, both of whom would later publish book-length collections of their own.

A third major book to appear during the bicentennial year was Walter McDonald's *Caliban in Blue*. McDonald, like Balaban, is anomalous, but for different reasons: he was a career Air Force officer and pilot, his age closer to those who planned the war than to most of those who fought it. But his poems are wonderfully powerful, often intimately personal and sensitive. In "Faraway Places," he writes:

> This daughter watching ducks knows
> nothing of Vietnam,
> this pond her only Pacific,
> separation to her
> only the gulf between herself
> and ducks that others feed.
>
>   ***
>   Strange prospect
> to leave such gold, he thinks,
> There is no gold for him
> in Asia.
>   Possession
> turns on him like swimming ducks,
> forcing his touch again.
> She does not feel his claim
> upon her gold
> that swirls upon her face but cannot blink
> her eyes
> so full of ducks.

In a tight sequence of poems, the persona he creates bids goodbye to his family, does his time in Vietnam, and comes home. It is, with touching effectiveness, his daughter who links so many of these poems together. In "Rocket Attack," he first describes the death of a young Vietnamese girl, then cries out:

> Daughter, oh God, my daughter
> may she never
> safe at home
> Never hear the horrible
> sucking sound a rocket makes when it

--and there the poem ends, abruptly as consciousness at the moment of impact. Finally, home at last, "The Retired Pilot to Himself" wonders:

> Bombs so long falling; after falling,
> what release?
>   O for tonight--
> my child
> with benediction
> sidling heel and toe in graceful
> rhapsody,
> acceptance of herself.

In one particularly striking poem, "Interview with a Guy Named Fawkes, U.S. Army," McDonald captures--as well as any young "grunt" could--the grinding frustrations of guerrilla war:

> --you tell them this--
> tell them shove it, they're
> not here, tell them kiss
> my rear when they piss about
> women and kids in shacks
> we fire on. damn.
> they fire on us.
>
>   ***
>
> what do they know back where
> not even in their granddam's days
> did any damn red rockets glare.

In addition, a number of very good non-Vietnam poems in *Caliban in Blue* attest to McDonald's great skill and expanding field of vision.

Gerald McCarthy's solid collection, *War Story*, appeared in 1977. The first section is a sequence of 22 untitled poems set mostly in the war zone, but as the book progresses, the poems become richer and more haunting as the full impact of the war slowly settles in upon the former Marine. In "The Sound of Guns," he writes:

> At the university in town
> tight-lipped men tell me the war in Vietnam is over,
> that my poems should deal with other things[.]
>
> ***
>
> At nineteen I stood at night and watched
> an airfield mortared. A plane that was to take
> me home, burning; men running out of the flames.
> Seven winters have slipped away,
> the war still follows me.
> Never in anything have I found
> a way to throw off the dead.

It would be another two years before Bruce Weigl would publish his first book-length collection, *A Romance*. Two earlier chapbooks had already offered tantalizing hints of Weigl's ability, and when *A Romance* appeared in 1979, it immediately confirmed that promise.

Again, one finds the particular hallmark of the very best of the soldier-poets: scattered among the war-related poems are numerous excellent poems on other topics, suggesting an ability to transcend Vietnam. Indeed, of the 36 poems, only ten deal with the war. Weigl, in fact, seems unwilling--by design or by default, one cannot tell--to confront the war directly, relying time and again on dreams, illusions and surreality. "Sailing to Bien Hoa" is typical:

> In my dream of the hydroplane
> I'm sailing to Bien Hoa
> the shrapnel in my thighs
> like tiny glaciers.
> I remember a flower,
> a kite, a mannikin playing the guitar,
> a yellow fish eating a bird, a truck
> floating in urine, a rat carrying a banjo,
> a fool counting the cards, a monkey praying,

> a procession of whales, and far off
> two children eating rice,
> speaking French--
> I'm sure of the children,
> their damp flutes,
> the long line of their vowels.

It is almost as if, even after eleven years, the war is still too painful to grasp head-on. Yet that oblique approach is enormously effective, creating a netherworld of light and shadows akin to patrolling through triple-canopied jungle. In "Mines," he writes:

> Here is how you walk at night: slowly lift
> one leg, clear the sides with your arms, clear the back,
> front, put the leg down, like swimming.

And in "Monkey," a complicated five-part poem, he writes:

> I like a little unaccustomed mercy.
> Pulling the trigger is all we have.
> I hear a child.
>
>   ***
>
> I'm tired of the rice
> falling in slow motion[.]

Each one of these ten poems, scattered as they are among the others, is like stepping into a punji pit or triggering a tripwire.

III

Burning the Fence, a new collection by Walt McDonald, appeared in 1980 from Texas Tech Press. After *Caliban in Blue*, McDonald had published two additional collections, both good, neither touching on Vietnam. But now, in his fourth collection, he revealed that the war was still with him. In "The Winter Before the War," he talks of raking leaves in late autumn, the approach of winter, the first snow and ice-fishing, concluding:

> The fireplace
> after dark
> was where we thawed.

> Chocolate steamed
> in mugs we wrapped
> our hands around.
> Our children slept.
> The news came on.
> We watched
> each other's eyes.

Only in "Al Croom," in fact, does he write of Vietnam directly, and the word "Vietnam" appears nowhere in the collection. But the war is there, nevertheless, like a dark and brooding presence.

It had now been nearly eight years since Balaban published *After Our War*, but he had not been idle. In the intervening time, he had published two collections of translations: *Vietnamese Folk Poetry* and the bilingual *Ca Dao Viet Nam*. And in 1982, his *Blue Mountain* ably demonstrated the growth of his own poetry over the years. Here are poems ranging from the American West to the southern Appalachians, from Pennsylvania to Romania, along with eloquent elegies to friends and family members.

Still, lingering memories of Vietnam persist. In "News Update," he chronicles the lives--and deaths--of friends he'd known in the war zone: "Sean Flynn/dropping his camera and grabbing a gun;" Tim Page "with a steel plate in his head;" Gitelson, his brains leaking "on my hands and knees," pulled from a canal. "And here I am, ten years later," he muses:

> written up in the local small town press
> for popping a loud-mouth punk in the choppers.
> Oh, big sighs. Windy sighs. And ghostly laughter.

In "For Mrs. Cam, Whose Name Means 'Printed Silk,'" he reflects on he dislocation of the refugee Boat People:

> The wide Pacific flares in sunset.
> Somewhere over there was once your home.
> You study the things which start from scratch.

And in "After Our War," he writes:

> After our war, the dismembered bits
> --all those pierced eyes, ear slivers, jaw splinters,
> gouged lips, odd tibias, skin flaps, and toes--
> came squinting, wobbling, jabbering back.

After observing wryly that "all things naturally return to their source," he wonders, "After our war, how will love speak?"

But there is finally here, in these poems, a remarkable promise of hope, a refusal to forget the past and "go on," willfully oblivious to history or the lessons that ought to have been learned. In "In Celebration of Spring," he insists:

> Swear by the locust, by dragonflies on ferns,
> by the minnow's flash, the tremble of a breast,
> by the new earth spongy under our feet:
> that as we grow old, we will not grow evil,
> that although our garden seeps with sewage,
> and our elders think it's up for auction--swear
> by this dazzle that does not wish to leave us--
> that we will be keepers of a garden, nonetheless.

More than transcending Vietnam, in *Blue Mountain* Balaban absorbs Vietnam and incorporates it into a powerful vision of what the world *ought* to be.

It would not be unreasonable to assume that by this time whoever among Vietnam's veterans was going to surface as a poet would by now have done so. It had been 21 years since Jan Barry first went to Vietnam, and even the youngest of the vets were approaching their mid-thirties. But the appearance in 1984 of D.F. Brown's *Returning Fire* proved that assumption to be false.

Former medic Brown is particularly interesting, having remained in the Army from 1968 to 1977, and one can only wonder why he stayed in and why he got out. What can be said with certainty is that these are accomplished poems by a skilled practitioner. All of them deal with Vietnam and its aftermath. "I can tell true stories/of the jungle," he writes in "When I Am 19 I Was a Medic":

> I sleep strapped to a .45,
> bleached into my fear.
> I do this under the biggest tree,
> some nights I dig
> in saying my wife's name
> over and over.
>
> ***
>
>   I never mention
> the fun, our sense of humor

embarrasses me. Something
warped it out of place
and bent I drag it along--
keep track of time spent,
measure what I think we have left.

In "Eating the Forest," he speaks of "soldiers/trained to sleep/where the moon sinks/and bring the darkness home[.]" In "Still Later There Are War Stories," he warns: "We grow old counting the year/in days,...The jungle/loaded, nobody/comes away in one piece." And in "Coming Home," he notices:

Someone has stacked his books,
Records, souvenirs, pretending
This will always be light
And zoned residential[.]

The shortest poem in the book is "L'Eclatante Victoire de Khe Sanh":

The main thing
to remember
is the jungle
has retaken the trenches--
think it forgiven
look on it healed
as a scar.

The longest poem, from which the book's title is taken, runs over three pages. In between are some of the best poems to come out of the war. Whether Brown will eventually expand his reach to include other subjects and themes remains to be seen, but *Returning Fire* is a strong beginning.

Bruce Weigl had already demonstrated his mastery of other subjects and other themes in *A Romance*, and his 1985 collection, *The Monkey Wars*, gives further proof of his considerable talents. Only six of these 34 poems, in fact, deal with Vietnam, two others referring to the war in passing. Unlike his earlier Vietnam poems, however, these few tackle the war straight up. Absent are the dreams and illusions, the surreality. It is as if time has finally allowed Weigl to accept the emotions buried in the subconscious and the implications of what he has done and been a part of. In the tellingly brutal and straightforward poem, "Burning Shit at An Khe," he describes in painful detail the repulsive task of cleaning makeshift outhouses:

> I tried to light a match
>   It died
> And it all came down on me, the stink
>   And the heat and the worthlessness
> Until I slipped and climbed
>   Out of that hole and ran
> Past the olive drab
>   Tents and trucks and clothes and everything
> Green as far from the shit
>   As the fading light allowed.
> Only now I can't fly.
>   I lay down in it
> And finger paint the words of who I am
>   Across my chest
> Until I'm covered and there's only one smell,
>   One word.

Even more chilling is "Song of Napalm," in which he tries to appreciate the wonder of horses in a pasture after a storm:

> Still I close my eyes and see the girl
> Running from her village, napalm
> Stuck to her dress like jelly,
> Her hands reaching for the no one
> Who waits in waves of heat before her.
>
>   ***
>
> So I can keep on living,
> So I can stay here beside you,
> I try to imagine she runs down the road and wings
> Beat inside her until she rises
> Above the stinking jungle and her pain
> Eases, and your pain, and mine.

But the poem continues, "the lie swings back again," and finally:

> ...she is burned behind my eyes
> And not your good love and not the rain-swept air
> And not the jungle green

Pasture unfolding before us can deny it.

Perhaps because he has come to terms with the worst, he can also now remember with a certain amusement "The Girl at the Chu Lai Laundry," who wouldn't give him his uniforms because they weren't finished:

> Who would've thought the world stops
> Turning in the war, the tropical heat like hate
> And your platoon moves out without you,
> Your wet clothes piled
> At the feet of the girl at the laundry,
> Beautiful with her facts.

These are wonderful poems, made more so by their juxtaposition with touchingly beautiful non-war poems like "Snowy Egret" and "Small Song for Andrew." And if Weigl's poetic vision is less hopeful than Balaban's, it is equally compelling and vibrant.

Best of all, poets like Weigl, Balaban, and Brown are still young and still producing. Weigl recently collected previous and new war poems in *Song of Napalm*; the title poem of that volume is already widely recognized as one of the finest poems to come out of the war. Balaban has written a novel and is currently translating into English the late eighteenth-century Vietnamese poet Ho Xuan Huong, and so continues to keep the Vietnamese people and literary tradition in view for American readers. Brown has been writing experimental long poems, including "The Other half of Everything" (Ironwood 31/32, 1988). McDonald has been amazingly prolific. He recently won two honors: the Elliston Prize for *The Flying Dutchman* and the Juniper Prize for *After the Noise of Saigon* both published in 1987. In 1988, *Night Landings* and *Splitting Wood for Winter* appeared. Yusef Komunyakaa, whose excellent poems have been appearing in magazines and anthologies, has recently published three collections, the last of which deals exclusively and imaginatively with Vietnam: *I Apologize for the Eyes in My Head*, *Toys in a Field*, and *Dien Cai Dau*. Who knows what else awaits the touch of a pen or the favor of a publisher?

IV

There remains, for now, only to speculate on why Vietnam has produced such an impressive body of poems (not to mention short stories, novels and personal narratives)--especially considering the relative paucity of poems arising from other modern American wars.

Korea produced almost nothing at all. From World War II, one can think of only a handful of poems, like James Dickey's "The Firebombing," Randall Jarrell's "The Death of the Ball Turret Gunner," and sections of Thomas McGrath's *Letter to an Imaginary Friend*. The contrast is even more remarkable when one considers how very few members of the Vietnam Generation ever actually served in Vietnam in any capacity at all. Where then do these poems come from?

Surely it has to do with the peculiar nature of the war itself. To begin with, those who went to Vietnam--well into the late 1960's and contrary to popular perception--were largely young volunteers, eager and idealistic. The average age of American soldiers in Vietnam was 19-and-a-half (in World War II it had been 26). They had grown up in the shadow of their fathers' generation, the men who had fought "the good war" from 1941 to 1945. Most had been in grade school or junior high school when John F. Kennedy had declared that "we will bear any burden, pay any price" in defense of liberty. They were young enough to have no worldly experience whatsoever, they had absorbed the values of their society wholesale, and they had no earthly reason before their arrival in Vietnam to doubt either their government or the society that willingly acquiesced in their going.

All of that was about to change forever. Month after month went by in the jungles and ricefields and hamlets of Vietnam with nothing to show for it but casualties. Men fought and died for nameless hills, only to walk away from them when the battle was over. Men taught to believe that American soldiers handed out candy to kids found themselves killing and being killed by those very kids. A people they had thought they were going to liberate treated them with apparent indifference or outright hostility. Progress was measured in grisly official body counts, and any dead Vietnamese was a Viet Cong. Torture, assault and battery, malicious destruction, murder and mayhem--the very things young Americans had always been taught only the enemy did--were widespread and tacitly or openly sanctioned. Worst of all, as time passed, it became obvious even to the most naive 18-year-old that the war was going nowhere.

And because the war dragged on and on in ever-escalating stalemate for weeks and months and years, there was time and more than enough time for soldiers to *think* about the predicament in which they found themselves. Who in the hell was fighting whom? Why?! And for what? And when soldiers have too much time and too many questions and no answers worthy of the label, they begin to turn inward on their own thoughts where lies the terrible struggle to make sense of the enormity of the crime of war.

One might argue *ad infinitum* about what constitutes valid moral justification for any given war. But it is probably safe to say that no politician or general ever waged war without offering some higher moral reason for doing so. Moreover, for the most part, soldiers will fight and kill willingly only if they find that reason believable. Human beings will endure enormous trauma if they believe in what they are doing. But the explanations given by those who'd sent the soldiers to fight in Vietnam became ever more surreal and absurd until they were revealed for what they were: nothing but empty words, bereft of reason or any semblance of higher moral authority.

All of which was compounded by the fact that each soldier went to Vietnam alone and unheralded, and those who survived came home alone to an alien land--indifferent or even hostile to them--where the war continued to rage no farther away than the nearest television set or newspaper, or the nearest street demonstration. Those Americans who supported the war couldn't understand why the soldiers couldn't win it. Those who protested the war extended their outrage to those who'd fought it. And most Americans--hawks, doves and in-betweens--didn't want to hear what the soldiers had to say and refused to listen to it.

In short, those who had been asked and ordered to pull the trigger were left alone to carry the weight of the entire disaster that was America's war in Indochina. The American people turned their backs on the war long before it ended. Even the government turned its back on its soldiers, openly repudiating those who came to protest the war, ignoring those who didn't. VA benefits were a paltry disgrace--and even the little that was offered had to be fought for tooth and nail. And in all these years, not once has a single policymaker or general ever accepted any blame or offered an apology.

Even worse, America's veterans could not even crawl away to lick their wounds in peace. Without even the illusion of a satisfactory resolution, the war ground on for years after most veterans had come home, and the fall of Saigon has been followed by one reminder after another: the boat people, the amnesty issue, Agent Orange, delayed stress, the occupation of Cambodia, the bombing of the Marine barracks in Beirut, the mining of Nicaragua's harbors. And the initial rejection of Vietnam veterans, and the long silence of the seventies which followed (during which time Vietnam veterans were routinely stereotyped as drug-crazed, emotionally unbalanced misfits), have only given way to Rambo, Chuck Norris, and the sorry spectacle of America's Vietnam veterans driven to build monuments to themselves and throw parades in their own honor.

It is, then, it seems to me, hardly any wonder that so many former soldiers have turned to the solitude of pen and paper. Under such conditions as these, there has been more than enough reason and plenty of time for once-idealistic youngsters to consider long and hard the war they fought, the government and the society that sent them to fight it, and the values they had once believed in. While many of these writers might be loathe to call themselves anti-war poets, few if any have anything good to say about their experience in Vietnam.

In 1963, John Kennedy said in a speech at Amherst College, "When power corrupts, poetry cleanses." Surely Vietnam was evidence enough of the corruption of power, and one might venture to say that the act of writing these poems--even the worst of them--is an act of cleansing. One would like to think that the soul of the nation might somehow be cleansed thereby, but that is hardly likely. More realistically, one hopes that in writing these poems, the poets might at least have begun to cleanse their own souls of the torment that was and is Vietnam. Surely, in the process of trying, the best of them have added immeasurably to the body and soul of American poetry.

Works Cited

Balaban, John. *After Our War*. Pittsburgh: University of Pittsburgh Press, 1974.

-----. *Blue Mountain*. Greensboro, NC: Unicorn Press, 1982.

-----. *Ca Dao Viet Nam*. Greensboro, NC: Unicorn Press, 1980.

-----. *Vietnamese Folk Poetry*. Greensboro, NC: Unicorn Press, 1974.

Barry, Jan, Basil T. Paquet, and Larry Rottmann, eds. *Winning Hearts & Minds*. Brooklyn: 1st Casualty Press, 1972.

----- and W.D. Ehrhart, eds. *Demilitarized Zones: Veterans after Vietnam*. Perkasie, PA: East River Anthology, 1976.

Berry, D.C. *saigon cemetery*. Athens: University of Georgia Press, 1972.

Brown, D.F. *Returning Fire*. San Francisco: San Francisco State University Press, 1984.

Casey, Michael. *Obscenities*. New Haven: Yale University Press, 1972.

Floyd, Byran Alec. *The Long War Dead*. NY: Avon, 1976.

Komunyakaa, Yusef. *Dien Cai Dau*. Middletown: Wesleyan University Press, 1986.

Layne, McAvoy. *How Audie Murphy Died in Vietnam*. Garden City, NY: Anchor Books, 1973.

McCarthy, Gerald. *War Story*. Trumansburg, NY: The Crossing Press, 1977.

McDonald, Walter. *After the Noise of Saigon*. Amherst: University of Massachusetts Press, 1987.

-----. *Burning the Fence*. Lubbock: Texas Tech University Press, 1980.

-----. *Caliban in Blue*. Lubbock: Texas Tech University Press, 1976.

-----. *The Flying Dutchman*. Columbus: Ohio State University Press, 1987.

-----. *Night*. New York: Random House, 1988.

-----. *Splitting Wood for Winter*. University of North Texas Press, 1988.

Weigl, Bruce. *A Romance*. Pittsburgh: University of Pittsburgh Press, 1979.

-----. *The Monkey Wars*. Athens: University of Georgia Press, 1985.

-----. *Song of Napalm*. Boston: Atlantic Press, 1988.

GONE TO FLOWERS:
THEATRE AND DRAMA OF THE VIETNAM WAR

Weldon B. Durham

In 1966, just two years after the Tonkin Gulf Resolution and the beginning of the buildup of American military presence in South Vietnam, there appeared at the La Mama Experimental Theatre Club in New York City the first and one of the most celebrated theatrical pieces about the war: Megan Terry's *Viet Rock: A Folk War Movie*. Terry ran the playwright's workshop of Joseph Chaikin's Open Theatre, and actors from the company created the play in improvisations based on news material and the performers' personal experiences. Terry then "solidified" these creations and formed them as a playscript. Her remarks on the origins of this play could well stand as a preamble to a discussion of the whole of drama and theatre focussed on the war in Southeast Asia:

> To deal with the bewilderment, shame, and confusion created by this war, I felt we had to explore our negative feelings, drives, and fantasies. . . . Also, we explored loss, grief, and regret. We tried to get at the essence of violence (21).

Terry's ensemble employed "transformational acting," a technique which has outlived the material it was designed to serve. Critic Richard Schechner observed about transformations in his introduction to *Viet Rock* that:

> The actor no longer plays out a continuity but a set of interrelated (and sometimes unrelated) actions, each of which is self-contained. He gets from one action to the next not by establishing for himself a logical, motivational connective but by following the "rules of the game" which say that at a certain time, on a certain cue, action A ends and action B begins (p. 11).

Transformational acting made *Viet Rock* resemble the nightly news television broadcast, as Robert Asahina suggests (32), but the resemblance is superficial. The idea of transformational acting is

332

rooted in a view of human consciousness as a pastiche of personal and communal experiences, an idea at least as old as August Strindberg's epochal "Preface" to *Miss Julie*, an idea given technical dimension in Sergei Eisenstein's theory and practice of cinematic montage and in Bertolt Brecht's theory and practice of *verfremdungseffekt* ("defamiliarization"). As implemented in *Viet Rock*, the technique of transformations "alienated" the audience. Onlookers were no longer able to identify the actor with a character. Undermining the appeal of the actor-character relationship undermined the appeal of "character," itself. When "character," as a repository of preconceptions about the roots of social behavior in "human nature," is undermined, the actor-action relationship is aggrandized, and the auditor is left with the consideration alone of the socio-political roots of social behavior, with the consideration alone of political choices.

Terry's play aimed, in both form and content, to attack the roots of our culture's sensibility and to disrupt through a shocking denial the very modes of perception that sustained that sensibility. Its critique of culture is evident in its orientation towards the centrality of the body, towards the "thinking" of the body, as evident in the spectacle of gesture, grimace, and movement and of the choreographic arrangement of masses of bodies. Terry insisted that "the visual images are more important than the words (21)." Indeed, as the play begins "the actors are discovered lying on the floor in a circle. Their bodies, heads inward, form a giant flower or a small target. They are still; bit by bit movement can be detected. First: as if flower petals are stirred by wind or are warming toward the sun (28)." As the play ends, Saigon Sallie's bar is blown to bits, and

> the bodies are massed together center stage,
> tangled and flailing in slow motion. They stab
> one another, shoot one another, and choke one
> another as they fall in a heap to the floor. . . .
> When all are dead they are in a tangled circle on
> the floor, the reverse of the beautiful circle of the
> opening image (102).

Between these two images of sculpted flesh, the audience is bombarded with sensual experiences, from the "sounds of children playing war games" to the sensation of being looked at and touched lovingly by a performer. The visual and aural images relate a "story" of little originality or distinction, but story-telling is not the aim of this performance experience. The audience witnesses the transformation of elements of the circle/flower into new babies (the men) and mothers (the women). A Sergeant leaps to his feet and yells "Ten-Hut!" and induction physicals begin. The women play doctors and a chorus which recites "U. S. Government Inspected Male," as each man receives an immunization shot. And so it goes until the males are shipped to Vietnam (with time out for an orgy in Shangrila!) then slaughtered in the explosion of Saigon Sallie's bar. Throughout, the war is a physical fact rather than a political abstraction, and the play is less an anti-war argument than it is an assault on the public's refusal to accept the war as anything more real than news film or video footage.

Mac Bird! (1966), by Barbara Garson, is a burlesque of Shakespeare's *Macbeth* focussed on the presidency of Lyndon Johnson, and it is wholly unlike *Viet Rock*, for *Mac Bird!* emphasizes a story told in a distinctly and almost exclusively verbal medium. In the early scenes Mac Bird, having been forewarned by three witches (a beatnik-type student demonstrator, a Negro civil rights protester, and an old-style radical in overalls and carrying a worker's lunch pail), accepts an invitation to join the ticket of John Ken O'Dunc, the party's nominee for the presidency. Mac Bird is distressed by the way his political expertise is ignored by the nominees and his brothers and other advisers. Later, Ken O'Dunc is assassinated in a ceremonial parade arranged by Mac Bird and Lady Mac Bird. President Mac Bird commissions the Earl of Warren to conduct a full investigation of the assassination, then announces the beginning of a "Pox Americana," which will unite all peoples in peace and freedom. He also announces his plans for a "Smooth Society," an orderly America "sweet with unity," to be achieved by stifling dissent. He orders Lord McNamara to stamp out the rebellion of the peasants in Viet Land. Wayne of Morse, in Quixote armor and carrying a lance, opposes the war, as does the "Egg of Head" (Adlai Stevenson). The nation rises in rebellion against Mac Bird and his programs, especially the war. Mac Bird goes to visit the Three Witches to see what he might do about the future. The Witches mix a noxious brew in a boiling cauldron. It includes:

> Taylor's tongue and Goldberg's slime,
> MacNamara's bloody crime
> Sizzling skin of napalmed child,
> Roasted eyeballs, sweet and mild.
> Now we add a fiery chunk
> From a burning Buddhist monk.
> Flaming field and blazing hut,
> Infant fingers cooked and cut,
> Young man's heart and old man's gut,
> Groin and gall and gore of gook

In our caldron churn and cook. (79)

Images of General Ky and Madame Nu emerge from the brew to urge Mac Bird to continue the war. Mac Bird struggles but yields to pressure and announces his plans to resign. However, he must be forcibly removed from office by John Ken O'Dunc's brother, Robert, who succeeds Mac Bird at the end of the play.

Apple Pie, three short plays by Terrence McNally, continues the theatre's tentative exploration of the implications of America's increasing involvement in the war in Southeast Asia. *Next* takes place in an "anonymous-looking" examination room decorated with an American flag. A woman, Sgt. Thech, administers a pre-induction physical to Marion, a fat man in his late forties. Marion passes the physical, despite his protests, but he fails a rudimentary psychological examination, to which he responds with apparent normality. When Sgt. Thech advises him he is unacceptable, Marion is stung, in part by the inhumanity of a system that evaluates then rejects whole man as unacceptable by narrow and inscrutable standards. Ultimately, Marion is reduced to bitter tears by the realization that he has lost any sense of the meaning and purpose of his country. *Tour* features not a tour of duty in a war zone, as the title might suggest, but an American couple, the Wilsons, being chauffeured through Italy. Their son is in Vietnam, but the couple, enthroned in the back seat of their rented car, is as removed from the reality of the war as their son is immersed in it. Moreover, their inane conversation reveals their inability to comprehend any aspect of the world in which they live. McNally uses Mrs. Wilson's hysteria as a means of blending into the dialogue images suggesting her preoccupation with the war in Southeast Asia. When they are lost ("We are too lost! *L-a-o-s*."), it is in an area like a rain forest. They get out of the car, but the chauffeur won't unlock the doors to let them back in. Beggars in robes suggesting the appearance of Buddhist monks assail them. The face of one is eaten away by leprosy or burned away by napalm. Mrs. Wilson wants to know why they keep burning themselves and she insists, "WE ONLY BOMB THE NORTH! BAD PEOPLE!" The phantasmagoric experience fails ultimately to arouse the Wilsons to full and responsible consciousness of their personal and geopolitical situation. In *Botticelli*, two soldiers await the emergence of a trapped enemy soldier. As they wait, they play a game revealing wide but superficial exposure to humanistic values. When the enemy appears, they gun him down, then return to camp, still arguing about the names and achievements of the painters and poets.

The intransigent indifference and comforting ignorance of the American public as regards the war is at the heart of McNally's *Bringing It All Back Home*, first produced in New York in 1969. The characters are types of the American middle class: Son (a junior-high-school druggie), Daughter (a promiscuous high-school cheerleader), Mother (a deeply disturbed woman, perpetually under the hair dryer, who worries about the signs of disintegration in the family), and Father (a bowling maven who worries about the masculinity of his younger son and makes obscene phone calls). The play opens in a swirl of activity designed to establish the intellectual and emotional barrenness of this American family. Two men bring in a large box holding the body of the older brother, Jimmy. Son and Daughter don't know how to respond, so they ignore the box. They hardly remember their brother, but then, Mother and Father pay no attention to the coffin either. Jimmy steps out of the coffin and, in direct address to the audience, corrects false impressions of his character formed by his family's remarks. An egregiously exploitive television reporter comes to do a story on the grieving family, and the family describes Jimmy in terms contradicting all the dead soldier has told the audience. The family members evade the reporter's question about the morality of the war. The reporter's interview reveals that the family's daily life is unaffected by the death of Jimmy, and that they were emotionally detached from him. They have some ideas about why he died, but they are superficial, thoughtless excuses. The reporter reveals that Jimmy didn't die immediately, but had 45 minutes of pain and terror while holding his intestines in his hands before losing consciousness. Mother is devastated by this information, but the rest of the family denies the news. The reporter demands: "Do any of you know *anything*? . . . Or *want* to?" Jimmy concludes to the audience: "The main reason I wish I was alive is so I could figure out why I was dead."

In *Muzeeka* (1968), John Guare carries on the theme of the intransigence of the majority when he presents a middle-class man who works at a company that pipes music into business establishment all over America. The man imagines himself in many morally ambiguous or untenable circumstances, including fighting in Vietnam, and manages to soothe his conscience with doubletalk and empty verbiage.

With the 1967 production of *Hair*, (book and lyrics by Gerome Ragni and James Rado, music by Galt McDermott), by the New York Shakespeare Festival, the Vietnam War, or more properly the spectacle of the apparently unwashed opponents of U.S. involvement in the war, emerged in a mainstream theatre. Two long-haired hippies, Claude Hooper Bukowski and George Berger, encounter all the impediments of their age, represented by two characters, "Mom" and "Dad," as they try to grow into free and whole men. Claude is drafted, but the extent of his political consciousness is suggested in the line: "I want to be over here doing the things they're defending over there" (55). He's afraid of being hurt, and he doesn't want to die. Berger is rightfully accused by his ex-girlfriend, a student protester, of being an "uncommitted hedonist jerk." Claude dies in Vietnam, but he has left his hair, shorn from his head by his lover, Sheila, in a paper sack. The army and its war in Vietnam represent death and repression for members of a youthful tribe wanting only to live in freedom. Of all the theatre devoted even marginally to the issue of the war, *Hair* was surely the most popular. Images of the hippie drug culture, with which the public was fascinated, and scenes of nudity and of simulated intercourse made the New York production and its several road-show clones exciting to a population indifferent to its minimal cultural critique. Productions were seen world-wide in a number of languages, and the cast album and singles from it were great hits. Not until the Milos Foreman motion picture based on the play was screened in 1979 did the political content of the piece become manifest.

Michael Weller's *Moonchildren* premiered under the title *Cancer* in London in 1970 and was first seen in America in 1972. This terrier version of *Hair* explores the lives of the rootless, aimless youth of the sixties. Five men and three women in their senior year of college demonstrate for justice and against the war, but without conviction. Their lives are pointless fantasies in which they merely indulge themselves.

The 1968 production of Ron Cowen's *Summertree* by New York's Repertory Theater of Lincoln Center, continued the interest of the mainstream theatre in the Vietnam war. But if the war was lost in a celebration of anarchistic hedonism in *Hair*, it was obscured under a film of sentiment in *Summertree*.

The scene is a deep, green glen containing a large, gnarled tree and the action is made up of the reveries of a twenty-year-old Vietnam war casualty in the moment of his death from a knife wound in the stomach. Interest in this pitiful spectacle of an unjust and pointless death grows out of an audience's sympathetic identity with the dying "Young Man" and his mother. The Young Man's relations with his father are rooted in a rigid code of masculinity, as are the Young Man's relations with the "Little Boy," alternately the Young Man at an early age and the Young Man's little brother. The play is almost wholly apolitical, raising no questions about the causes of the conflict. Tension in this essentially lyric piece centers on the relationship, only casually developed, between the Father and the Young Man.

In implicit acknowledgement of the obstinacy of the theatre-going public, Arthur Kopit disguised his effort "to put the Vietnamese situation into a context of American history and American method ("Dialogue") as a political allegory in *Indians* (1968). Here the setting is a circus arena where Buffalo Bill is about to introduce one of his famous Wild West shows. Instead, he tries compulsively to rationalize the cruelty done the American Indian. Guilt for the slaughter of the buffalo and the obliteration of Indian culture must be shared by Bill and his contemporaries with the modern audience, who must also recognize the consubstantiality of the Indian and the Vietnamese.

David Rabe argues in his introduction to *Sticks and Bones*, first produced at Villanova University in 1969, then at the New York Shakespeare Festival's Public Theater in 1971 and on Broadway in 1972, that one of the major conflicts of the play "is whether the world is ordinary, stereotypical, or poetic" (xx). The mixture of modes in the play is problematic, for it sets the clash of the guilt-racked and physically disabled veteran with his uncomprehending family in a context embracing both the ghostly image of a Vietnamese woman and the farcical antics of television's Nelson family. The characters are Ozzie and Harriet, sons Rick and David, and Zung, a Vietnamese girl visible only to David. A Sergeant Major delivers a blind David to the family home on his way to deliver broken young men to family homes all over America. David's blindness is at once an image of the psychological condition of the family and the surreal culture it represents and an expression of Rabe's identity with his hero. Rabe, veteran of a two-year tour with a hospital support unit in Vietnam, would seem to be burdened with such guilt and corrupted with such awful hatred that his impulse in writing for the theatre parallels David's in living with his family as a blind Tiresias-a seer whose sayings make him a criminal and a pariah.

The point of the play is brutally clear. Rabe has maintained that "Mom and Dad are not concerned that terrible events have occurred in the world, but rather that David has come home to behave in a manner that makes him no longer loveable" [*The Basic Training of Pavlo Hummel* and *Sticks and Bones* (New York: Viking Press, 1973, p. 225)]. An America deeply committed to the bogus myth of the family and anesthetized by false imagery of happiness, simplicity, and love simply could not cope, in Rabe's view, with the ugly reality of Vietnam. Neither the trickle of broken bodies and the planes loaded with caskets and nor the acidic stream of news from the war zone had seared through the facade of peace with honor behind which so many Americans had taken refuge. And the play is another, with *Orphan* (1970), of Rabe's examinations of the myth of the family as the perfected locus of our identity as individuals and, ultimately, of our identity as a society.

The second of Rabe's three Vietnam plays, *The Basic Training of Pavlo Hummel*, existed in a completed first draft in the fall of 1968, when a draft of *Sticks and Bones* was not so far along. It was first produced at the New York Shakespeare Festival's Public Theater in May 1971. Early rehearsals of the unrevised version revealed a first act rooted in documentary realism and a fragmentary and impressionistic second act. Impresario Joseph Papp, director Jeff Bleckner, and Rabe revised the play, making the whole more theatrical.

Ardell, an angel of death, a black soldier wearing sunglasses, bloused boots, and a strangely unreal uniform with black ribbons and medals, attends to Pavlo, drifting in and out of the play as needed. Pavlo yearns to be an efficient soldier; he strives to please his superiors and to find a model for his military life. He lies about his past, trying to make himself seem dangerous and worldly. He is despised and ridiculed by the other trainees, accused of stealing from them, then beaten. Nevertheless Pavlo wins a pair of sunglasses from Ardell. The progress of the training is suggested by the increasing skill with which the trainees go through the manual of arms.

In Act II training ends and Pavlo goes home to tell his brother Mickey he doesn't need him any longer, because he has real brothers in the army. Despite his fantasy of being sexually attractive, Pavlo is repeatedly rejected in bars where he wears his uniform, and he makes a fool of himself when he gets drunk and calls on an old girlfriend. Pavlo's mother finds her son is a stranger, so Pavlo's home leave is the negative of the experience the young soldier of American tradition could expect.

Pavlo is shipped to Vietnam and assigned to a field hospital as a medic. Pavlo goes to a brothel, and the scene there is interwoven with a scene in which a neurotically despondent multiple amputee begs Pavlo to help him die. Pavlo has sex with Yen, a Vietnamese whore, while Sergeant Power instructs trainees in the use of an M-16 rifle. Pavlo transfers to a combat unit and gets wounded three times. The army denies his request to get out of Vietnam because of his multiple wounds. Pavlo goes to the bar and claims Yen, who is with Sergeant Wall. Pavlo beats Wall, who then tosses a grenade into the room and kills Pavlo.

Rabe suggests that basic-training is a metaphor for an essential training that includes more than the training given by the army (xiii). Pavlo's training increases his mental and physical efficiency, but he never gains any real insight (110). In kind with *Sticks and Bones, Pavlo Hummel* directs a withering gaze at nurture as it is practiced in our culture. *Sticks and Bones* focuses on the nurturing function of the family, while *Pavlo Hummel* establishes the military as a symbol of the nurturing institution beyond the home. *Pavlo Hummel* is a simple play, but potentially effective if the role of Pavlo is cast properly, for the "message" of the play is richly and completely embodied in the title role, an emblem of a stratum of young American manhood in the late sixties. Pavlo believes that manhood and full personhood is replete with brutality, the power of life and death over other people, and with sexual conquest. Sexuality and death are imaginatively commingled in the imagery of the play.

Rabe's third Vietnam play, *Streamers*, was written at the same time as *Sticks and Bones* and *Pavlo Hummel*. Rabe registered a copyright for *Streamers* as an unpublished work in 1970, though it was not professionally produced until 1975. The play is set in the cadre room of a barracks on an army base which functions as a replacement center servicing combat units in Vietnam. The base is near Washington, D.C. The time is the summer of 1964. The play is about five young soldiers: two blacks, Roger and Carlyle; and three whites, Richie, a homosexual, and Martin and Billy. As the play begins, Martin has mutilated himself to express his loathing for the army. Carlyle feels isolated and afraid because there are so few blacks on the base. He hates the army and is afraid of going to Vietnam, so he's confused by Roger's apparent acceptance of the army. Billy and Roger are compulsively disposed to mop and clean their quarters and to exercise and keep fit.

Cokes and Rooney, very drunk, come in looking for fun. Cokes has just returned from Vietnam; Rooney is on the way. Both are former "Screaming Eagles" of the 101st Airborne Battalion, and, to prove it, they scream like eagles and show the boys how men jump out of airplanes. Cokes tells of the death of O'Flannigan ("The guy with his chute goin' straight up above him is a streamer, like a tulip, only white, you know."), and he illustrates with a whiskey bottle dropped on bed as he sings "Beautiful Streamer" to tune of Stephen Foster's "Beautiful Dreamer." It turns into a song about all those who are about to die. Cokes falls down, which he has done frequently of late. He's been sent back from Vietnam by doctors who think he has leukemia. Rooney and Cokes make the young men disrobe and go to bed, and Cokes, the demolitions expert, threatens to blow them all up if they don't obey.

A quiet interlude follows in which Billy tries to get Richie to explain why he's a homosexual. Then, Carlyle bursts in making sounds of machine guns and cannons. The play is packed with imagery of explosions, and explosive moments alternate sharply with quiet, probing moments. Carlyle is drunk, and his assault turns to boasting, then to recriminations, then to a rage that explodes out of grief. When he passes out, he boys let him sleep on the cadre room floor. As taps is played, Billy makes a final effort to understand Richie.

Act Two continues with more development of the interlocked themes of pent-up homosexuality and explosive violence and death. The sexually explicit banter culminates in which Richie and Carlyle become involved in foreplay. When Richie asks the others to leave the room, Billy and Roger, frightened, refuse to leave. The situation escalates through sexual anxiety to racial hatred and explodes in violence as Carlyle stabs and kills Billy. Rooney happens in, looking for Cokes in a silly game of hide and seek, and tries to break up the fight with his eagle scream. He frightens Carlyle, who runs out, but he soon returns and fatally stabs Rooney. The Military Police arrest Carlyle and remove him. Roger starts to mop up, when Cokes arrives, looking for Rooney. He tries to comfort Richie and Roger by singing "Beautiful Streamer" in a pseudo-Oriental language. His performance and the play ends with "the soft, whispering sound of a child imitating an explosion."

Again Rabe has mingled death and sexuality in a close-up treatment of the rituals by which masculinity is confirmed in a militaristic culture. He has also situated a source of military discipline in anxiety about homosexuality. But the artistic achievement of this play, the best of Rabe's Vietnam trilogy, resides not in the power or precision with which these themes are asserted, but in the thoroughness with which Rabe has invested the play with explosive images on impact with the earth; when trapped in a spider hole with a live grenade; in frustration, rage, grief, or sexual excitement.

Rabe has recalled an effort in Vietnam to keep a journal of his experiences. He abandoned the journal when he became "aware acutely, and in a way that makes writing impossible, of the existence of language as mere symbol." He couldn't detach himself from an obsession with events that seemed "huge and continual," beyond the reach of language (xvii-xviii). Rabe's trilogy is evidence that his struggle to discover a dramaturgy equal to his vision developed through stages toward a conceptually sound, stylistically integrated and emotionally touching drama in *Streamers*.

Vietnam Campesiño (1970), the first part of a trilogy by Luis Valdez and El Teatro Campesino, a theatre collective dedicated to agitation for the rights of migrant farm workers, had its source in a reassessment of the goals and strategies of activism occasioned by the death of Ruben Salazar, prominent Chicano journalist, in a violent demonstration during the Chicano Moratorium on the Vietnam War (19 August 1970) in Los Angeles (29). This broadly farcical *acto* focused the attention of the troupe's audience of workers on blatant wartime profiteering by agri-business interests which colluded with a discriminatory selective service system claiming thousands of Chicano youth for combat service. The play also indicted the white race for willful destructiveness in pitting two brown races against each other.

A mute death figure, labeled (as are most characters in the *actos*) with a sign reading "The Draft," easily captures the teenage son of a farm worker, while the last-minute intervention of an Army general saves the plantation owner's son. The final scene features a battle between campesinos and Vietnamese farmers.

Soldado Razo (1971) focuses on the emotional turmoil of a *barrio* family as a son prepares to depart for the war. Valdez explores the Latin fascination with the military and the expectation that each young man prove his "manhood." Here the death figure is a jovial, wisecracking, bilingual person known simply as "La Muerte." The death figure orchestrates the play, anticipating where it will lead by several times applying white make up to parts of the hero's face, until at the end his face is totally white, an indication of the inevitability of his death. The hero's parents are monolingual, and their social status is indicated not by signs, as in the *actos*, but through dialogue and behavior.

The dramaturgy of *Dark Root of the Scream* (1971) becomes even more sophisticated than that of its predecessor. As did *Soldado* and *Vietnam Campesiño*, *Dark Root* treats war as the ultimate form of exploitation, but its genre is that of the *mito*, a play based on the Aztec and Mayan roots of Mexican-American heritage (Brown, p. 30-36). The play centers on a wake for a Chicano Congressional Medal of Honor winner. The dead hero is a former Chicano rights activist and *barrio* leader know as "Indio." Other characters are named after animals (the men) or flowers (the women). The script calls for a set modeled after the pyramidal temples for the Aztecs and Mayas. At the brightly lighted base of the pyramid is the *barrio*. At the more dimly lighted mid-region of the pyramid are found artifacts of the Hispanic Christian tradition, while the faintly lighted apex of the structure is decorated with emblems of ancient Indian civilizations. The play structures time to reflect this arrangement of the stage space: action moves from the urban present, through the Hispanic colonial era, and back to pre-Columbian Mexico. The dramatis personae are similarly formatted: some represent the violent, alienated elements of the *barrio*. A priest and one of the women represents the Christianized *mestizo* culture. Two characters, a man and a woman, personify ancient ideals and a new socio-political consciousness based on rejection of the Anglo world and its god. Characters also represent various strategies for adapting to life in the *barrio*. The play ends with the dead Vietnam hero transfigured into the resurrected Aztec god for whom he was named, for Indio's true name is found to be Quetzalcoatl Gonzales.

The Trial of the Catonsville Nine (1971), by Daniel Berrigan, was created in the experimental New Theatre For Now program of the Center Theatre Group at the Mark Taper Forum, Los Angeles, in August, 1970. It was first produced in New York in 1971. The script is an edited and condensed transcript of the Federal-court trial in 1968 of nine persons accused of destroying government property in removing and burning some of the records of the Selective Service office in Catonsville, Maryland. The central issue of this long one-act play is the exclusion of moral passion as an operative element of American justice, a system based on civil and criminal codes. The defendants admit breaking the civil law in their action, but they argue the existence of a higher law, which compelled them as Christians to oppose the war with force. Along the way, the testimony of the defendants situates the anti-war movement in the context of the agenda of the American left, particularly as that agenda is worked out in liberation-theology-based mission work in Africa, Central America, the Caribbean, and in poverty-stricken areas of the U. S.

Romulus Linney's *The Love Suicide at Schofield Barracks* (1972) is an enactment of the military inquiry into a double suicide at a Halloween dance in 1970 at the officer's club at Schofield Barracks, Hawaii. A Major General of the U. S. Army and his devoted, patriotic wife commit suicide while wearing Japanese gowns and masks of the classical Japanese Noh theatre. Moreover, the party was on the agenda of the President of the United States who was to have come to the islands to confer with America's allies in Southeast Asia.

What seems at first a senseless act of violence turns out to be an expiation of guilt and a statement by the deceased of their beliefs about war, killing, and individual responsibility. One of the witnesses remarks that "military parties would make an excellent substitute for war itself." The inquiry reveals that the general and his wife had written a *shinju*, a "kind of play in which lovers, who cannot bear the cruelty of the world, commit suicide together." Their play had been modeled after *The Love Suicides at Sonezaki* by the eighteenth-century Japanese playwright, Chikamatsu. Furthermore the general had commissioned a *liebestod* to be written on his behalf, and had told his doctor that "he was going to heaven, where he would stop the war."

The general and his wife had lost their son, a Marine killed in action in 1965 near Danang. The General had become convinced he was responsible for his son's death. He had ordered the inquiry following his death by suicide, and he had carefully selected the players to participate in it, for each of them qualified by virtue of having lost a son.

It is argued in the end that the suicide was but a part of the general's plan, which was to have included the execution of an Oriental-American child, the drenching of the President in the boy's blood, then the assassination of the President, followed by the double suicide. A witness, whom the general and his wife had saved from a suicidal situation, testifies that "They were too God-damned good for their own stinking country, that's why, and after fifty years of believing in it, they found that out!"

The authorized edition is supplemented by a lengthy prologue describing preparations for the inquiry, an interlude that is a transcript of a deposition by a witness, and an epilogue in the form of a lengthy diary in which the officer who conducted the inquiry probes the motive and character of the deceased and the witnesses. The play is an interesting conflation of dramatic, lyric and narrative modes, but it is clearly designed more for the page than for the stage.

The Dramatization of 365 Days (1971), by H. Wesley Balk, is based on the book by Ronald J. Glasser, a physician assigned to an Army hospital in Japan during the period when American casualties in Vietnam were running as high as 14,000 a month. Glasser wrote in *365 Days* (1971) of events he witnessed and stories he heard. Balk, the author-director, blended words selected from the book and spoken by performers, with music, mime, and dance-movement to create what could be more accurately called a "theatricalization" of the book. Balk's treatment brings together the harsh but cold and distantly mediated virtual past of the narrative with a gentle, warm, and immediate human experience in a virtual present created by living performers. The tension between the pastness of Glasser's narrative (the "text") and the immediacy of the performance stylization (the "context") is the chief source of the appeal of the dramatization.

David Berry's *G. R. Point*, was drafted in 1975 as *Spiders Talk Upon the Lawn*. It was first presented as a staged reading at the Eugene O'Neill Playwrights' Conference in 1976, then professionally produced in New York City in 1977. Berry points out in his 1979 preface to the play that "*G. R. Point* deals significantly with the *ensemble nature of survival*--a quality of life in which I deeply believe, and a salutary lesson for our times and that "*G. R. Point* is a play of reconciliation, in the service of peace and understanding" (6, 7).

The setting is a small military compound in Tay Loi, South Vietnam: a hootch (barracks), the Graves Registration building (G. R. Point), and a yard. Graves Registration is the last stop before a body is shipped to the Saigon Morgue for trans-shipment to the U. S. The characters in the play clean up and bag bodies, collect personal effects, and escort the dead to Saigon. A college-educated WASP from an old-line Maine family is assigned to the unit. It is populated by a WASP officer and six enlisted men: a Puerto Rican, three blacks, a Greek, and a Pole. The unit is served by a middle-aged Vietnamese woman. The play begins on the day in Vietnam coinciding with Easter Sunday in the U. S. and continues to account for the transformation of Micah Bradstreet, the insular and bigoted WASP with certain intellectual and moral pretensions, into a man who knows himself and who can accept flaws and inconsistencies in himself and in others with greater ease and grace. Of the plays examined in this essay, it alone locates a modicum of value in the war experience.

Reconciliation is impossible for the hero of Tom Cole's *Medal of Honor Rag* (1976). Cole's play is based on the case of Dwight Johnson, a black who won the Congressional Medal of Honor for bravery in combat in Vietnam only to be gunned down while holding up a supermarket in Detroit in 1971. Cole writes an inquiry into why the man died and what his death might mean, if it means anything. At the Valley Forge Army Hospital, a psychiatrist interviews a black patient, Dale Jackson, to discover the cause of his pain, anguish, and alienation. The doctor's efforts to induce a healing abreaction in the patient are turned on the psychiatrist, a man untested by anything but the American educational system. Christopher Durang's *The Vietnam-ization of New Jersey* (1977) is a two-bladed (at least) satirical sword directed against America's Bicentennial Celebration and against David Rabe's *Sticks and Bones*. The satire extends, through the medium of Rabe's play, which was rooted in American TV culture, to television, motion pictures, and popular stage musicals, and, through the medium of the bicentennial celebration, to American political myths.

The humor is sophomoric, but delightfully so, at once like an extended "Laugh-In" sketch and a Henry Fielding or John Gay burlesque of cultural icons. Periodically, the action halts for a "Bicentennial Minute" delivered by one of the characters: Hazel's, in act II, is typical:

> When in the course of human events it become necessary for one Thomas Jefferson to dissolve the political bands Glenn Miller, Benny Goodman and to assume the powers based on the theory of natural rights, ours not theirs; then it comes to pass that we hold these truths to be self-evident-that all men are created evil, that they are endowed by their Creator with certain

> unavoidable blights, that among these are the
> cities, the politicians, the Nixon years, the
> Johnson years, Mr. Wipple commercials, plague,
> pestilence, famine . . . (48)

An exchange in Act II, scene 2, suggests the pace and depth of the
humor:

> DAVID. [To Larry, who has rescued the family
> home from the repossession men] What did you
> do before you were in the Mafia?
> LARRY. (*Pauses, stares at him.*) I manufactured
> napalm.
> DAVID. (*Becomes hysterical.*) Mother, we can't
> accept his money. It's contaminated. We've got
> to send the walls back!
> OZZIE. Davey, calm down, there are lost of
> peaceful uses of napalm too.
> DAVID. Like what?
> OZZIE. I don't know. Burning crops, heating
> homes, that sort of thing.
> DAVID. This house is evil! (*Larry gets David in
> a neckhold.*)
> LARRY. We got to teach you some manners for
> your elders, sonny boy. Hazel, keep these hot
> cakes *hot.*
> ET. You know, the way that Uncle Larry and
> Davey don't get on is rather like the difficulties
> the generations had getting on in America,
> particularly in the late 60's, Kent State, etc. . .
> (42)

Fifth of July, by Lanford Wilson, was first produced by the Circle
Repertory Company, New York City, in 1978 as *5th of July* and
published in the same year. An edition revised for production in Los
Angeles was published in 1982.

The play occurs on the Talley Place, a farm near Lebanon,
Missouri, during the early evening of Independence Day, 1977, and on
the following morning. The central character is Ken Talley, Jr., a 32-
year-old teacher/disabled veteran who lost both his legs to wounds
suffered in Vietnam. The play centers on Ken's decision to effect his
independence by forgetting his bitterness about his physical condition
and his disappointment at being abandoned by John Landis, his
childhood friend. Through retrospective exposition, we learn that John,

Ken, and Gwen, John's wealthy, racy wife, had, while students at Cal-Berkeley in 1968, been involved in a *ménage a trois*. Their relationships were complicated by Ken's unacknowledged and unrequited love for John. Ken, Gwen, and John had planned for six months before graduation to flee to Europe to avoid the draft. At a critical moment just before graduation, John, wanting to extract himself and Gwen from "the whole steamy situation," tells Gwen than Ken has changed his mind about avoiding the draft. John then persuades Gwen to elope with him. Ken languished in Oakland for nearly three months, then submitted to induction into the army. Ultimately, Ken has to accept the fact that he went into the army in a self-destructive fit of pique designed unconsciously to punish John and Gwen for abandoning him and to confirm his own sense of his identity as a victim. Fortified by newly acquired knowledge of his complicity in his fate, sustained by the loving acceptance of his eccentric aunt and the affection of his lover, Jed, Ken is able to commit himself to a high-school teaching position he has been offered. Just as Ken is able to break his emotional attachment to the losses he has suffered and move on to a stage of new independence, so also do other characters free themselves from disabling emotional fixations. The widowed Aunt Sally is able to scatter the ashes of her husband on Jed's rose garden, while Ken's sister June stages a successful but long-dreaded defense of her right to the custody of her daughter by John Landis.

Wilson's play focuses on the independence of the Vietnam veteran from his self-imposed identity as a victim, but its appeal to the general audience is rooted in the broadly generalizable question of what one does the day after one proudly declares one's independence of disappointments, fears, and loses of the past. How does one cope with freedom and independence after a long history of being incapacitated by soul-deadening wounds?

Here, but three years after American withdrawal from Vietnam, one finds that the emotional wounds of the ten-year conflict have become of a kind with others nearly as debilitating. The corpse of the war is turning to a fertile dust and ash in which poetic impulses can root to produce expressions, such as Durang's and Wilson's, not specifically or pointedly about the war.

Still Life (written 1979, first produced 1980), by Emily Mann, as did Wilson's *Fifth of July*, uses the Vietnam War as a backdrop against which are presented the lineaments of a crucial social issue, violence in the home. The play, a distillation of interviews, takes the form of a tapestry of documents made up of overheard speech that functions less as dramatic dialogue, since the characters speak directly to the audience, than as an extended composition for three voices. The title suggests the "stillness" of a composition rendered without recourse to conventionally confrontational dramatic scenes. It also suggests the cruel life-likenesses that do emerge. Just as the title suggests distinctive formal features of this theatrical piece, it also adroitly calls attention to the primal paradox out of which is generated this culture's blood-soaked past, present, and apparent future. Stillness is the mystery of death with which a materialistic and pragmatic society cannot cope. Life is the equally unfathomable quality with which we cannot deal because of our disabling ignorance of the meaning of death. Mark, a deeply traumatized Vietnam veteran, is an artist who creates assemblages in bottles. His creations express his obsession with violence, but so also does his life with his battered wife, Cheryl, and his affair with Nadine, a woman who gets drunk and beats her husband. Ultimately Mark confesses to the murder of a Vietnamese family, but neither this confession nor Mark's ability to name his friend, R. J., killed in a bank robbery in Chicago, as one of the causalities of Vietnam, suggest that redemption is possible for these characters or for the myriads they represent. The final of many still life slides projected on screens above the characters is of two grapefruits, an orange, a fly on the fruit, a broken egg, and some bread, with a grenade in the center of a dark background. The slide is occasioned by Mark's account of how the Marine Corps rewards a unit with special rations after it has suffered heavy combat losses, and it is the final image left with the audience--an image of an instrument of cruelty and violence in the midst of an image of plenty.

How I Got That Story (1979), by Amlin Gray, is about how the press is co-opted by the events its seeks objectively to represent. The case in point is the Vietnam War. Amlin carries out his mission with but two performers. One plays The Reporter, an eager young man in his twenties, and another portrays The Historical Event, an older man, appearing at times as the entire Event, at other times as people who make up the Event. The playwright's casting notes suggest the Reporter should not appear to be lacking in experience "so much as in connection to experience" (49). He is not unintelligent, but he hasn't the tools to cope with this situation. "He is like a sexologist who retains his virginity in the thought that he will thereby achieve objectivity towards his subject" (50). The action of the play is the enactment of the absorption of the Reporter into the Event, a process paralleled by a large, projected photo of the Reporter which gradually dissolves into a photo of the Event. When the Reporter arrives in Am-Bo Land to begin new job with TransPanGlobal Wire Service, he learns that the press is accredited to report the war only under condition that reports reflect favorably on the host government, headed by Madame Ing.

Mysteriously, a tip on a news story appears in the Reporter's pocket. He goes to a rendezvous where a Buddhist priest immolates himself. The Reporter tries but fails to be objective and to subdue his sense of horror. Later, the Reporter talks to the Reverend Father of the Han Sho Street Pagoda and learns why the monk killed himself. The Reporter writes down the words spoken by the elder priest, but he can't understand them.

He is summoned to an audience with Madame Ing. She "convinces" him that he bribed the monks to burn one of their own, then she dances for him, enacting a Peking Opera version of a war in which the Paramilitary Girl fights and defeats a guerrilla man. The Reporter tries to interview a grunt, but can't learn much except that he has to go into the jungle to learn what the war is really like. He meets the commander of an airborne unit who has learned how to kill and how to swear and a PFC who tells him how to stay alive, where to walk and how to keep from being taken for someone important a sniper might want to shoot. When the Reporter is slightly wounded, he learns that the news service means to exploit his condition in order to increase the value of the copy it can sell. The Reporter refuses to cooperate and tries to leave the country. He misses his plane, but he meets a dope-crazed photographer who has sacrificed a couple of limbs for good pictures. The photographer persuades the Reporter to join him on a bombing mission. They attack, they're hit; the Reporter ejects and gets lost in the jungle. He observes an Ambonese Psychological Warfare Officer introducing villagers to defoliant. The officer washes his face and hands in it, puts it on his rice and, and drinks it. The Reporter is captured by the enemy, then ransomed to the wire service. His bosses plan a series of stories on his capture and rescue, with most of the details invented to make it more exciting and saleable. Movie rights will fetch a big price as well. All the while, the features of the Reporter are being absorbed into those of the Event on the up-stage screen. Sardonic humor abounds in this highly theatrical expose of the flaws of journalistic reporting. The war is, however, but a type of event, albeit the most recent and most obvious one, which exceeds, in its complexity and density, the capacity of objective reporting to ensnare it.

Robert Auletta's *Rundown* was presented at the American Repertory Theatre in Cambridge, Massachusetts in 1982 and was performed in Israel during ART's summer 1982 tour. The play is an account of Pay's passage through a night given over to his effort to "visit his mother," to get back to the source of his being, after having experienced the alienating, disintegrating shock of Vietnam, and of killing so aimlessly while there. His is a journey toward self-forgiveness and re-integration. Pay is afflicted with guilt: "Underneath the guises, all the middle class guises, Lassie dog, and the ol' white frame house. (Pause) I don't trust anybody anymore. . . . Not that I'm any better than the rest of them. No sir. There's blood all over my white frame house soul, too (p. 1-23)."

Along the way he must cope with Spear, a type of anti-war terrorist, one who challenges Pay's motives for letting himself be drafted. Part of the rite of liberating Pay involves the death of his "brother," Spear, and the rejection, by Page, of his "sister/lover," Laure. Laure is a woman toward whom he is attracted and by whom he is repulsed. She seems to be an emblem of all women and all love relationships. Tracer is a "friend," but a nemesis who threatens Pay, victimizes him, and becomes his victim. All the male characters were once members of a group called "The Runaway Boys." This was not a band of the usual sort, however, for their pastime was to walk blindfolded into street and freeway traffic.

Pay's stream of consciousness leads to talk of America changing, just as Pay must, but needing to go through more hell to become "as beautiful as she must." Laure urges Pay to join her in changing the heart of America. Pay declines: "No! The Runaway boys have been blasted out of the air. Fire, rockets, tracers blasting their runaway, rundown, rundown, rundown fucking lives" (1-15).

Pay's nightmare journey toward the hard, dry redemption awaiting him is accomplished in an open, flexible space, designated simply as the "road." It concludes with "I'm not proud of everything I did over there. But I am proud of some things, some service, some selflessness. And I am proud of the men I was with. I'm very proud of them. . . . The book's closed" (2-59). Pay's last monologue to is about his encounter with a disabled male veteran and a woman, also a veteran, making a living as street musicians. Their rendition of "Dixie" is wonderful: "I've never heard that song played that way. It tore through their bodies. It had no mercy on them. But they didn't ask for it. They didn't need it. They had lost the war, but they had won something" (2-59). When he gets to his mother's house, he learns she has died and the funeral has already happened. He gets high and remembers the parties of old: "I mean, in those days: nothing could stop us! Because we came from the heart, straight from the heart! America in all her possibilities lay before us. All her infinite beauty wonder possibilities would soon be ours! . . . It was only later we learned otherwise, different: that the heart is not enough" (2-60). Still later, he sees the street musicians once again, but he "just walked right by."

Stephen Metcalfe's *Strange Snow*, produced at the Manhattan Theatre Club in 1982, carries on the task of integrating the guilt-laden veteran into society rapidly forgetting the conflict that was the source of his guilt. Megs (Joseph Megessey) shows up on David Flanagan's front porch before dawn on a crisp spring day, ostensibly to rouse his old friend from Vietnam for the first day of the trout fishing season. Megs meets Dave's sister, Martha, an emotionally blocked school teacher with a bad self-image. Dave, a truck driver, is a heavy drinker and very hung over this morning. Megs is as prone to self-mutilation (he thrusts his fists through panes of glass) as to cathartic self-revelations. Megs wants to talk about his grief, get it out in the open; Dave wants to hide it in booze. Megs is attracted to Martha and seems to be breaking through her protective facade of shyness and indifference to life. She seldom laughs or cries, she says, though Megs' stories of how he and Dave and Bobby, their best friend and protector who was killed in action, makes her want to do both. The source of the grief Dave and Megs share but cannot assimilate is a combat incident. Their squad is in a helicopter thirty feet over a landing zone, and they have to jump to the ground in the middle of a fierce firefight. Dave is frightened and has to be pushed from the 'copter. He lands wrong and breaks his ankles. Bobby and Megs (he's called "Jackknife" because he wrecks eighteen-wheelers--he's also a crazed, violent killer) have to rescue Dave. Megs is seriously wounded. Bobby saves Dave, and Dave tries to get Bobby to leave Megs behind. Bobby goes back to save Megs and gets killed.

At the end of this opening day, while Megs and Martha are drinking and talking after the dinner Martha has prepared for Megs, Dave, nicknamed "High School" because of his obsession with his own high-school athletic exploits, goes to a bar and picks a fight with a gang of 18-year-old boys. He comes home, bloodied and remorseful. Martha asks Megs to spend the night with her. He refuses at first, exits, then quickly relents, and they play out their fantasy of being seniors at the high school prom. The play ends as snow falls near dawn of the day after the opening of trout season, and Megs and Martha head up the stairs to the bedroom.

If *Strange Snow* appeals at all, it does so because of its implicit nostalgia for the innocence of high school, and for the first opportunities there to be a whole adult. It is nostalgic, too, for the rending, suicidal experiences of a war that at once fragments the young and stunts their growth while promising occasions for the bittersweet shocks thought by romantic youth to confirm one's maturity.

In Larry Kerton's *Asian Shade* (1983) it is June, 1967, and two 20-year-old recruits just out of infantry school, are at home on leave in East Tennessee at the lake house of a wealthy man who has loaned them his place for a fling before they go to Vietnam. They encounter two girls with whom they try to score, but they can't. The wealthy man

promises them a way out of going to Vietnam if he can get an
influential friend at the debarkation point in California to assign them
to Military Police at the post. His efforts fail, and the young men have
to go off to war. One returns in the last scene, a year later, much
changed. He meets the daughter of the wealthy man and seems to be
about to strike up a relationship with her as the play ends. *Asian
Shade* is a diffuse and unsuccessful effort to import the tension of
combat into the waiting to go off to war.

Larry Shue wrote *The Nerd* in 1980. It was first produced in 1981
by the Milwaukee Repertory Theatre, then published in 1987 after a
brief run on Broadway. Rick Steadman, a chalk inspector, comes to
visit Willum Cubbert, an architect, and he stays. Rick had saved
Willum's life in Vietnam, though they hardly knew each other. Now
Rick, thrown out of his home by his brother, comes to Willum, who
feels he must repay his rescuer. Rick, the title character, is hopelessly
inept and impervious to reconstruction. That Rick is a Vietnam veteran
seems a dramaturgical convenience to justify the obligations Willum
feels toward Rick. The play is interesting in the context of an
examination of Vietnam war drama because it features a character who
is a comic fool despite the stigma of Vietnam on him. The popularity
of this play in regional and community theatres all over American is a
testament not only to Shue's mastery of the techniques of the stage
farce, but also to the degree to which the Vietnam veteran and the war
in which he fought has been domesticated.

Tracers was conceived by John DiFusco and created by a group of
actors and one writer, all Vietnam veterans. It is based on personal
experiences first given dramatic form through improvisation, rap
sessions, psychodrama, physical work, and ensemble work. Reports and
transcripts of these sessions were further shaped by DiFusco and writer
Sheldon Lettich. It was performed as a work-in-progress performance
in Los Angeles on July 4, 1980, some three months after the group
started work on the piece. The final form of the play was achieved in
October, 1980. After a lengthy run in Los Angeles, it was produced by
the Steppenwolf Theatre Company of Chicago in January 1984, then by
the Vietnam Veterans Ensemble Theatre Company at the Public
Theatre, New York City, in 1985.

Tracers bears many superficial resemblances to *Viet Rock*. Time
fluctuates between 1980, to a period just after the war, and to moments
during the war. The ensemble speaks a poem as a prologue, ending
with repeated question, "You were there?" The script calls for recorded
music from the eighties and from the sixties. The ensemble does a
dance "which is both an interpretation of the song and a statement of
camaraderie" (6) to "Walkin' on a Thin Line," by Huey Lewis and the

News. Bruce Springsteen's "Shut Out the Light" underscores the beginning and ending of several monologues spoken by characters named Scooter, Little John, Baby San, Dinky Dau, Habu, and The Professor. Scooter dreams of a war in which nobody dies and nobody gets to go home. Little John can't adjust to civilian life. He is restless and alienated, feeling that he was only truly alive in Vietnam. Dinky Dau rages against American women, while acknowledging his drug problem and his fond memories of Vietnamese women. Habu notes that the violence and alienation of rootless high school youth prepares them well for the violence of Vietnam. The rows of red lights he runs in his speeding Camaro are like tracer streaks. The Professor suffers delayed stress syndrome which binds him to painful memories:

In basic training, the recruits encounter an abusive drill instructor to whom they are all "maggots." The DI explains to the draftees: "Ten Percent are fighters. One in one hundred is a warrior. Eighty percent are targets." They realize as does the audience that they will be undertrained and inappropriately equipped and organized to fight a guerrilla war. The troops arrive in Vietnam to the sound of "Fixin' to Die Rag," by Country Joe and the Fish, mixed with Vietnamese music and chopper sound effects. "I lost my sense of judgment yesterday" by Baby San is a prose poem on the shock of initiation into Vietnam and into killing combat. The Rolling Stones' "Sympathy for the Devil" plays under the slow, catlike pantomime of a patrol. Dinky Dau describes contact with the VC and the hyper-brutal celebration of their little victory as they kill eight or nine of the enemy without losing one of their own. In a heroine-induced daze, they watch the tracers and flares around the perimeter of their compound. This is an ironic Fourth of July fireworks display underscored by a rendition of "Yankee Doodle Dandy" and "The Star-Spangled Banner."

The most touching sequence in the play is the Professor's tale of his relationship with the medic, Doc, a classic hippie GI who reads *Steppenwolf*. The Professor gets a rat bite on the finger, for which he must have a series of anti- rabies shots for fourteen days. Doc and The Professor get high and talk about Pirandello's metaphysics.   The Professor explains how he uses meditation and fantasies of the war as opera to keep the experience at a manageable distance. He also avoids friendships, but he continues to visit Doc and they become close friends. When Doc kills himself, the Professor tries to weep but can't. "The 'machine' just refused to shut itself off." The Professor explains that the "machine was a defense mechanism I dreamed up in boot camp. When things got tough, I would just turn my mind off and become a machine."

In a series of monologues set in the future (1984), we learn that the Professor returns to Southeast Asia to get relief from guilt and trauma of war. Little John is dying of cancer from Agent Orange and his children are birth defective. Baby San is a prosperous world traveler, concerned, but not much, about the child he left in Vietnam. Habu is a career Army man with service in Lebanon and the sure knowledge that nothing has changed for the army, which remains "the unwilling led by the uneducated to do the impossible for the ungrateful." He wonders if they'll build another wall in Washington for the kids in Beirut. Dinky Dau excoriates his ex-wives and battles his disabling memories. Scooter, just out of prison, visits the Vietnam Memorial in Washington and tells of his dream of all the boys in his high-school graduating class in body bags. They are reborn, however, and go through a ticker tape parade in the home town. In a surreal scene called "Ambush," all are killed or mutilated. In "The Resurrection (The Ghost Dance)," they are ritually raised from the dead and made whole to pay tribute at the Vietnam Memorial.

   Eleven-Zulu (1983), by Sean Clark, is a murder mystery set in a sandbag bunker in the high country of Vietnam in 1971. The play begins on a gravel path in a public park in the U.S. in 1981. Ten years after the incident featured in the play, Robert Dobbs, one of the survivors of the patrol and now a high school history teacher, is jogging at night, when he is frightened by the play of shadows across his path. The fright stirs intense memories of his experience in Vietnam. He huddles in a near-catatonic state by the side of the path until his wife, Yvonne, a high school guidance counselor, comes out to look for him. They are black.

   Robert tells Yvonne of the day when four men in his squad were killed. His unit (their army job code is Eleven-Zulu for Infantry, Armored Reconnaissance) was on patrol in an armored personnel carrier. Tension mounts with the mysterious death of McKee, a black PFC killed, apparently, by sniper fire after the squad had abandoned its disabled APC and occupied an abandoned French-built bunker on a nearby hill. McKee was on his way from the APC to the bunker when he was hit. Robert was on the way down to the APC at the same time. Later, another black soldier, Jackson, is killed when he discovers and tries to move McKee's body, which has meantime been booby-trapped by the Viet Cong.

   Blame for McKee's death shifts from the VC to the soldier McKee was on guard with, Phillips, a sadistic, racist punk. Phillips hates the squad leader, Sergeant Ruiz, who has caused Phillips to be broken in rank and humiliated for brutally beating a Vietnamese laundry woman. Phillips tries to pin the responsibility for McKee's death on the Latino sergeant. At a particularly tense moment, when they are apparently being stalked by the VC, Phillips provokes Ruiz to fight, then knifes

him. Hoover, a young black soldier then kills Phillips. Dobbs and
Hoover, along with Jonsson and Smitty, a pair of white PFC's, decide
to cover up the deaths by making it look like the men were killed by
VC sappers. They all agree to tell a story that will blame nobody.

At the end of the play, Robert Dobbs is finally able to confront and
reveal the fact that he had killed McKee after mistaking him for an
enemy soldier. He was never able to tell anyone that his mistake
sparked the chain of events leading to the deaths of three more
soldiers.

The play is built on two sources of tension: the threat of a silent
and stealthy enemy who terrifies this squad of boy-soldiers, and the
threat of racial violence which eats as the squad from within. Dobbs'
memories are stimulated by the professional probing of his deeply
concerned wife, who has recognized in her husband a man with a load
of grief and guilt that is about to ruin their marriage and his life. Each
of the other squad members is paired with a woman of memory or
fantasy. Smitty and Jonsson have girl friends back home who think of
them as they read letters from the war zone and who write to them.
Ruiz is obsessed with onanistic fantasies of Christine, a Playboy
centerfold who visits him when he tries in his dim-witted way to plot a
strategy to cope with the squad's dangerous situation. Hoover is
comforted by the ministrations and guided by the moral instructions of
his powerful mother, while Phillips is piqued to new heights of paranoid
hysteria by memories of his emotionally manipulative and overly-
protective mother. Scenes with the women are woven into the texture
of the tightly constructed murder plot, providing relief from its tensions
while offering illuminating views of the psychology of each of the
suspects in the murder case.

The play is especially effective in dramatizing in covert and overt
ways the terror of the boy-soldiers. Clark has infused the fiber of the
murder-mystery with subtle inferences and explicit verbal references to
bodily fluids and substances, the presence of which gives the experience
of the play an immediacy that can only be suggested here. The soldiers
spit and sweat, they urinate, ejaculate, and defecate, they bleed and cry.
The excrescences of the flesh fairly explode through the skin, just as
Robert's long pent-up guilt and self-loathing bursts forth from deep in
his unconscious mind. This is a play, like *Rundown* and *Tracers*, of the
"forgive-and-forget" variety. Like them it sets the price of peace
according to the cost of our recognizing the blind and stupid self-
destructiveness of the Vietnam War.

Lawrence O'Sullivan's *The Grunt Childe* (1984) continues the
project of reconciliation carried on in post-war plays from David Berry's
G. R. Point to Sean Clark's *Eleven-Zulu*. It is one of the most

interesting of the Vietnam war plays--not the best written, but certainly one of the most daring structurally and one of the most exciting, theatrically. It is over-written, too long in the middle. The central character, the Grunt Childe, is a suffering victim rather than an active agent, but his lyrical function is powerfully realized. The chorus of Grunts makes a penetrating statement through their mocking commentary delivered in the army's marching cadence.

> The grunt Childe was our point
> 'Til they bent him outa joint
> Canned his ass an' flagged his file
> Now they got him standin' trial. (1-13)

The play is crafted on the model of Tom Stoppard's *Travesties* in which the characters of Oscar Wilde's *The Importance of Being Earnest* and their apparently pointless fripperies are the theatrical base for exploring the relationship of art and politics. *The Grunt Childe* joins the style of the late-night celebrity talk show with the content of the court-martial of an Army private charged with the murder of a French newswoman and her camera man in a Vietnam war zone. The "grunt," as infantrymen were called in Vietnam, has been charged with a number of serious violations of the Uniform Code of Military Justice. He is cleared of the murder, but found guilty of desertion in the face of the enemy, for which he is executed.

The play features a news media celebrity, Bernard McElroy, who anchors a news program taped in a television studio in Saigon in the last days of the war. The show asks the "Why" of "What Happened Yesterday" in Vietnam. McElroy's guests include two Unites States Senators, one a dove, and one a hawk, as well as a Joyce Brothers-type pop psychologist. The court-martial is convened by General Harold Glaspey; a prosecutor and a counsel for the defense; the defendant, Private Nathaniel Childe (age 19 and "ethereal"); several witnesses, including members of Childe's squad, a chorus of grunts who announce the entrance of each person to the courtroom/television studio by chanting "Incoming, incoming"; military police, stagehands and television production people. Childe seldom speaks, but he often whistles in response to the situation. O'Sullivan says his whistle "should have a haunting quality, a sound which many of us may have heard as children and which evokes what in our youth was warm, comfortable, secure and loving; HE reaches out with love" (1-12).

Act I is called "Sergeant Drummond," after the Special Forces soldier who bursts into the trial/television studio, wearing his Congressional Medal of Honor about his neck, and therefore commanding respect from even the highest ranking officer. Drummond claims he is a witness, though neither the defense nor the prosecution has called him, and he is silent about his reasons for appearing. As the testimony is haltingly brought in, it becomes clear that Childe is a hero, and that he has been extraordinarily stressed by the fatal and grotesque wounding of Private Dudley Watson. Watson and Childe are described by one of the grunts, Medicine Man:

> They were blessed, born of the earth and the four winds. Where they walked, they walked in the center of the universe and all things revolved around them because they became all things, the earth and the four winds, and they carried us through darkness of days of death with their love and magic because they were spirits freed from fear while we were flesh afraid of the dark. (1-27)

Dudley's wounding pitches the squad into a frenzy of revenge, and it's in this mood that they encounter the French journalists. The journalists witness a couple of the grunts "roughing up" a young Vietnamese girl and try to take pictures. Childe tries to stop them; they resist, striking Childe. As he falls in a semi-conscious stupor, a burst from his weapon kills both the journalists (and destroys their camera and the pictures they were taking).

Drummond intercedes in the testimony to explain that Childe saved his life while the two of them were on a secret mission shortly after the deaths of the French journalists. Drummond really speaks to the issue of what kind of war this is, comparing it to World War II, and explaining forcefully that the death of these two journalists is no atrocity at all in comparison to the death of thousands of innocent victims at Hiroshima. Drummond also stages a mock execution of Childe that looks like the famous photo of an ARVN officer executing a Viet Cong prisoner with a single shot to the head. He asks McElroy to play the ARVN officer, gives him a gun that seems to be unloaded, then he reveals to McElroy at the last moment that he has almost killed Childe. After Drummond tells how Childe saved his life, he stages a decoration ceremony in which Childe is given a medal. Childe responds by nearly crushing the hand of the awarding officer in a fierce and demented handshake.

The final episode of the act involves the death of Dudley (enacted by Childe in a straitjacket to emulate the bandages swathing the badly burned Private Dudley). Childe is attended by Nurse Paulson who comforts him by releasing him from the straitjacket and holding him to her bared bosom. The lunatic action of Act I ends with the chaotic exit of all from the studio after the show is disrupted by Nurse Paulson's behavior. The prosecuting officer and Childe are left on stage in pools of light as "the sound of the shepherd's pipe is heard. . . ," a sound associated with Childe.

Act II begins with a scene that functions as does the *parabasis* in the Aristophanic comedy of ancient Greece, where a spokesman for the author makes a naked plea for the political point of view the play is trying to establish in a dramatic, comedic form. Drummond explains that he came back to Vietnam after he saw how the American public has treated the Vietnam veteran: "Me and the grunts have been abandoned by our own country, Counselor, that's why I came back to Vietnam." He explains that press exploitation of the war has given the public "combat fatigue," that the unrelieved exposure of civilians to the horror of war through television reporting is more lethal to the American soldier than the VC and his weapons.

The psychologist interviews Childe who reveals that he "was born in the field out back between the street and way over there when [he] was nine years old . . . , under a crab apple tree. And then, all of a sudden, a golden spider wove a web of wonder about my brow and bit my brain into being. He was a funny-looking little guy. And he was playing a shepherd's pipe" (2-1-62). The grunts then introduce the characters and the trial is resumed. McElroy's updating summary for the television audience makes it clear that he's out to see that Childe is found guilty and executed. The defense counsel objects then goes on to make a case for the dismissal of murder charges against Childe. Gradually the charges are changed until Childe stands accused of desertion, for he left his post to accompany Drummond on the so-called secret mission.

The prosecutor rests his case with an attack on the "mature minds" that lead America into the war, making all of us victims. No soldier should be convicted of committing an atrocity in Vietnam "without calling to account the mature minds which bent their young minds to murder, . . ." (2-1-81).

The Senators make brief, self-serving speeches, then pronounce Childe guilty and consent to his execution on television. Nobody wants to pull the trigger. However, Drummond is ordered to administer the *coup de grace*, and he follows his orders. Drummond persuades the grunts to function as a firing squad, then he rushes into the line of fire at the last instant and is killed. Word comes that the peace talks have ended and the President has ordered the complete and immediate withdrawal of all American forces from Vietnam. The "Red Bird" helicopter comes to get the grunts, who are seen in a final tableau, with Childe, who cradles Drummond in his arms. *The Grunt Childe* is a brash and risky effort to imbue military characters caught in the coils of self-serving politicos and media stars with a heroism neither tragic nor mocking.

James Duff's *Home Front* was first produced under the title, *The War at Home*, in London in 1984. Its New York premiere was January 2, 1985. The story line and tone of the play reminds one of *Sticks and Bones*, though the stylization of *Home Front* is nearly hyper-realistic.

Home Front takes place in the Collier home in suburban Dallas-Fort Worth on Thanksgiving Eve and Thanksgiving Day. Contempt for the life style represented by the Colliers exudes from the author's description of the setting: "residential sprawl," "fortress fencing," "somewhere, mercifully not visible on-stage, a black velvet portrait of a gored Mexican bullfighter." A bookcase filled with Reader's Digest Condensed Books is an emblem of superficiality; a full set of World Book Encyclopedia betokens the family's hopeful but misguided effort to provide the trimmings of a full and effective education for the children. The kitchen, visible upstage through a pass-through window at first shuttered away from view, is "beautifully tiled and papered, . . . highly polished and extremely well-kept," which alerts us to the emotional repressiveness pervading family life in this house.

Jeremy is a 23-year old Vietnam veteran making a very difficult readjustment to life with his family. He brawls with his mother over his dress and demeanor and with his father about his failure to get a job. At the end of this predictable rehearsal of well-known characters in situations long ago drained of their dramatic potential, Jeremy, who had been ordered to execute a prisoner of war in Vietnam, puts a gun to his father's chest and pulls the trigger. The weapon misfires. The father orders Jeremy out of the house, then explains to Jeremy's distraught mother how they'll live down this moment: "We'll just forget about it. We'll forget about it and go on." His words would seem to suggest Duff's sense of the position taken by the American public by 1985 as regards the Vietnam War and its victims.

Works Cited

Asahina, Robert. "The Basic Training of American Playwrights: Theater and the Vietnam War," *Theater*, 9, ii (1978):30-37.

Auletta, Robert. *Rundown*. Manuscript circulated by *Plays in Process*. New York: Theatre Communications Group, Inc., 1982.

Balk, H. Wesley. *The Dramatization of 365 Days*. Based on the book *365 Days*, by Ronald J. Glasser, M.D. Minneapolis: University of Minnesota Press, 1972.

Berrigan, Daniel. *The Trial of the Catonsville Nine*. New York: Samuel French, Inc., 1971.

Berry, David. *G. R. Point*. New York: Dramatists Play Service, Inc., 1980.

Brown, Edward G. "The Teatro Campesino's Vietnam Trilogy," *Minority Voices*, 4:2 (Spring 1980): 29- 38.

Clark, Sean. *Eleven-Zulu*. New York: Samuel French, Inc., 1984.

Cole, Tom. *Medal of Honor Rag*. New York: Samuel French, Inc., 1977.

Cowan, Ron. *Summertree*. New York: Dramatists Play Service, Inc., 1968.

DiFusco, John. *Tracers*. New York: Hill and Wang, 1986. Conceived by DiFusco; written by original cast: Vincent Caristi, Richard Chaves, John DiFusco, Eric E. Emerson, Rick Gallavan, Merlin Marston, Harry Stephens, and Sheldon Lettich.

Duff, James. *Home Front*. New York: Dramatists Play Service, Inc., 1985.

Durang, Christopher. *The Vietnamization of New Jersey*. New York: Dramatists Play Service, Inc., 1978.

Garson, Barbara. *Mac Bird!* New York: Evergreen Press, 1966.

Gray, Amlin. *How I Got That Story*. Revised edition. New York: Dramatists Play Service, Inc., 1981.

Guare, John. *Muzeeka*. New York: Dramatists Play Service, Inc., 1968.

Kerton, Larry. *Asian Shade*. New York: Dramatists Play Service, Inc., 1983.

Kopit, Arthur. *Indians*. New York: Bantam Books, 1971. Includes "A Dialogue with Arthur Kopit and John Lahr, theatre critic of *The Village Voice*."

Linney, Romulus. *The Love Suicide at Schofield Barracks* and *Democracy and Esther*. New York: Harcourt Brace Jovanovich, Inc., 1973.

McNally, Terrence. *Bringing It All Back Home*. New York: Dodd, Mead & Company, 1976.

-----. *Tour*. In *Collision Course*, Ed. Edward Parone New York: Vintage Books, 1969; *Next* and *Botticelli* appear in Terrence McNally, *Sweet Eros, Next, and Other Plays*. New York: Random House, 1969.

Mann, Emily. *Still Life*. In *New Plays USA 1*, ed. James Leverett. New York: Theatre Communications Group, Inc., 1982.

Metcalfe, Stephen. *Strange Snow*: New York: Samuel French, Inc., 1983.

O'Sullivan, Lawrence. *The Grunt Childe*. Manuscript circulated as *Plays in Process*. New York: Theatre Communications Group, Inc., 1984.

Rabe, David. *The Basic Training of Pavlo Hummel* and *Sticks and Bones*. New York. Viking Press, Inc., 1973.

-----. *Streamers*. New York: Alfred A. Knopf, 1977.

Ragni, Gerome, and James Rado. *Hair*. Music by Galt McDermott. New York: Pocket Books, 1969.

Shue, Larry. *The Nerd*. Garden City, N.Y.: Nelson Doubleday, Inc., 1987.

Terry, Megan. *Viet Rock: A Folk War Movie*. Music by Marianne de Pury. Produced 1966 at Cafe La Mama Experimental Theatre Club, New York. Published New York: Simon and Schuster, 1967.

Valdez, Luis. *Dark Root of the Scream*. In *From the Barrio: A Chicano Anthology*, Ed. Omar Salinas and Lillian Faderman. San Francisco: Canfield, 1973.

-----. *Soldado Razo*. In *Actos*. San Juan Bautista, California: Menyah Productions, 1971).

------. *Vietnam Campesiño*. In *Actos*. San Juan Bautista, California: Menyah Productions, 1971; and in *Guerilla Street Theatre*, Ed. Henry Lesnick . New York: Bard Books, 1973.

Weller, Michael. *Moonchildren*, authorized, revised edition. New York: New American Library, 1982.

Wilson, Lanford. *Fifth of July*. New York: Dramatists Play Service, 1982.

TELLING IT LIKE IT WAS: THE NONFICTION
LITERATURE OF THE VIETNAM WAR

Jacqueline E. Lawson

In a review published in the June 1984 issue of *Harper's* magazine, C. D. B. Bryan, author of the critically-acclaimed Vietnam narrative *Friendly Fire*, tried to "get a bead" on a small but distinguished body of personal narratives produced by the veterans of the Vietnam war.[1] Of the eight books Bryan reviewed, five were works of witness-bearing of varying types (memoirs, oral histories, anthologies), one of which--Ron Kovic's searing autobiographical memoir *Born on the Fourth of July* (1976)--was already out of print. Among the handful of nonfiction narratives showcased in Bryan's review were Ron Glasser's *365 Days* (1971), an anthology of "true sketches" drawn from Glasser's experiences as an Army physician at an evac hospital in Japan[2]; Philip Caputo's *Rumor of War* (1977), one of the most self-consciously literary of the war's memoirs, borrowing chapter epigrams from sources as disparate as Shakespeare and Siegfried Sassoon; Michael Herr's *Dispatches* (1977), a *tour de force* of war reportage culled from Herr's 1967 "tour" in Vietnam as an *Esquire* correspondent; and Mark Baker's oral history *Nam* (1981), a compendium of transcribed interviews aimed at bringing Vietnam to life through "the words of the men and women who fought there." After remarking on the excruciating intensity of these works, an intensity "similar to that which pervades the literature of the Holocaust," Bryan summed up his feelings about this remarkable body of war narratives: "the voice of Vietnam literature," he declared, "is that of a barely suppressed scream. . . . one is always conscious of the authors' efforts to stay calm, to contain the shriek" (71). This is the best description of Vietnam's nonfiction canon that has been written to date and Bryan is to be credited, among other achievements, for getting precisely the right "bead" on one of the most riveting bodies of texts to emerge from the war.

Readers approaching this body of narratives for the first time are advised to suspend prior judgment about what war memoirs are or ought to be. These works are manifestly more than mere war stories; they are meditations on culture, personal reflections on illusions lost and myths shattered, elegies to the American dream. They are dirges to lost innocence, the intimate and often anguished reflections of the youngest, and without question, most idealistic group of soldiers America has ever sent off to war. These adolescent soldiers hailed from places like rural Minnesota, inner-city Brooklyn, and suburban Westchester, Illinois. As kids, they launched commando raids in their neighborhoods, waged imaginary battles in their backyards, and spent Saturday afternoons at the movies, watching wide-eyed as John Wayne and Audie Murphy played out the decisive battles of World War II. They learned about war from their fathers in the patriotic milieu of the fifties; they were "the offspring of the great campaign against the tyrants of the 1940's . . . fed by the spoils of 1945 victory" (O'Brien 20). The America of their childhood was prosperous, strong, and invincible, and they were its soldiers-in-waiting: they "joined the cub scouts and marched in parades on Memorial Day, made contingency plans for the cold war and built fallout shelters out of milk cartons" (Kovic 56). Young, restless, and fed on the myths of America's heroic past, they readied themselves for their country's next war, and when the call to arms finally came, delivered by America's most youthful and charismatic president, the youngest combatants in America's history--average age, 19.2 years--were ready to play out their fantasies in the jungles of Vietnam. In the words of Philip Caputo, "we went overseas full of illusions, for which the intoxicating atmosphere of those years was as much to blame as our youth" (Caputo xiv). These youthful apprentice soldiers left for Vietnam without literary pretensions and with no desire to publicize their experiences. They returned to 'the World' disillusioned, haunted, and angry--determined to tell the truth about this war, to tell it like it was.

I

Like the progress of the war itself, veterans' accounts of the war emerged in singularly strategic stages: they began appearing sporadically, as though in an advisory capacity, in the mid-to late-sixties; escalated with increasing urgency throughout the seventies; and have since undergone a veritable explosion, proliferating at so rapid a rate that new titles are appearing faster than scholars can catalogue them. Indeed, so marked has been the recent proliferation of "true" stories about the war that we can now confidently speak of a large and well-established canon of Vietnam narratives, a body of works whose range and diversity encompass virtually every aspect of the war.

Some of the most interesting if neglected narratives emerged during the earliest years of America's presence in Vietnam, carving out the broad parameters of the canon and introducing the distinctive style and tone that would come to mark the best of the war's later nonfiction writing. Among these early works are Richard Tregaskis's *Vietnam Diary* (1963), a civilian writer's eyewitness account of the role of American military advisors in Vietnam during the pivotal years of the war's build-up[3]; David Parks's *G.I. Diary* (1965), the first view of the ground war by a black American infantryman; John Sack's *M* (1966), a journalistic compilation of scenes from the war, many of which have the surreal, disjointed quality we have come to associate with Michael Herr's *Dispatches*; and Bill Adler's *Letters From Vietnam* (1967), the first published collection of letters from the war zone. Published at the end of the decade were Ward Just's *To What End?* (1968), Martin Russ's *Happy Hunting Ground* (1968), and Charles Coe's *Young Man in Vietnam* (1968), three works of witness-bearing by reporters or veterans who served in the critical years of the war's escalation phase; two "real battle" accounts, *West to Cambodia* (1968) and *Ambush* (1969), by noted military historian S. L. A. Marshall; and Larry Hughes's soldier-memoir, *You Can See a Lot Standing under a Flare in the Republic of Vietnam* (1969).

When judged by the rigorous standards of literary exegesis these pioneering texts--with the notable exception of Sack's *M*--do not represent a seminal achievement in the canon as a whole. Unpolished, unsophisticated, and primitive--most are leagues away from the searching and self-reflective chronicles of the later period--they provide little in the way of personal introspection or narrative probing into the "hows" and "whys" of the war. Few succeeded in capturing an audience when they were first published, and most went quickly out of print. Yet these works are important and those that are currently unavailable ought to be reissued, if not for their analytic impact (most are merely encyclopedic compilations of factual data rather than works of reflective narration) then simply because they are the first body of eyewitness accounts to document, factually and largely from the perspective of the foot soldier, the earliest and arguably most critical phase of America's growing military presence in Vietnam. What emerges most distinctly from these works is an unfiltered ground-level portrait of what Tregaskis had prophetically described in October of 1962 as "the strange, off-beat, new-style war in which we find ourselves engaged in the miserable little jungle country called Vietnam."[4] As the war's first chroniclers were at pains to demonstrate, even from its earliest phase, Vietnam gave every appearance of being a different kind of war, a war that was as young, brash, and unconventional as those who would fight it, a war that would demand new forms of narrative assessment and appraisal, a war worth writing about.

The following decade saw a steady increase in both the quantity and quality of Vietnam narratives. The seventies produced an impressive array of personal narratives, most of them memoirs, and it was during this fertile period in the canon's development that some of the most durable and acclaimed works emerged. Among the books published during this period were Ron Glasser's *365 Days* (1971), one of the war's most harrowing narratives, mentioned in Bryan's review for its unforgettable scenes of wounded boys screaming; Charles Anderson's *The Grunts* (1976), a no-frills "grunt's-eye" view of the ground war ("Nam. Bravo Company. The Real Story"); Bryan's own *Friendly Fire* (1976), an exposé of the death of Michael Eugene Mullen, killed in an artillery strike called down by his own forces; Benjamin F. Schemmer's *The Raid* (1976), an account of the Army's unsuccessful attempt to free seventy American POWs from the Son Tay Prison Camp; and Frederick Downs' *The Killing Zone* (1978), a gritty personal narrative chronicling a year in the bush with infantry platoon Delta One-Six. These works from the canon's "middle range"[6] deserve mention, especially since they have been so vastly overshadowed by the other narratives produced in the seventies.

Also published during this period were four of the war's most highly-acclaimed memoirs, works which have continued to occupy a central place in the hearts and minds of scholars, teachers, and students intent on "getting a bead" on the lessons of the Vietnam war. These are Tim O'Brien's eloquent soldier-memoir *If I Die in a Combat Zone* (1973), portions of which first appeared in magazines and newspapers between 1969 and 1972; Ron Kovic's *Born on the Fourth of July* (1976), one of the most heartbreaking texts to emerge from the war, written in the tradition of Dalton Trumbo's *Johnny Got His Gun*; Philip Caputo's stylized remembrance *A Rumor of War* (1977); and Michael Herr's *Dispatches* (1977), a text which defies conventional categorization[6]. These four works, to which I will return, mark the apogee of the war's literary achievement. They are the acknowledged "classics" of the Vietnam war, the works which set the standard for Vietnam's nonfiction canon, the works most frequently taught, discussed, analyzed, and cited, and the works whose influence can clearly be seen in the avalanche of diaries, journals, memoirs, chronicles, anthologies, oral histories, textbooks, films, and television series with which we have been inundated in recent years.

Over the past decade the number of nonfiction narratives has grown exponentially, swelling the number of available titles and significantly altering the canon's range. The eighties have not only witnessed a proliferation of personal accounts of the war but have also seen a concomitant narrowing of their scope as authors and editors have self-consciously sought for their texts a more specialized identity. Thus, we now have memoirs whose aims are overtly polemical (W. D. Ehrhart's *Passing Time*, 1985); memoirs by wounded veterans (Rick Eilert's *For Self and Country*, 1983); memoirs by Army nurses (Lynda Van Devanter's *Home Before Morning*, 1983); POW memoirs (Jim and Sybil Stockdale, *In Love and War*, 1984); memoirs by Medal of Honor winners (Timothy S. Lowry, *And Brave Men, Too*, 1985); after-the-war memoirs (Joe Klein, *Payback*, 1984); return-to-Vietnam memoirs (William Broyles, Jr., *Brothers in Arms*, 1986); memoirs from every service branch (Shelby L. Stanton's *Green Berets at War*, 1985; Zalin Grant's *Over the Beach: The Air War in Vietnam*, 1986, and Frank Camper's *L.R.R.P., The Professional*, 1988); great battle narratives (Robert Pisor's *The End of the Line: The Siege of Khe Sanh*, 1982); true adventure narratives (Jack Broughton's *Thud Ridge*, 1985); tactical duty narratives (Ralph Zumbro's *Tank Sergeant*, 1986, and Robert Mason's *Chickenhawk*, 1983); collected letters from the war zone (Bernard Edelman's *Dear America: Letters Home from Vietnam*, 1985), the home front, and the Wall (Laura Palmer's *Shrapnel in the Heart*, 1987); and oral histories of black veterans (Wallace Terry's *Bloods*, 1984), women veterans (Keith Walker's *A Piece of My Heart*, 1985), even veterans from Oklahoma (Stanley W. Beesley's *Vietnam: The Heartland Remembers*, 1987).[7] Clearly, literary production on the war in Vietnam has burgeoned into a thriving industry, and the veterans' personal narratives have contributed in large measure to the public's growing fascination with Vietnam.

While this outpouring of new titles has succeeded in popularizing the Vietnam narrative--thereby granting to the war's stories the recognition denied to the war's returning veterans--the sheer size of the canon inevitably creates problems, not the least of which is market saturation. With scores of veterans now publishing their memoirs, it is becoming difficult to differentiate between works and "Vietnam, the true story" is currently in danger of falling victim to its own success. Moreover, the canon's proliferation creates additional problems, especially for scholars wishing to use selected texts as a means of studying or teaching the war. How are we to distinguish quality in a canon numbering well over one hundred titles and proliferating at the rate of several new volumes a day? What constitutes a "good" Vietnam narrative? Have demonstrably "bad" works been published? Finally, what importance do these texts hold for a generation of young Americans born while the war was still raging and for whom Vietnam signifies little more than a night at the movies with Rambo? These are some of the questions raised by these texts that the remainder of this study will attempt to address.

II

Vietnam's nonfiction literature falls roughly into three generic categories: works of confession and meditation (memoirs), of wartime witness (diaries, journals, chronicles), and of post-war remembrance, both individual and collective (oral histories and letters). The most successful of these is the Vietnam memoir. Meditative in tone, narrated by a single speaker, and spanning both the pre-war and post-war experience, the Vietnam memoir is an autobiographical account of personal experience that seeks to place Vietnam in a larger context of myth, culture, memory, and meaning. Of the works in this genre, most are overtly didactic, many are polemical, and almost all put forth an anti-war message. These memoirs hold out a warning, to the next generation of veterans, of what war is and what it does. Exemplary texts the combat memoirs of Tim O'Brien, Ron Kovic, and Philip Caputo, Michael Herr's *Dispatches*, and a number of lesser-known but no less powerful works, among them two memoirs by noted Vietnam poet-veteran W. D. Ehrhart, *Vietnam-Perkasie*: *A Combat Marine Memoir* (1983) and *Passing Time* (1986), and John Ketwig's *And A Hard Rain Fell* (1985), one of the war's most underrated memoirs.

The impetus behind virtually every Vietnam memoir is personal catharsis, the overwhelming need on the part of the war's veterans not merely to tell their story but to expunge the memories, to exorcise the demons, to free themselves from "a world of hurt." Accordingly, many of the texts open with an emotionally-laden personal confession, often taking the form of an apologia: "I didn't set out to write a book. I've never written more than an occasional letter to the editor in my life. My twisted insides had spawned ulcers. The nightmares were more frequent. I needed to get Vietnam out into the open . . ." (Ketwig xi). For John Ketwig, as for so many of Vietnam's veterans, writing about the war marked the first step on the road to healing, "like squeezing pus out of an infected wound" (Ketwig xii). The wounds of Vietnam continue to fester. The need of America's veterans to "assimilate the realities of Vietnam" (Ketwig xiii) reflects our nation's larger need to understand what the war did to all of us. Reading the veterans' accounts can thus be a means of expiating our nation's sins, of confronting our collective responsibility, not only for our conduct in the war but for our conduct toward its warriors. The veterans' anguish is also our own, and reliving their memories can help "bring our nation closer to a diagnosis and a cure" (Ketwig xiii).

At its best, the Vietnam memoir has a transcendent quality that places the narrative beyond the wartime experience it centrally describes. What distinguishes the works of O'Brien, Kovic, Caputo, and Herr from the scores of Vietnam memoirs published over the past twenty years is these writers' ability to see, not the war, but rather their own delusions about the war--and ultimately their own complicity in it-- as the catalyst for the anguish, rage, and despair that is so much a hallmark of the canon as a whole. The war's best memoirs are not really *about* Vietnam at all. They are about America, about young boys coming of age in a nation that believed too much in itself; they are about life in the fifties, about growing up and growing old. They are narratives of de-initiation and deculturation in which the narrator's adolescent quest for identity is abruptly truncated, propelling him from a dream-marked boyhood to a premature middle age.

A number of memoirs, like W. D. Ehrhart's *Passing Time*, begin on a stirring note of adolescent optimism: "I'd enlisted in the Marines in the Spring of 1966 with visions of brass bands, victory parades, free drinks in bars, and starry-eyed girls clinging to my neck like so many succulent grapes" (Ehrhart 8). Yet virtually all end with an embittered cry of anguish, the dirge to lost innocence that was the requiem of the war: "I knew at last that nothing I had ever done in Vietnam would ever carry with it anything but shame and disgrace and dishonor; that I would never be able to recall Vietnam with anything but pain and anger and bitterness; that I would never again be able to take pride in being an American. And the rage and sorrow and tragedy of it all was overwhelming" (Ehrhart 247). Vietnam was a war that robbed its soldiers of their ideals, illusions, convictions, and above all, their youth. As Caputo remarks in *A Rumor of War*, "I was left with none of the optimism and ambition a young American is supposed to have, only . . . an old man's conviction that the future would hold no further surprises, good or bad" (Caputo 4). Thus, it is a sense of loss, and anger over this loss, that gives these memoirs their narrative power. "None of us was a hero," notes Caputo, "we would not return to cheering crowds, parades, and the pealing of great cathedral bells. We had done nothing more than endure. We had survived, and that was our only victory" (Caputo 320).

A second, and comparatively less effective category of narrative, are chronicles of a type that can best be characterized as "gung-ho." Included in this group are a number of the great battle, true adventure, and tactical duty narratives cited earlier.[8] More constricted in scope, less self-reflective in tone, these works tend to privilege the combat experience and are less explicitly concerned with using that experience to derive lessons, draw conclusions, or relate the war in any meaningful way to the larger cultural forces that produced it. At their worst, these works present a distorted view of the war, leaving readers with the mistaken impression that the war in Vietnam consisted chiefly of a series of "big battles" and sweeping strategic maneuvers; moreover, many tend to be self-aggrandizing, overtly racist and sexist, and exploitive of the war. Yet works of this type bear mentioning because there are so many of them; they are easy to spot on bookstore shelves since most are published by popular mass-market presses, endorsed by military bookclubs and carry titles like *Marine Sniper*, "The Explosive True Story of a Vietnam Hero. 93 Confirmed Kills." Perhaps the most commercially successful of this category of narrative is the Vietnam "trilogy" by Michael Lee Lanning: *The Only War We Had: A Platoon Leader's Journal of Vietnam* (1987), *Vietnam, 1969-1970: A Company Commander's Journal* (1988), and *Inside the LRRPS: Rangers in Vietnam* (1988), all published by Ballantine Books. Scholars interested in researching or teaching the war are urged to read Lanning's works, if only as a means of assessing the vastly disparate range in the quality of the war's nonfiction literature; one might even consider adopting one or more of his texts for classroom use, to be read mainly for comparative purposes in conjunction with O'Brien, Kovic, and Caputo.

A third type of narrative that has gained in popularity in recent years is the oral history, a collection of transcribed interviews that have been professionally edited and strategically arranged, often around the war's familiar calendar, the 365 days that constituted every participant's tour of duty in Vietnam. Editors of oral histories have relied heavily on this organizational structure, since the one-year tour of duty provides a convenient way to frame a large and disparate body of material. Mark Baker's *Nam: The Vietnam War in the Words of the Men and Women Who Fought There*, published in 1981, is paradigmatic of the genre. Baker's text consists of over 175 transcriptions of interviews with Vietnam veterans, the longest running nearly ten pages, the shortest only two or three sentences. All of these "histories" are anonymous, although a careful reader can distinguish the speaker's gender, race, and even home state, since the transcriptions have sought to retain as much of the speaker's individual identity (accent, inflection) as possible. Baker's text is less a series of personal reminiscences than a tightly controlled, highly selective archive of the war's "major" events and "important" subjects, arranged chronologically from "Initiation" to "The World." The text is further sub-divided into eight smaller categories designed to illustrate distinct stages, themes, and phases of the war. Thus, Section I, Initiation, consists of two "chapters," "Ask Not . . ." and "Baptism of Fire" and encompasses pre-induction, boot camp, and the initiation into war; Section II, "Grunts" and "Martial Arts," seeks to replicate the combat experience; while Sections III and IV, "Victors" and "Victims," "Homecoming" and "Casualties" describe the end of the tour and coming home.[9] While these divisions are useful in providing an overview of the Vietnam experience, from pre-induction to the war's aftermath, overall, such categories are artificial, especially since all of the interviews in Baker's text have been pre-selected and heavily edited.

Perhaps the most successful oral history is Kim Willenson's *The Bad War*, published in 1987 by *Newsweek* magazine. With the assistance of *Newsweek's* Southeast Asia correspondents, Willenson has compiled an exhaustive cross-section of interviews with Vietnam veterans, journalists, government officials, North and South Vietnamese civilians and combatants,[10] American college students and even anti-war protestors. Willenson's work is one of the most ambitious and balanced attempts to historicize the war through oral remembrance and thus may be an effective teaching aid, particularly since it contains a useful "Vietnam Chronology" and a comprehensive index. Of related interest is Bernard Edelman's *Dear America: Letters Home From Vietnam* (1985), collected correspondence of American veterans. Edelman's text suffers from many of the same problems as Baker's *Nam*, notably its insistence on treating the war as a highly readable "story" complete with chapter headings, such as "Cherries: First Impressions," "Humping the Boonies," "Beyond the Body Count," and so forth. Nonetheless, *Dear America* is a moving testament to the homesickness of the American combatant in Vietnam, and it does succeed in capturing a unique dimension of the war not presented in some oral histories. Edelman's text has recently been made into a film and could easily be incorporated into a course on the war; some viewers, however, may feel that the film lacks much of the power of the original text.

III

While these generic differences bear noting they should not be overemphasized, for despite its range and diversity the most striking feature of the canon as a whole is its remarkable homogeneity. The hallmark of Vietnam's nonfiction literature is its overriding uniformity--of structure, tone, aim, purpose, and above all, of experience. Individually, the Vietnam narrative is an intensely personal statement written out of each veteran's desperate need to give shape, definition, meaning, and purpose to an experience that was, for most of the war's participants, inscrutable, surreal, fragmented, terrifying, devoid of meaning and filled with anguish. Collectively these works offer a numbing recital of the heat, stench, boredom, exhaustion, carnage, terror, and exhilaration that were the common denominators of the war.

The texts themselves are largely formulaic. The Vietnam narrative has recognizable antecedents in the bildungsroman, a novel of initiation tracing a youthful protagonist's search for meaning and identity in a terrifying and alien world. The conventional bildungsroman follows a young male on a mythic journey from innocence to experience, a rite of passage fraught with peril though out of which comes acceptance by the adult world. Not surprisingly, the bildungsroman has been the favored vehicle of generations of war chroniclers from Homer to Stephen Crane,[11] the trials of the battlefield providing, in literature as in life, the mythic rite of passage from boyhood to manhood. Yet while appropriating the bildungsroman's contours, the Vietnam narrative baldly subverts its aims, reshaping the traditional quest for meaning to suit *its* war's essential meaninglessness.

The Vietnam narrative traces a process of deterioration, an erosion of belief and a disintegration of illusion experienced by nearly all the war's participants. In the words of W. D. Ehrhart, "From the time I was a little boy, I'd wanted a medal. A Red Badge of Courage. A sign that I was a hero in the company of Stephen Decatur and Alvin York. Now that I had them, what did they mean? I could never hang them on my wall in a tasteful wooden display case, tacitly saying to friends and visitors, 'Look, this is what I've done for my country; this is the man I am.' I could never be proud of them" (*Passing Time* 171).

As its veterans are at pains to remind us, Vietnam was a shatteringly different war from what they had been led to expect and the events recounted in the pages of their narratives bear about as much resemblance to *The Sands of Iwo Jima* as America's teenaged soldiers did to John Wayne. "We didn't have no flame throwers. I didn't see no tanks in Saigon," recalls a speaker in Mark Baker's *Nam*. "They didn't have things like you see in the movies on TV about World War II. It surprised me. I was expecting for the tank to come up there and do the John Wayne type of things" (Baker 83). As its soldiers quickly discovered, Vietnam was not World War II and "the John Wayne type of things," allusions which run like a torrent through the veterans' narratives, were fictive images that had no place in a guerrilla war. "There were no Normandies or Gettysburgs for us," observes Caputo, "no epic clashes that decided the fates of armies or nations" (Caputo xiv). Vietnam was a war of body counts and kill ratios, of "enduring weeks of expectant waiting and, at random intervals, of conducting vicious manhunts through jungles and swamps where snipers harassed us constantly and booby traps cut us down one by one" (Caputo xiv, xv). The war limned its own reality, a reality in sinister opposition to the myths which informed it. As another of *Nam's* speakers recalls, "[the war] shattered my whole image of the United States, of freedom and democracy, of the world we live in, all the ideals I had gone to Vietnam with. The sacrifice was a lie" (Baker 310). The veteran's bitterness is characteristic and says much about this war's power to undermine belief. Thus, the bildungsroman's mythic journey from innocence to experience is subverted in these narratives, replaced by a terrifying movement from naivete to cynicism.

There is an addictive quality to this body of narratives that distinguishes them from the more imaginative depictions of the war. As their authors persistently remind us, these stories are "true" and because they are "true" we are compelled to keep reading them. To read a number of Vietnam narratives is to be assaulted by a riot of voices all speaking the same language, all describing the same feelings, all enduring the same conditions, all serving the same time--in effect, all saying the same thing. Thus, it is the war's grinding sameness, even more than its differences, that gives this canon its essential cohesion. The voices that resonate in text after text are haunted, wounded, lyrical and angry, a greek chorus of 'old kids' whose memories of the war will break your heart and make you wince. Memoirist John Ketwig recalling the terror and loneliness of his first firefight: "Thousands of guys were kneeling in the mud, peering into the shadows and awaiting death . . . .To my left a voice cut through the damp fog. 'Holy Mary, Mother of God . . .' Were the others as scared as I?" (Ketwig 61); paralyzed veteran Ron Kovic, "cr[ying] inside for a woman, any woman, to lie close to him" (Kovic 120); author Tim O'Brien, pausing in the midst of his reveries to pay tribute to a fallen comrade: "He died in such a way that, for once, you could never know his color. He was wrapped in a plastic body bag, we popped smoke, and a helicopter took him away, my friend" (O'Brien 125). The power of Vietnam's meditative literature lies in its cumulative narrative impact, the steady accretion of fact and detail that serve to corroborate for the reader the terrible "truths" held out by these texts. In the words of Tim O'Brien,

> Now, war ended, all I am left with are simple, unprofound scraps of truth. Men die. Fear hurts and humiliates. It is hard to be brave. It is hard to know what bravery *is*. Dead human beings are heavy and awkward to carry. . . .Is that the stuff for a morality lesson, even for a theme? Do dreams offer lessons? Do nightmares have themes, do we awaken and analyze them and live our lives and advise others as a result? Can the foot soldier teach anything important about war, merely for having been there?. . . He can tell war stories. (O'Brien 31, 32)

O'Brien's meditation is a fitting epilogue to a war whose lessons we have only begun to learn. Through their remembrances of the war, Vietnam's veterans are helping to teach these lessons. As Bill Ehrhart has remarked, "If I could use my experience to convince others that the war had to end. . .if I could keep others from having their lives shipwrecked and their dreams and bodies and minds broken, if I could help my country regain its moral balance, its perspective on itself, and Vietnam and the world--then, perhaps, in some small but real way, my own experience might gain some positive meaning after all" (Ehrhart 247). In the personal narratives of Vietnam's veterans reside the "truths" that may prevent another generation of Americans from fighting the next war.

Notes

1. C. D. B. Bryan, "Barely Suppressed Screams: Getting a bead on Vietnam War literature," *Harper's*, June, 1984: 67-72.

2. For further discussion of Glasser's text see Philip D. Beidler, *American Literature and the Experience of Vietnam* (Athens, Georgia: The University of Georgia Press, 1982), pp. 24, 27, 87, 98-99. Although Beidler is one of the few scholars to accord *365 Days* close critical attention, he inexplicably refers to the work as a collection of "short fiction" (87), despite the fact that Glasser is at pains in his Foreword to emphasize that "the stories . . . here are true" (xi). I have suggested elsewhere that the work is an oral history, in the same genre as Mark Baker's *Nam* and Al Santoli's *Everything We Had*, see "'Old Kids': The Adolescent Experience in the Nonfiction Literature of the Vietnam War" in *Search and Clear: Critical Responses to Selected Literature and Films of the Vietnam War*, ed. William J. Searle (Bowling Green, Ohio: The Popular Press, 1988), pp. 26-36. Technically, neither of us is correct since what Glasser seems to have assembled is a work of "new journalism," a series of "true sketches" drawn from fact but presented as fiction. The problem of reliability, and the related problem of genre-typing, in texts which purport to be authentic is endemic to Vietnam's nonfiction canon and will no doubt continue to be a major source of difficulty for scholars working in this field.

3. Tregaskis is the author of a number of wartime accounts, including the celebrated World War II chronicle, *Guadalcanal Diary*.

4. Cited in *Vietnam Voices: Perspectives on the War Years 1941-1982*, compiled by John Clark Pratt, (New York: Penguin Books, 1984), p. 113.

5. Beidler identifies three distinct "movements" in the emergence of the war's literature: Early Writing, 1958-1970; the Middle Range, 1970-1975; and the New Literature, 1975-1982, and his discussion of the texts follows this chronology. His study encompasses a wide range of the war's literature, including novels, poetry, and drama. For a more recent survey of the Vietnam canon see Tom Myers' *Walking Point: American Narratives of Vietnam*, (New York and Oxford: Oxford University Press, 1988), which treats many texts published since 1982.

6. Since its appearance in 1977, Michael Herr's *Dispatches* (New York, Alfred A. Knopf) has been hailed by a host of critics and reviewers as the single most influential work to emerge from the war; see, for example, Beidler's comment that "by general consent, *Dispatches* [is] one of the most fully wrought and authoritative works to emerge from all the literature of Vietnam" (141); Myers likewise places Herr's text at the forefront of "some of the finest Vietnam prose narratives" (32, 33), later remarking that *Dispatches* "has been the subject of so much lavish praise that it seems to have been with us for decades" (76). There is no denying that Herr's *Dispatches* is an a unprecedented achievement in war reportage and I have no wish to minimize its importance in the larger canon of Vietnam narratives. It is perhaps worth stressing, however, that *Dispatches* is not, strictly speaking, either a combat memoir or a veteran's narrative. Herr's privileged position as a war correspondent placed him outside the pale of the grunt's experience; as he admits, "there wasn't a day when someone didn't ask me what I was doing there. . . what I was *really* doing there" (19). Indeed, it is Herr's ubiquity that gives *Dispatches* its air of authenticity and its unbridled sweep; he becomes, in the text, both observer and participant.

7. Attempting to survey the complete collection of Vietnam-inspired memoirs, oral histories, and letters produced over the past twenty years is a little like re-fighting the war--an exercise more of attrition than definition, of exhaustion more than exhaustiveness. This study makes no attempt to be exhaustive; indeed, such a study would have to wait until the literary output on the war is itself exhausted, and given the public's growing appetite for "true" stories about Vietnam--and the veterans' unstinting determination to keep publishing their accounts-- that is not likely to happen soon. This list of titles is intended only to be illustrative and referential. I have omitted a number of titles, and have no doubt included works under thematic categories that other readers may dispute. Individual readers are encouraged to make their own emendations.

8. I do not mean to suggest that all adventure chronicles, great battle accounts, and tactical duty narratives are "gung-ho." Three excellent works depicting the combat experience are Keith William Nolan's *Battle for Hue: Tet, 1968* (New York: Dell Publishing Company, 1983); Robert Pisor's *The End of the Line: The Siege of Khe Sanh* (New York: Ballantine Books, 1982), and Robert Mason's *Chickenhawk* (New York: Viking Press, 1983), an extraordinary personal chronicle of a helicopter assault pilot.

9. Al Santoli's *Everything We Had* (New York: Ballantine Books, 1981), is similarly divided by descriptive subheadings, for example "Gathering Clouds," "Sand Castles," "Peaks and Valleys," "Barren Harvest," and "New Wind," while Ron Glasser's *365 Days* announces its intention to calibrate the war even more explicitly. A number of recent oral histories with more specialized appeal have departed from this format. See, for example, Wallace Terry's *Bloods: An Oral History of the Vietnam War by Black Veterans* (New York: Random House, 1984); Keith Walker's *A Piece of My Heart: The Stories of Twenty-Six American Women Who Served in Vietnam* (New York: Ballantine Books, 1985); Kathryn Marshall's *In the Combat Zone: An Oral History of American Women in Vietnam, 1966-1975* (Boston and Toronto: Little, Brown and Company, 1987); Matthew Brennan's *Headhunters: Stories from the 1st Squadron, 9th Cavalry in Vietnam, 1965-1971* (Novato, California: Presidio Press, 1987); and Stanley Beesley's *Vietnam: The Heartland Remembers* (Norman, Oklahoma and London: University of Oklahoma Press, 1987). Most of these oral histories resist the impulse to "order" the war and all identify their speakers by name, rank, service branch, and in some cases, photographs; the identification of the speakers helps authenticate the narrative and it is left to the reader to make judgments, draw conclusions, and ponder implications.

10. Al Santoli's second oral history, *To Bear Any Burden*, (New York: Ballantine Books, 1985), also incorporates the Vietnamese perspective, though not nearly as successfully as Willenson's *The Bad War*. Readers interested in obtaining a more complete perspective on the war are encouraged to read the growing body of memoirs by Vietnamese soldiers and Cambodian refugees, many written after the fall of Saigon and all published in translation. See, for example, Truong Nhu Tang, *A Vietcong Memoir* (New York: Vintage Books, 1985); General Van Tien Dung, *Our Great Spring Victory* (New York and London: Monthly Review Press, 1977); Molyda Szymusiak, *The Stones Cry Out: A Cambodian Childhood, 1975-1980* (New York: Hill and Wang, 1986); Joan D. Criddle and Teeda Butt Mam, *To Destroy You Is No Loss*:

The Odyssey of a Cambodian Family (New York: The Atlantic Monthly Press, 1987); Haing Ngor, *A Cambodian Odyssey* (New York: Macmillan Publishing Company, 1987); David Chanoff and Doan Van Toai, *Portrait of the Enemy* (New York: Random House, 1986); Nayan Chanda, *Brother Enemy: The War After The War* (San Diego, New York, London: Harcourt Brace Jovanovich, 1986); and Sydney H. Schanberg, *The Death and Life of Dith Pran* (New York: Penguin Books, 1985), the basis for the film *The Killing Fields*.

11. Myers ably traces the bildungsroman's influence on American war literature from the Civil War through Vietnam, notably its application in the Vietnam novels, see pp. 108-139. For further mention of the bildungsroman structure in the Vietnam narrative see John Clark Pratt's Foreword to W. D. Ehrhart's *Vietnam-Perkasie: A Combat Marine Memoir*, (Jefferson, N.C.: McFarland and Co., 1983), pp. ix, x.

Works Cited

Adler, Bill. *Letters From Vietnam*. New York: Dutton, 1967.

Anderson, Charles R. *The Grunts*. 1976. New York: Berkley Books, 1987.

Baker, Mark. *Nam: The Vietnam War in the Words of the Men and Women Who Fought There*. 1981. New York: Quill, 1982.

Beesley, Stanley W. *Vietnam: The Heartland Remembers*. Norman, Oklahoma and London: University of Oklahoma Press, 1987.

Beidler, Philip D. *American Literature and the Experience of Vietnam*. Athens, Georgia: The University of Georgia Press, 1982.

Brennan, Matthew, ed. *Headhunters: Stories from the 1st Squadron, 9th Cavalry, in Vietnam*. Novato, California: Presidio Press, 1987.

Broughton, Jack. *Thud Ridge*. New York: Bantam Books, 1985.

Broyles, William, Jr., *Brothers in Arms: A Journey From War to Peace*. New York: Alfred A. Knopf, 1986.

Bryan, C. D. B. "Barely Suppressed Screams: Getting a Bead on Vietnam War Literature." *Harpers*. June, 1984: 67-72.

_____. *Friendly Fire*. New York: G. P. Putnam, 1976.

Camper, Frank. *L.R.R.P., The Professional*. New York: Dell, 1988.

Caputo Philip. *A Rumor of War*. New York: Ballantine Books, 1977.

Chanda, Nayan. *Brother Enemy: The War After The War*. San Diego, New York, and London: Harcourt Brace Jovanovich, 1986.

Chanoff, David and Doan Van Toai. *Portrait of the Enemy*. New York: Random House, 1986.

Coe, Charles. *Young Man in Vietnam*. New York: Four Winds Press, 1968.

Criddle, Joan D. and Teeda Butt Mam. *To Destroy You Is No Loss: The Odyssey of a Cambodian Family*. New York: The Atlantic Monthly Press, 1987.

Downs, Frederick. *The Killing Zone*. New York: W. W. Norton-Berkley Books, 1978.

Edelman, Bernard, ed. *Dear America: Letters Home From Vietnam*. New York: Pocket Books-Simon and Schuster, 1985.

Ehrhart, W. D. *Passing Time*. Jefferson, NC: McFarland and Company, 1986.

_____. *Vietnam-Perkasie: A Combat Marine Memoir*. Jefferson, NC: McFarland and Company, 1983.

Eilert, Rick. *For Self And Country*. New York: Simon and Schuster, 1983.

Glasser, Ronald J. *365 Days*. 1971. New York: George Braziller, 1980.

Grant, Zalin. *Over the Beach: The Air War in Vietnam*. New York and London: W. W. Norton, 1986.

Henderson, Charles. *Marine Sniper*. New York: Berkley Books, 1986.

Herr, Michael. *Dispatches*. New York: Alfred A. Knopf, 1977.

Hughes, Larry. *You Can See a Lot Standing Under a Flare in the Republic of Vietnam*. New York: William Morrow, 1969.

Just, Ward. *To What End?* Boston: Houghton Mifflin, 1968.

Ketwig, John. *And A Hard Rain Fell: A GI's True Story of the War in Vietnam*. New York: Pocket Books-Simon and Schuster, 1985.

Klein, Joe. *Payback: Five Marines After Vietnam*. New York: Alfred A. Knopf, 1984.

Kovic, Ron. *Born on the Fourth of July*. New York: Pocket Books-McGraw Hill, 1976.

Lanning, Michael Lee. *Inside the LRRPS: Rangers in Vietnam*. New York: Ivy Books-Ballantine, 1988.

_____. *The Only War We Had: A Platoon Leader's Journal of Vietnam*. New York: Ivy Books-Ballantine, 1987.

_____. *Vietnam, 1969-1970: A Company Commander's Journal*. New York: Ivy Books-Ballantine, 1988.

Lawson, Jacqueline E. "'Old Kids': The Adolescent Experience in the Nonfiction Narratives of the Vietnam War," in *Search and Clear: Critical Responses to Selected Literature and Films of the Vietnam War*. Ed. William J. Searle. Bowling Green, Ohio: The Popular Press, 1988.

Lowry, Timothy S. *And Brave Men, Too*. New York: Berkley Books, 1985.

Marshall, Kathryn, ed. *In the Combat Zone: An Oral History of American Women in Vietnam*. Boston and Toronto: Little, Brown and Company, 1987.

Marshall, S. L. A. *Ambush*. 1969. New York: The Battery Press, 1983.

_____. *West to Cambodia*. 1968. New York: The Battery Press, 1984.

Mason, Robert. *Chickenhawk*. New York and Harmondsworth, Middlesex, England: Penguin Books, 1983.

Myers, Thomas. *Walking Point*: *American Narratives of Vietnam*. New York and Oxford: Oxford University Press, 1988.

Ngor, Haing. *A Cambodian Odyssey*. New York: Macmillan Publishing Company, 1987.

Nolan, Keith William. *Battle for Hue*: *Tet, 1968*. New York: Dell, 1983.

O'Brien, Tim. *If I Die in a Combat Zone, Box Me Up and Ship Me Home*. 1969. New York: Dell, 1979.

Palmer, Laura, ed. *Shrapnel in the Heart*: *Letters and Remembrances from the Vietnam Veterans Memorial*. New York: Random House, 1987.

Parks, David. *G.I. Diary*. New York: Harper and Row, 1965.

Pisor, Robert. *The End of the Line*: *The Siege of Khe Sanh*. New York: Ballantine Books, 1982.

Pratt, John Clark, ed. *Vietnam Voices*: *Perspectives on the War Years, 1941-1982*. New York and Harmondsworth, Middlesex, London: Penguin Books, 1984.

Sack, John. *M*. 1966. New York: Avon Books, 1985.

Santoli, Al, ed. *Everything We Had*: *An Oral History of the Vietnam War By Thirty-Three American Soldiers Who Fought It*. New York: Ballantine Books, 1981.

_____. *To Bear Any Burden*: *The Vietnam War and its Aftermath in the Words of Americans and Southeast Asians*. New York: Ballantine Books, 1985.

Schanberg, Sydney H. *The Death and Life of Dith Pran*. New York: Penguin Books, 1985.

Schemmer, Benjamin F. *The Raid*. New York: Avon Books, 1976.

Stanton, Shelby L. *Green Berets at War: U.S. Army Special Forces in Southeast Asia 1956-1975*. New York: Dell, 1985.

Stockdale, James B. and Sybil B. *In Love and War: The Story of a Family's Ordeal and Sacrifice During the Vietnam Years*. New York: Harper and Row, 1984.

Szymusiak, Molyda. *The Stones Cry Out: A Cambodian Childhood, 1975-1980*. New York: Hill and Wang, 1986.

Tan, Truong Nhu. *A Vietcong Memoir*. New York: Vintage Books, 1985.

Terry, Wallace. *Bloods: An Oral History of the Vietnam War by Black Veterans*. New York: Random House, 1984.

Tregaskis, Richard. *Vietnam Diary*. New York: Holt, Rinehart and Winston, 1963.

Van, General Tien Dung. *Our Great Spring Victory*. New York and London: Monthly Review Press, 1977.

Van Devanter, Lynda. *Home Before Morning: The Story of An Army Nurse in Vietnam*. New York: Warner Books, 1983.

Walker, Keith, ed. *A Piece of My Heart: The Stories of Twenty-Six American Women Who Served in Vietnam*. New York: Ballantine Books, 1985.

Willenson, Kim, ed. *The Bad War: An Oral History of the Vietnam War*. New York: New American Library-*Newsweek*, 1987.

Zumbro, Ralph. *Tank Sergeant*. New York: Pocket Books-Simon and Schuster, 1986.

NOTES ON CONTRIBUTORS

NANCY ANISFIELD is a graduate of Lafayette College and Middlebury College. She is currently an Instructor in English at St. Michael's College and at the University of Vermont, where she teaches Vietnam War literature and comparative war literature courses. She has published several articles on the fiction and poetry of the Vietnam War and is the editor of *Vietnam Anthology: American War Literature* (Popular Press, 1987). She is currently working on a collection of critical essays on literature in the nuclear age for Popular Press.

MILTON J. BATES served with the Americal Division in Chu Lai, Vietnam, in 1970-71. Currently an Associate Professor of English at Marquette University, he is the author of *Wallace Stevens: A Mythology of Self* (1985) and the editor of *Sur Plusieurs Beaux Subjects: Wallace Stevens' Commonplace Book* (1989) and the revised edition of Stevens' *Opus Posthumous* (1989).

PHILIP D. BEIDER is Professor of English at the University of Alabama. He is the author of articles on American Literature from the colonial and classical periods to the present and of *American Literature and the Experience of Vietnam*. He is also the editor of *The Art of Fiction in the Heart of Dixie: An Anthology of Alabama Writers* and of a forthcoming reprint of William March's classic novel of war, *Company K*. He is currently completing a new book entitled *Re-Writing America: Vietnam Authors in Their Generation*.

MICHAEL BELLAMY has been teaching American literature at the College of St. Thomas in St. Paul, Minnesota, for ten years. He has published articles on Iris Murdoch, John Fowles, William Dean Howells, Saul Bellow, and Flannery O'Connor. He is planning to write a critical bibliography of his great-grandfather, Edward Bellamy. He spent two of the Vietnam War years, 1968-69, in the Peace Corps in India.

ROBERT E. BOURDETTE. JR. is Professor of English at the University of New Orleans. He is the author, with Michael Cohen, of *The Poem in Question* and of numerous articles on Milton, Shakespeare, and seventeenth-century poetry.

CATHERINE CALLOWAY is a graduate of the Ph.D. program at the University of South Florida and is currently an Assistant Professor of English at Arkansas University, where she teaches courses in fiction,

American literature, and world literature. She has published a bibliography of secondary sources on the literature and film of the Vietnam War as well as critical articles on modern and contemporary writers.

DAVID DeROSE is Director of Undergraduate Theatre Studies at Yale University. His dramatic criticism has appeared in *Theater, Theater Journal*, and *Vietnam Generation*. He is currently at work on a book-length study of Vietnam War drama, *Stages in the War*.

MARILYN DURHAM teaches the literature of the Vietnam War in her literature and composition courses at the University of Wisconsin-Whitewater.

W.D. EHRHART, a Marine veteran of Vietnam (1967-68), contributed poems to *Winning Hearts and Minds* and co-edited *Demilitarized Zones* with Jan Barry. More recently, he edited *Carrying the Darkness: The Poetry of the Vietnam War* and *Unaccustomed Mercy: Soldier-Poets of the Vietnam War* (both from Texas Tech University Press, 1989). His own collections of poems include *To Those Who Have Gone Home Tired: New and Selected Poems* (Thunder's Mouth Press, 1984), *The Outer Banks and Other Poems* (Adastra Press, 1984), and *Winter Bells* (Adastra Press, 1988). He is also author of the nonfiction books, *Vietnam-Perkasie, Going Back,* and *Passing Time* (McFarland & Co., Inc., 1983, 1987, and 1989 respectively). Due to the obvious conflict of interest, W.D. Ehrhart has not included a discussion of his own work in "Soldier-Poets of the Vietnam War."

CYNTHIA J. FUCHS received her Ph.D. at the University of Pennsylvania and has written journal articles on film and contemporary culture. She is an Assistant Professor of Film Studies at George Mason University.

OWEN W. GILMAN, JR. teaches writing and American literature at Saint Joseph's University. In addition to articles on John Dos Passos, Herman Melville, and E.A. Robinson, he has written frequently about the place of Vietnam in American culture. His most recent publications are "Vietnam and the South," for the *Encyclopedia of Southern Culture* (1989) and "Vietnam Writing and the Paradoxical Paradigm of Nomenclature," in *Search and Clear* (1988), ed. William Searle.

VICENTE F. GOTERA teaches American literature and creative writing at Humboldt State University in northern California. His doctoral dissertation, *Radical Visions: Poetry by Vietnam Veterans*, was completed at Indiana University. Gotera also holds the MFA degree in creative writing and is at work on *Pacific Crossing*, a book of poems on Filipino-American experience and popular culture.

H. PALMER HALL, Library Director at St. Mary's University in San Antonio, Texas, served in Vietnam as a Vietnamese interpreter/translator from 1967-68. His dissertation, *The Enlisted Man's War: A Study of the Vietnam War Novels*, was completed at the University of Texas in 1984. He has presented papers on Vietnam War literature at the national conference of the Popular Culture Association and at various Texas meetings.

PHILIP K. JASON is the author of two collections of poetry and the executive editor of *Poet Lore*, a poetry quarterly. He has edited the *Anais Nin Reader* (1973), *Shaping: New Poems in Traditional Prosodies* (1978) and *Landing Zones: Approaches to Literature of the Vietnam War* (forthcoming). With Alan B. Lefcowitz, he authored the Prentice-Hall *Creative Writer's Handbook* (1990). His annotated bibliography of secondary sources on nineteenth-century American poetry will be published by Salem Press.

JACQUELINE LAWSON received her Ph.D. from Brown University and is currently an Assistant Professor of English at the University of Michigan-Dearborn. Her research specialty is the nonfiction literature of the Vietnam War, notably veterans' memoirs and oral histories. She has articles appearing in the *Journal of American Culture* and in collections published by the Popular Press and the University of Iowa Press, and is currently at work on a book-length study of the misogyny of war and the rhetoric of mass culture. She is on the National Advisory Board of *Vietnam Generation: A Journal of Recent History and Contemporary Issues* and served as guest editor of a special issue on gender and the war (Dec 89). Professor Lawson serves as Vietnam Area Chair for the Popular Culture Association.

J.T. HANSEN is Professor of English at the University of Puget Sound in Tacoma, Washington. His teaching and research have centered on modern and contemporary American literature, and, since 1984, Vietnam War literature. "Vocabularies of Experience" is a chapter from a work-in-progress, *There It Is: Demystifying Vietnam Narratives*.

KATE BEAIRD MEYERS is a Visiting Lecturer in English at the University of Tulsa. She earned the Ph.D. in English from that

University in 1987. She has published an article on Vietnam War histories in *Genre* and has presented several conference papers on the subject of the importance of admitting "marginal" voices to the canon of Vietnam literature. She is currently editing a collection of essays concerning women writers and the Vietnam War.

WILLIAM J. PALMER is a dual specialist in the novel and in film studies. He has written books on the fiction of John Fowles and on *The Film of the Seventies: A Social History*. He is presently working on *The Films of the Eighties: A Social History*. He has also published scholarly essays on Samuel Richardson, Dickens, Hardy, Camus, Stendhal, Faulkner, and Fowles, plus film essays on the Vietnam War films, sports films, and Antonini's *Blow-Up*. An Associate Professor of English at Purdue University, he has taught since 1979 a course on the literature and film of the Vietnam War.

DONALD RINGNALDA teaches English at the College of St. Thomas in St. Paul, Minnesota. Among his articles on Vietnam War literature are "Chlorophyll Overdose: Stephen Wright's *Meditations in Green*" (*Western Humanities Review*) and "Fighting and Writing: America's Vietnam War Literature" (*Journal of American Studies*).

ROBERT M. SLABEY teaches courses in American literature at the University of Notre Dame. He has held Andrew Mellon and Fulbright fellowships and has published thirty essays on American novelists including James, Faulkner, Hemingway, Salinger, Ellison, and Cheever.

LORRIE SMITH teaches American literature at St. Michael's College in Vermont and specializes in contemporary American poetry, women's literature, and the literature of war. Recent articles on Vietnam War literature have appeared in *American Poetry Review*, *Vietnam Generation*, *Poetry Wales*, and *Landing Zones* (ed. Phillip Jason). Her work on Vietnam War literature is part of a critical study of politics and poetry in America, and she is working on an anthology of contemporary politically-engaged poetry.

MATTHEW STEWART teaches Humanities in the College of Basic Studies at Boston University. His dissertation is entitled *Making Sense of Chaos: Prose Writing, Fictional Kind and the Reality of Vietnam*. Among the works it treats are *Dispatches*, *Meditations in Green*, *The Short-Timers*, *Going After Cacciato*, and *In Country*.

DAVID E. WHILLOCK teaches courses in film history, theory, and critical analysis at the University of Alabama in Huntsville. He has presented several papers on the subject of Vietnam War films and has published articles in *Journal of American Culture* and *Literature and Film Quarterly*.